“AFTER YOU!”

BIBLIOTHECA
EPHEMERIDUM THEOLOGICARUM LOVANIENSIUM

UNIVERSITÉ CATHOLIQUE DE LOUVAIN
LOUVAIN-LA-NEUVE

KATHOLIEKE UNIVERSITEIT LEUVEN
LEUVEN

BIBLIOTHECA EPHEMERIDUM THEOLOGICARUM LOVANIENSIUM

CCLVIII

"AFTER YOU!"

DIALOGICAL ETHICS AND THE PASTORAL COUNSELLING PROCESS

EDITED BY

A. LIÉGEOIS – R. BURGGRAEVE – M. RIEMSLAGH – J. CORVELEYN

UITGEVERIJ PEETERS
LEUVEN – PARIS – WALPOLE, MA
2013

A catalogue record for this book is available from the Library of Congress.

ISBN 978-90-429-2898-5
D/2013/0602/68

TABLE OF CONTENTS

INTRODUCTION

"AFTER YOU" AND THE ASYMMETRIC RECIPROCITY OF PASTORAL COUNSELLING

The subject of this book is pastoral counselling as a particular form of pastoral care in the Christian context.

Formally speaking, pastoral counselling is a conversation whereby a pastor, in the framework of his pastoral task, engages in verbal contact with a conversation partner, likewise called the client or counsellee. With this, however, its most specific, qualifying aspect has not yet been named. After all, pastoral conversation is about a conversation that is 'pastoral' in nature. This means that it offers the client the space and possibility to bring up existential questions and experiences with regard to meaning and/or the Christian (religious) faith in discussion with a pastor who, from a Christian perspective, listens and speaks. Its goal is that in this conversation the client receives acknowledgement and support or advice, both on the level of insight as well as on the level of conviction, experience and practice. We can also call this the 'subject' or the 'content' of pastoral counselling.

In this book, we examine the actions of the persons involved in pastoral counselling, namely the event of the conversation itself or that which we call the 'counselling process'. Our attention is thereby directed not primarily at the technique or manner but at the ethical dimension, particularly at the ethical foundation and orientation of the pastoral conversation as a precondition for an authentic and fruitful conversation. Hence we can describe the theme of this book synthetically as 'the ethics of the pastoral counselling process'.

I. Encounter, Dialogue and Ethics: An Interdisciplinary Approach

In order to target this theme as adequately as possible, we need a view on conversation itself and its ethical dynamics. For this reason, attention is paid in the first part to the conversation event, "the discourse that persons facing each other hold between them, summoning one another and exchanging statements and objections, questions and answers"[1]. There the emphasis lies not primarily on the content but on the conversation as an 'event of encounter'. At the same time, it is obvious that the exploration and deepening of the conversation as an 'event of encounter' relies on the well-known 'philosophy of dialogue'[2], that deals not only with conversation but likewise describes being-human itself as relational, meaning to say as 'standing-in-relationship' ('in-Beziehung-stehen') (Martin Buber), namely as a dialogical condition that precedes the factual dialogue: "the intersubjective nexus, deeper than the language. Gabriel Marcel speaks of an 'originative communication', from which the verbal communication is coming forth"[3].

This basis for the phenomenology of conversation as encounter brings us directly to the ethical dynamics that is essentially interwoven with it. We thus gain access to that which makes conversation an authentic encounter. At this, ethics is interpreted not in the classic sense of the word as an entirety of values and norms that are applied via universal reason to actions: "ethics as subordinated either to prudence, or to universalization of the maxim of action [Kant], or to the contemplation of a hierarchy of values communicated like a Platonic world of ideas"[4]. In contrast to that,

1. E. LEVINAS, *Of God Who Comes to Mind*, Stanford, CA, Stanford University Press, 1998, p. 137.

2. *Ibid.*: "The value that an entire series of philosophers, theologians and moralists, politicians, and even public opinion, attach to the notion, or to the practice – and, in any case, to the word – of dialogue, (...) attests to a new orientation toward the idea that Western society has had of the essence of the meaningful and the spiritual. This is perhaps a result of the trials of the twentieth century since the First World War. It is thus not out of the question, in our time, to speak of a philosophy of dialogue (...). The work of Martin Buber and Franz Rosenzweig in Germany, that of Gabriel Marcel in France, and their influence in the world – but also the many remarkable works signed by less illustrious names – justify this manner of speaking". Cf. also ID., "Martin Buber, Gabriel Marcel and Philosophy", in ID., *Outside the Subject*, London, The Athlone Press, 1993, p. 20: "*I and Thou*, published in 1923, revealed the existence in Germany of a whole current of thought that, whether anticipatory or reminiscent, more or less converged with Buber's ideas. Texts conceived along the same lines preceded or followed the publication of his book by a short interval. They were signed by Ferdinand Ebner, Hans and Rudolf Ehrenberg, Eugen Rosenstock-Huessy, Eberhard Griesbach and a few others. These authors, however, belonged to the same cultural sphere. The encounter between the work of Martin Buber and that of Gabriel Marcel is a more conclusive indication of a spiritual reality independent of the accidents of discourse. When Gabriel Marcel was writing his *Metaphysical Journal*, he did not know Martin Buber. He came from the intellectual tradition far removed, at that time, from the German academic atmosphere". For further information regarding the philosophy of dialogue, see in this book the contribution of Burggraeve, part I: In Line with Dialogical Thought.

3. E. LEVINAS., *Otherwise than Being or Beyond Essence*, The Hague – Boston, MA – London, Martinus Nijhoff Publishers, 1981, p. 27.

4. ID., *Of God Who Comes to Mind* (n. 1), pp. 149-150.

ethics is understood as a dimension of the intersubjective encounter itself, not as something external that is added to it but as something internal that is entirely woven into it. In this regard, we are actually talking of "an ethics [as foundation] before ethics [as application]". Hence the ethical 'essence' of the encounter should not in any way be conceived of as static, like a pre-given and permanent substance. On the contrary, it realises itself as an interactive event that develops as direction and conversation – as speaking and listening and responding, or as 'contra-dicting' and answering differently – in an 'infinitely dynamic' manner.

The title of the first part reads: "Dialogue and ethics as preconditions for pastoral counselling". The manner in which phenomenology and ethics are introduced in the different contributions is indeed diverse. On the one hand, different thinkers serve as sources of inspiration like, among others, Emmanuel Levinas (1905-1995), Martin Buber (1878-1965), Mikhail Bakhtin (1895-1975), Lev Vygotsky (1896-1934). On the other hand, the authors' personal views on the 'event of dialogue' are illustrated on the basis of different forms and fields of conversation that come from both the pastoral as well as the therapeutic setting or that are involved in moral formation and education. The different contributions of the first part will be reviewed one by one, with an eye to the plan and development of the author's own view on 'conversation' as 'discourse' and 'authentic encounter'.

In her contribution Sheila McNamee searches for the main lines of 'a relational ethic', where at the same time the conditions for dialogue can be defined (chapter I). For that purpose, she starts with Bakhtin, who claims that dialogue is a responsive activity. When we are responsive to others, our words and actions are not entirely our own, they carry our history of relationships and the beliefs and values these relationships have crafted. This responsivity of dialogue situates the professional practitioners of dialogue, in different forms of guidance and counselling, within a relational ethic where attentiveness to the process of relating is centered, rather than adherence to some abstract, decontextualized set of principles. Dialogue, as an ethic of relationally sensitive practice, respects the diversity of locally situated beliefs and values. Thus, dialogue allows practitioners to let go of imposing judgment, assessment and evaluation of others' actions and opens the door for attentiveness to the coordination of diverse social orders.

Among the various domains of dialogic study, there is for the most part a remarkable silence when it comes to listening. Whichever way it is glossed – as rhetoric, dialogue, language, or argumentation – the western conception of *the logos* emphasizes speech at the expense of listening. And the problem with conceiving language in terms of speech and speaking is not only that it obscures and minimizes the importance of listening, but also that it conceals the ways in which listening is the event, occurrence, and performance of the ethical relation. Without it, no ethical relation can exist. Drawing upon three central ideas – alterity, intersubjectivity, and responsibility – in Martin Buber's and Emmanuel Levinas's dialogic philosophy, Lisbeth Lipari builds the case in her essay for listening as the nascent origin of the ethical relation (chapter II). Moreover, as she will argue, listening is a form of conjuring wherein the (in)vocation of dialogic ethics is a process that listens others to speech.

In her contribution Marie-Cécile Bertau concentrates on the notion of voice as polyphonic, namely as voices of others for the self, *and* as voices of others in the self (chapter III). The notion of voice introduced is based on certain ideas about language and speaking/listening subjects derived from a specific notion of fundamental human alterity. Alterity is, in this understanding, a developmental as well as a relational movement, thus it is performed and vividly experienced. The form this takes is language as spoken and listened to by the other, so the voice uttered and listened to is of central importance. Voice is seen as a psychophysical phenomenon, manifesting individual as well as socio-cultural meanings and value accents, bound to an utterance and thus transcending the speaking body and leading to a multivoiced self. Alterity and performed language are inseparably related, which leads to the formulation of the basic position of the subject as addressed and affected. Dialogue is then the means of a development from and to the other and the self, a means through which the subjects distinguish and relate themselves and each other in terms of positions and voices. These basic notions can be grasped in ontogenetic development as well as in adulthood in the acquisition and performance of a multiplicity of voices and positions characteristic for social as well as individual language usages. This multiplicity is effective on the communicative as well as on the self-reflective and self-developmental level. Polyphony, as representation of a simultaneity of voices forming a perceivable 'Gestalt', corresponds to the pervasive multivoicedness of socialized individuals, its improvement can be said to be a means and resource for constructing and reconstructing social reality.

In his essay Peter Rober pleads for paying special attention to the client's 'no' in every kind of counselling and particularly in marital and family therapy (MFT) (chapter IV). Dialogue in MFT is by definition a multi-actor dialogue: marital therapy is a dialogue between the therapist with two partners of the same generation, and family therapy is a dialogue between at least two family members of at least two different generations. This raises important challenges for therapists since this means that the conversation is often tension-filled and can have dramatic real life consequences for the family members. In the first part of the essay a conceptual frame is developed, relying on MFT literature on the subject as well as on the conceptual discussion in the field around the concept of not-knowing. The therapeutic effectiveness of the therapist's egalitarian intentions and the concept's implicit idealistic view of dialogue that heals naturally are questioned. The validity of some of Mikhail Bahktin concepts (addressivity, responsivity, ...) to address the specific complexities of the MFT encounter is especially highlighted. Then a case study is presented in which the reflection is limited to a micro-analysis of the first minutes of a first session of a marital therapy. The third part of the essay discusses what can be learned from the case-study against the background of some of the central concepts and ideas developed in the first part of the essay. This leads to the conclusion that the marital and family therapist cannot escape the uncomfortable position of being responsible for finding ways to contribute actively to a fruitful dialogue that is not a natural given at all, but rather a project not only in the technical but especially in the ethical sense of the word.

We round off the first part with two contributions that in their own way pay attention not only to a 'clinical, therapeutic counselling and guidance context' but also and especially to moral formation and education, and to the view on the human and on morality that are implied therein.

In the fifth chapter Vangie Bergum explores the relational space between persons (professional and client, teacher and student) as the place that quickens ethical action. Using experiential and theoretical knowledge, the ethical space is shown as a vibrant interactive environment, full of possibility for all participants within the space. Actions in ethical space are embodied, where respect for the personhood of each person is seen as the primary ethical principle. The embodied experience of quickening shows the moral moment of touching and being touched by others. Through recognizing the needs of both self and other, the ethical process of listening and talking together – dialogue – can continue. Ethical space, as a moral geography, is a place where participants grow and change by grappling with what is ethically fitting in each moment, encounter and challenge. Two examples, one from the end of life and one from the beginning, show that ethical action is a process, in which ethical decision-making must consider all forms of ethical knowledge – theory, principles, and personal experience (narrative, intuitive, emotive, and informal). The ethical space, found in both classroom and clinic, is enhanced by skills such as engagement, improvisation and interdependence that contribute to professional ethical action. Exploration of the difference between 'curriculum as planned' versus 'curriculum as lived' demonstrates the necessity of using personal experience, theatre, drama and art, as well traditional ethical theory in education. Dialogue is inherent to the exploration of ethical spaces and relationships both in the educational setting as well as in clinical practice.

In her essay Darcia Narvaez reflects on the neurobiological development of morality and moral functioning (chapter VI). A discussion of moral development often begins with questions philosophers ask: Is morality innate (Emerson, Rousseau, Thoreau) or are humans innately evil (Augustine, Hobbes, Machiavelli)? Can morality be taught explicitly through reason (Plato), or is it a matter of learning from experience (Aristotle)? In order to answer these questions the author uses an interdisciplinary and empirical approach. It may be best to begin with Socrates' (or the Oracle of Delphi's) insight, *Know thyself.* What do we know about humans from empirical science? What has evolved in human nature, that is, what is genetically determined, and what is 'plastic', or developed from experience? Can experience influence human moral nature? In the essay the current state of knowledge about the evolution and ontogeny of morality is examined. The essay concludes with suggestions for how to cultivate compassionate or 'dialogical' morality, based on supportive relationships.

II. Pastoral Counselling as Ethical Process

After having provided in the first part a number of building blocks for an interdisciplinary, critical reflection on every form of counselling as a qualitative event of conversation, the second part of this book will focus on the pastoral conversation as 'event of conversation' whereby our 'dialogical human condition' takes shape in its own manner. In addition two seemingly contradictory characteristics are linked with each other, namely asymmetry and reciprocity.

In the footsteps of Levinas it has been suggested that pastoral counselling, indeed like every other guidance and counselling, is not only marked factually by various forms of asymmetry, for instance that of power (and all the inherent risks of abuse of power and imbalances of power), but it is in particular based on a radical form of ethical asymmetry as well. The uniqueness of the other – the 'counsellee' – deserves to have priority because pastoral conversation starts from the presence and the question or the distress of the other. It is this priority of the pastoral 'client' that orientates the approach – the outreach – of the pastoral counsellor. It is the alterity of the other that leads the counsellor to give absolute priority to the other: 'after You'. In the words of Levinas we can state that pastoral conversation, as the face-to-face through the other-I-dialogue, "signifies the worth of the other person or, still more precisely, insofar as within the immediacy of the relation to the other person alone (and without the recourse to some general principle [to be applied]), a meaning such as 'be worth' (*valoir*) is sketched out. This is a worth attached to the human being coming out of the value of the other, or the human being who is other; a value attached to the other as other [*autrui*]"[5]. We can also call it the ethical 'urgency' that arises at the moment the pastoral counsellee and counsellor come into contact with each other – an ethical urgency that is expressed in the ethical 'politeness' of the 'after You' proceeding from the pastoral counsellor directed towards the pastoral counsellee: "Is not the very opening of the dialogue already a way for the *I* [*pastoral counsellor*] to uncover itself, to deliver itself, a way for the *I* to place itself at the disposition of the *You* [*pastoral counsellee*]?"[6].

This ethical asymmetry that not only characterises but also lies at the foundation of pastoral conversation does not contradict the reciprocity of the conversation itself. On the contrary, ethical asymmetry is the basis for reciprocity in the sense that by giving acknowledgement to the other the pastoral counsellee is not only enabled to tell his or her story, to express his or her distress or existential questions, but the counsellee also comes into contact in a real way with the pastoral counsellor as an other *and* throughout this contact – throughout this conversation – can find answers or inspiration or meaning in his or her own way. On the basis of this fundamental ethical asymmetry the pastoral counsellor and counsellee do not enter into a subject-object-relationship but on the contrary into a subject-subject-relationship whereby – thanks to the encounter and the conversation – a reciprocal involvement arises, but without eradicating or rather without allowing for the eradication of ethical asymmetry. Acknowledgement and reciprocity are only possible when the 'I' (the pastoral counsellor) relinquishes his "claim to know", in other words withdraws himself from his (professional) position of power in order to open up space for the other and to listen to the other's appeal. In that sense listening comes before speaking with the pastoral counsellee, the core of all invocation as interpellation. Or rather the face-to-face of the pastoral conversation is essentially interpellation as 'vocative': You (in

5. *Ibid.*, p. 150.
6. *Ibid.*

the second person), and not 'he/she' (in the third person). "The recognition of alterity does not consist in forming an idea of alterity. The adequate access to the alterity of the other is not a perception, but the saying of Thou. I speak *to* the other before speaking *of* the other. The immediate contact in and through this invocation is an original relation, or the 'relation by excellence' as it is called by Buber. Speaking to the other as You is thus tantamount to let her/his alterity be fulfilled"[7]. Or put differently: the ethical asymmetry of the 'other-I'-relationship is the condition of possibility for the reciprocity of a respectful conversation wherein the 'partners' – in their ethical but also factual asymmetry – give each other acknowledgement and thus are truly 'present' to each other.

That asymmetry and reciprocity (as a form of symmetry) do not exclude but rather include each other is articulated in the title of this *Introduction:* "Asymmetric reciprocity of pastoral counselling". Both are treated in a majority of contributions in the second part of this book in various modalities and levels. Inspiration is taken not only from the basic authors we already mentioned, Levinas and Buber, but also from other authors like Axel Honneth (°1949), Ivan Boszormenyi-Nagy (1920-2007), Pamela Cooper-White (°1955), Aat van Rhijn (1930-2002) and Hanneke Meulink-Korf (°1948) in particular in order to discuss thoroughly their own accents on acknowledgement and reciprocity in a context of ethical asymmetry.

In the first contribution of the second part, Marina Riemslagh, inspired by Levinas and Buber, searches for an ethically qualitative and effective pastoral counselling (chapter VII). What is the correct 'interaction' between pastoral counsellor and counselling partner in professional pastoral dialogue? What does a pastor owe a counselling partner in the context of a pastoral relationship? In her essay the author aims to find out what is correct in pastoral counselling and what is 'against doing justice' to the counselling partner. For Levinas doing justice has to do with giving priority to the counselling partner and to suffer with the suffering of the other. For Buber it means that the pastor and the counselling partner build up an authentic person-to-person relationship. This chapter discusses and compares the philosophy of Levinas and Buber for use in founding and orienting pastoral counselling. In Levinasian literature Levinas and Buber are usually pitted against each other and Buber is often criticised from the standpoint of Levinas. In this essay another path is taken: Levinas' ethical view on conversation – and thus on pastoral conversation as 'asymmetric revelation' – is connected with Buber's

7. E. LEVINAS, *Proper Names*, Stanford, CA, Stanford University Press, 1996, p. 22.

concept of reciprocity: 'asymmetric and reciprocal revelation'. Furthermore, Buber not only describes the singularity and originality of the encounter (Ich-Du-Beziehung – I-Thou-relationship) but likewise investigates that which makes this interpersonal treatment into an 'authentic' encounter, and thus into what promotes or hinders the other-I-encounter. Valuable insights for a qualitative – humane and humanising – pastoral relationship are contained therein.

In her contribution Carrie Doehring intends to outline how the relational ethics of Levinas informs the intercultural approach to pastoral care (chapter VIII). She describes this intercultural approach as a three-part process. First, pastoral counsellors must be able to use a comparative approach to religion that highlights what is different about each person's religious faith – the 'strangeness of the other, his irreducibility to the I, to my thoughts and possessions', such that 'the absolutely foreign [aspects of those seeking care] can instruct us'. Second, pastoral counsellors must cultivate a critical self-awareness of who they are spiritually and theologically, so that they do not unwittingly impose their religious meaning making and practices on those seeking care. Such self-reflexivity and other-awareness will de-center pastoral counsellors and reveal the careseeker as stranger and 'other' in the *infini* (infinity), such that 'the epiphany of the face as face opens up humanity'. When this remarkable relational space opens up, the third and culminating moment of intercultural care is possible. This is when pastoral counsellors and care seekers co-create contextual provisional meanings and ways of experiencing holiness.

In the contribution of Annelies van Heijst attention is given to acknowledgement as an important form of 'asymmetric reciprocity' (chapter IX). The main argument in her essay is that pastoral counselling is pointless, unless the 'client' draws from it a feeling of being recognized, i.e. feels valued as someone who is entitled to receive support and as a person who really matters to others. The concept of recognition (expressed as love, respect and social appreciation) as it was coined by Axel Honneth and complemented by his critics, offers a novel view of the way humans are interdependent – not only on a material level but also with regard to the place they occupy in the community and to their sense of being loved, respected and appreciated. When searching for an ethics to ground pastoral care and counselling, the dynamics of recognition can be an asset, since it goes beyond the dichotomy of the powerful professional who helps as opposed to the client who occupies the role of a mere receiver. This is especially relevant to the present condition of the health care and welfare sector, in which much pastoral care and counselling is given.

Pastors are now pressed to give account of their work in terms of product output, effectiveness and efficiency and need another frame of reference to express what their work is actually all about.

In his essay Axel Liégeois aims to make a critical ethical reflection on asymmetry and power in pastoral counselling (chapter X). The research question is how pastors can deal in an ethical and responsible way with the asymmetric relationship and the power imbalance in pastoral counselling. His reflection is based on a study of literature and on experiences in the field of pastoral counselling. First the asymmetric positions and the subsequent imbalances of power in the pastoral relationship are described. This power imbalance is structural and premoral, and becomes morally qualified depending on the way the pastor and the conversation partner deal with it. Because the pastor has the greatest power, he or she bears the greatest responsibility, namely not to abuse the power but to empower the conversation partner. Then one possible response to this challenge is presented, namely the development of a coherent pattern of ethical attitudes for the pastor. Attitudes are the driving force of human acts, the pastor's motivation and inspiration in pastoral counselling. The author discerns three sets of three attitudes: openness, attentiveness and mildness; recognition, responsibilization and truthfulness; wisdom, self-reflection and integrity. The pastor's ethical attitudes are a good way to prevent the abuse of power and to enhance empowerment in pastoral counselling.

For Annemie Dillen it is important to search for a 'just counselling relationship' or a just relationship of pastoral care (chapter XI). Therefore she focuses on how the contextual thought of the American-Hungarian family therapist Ivan Boszormenyi-Nagy can contribute to this subject and how it is related to other theories about pastoral counselling, such as the work of Pamela Cooper-White and reflections on 'power'. The essay concretely shows how various concepts, elaborated by Nagy, shed new light on dynamics within pastoral dialogue. Contextual pastoral care, as developed in the Netherlands by Aat van Rhijn and Hanneke Meulink-Korf, aims at stimulating the development of people, among other things, by motivating them to work on more justice in their primary (family) relations. The essay discusses among others the concept of 'direct address' in light of theories about 'transference' and 'countertransference' and within a broader framework of power dynamics in pastoral relationships. 'Direct address' is the 'cornerstone' of real dialogue and worth striving for in order to come to justice in relationships, not only in primary but also in so-called 'secundary' relationships like different forms of counselling and supervision. In order to come to a form of pastoral counselling that does justice to everyone involved in the counselling process it is important to strive for 'connection', but to notice at the same time one's own subjectivity. Multidirected partiality is one of the attitudes that can help a pastoral counsellor to reach this goal within the counselling process itself and to stimulate it in the life of all those involved or affected by the pastoral counselling.

In his contribution Roger Burggraeve sheds light again on pastoral conversation as an ethical event from the perspective of Emmanuel Levinas' vision on the face and responsibility (chapter XII). The essay can be seen as an inclusion to that of Marina Riemslagh. The following foundational aspects of pastoral conversation are discussed: the otherness and the mastership of the client; and the ethical dynamics of the pastoral face-to-face, beginning with the vulnerability of the other and the temptation to violence in the pastor. This violence has many faces: diagnostic reduction, rhetoric, dominance and tyranny or even terror. This means that the pastoral responsibility for the client starts with the prohibition 'thou shall not kill' and the negative movement of restraint, namely the decision not to inflict pressure, direct or indirect violence on the client. This self-emptying 'withdrawal' opens the perspective for positive forms of responsibility, starting from a simple 'good morning', a first form of ethical courtesy, through acknowledgement and respect, attention and listening, goodness full of longing, not letting the client alone in his or her suffering and dying (true consolation), to the responsibility for the responsibility of the client, not only for him or herself but also for others.

In the final essay (epilogue) Kenneth and Mary Gergen offer a critical retrospective, paying attention to the so-called 'missing voices' in the relational ethics elaborated throughout the different essays in the book (chapter XIII). In a 'fully relational ethic', that is at the same time realistic, we should not fall into the trap of a 'romanticised' conceptualisation of the other by means of emphasising only his or her phenomenological and ethical alterity and pay no attention to the factual other. However radically different the other may be in essence, and whatever amount of respect he or she may deserve, we cannot simply sweep under the rug that the other – the [pastoral] client – can maintain a value system or life pattern that is distasteful, unethical or evil. It surely cannot be that we lend an empathic and confirming ear to a tyrannical and abusive or bully client, a sexist and racist counsellee, a pedophile, a fundamentalist and/or 'terrorizing' faithful. It is indeed unacceptable that we approach only with acknowledgement and empathy and not with a sharp critical sense at the same time those counsellees who engage in behavior that they may consider to be perfectly acceptable or justifiable to themselves, but not at all for the counsellor nor to others (group, community, society). Care-givers and (pastoral) counsellors cannot remain silent, curious, accepting, and hoping only to make a contribution to the client's good in his or her own terms. If the pastoral or therapeutic relationship is truly a dialogue, then the care-givers may expect the client to grant to them the right to voice. Their 'face' should not be obliterated in the inter-change! Therefore in the essay two types of moral action are delineated, namely first and second order morality. 'First order morality' is concerned with the ethical order within a particular subgroup. Social conflict results from the conflict among first order moral systems. 'Second order morality' concerns itself with conflicts between competing moral visions, and with generating relational processes that keep alive the possibility for making mutual morality. Applied to care-giving and (pastoral) counselling, it is important that all parties recognize the relational processes that are necessary in order for ethical action to take place, and to honor the kinds of second order moral processes that bring otherwise alien moralities together. Several micro-practices that promote such outcomes in the care-giving and counselling relationship are discussed.

III. A Relationship without Tyranny, in Two Directions

This critical and retrospective contribution brings us to the end of this *Introduction* with a plea for an "order without tyranny"[8], namely a 'non-tyrannical' (pastoral) counselling in two directions. The ethical acknowledgement of the one (the counsellor) for the other (the counsellee) consists in questioning and avoiding all abuse of power and tyranny towards the other. In this sense the 'after You' expresses the exigency to approach the other non-violently. The non-tyrannical relationship, however, cannot come from one side only, namely only from the side of the pastoral counsellor. It must likewise come from the counsellee. The client as other is vulnerable, indeed, simply by means of the fact that he or she appeals to a care-giver or a counsellor. But the client can also abuse this vulnerability and even use it as a weapon of power not only to influence the counsellor (which can still be positive) but also to force the counsellor to take certain pronouncements, agreements or actions by means of some form of manipulation, humiliation, if not subtle terror. Hence, pastoral

8. E. Levinas, *Freedom and Command*, in Id., *Collected Philosophical Papers*, translated by Alphonso Lingis, Dordrecht – Boston, MA – Lancaster, Nijhoff Publishers – Kluwer Academic Publishers Group, 1987, 15-23, p. 23.

counselling must be reciprocal on the ethical level: from both sides – not only from the counsellor but also from the counsellee – it must be non-tyrannical and non-violent. In that, both pastoral counsellor and counsellee are radically equal and their relationship and conversation must therefore be based on mutual respect: "I recognize the other [the counsellee]; that is, I believe in her/him. But if this recognition were a submission to the other, the submission would take all its worth away from my recognition; recognition by submission would annul my dignity, through which recognition has validity. (...) The term respect could be taken up here, provided that it be emphasized that the reciprocity of this respect is not an indifferent relation, and that it is not the outcome of, but the condition for ethics. (...) To show respect cannot mean to subject oneself. (...) The one respected is not the one to whom, but the one with whom one renders justice. Respect is a relationship between equals. And justice presupposes this original equality. (...) All the slackness of the world filters in through friendly faces as soon as the relationship of mutual responsibility is suspended"[9]. Only in and through this ethical reciprocity does the 'after You' of the title of this book acquire its full and correct significance, coming from me towards the other *and* proceeding from the other towards me.

We hope and wish that this book may find its way to both therapists and all psycho-social care-givers as well as to pastoral and spiritual counsellors.

IV. Acknowledgements

First of all we want to thank all the contributors who presented their essay during the interdisciplinary Expert Seminar 'After You', held on 11-13 February 2010 at the KU Leuven, Department of Pastoral Theology of the Faculty of Theology and Religious Studies. A special word of thanks goes to Marina Riemslagh (and her family members) for the organization, realization and follow-up of the expert seminar, in close consultation with the promoters of the research project 'The ethics of the pastoral counselling process', financially supported by the Flemish Fund for Scientific Research. Thanks also to Roger Burggraeve for the editing work of this volume. Our gratefulness goes also to Prof. Joseph Verheyden, General Editor, and to the Board of the series *Bibliotheca*

9. Id., "The Ego and the Totality", in Id., *Collected Philosophical Papers* (n. 8), pp. 43-44.

Ephemeridum Theologicarum Lovaniensium, for their willingness and support to publish this volume. Thanks to Rita Corstjens, editorial assistant, for the technical competence in preparing the volume for publication. Thanks to Ann Milton for reviewing the English and to Edmund Guzman for some translations. We thank Monique Tersago for having designed and rendered the water colour painting on the cover of the book especially for the theme 'After You'. Thanks to the publisher Paul Peeters for his eagerness to publish the book. In a word, we want to thank all who contributed to the project and the book, by discussing the theme, by the particular content elaborated, and – last but not least – by all the practical and technical assistance.

Axel LIÉGEOIS
Roger BURGGRAEVE
Marina RIEMSLAGH
Jozef CORVELEYN

PART I

DIALOGUE AND ETHICS AS PRECONDITIONS FOR PASTORAL COUNSELLING

THE DIFFERENCE OF DIALOGUE

TOWARD A RELATIONAL ETHIC

In her foreword to "Dialogue: Theorizing Difference in Communication Studies", Julia Wood says, "Genuine dialogue depends less on self-expression and other transmissional aspects of communication than upon responsiveness ... [which] arises out of and is made possible by qualities of thought and talk that allow transformation in how one understands the self, others, and the world they inhabit"[1]. If we are responsive to others – particularly to others who seek our "expert" opinion – then we are also open to altering our own commitments and beliefs. The responsivity of dialogue requires questioning one's own world view just enough to allow space for the *rationality* of the other's view. The focus is on making space for multiple rationalities. In professional practice, this means that our job is not to impose our "expert" understanding on the other but to create a space where multiple (and often diverse) understandings can co-exist.

I. What Is Dialogue?

Bakhtin describes dialogue as a *responsive* activity[2]. Dialogue is not limited to self-interest, psychological or relational improvement, nor to crafting cooperative, conflict-free ways of "going on together"[3]. Dialogue is about responsivity. In dialogue,

> (1) communication is ... a fluctuating, unpredictable, multivocal process in which uncertainty infuses encounters between people and what they mean and become, ...; (2) interlocutors are immersed in a process that shapes and forms them even as they shape and form it and one another in ways that are not entirely predictable or finalizable, ...; (3) tension is inherent ... and integral to (the process) ...; (4) (there is no attempt to) idealize or seek common ground, ... and (5) (participants) are realized in the *process*...

1. R. Anderson – L.A. Baxter – K.N. Cissna (eds.), *Dialogue: Theorizing Difference in Communication Studies*, Thousand Oaks, CA, Sage Publications, 2004, p. xvi.
2. M. Bakhtin, *The Dialogical Imagination*, Austin, TX, University of Texas Press, 1981.
3. L. Wittgenstein, *Philosophical Investigations*, Oxford, Blackwell, 1953, pp. xvii-xviii.

Yet, I must be clear. Bakhtin's responsivity should not be equated with assumptions of equal partners with equal values seeking equal outcomes. To Bakhtin, as to Buber[4], dialogue occurs when conditions of *curiosity* are fostered, despite differences in values and beliefs. Participants in dialogue engage with respect and curiosity.

In contrast to dialogue, Bakhtin, Sampson[5] and others would describe our common, individualist understanding of communication as *monologic*. Monologism is characterized by a focus on what Sampson calls the *self contained individual*. To understand communication, one only needs to understand the person – his or her motives, beliefs, intentions, and cognitive abilities. Dialogism, as proposed by Bakhtin, offers us a very different understanding of human interaction. As Sampson says, in dialogism "*the most important thing about people is not what is contained within them, but what transpires between them*"[6]. Further, Sampson tells us that in dialogue, the "emphasis (is) on the idea that people's lives are characterized by the ongoing conversations and dialogues they carry out in the course of their everyday activities"[7].

Monologism, which is also our taken-for-granted way of being in the world, focuses on the individual and his or her private meanings, feelings, and motives. There is no concern for the ways in which conversational partners make meaning together. It is a "mentalist" approach where the assumption is that one must "get their ideas out on the table" (where "out" refers to out of the private recesses of a person's mind) in order for any sort of coordination to transpire. This is very much the model of most professional practice; it holds individuals accountable for their own private meanings and intentions. Yet, the dialogic understanding of meaning that Bakhtin, Sampson and a host of others are proposing is concerned first and foremost with appreciating the complex processes by which our worlds are made.

These processes start when people coordinate their activities with others in interaction. From these coordinated patterns, rituals quickly emerge. These rituals generate a sense of standards and expectations that we use to assess our own and others' actions. With these standardizing modes in place, values and beliefs are generated; in other words, entire realities are constructed. Thus, from the very simple process of coordinating our

4. M. BUBER, *I and Thou*, New York, NY, Scribners, 1970.

5. E.E. SAMPSON, *Celebrating the Other*, Chagrin Falls, OH, Taos Institute Publications, 2008.

6. *Ibid.*, p. 20 (italics original).

7. *Ibid.*

activities with each other, we develop entire belief systems, moralities and values.

If we are blind to this process (as traditional, monologic modes of being are), we can easily locate meaning, intentions, values, moralities, and all that is meaningful in our lives to the private world of the mind. And, in so doing, our attempts to move beyond personal or relational conflict toward some sort of livable future is thwarted because the decisions about how we should live, the decisions about what counts as "normal", and about what counts as equity, will remain in the hands of those in positions of power (professionals) who are granted the ability to make these complex decisions because the presumption is that they know how to preserve the right values. But, the question must be asked: *By whose standards are we determining the right values? What are the standards by which professionals claim their position of authority (over someone else's life)?*

Dialogue is not a constant, nor a common, form of relating. As Anderson, Baxter, and Cissna describe, dialogue "exists in moments rather than extended states, cannot be lionized, cannot become business as usual, and cannot be planned precisely or made to happen"[8]. To engage in dialogue is not to impose our professional knowledge on others. Dialogue requires that we extend our curiosity about the profuse and diverse realities that emerge when people come together and coordinate their activities. We must extend that curiosity to those with whom we work, opening possibilities to explore alternative understandings of a person's life situation.

Robin Penman[9] writes about the ways in which various types of interaction and communication allow for genuine participation, and how they influence the wellbeing of participants – whether that wellbeing refers to their private lives or issues of broader public concern. She discusses "good communication" from a dialogic orientation as necessarily implying a morality: communication is "good" when it is human and good to people, *not when it is clear and concise*. This last statement distinguishes a dialogic understanding of human communication from a popular, technique-oriented approach to communication – an approach associated with a modernist, individualist understanding of communication and meaning.

A dialogic interaction must acknowledge those present and the values and beliefs they bring to the conversation. The most important aspect of any conversation is the *interactive moment* – what those present are doing

8. ANDERSON – BAXTER – CISSNA (eds.), *Dialogue* (n. 1), p. 15.

9. R. PENMAN, *Reconstructing Communication: Looking to a Future*, Mahwah, NJ, Erlbaum, 2000.

now and the histories, cultures, and traditions they bring with them. In addition, any conversation must remain open to the possibilities that emerge within the interactive moment; there is no prescribed route toward a pre-determined goal. In other words, dialogue is not focused on any particular technique or content. In dialogue we are more attentive to *what we are doing together*. Additionally, dialogue is marked by openness to diverse understandings, which are the by-product of coordinations among participants. Finally, no meaning, no conversation is ever ultimately complete. Meaning is always open to further supplementation and thus to the construction of new understandings.

Positioned with this relational ethic, we are less focused on the content of what people are doing and saying and more attentive to the *processes* in which they engage and *how their actions* invite each other into particular rituals and relationships. This is not to say that content does not matter. Of course it does – particularly in the workings of our daily lives. However, the dialogic focus I am proposing here encourages a "pause", if you will, in our attention to content. The emphasis in dialogue is on *building a conversational domain where people can talk in different ways about the same old issues*. This means that our first task is to explore ways of creating a context (physical, relational, and personal) that invites participants to talk differently about "the same old topic". This does not mean that differences of opinion, conflict or competing worldviews must be suppressed. This also does not imply that differential power positions are ignored nor that professional expertise is put aside. Rather, to be in dialogue is to engage in the tensionality produced when one holds one's own position while simultaneously remaining open to the position of the other[10].

The risk of holding one's own position while allowing others – often with opposing views – to do the same, and to be open and curious about the *coherence* of those very different positions, creates a very unique relational context. It is a context that is more democratic and concerned with broader issues of human and social wellbeing. It is, in other words, a useful process for professional practice. Dialogue, and the relational ethic it embodies, places our attention on what we are co-creating with others. This is a radically different focus from traditional professional ethics where being ethical means using professional tools and knowledge to make assessments and chart a course of action for remedying problems.

10. J. STEWART – K. ZEDIKER, *Dialogue as Tensional, Ethical Practice*, in *Southern Communication Journal* 65 (2002) 224-242.

Dialogue implies that we begin by presuming the other's *rationality*. In other words, the challenge is to find a way to approach the other as an other who is coherent and rational within his or her own community of significance. As mentioned, this stance moves our focus away from *assessment* of who is right and who is wrong or who is a good person and who is not. It places our focus on understanding very different life forms *on their own terms and temporarily suspending evaluation*. Such a stance invites space for multiple rationalities as opposed to persuasive rhetoric where securing the rightness of our own form of life is our main concern. This is not to suggest that preferred forms of action or preferred "ways of being" are ignored or avoided. The point is to open professional practice to the co-construction – the relational achievement – of "preferred" forms of action. The main question to explore is how professional practice unfolds if we begin our work by confronting others dialogically. From this different origin, new possibilities for coordination can emerge.

So, our challenge is to create opportunities for dialogue.

II. Creating Conditions for Dialogue

The first task is to explore ways of creating a context that *invites* a different form of conversation – a form of conversation that embodies the tension of dialogue. As described, a dialogic stance brackets the typical persuasive moves professionals are trained to adopt where the very act of being a professional seems to require imposing common standards of good and bad, right and wrong on the situation and/or actions of the other.

In the remainder of this essay, I offer some resources for action that can assist us in creating the very different conversational space of dialogue; a space that opens possibility for new understandings while simultaneously not terminating with easy answers about what is moral or good or right and what is not. In other words, these resources for action remind us that diversity of meaning is part of the human condition and engaging diversity with respect and curiosity helps us appreciate the power we each have to construct liveable futures together. Let me offer a set of practices that I believe direct our attention to the process of constructing bridges among competing meaning-making communities. This is not to suggest that all forms of life are acceptable, viable, or in any way condonable. It is simply to refocus our attention on how a life form emerges and in focusing on this process, creating the opportunity for a conversation where new understandings can be generated.

Bakhtin claims that language is never a representation of the world as it is but is, rather, a creation of the world as we construct it[11]. If we take seriously the relational sensibility required of dialogue, we might enter into our daily activities in very different ways. We might, for example, enter into a counselling session with curiosity about *how* the client's problem emerged and what purpose it was serving, rather than from the perspective of *why* it was occurring and who or *what* was at fault. And similarly, we might enter into a smoothly flowing relational moment with a fresh curiosity for how, among all the complexity of human affairs, we manage to become engaged in such preferred performances. The relational ethic of dialogue is rich with potential, opening interactions to the continual reconstruction of meanings.

Shotter suggests, "for something to make a difference that matters to us, something must surprise us, be unanticipated, unexpected, fill us with wonder"[12]. I would like to propose some general notions that, I believe, orient us toward the creative possibilities of dialogue and thereby position us within a relational ethic. These resources are by no means exhaustive. I offer these as only an opening into the imaginative construction of further dialogic potentials.

1. *Reflexive Critique*

First, and probably most contrary to our traditional, individualist orientation to the world, is the constant use of reflexive critique. Here, the attempt is to entertain doubt about our own certainties. Reflexive critique can take many forms in any interactive moment. We might, for example, pause at the moment we *know* we are correct, we *know* we have the best method or plan, we *know* how something should be. If we pause and ask ourselves, "how else might this be", "what else could I do at this moment", "is there a different way to make sense out of the other person's comments or actions", we open ourselves to the sort of inquiry that invites alternative meaning[13].

This is just the sort of inquiry Jaakko Seikkula and his colleagues engage when they respond to a psychiatric crisis[14]. Rather than assume

11. M. Bakhtin, *Speech Genres and Other Late Essays*, Austin, TX, University of Texas Press, 1986.

12. J. Shotter, *Contests of Identity*, Thousand Oaks, CA, Sage Publications, 2004.

13. S. McNamee – K.J. Gergen, *Relational Responsibility: Resources for Sustainable Dialogue*, Thousand Oaks, CA, Sage Publications, 1999.

14. J. Seikkula – J. Aaltonen – B. Alakara – K. Haarakangas – J. Keranen – M. Sutela, *Treating Psychosis by means of Open Dialogue*, in S. Friedman (ed.), *The Reflecting Team in Action*, New York, NY, Guildford Press, 1995, 62-80.

they, as the professionals, should provide a diagnosis and treatment plan, Seikkula and his team gather all interested parties together (the person in crisis, family members, friends, neighbors, medical professionals – anyone who might have something to contribute). Collaboratively they develop a plan of action that is responsive to the multiple ways of approaching and understanding the situation. The person in crisis is an active participant in this process. Seikkula calls this process *open dialogue*. It requires a suspension of the professional's certainty that s/he can provide an accurate diagnosis from which a successful treatment plan can be developed.

When we engage in self-reflexive critique like this, we avoid certainty. And, while certainty (as one hallmark of the competent individual) logically sounds appealing to us, it is precisely the stance that closes us to alternative views. Certainty also separates participants by establishing levels of expertise. Ironically, one of the very qualities we are trained to develop – certainty – inhibits our ability to act in ways that encourage transformation – in other words, in ways that are relationally ethical.

2. *Give Voice to Life Stories*

Another resource I find useful, as I mentioned earlier, is to avoid speaking from abstract positions. As with the stance of certainty, abstractions invite hierarchy and thus, separation – features not found in dialogue. Principles, values, and beliefs are crafted out of our day-to-day engagement with others. Understanding the principles from which you speak, the values that so strongly shape your position, or the beliefs that you hold dear, requires some sense of the relationships, the communities, the situated activities that have given these abstractions meaning for you. If you tell me a story about your family's rituals, I am more likely to appreciate how you raise your own children. Such appreciation does not require agreement. Yet, the difference between acknowledging the coherence of your beliefs or values and simply declaring them wrong, evil, or bad (because they do not fit with dominating cultural or communal beliefs or values) is tremendous.

This is aptly illustrated in the work of the Public Conversations Project[15]. They show us how dialogue, among people with incommensurate views, is facilitated by inviting them to talk about the relational communities within which their beliefs (i.e., abstract positions) have been

15. E.g. R. Chasin – M. Herzig, *Creating Systemic Interventions for the Sociopolitical Arena*, in B. Berger-Could – D.H. DeMuth (eds.), *The Global Family Therapist: Integrating the Personal, Professional and Political*, Needham, MA, Allyn and Bacon, 1992.

constructed. We can remain in dialogue if we appreciate the situated coherence of each other's position. And, in order to craft a reality together, remaining in dialogue is necessary. Thus, we can see that speaking from abstract positions closes our opportunities to *go on together* and locks us in endless attempts to achieve agreement (which we may never achieve). Avoiding abstraction helps us focus on recognizing the *local* significance of opposing views and in that recognition lies the potential to remain in dialogue. Specifically, the interaction (and thereby the relationship) shifts from one where the professional provides expert advice to one where the professional engages in *generous listening* to the narratives that lend coherence to the client's current situation. A professional might disagree with the values or actions described by a client but by listening to the client's story, the professional can understand how it is that this action or belief makes sense to the client. The professional no longer sees the client as crazy or evil or wrong. The client is viewed as having a different story, a different rationale, a different history of relationship. The professional is much better equipped to continue the conversation with this form of understanding.

3. *Coordination of Multiplicity*

Another relational resource for ethical action is attention to the coordination of multiplicities. When we confront difference, our tendency is to find any means to move toward consensus. Yet, consensus has its problems. Frequently, consensus is reached by participants removing from consideration the issues about which they are most passionate (and by association, the issues upon which their different world views emerge). The "common ground" or consensus that emerges from the process of negotiation most often focuses on smaller, less significant issues and thus, issues with which participants have little investment. To this end, consensus works to accelerate distrust and conflict rather than dissolve either. Consensus privileges problem solving over dialogic connection with the other. If the problem can be solved, there is little need for relational responsibility and attentiveness to the other.

Rather than approach problems as opportunities to develop consensus, in transformative dialogue we attempt to coordinate multiple discourses. The challenge is to become curious about all forms of practice and to explore the values and beliefs that give rise to them without searching for universal agreement. Can we create dialogic opportunities that invite *generous listening, curious inquiry, and a willingness for co-presence*?

4. *Using the Familiar in Unfamiliar Ways*

We might also explore using our familiar forms of action in unfamiliar contexts. Often when we feel that we lack the resources to be attentive to others' needs, we search for new tools or strategies that will create the desired change. In fact, one of the reasons counsellors and therapists are in such high demand is because culturally we believe that experts can teach us successful strategies for change. Yet, I would like to suggest that learning new strategies for coordinating conflict might not be necessary. Gregory Bateson talks about "the difference that makes a difference"[16] and Tom Andersen sees this difference as introducing "something unusual but not too un-usual"[17]. Here, I am suggesting a variation on this theme.

We all carry with us many voices, many differing opinions, views and attitudes – even on the same subject. These voices represent the accumulation of our relationships (actual, imagined, and virtual). In effect, we carry the residues of many others with us; we contain multitudes[18]. Yet, most of our actions, along with the positions we adopt in conversations, are one-dimensional. They represent only a small segment of all that we might do and say. The challenge is to draw on these other voices, these conversational resources that are familiar in one set of relationships and situations but not in another. In so doing, we achieve something unusual.

Using familiar resources in contexts where we do not generally use them invites us into new forms of engagement with others. If we think of all our activities as invitations into different relational constructions, then we can focus on how utilizing particular resources invites certain responses in specific relationships and how it invites different responses and constructions in others. All represent various attempts to achieve coordinated respect for the specificity of a given relationship and situation. If we can encourage ourselves (and others) to draw broadly on the conversational resources that are already familiar, perhaps we can act in ways that are *just different enough* to invite others into something beyond the same old unwanted pattern. To the extent that we can invite the use of the familiar in unfamiliar contexts, we are coordinating disparate discourses. What we are avoiding is co-opting one discourse as right and another as wrong. The novelty of enacting the old in a new context

16. G. Bateson, *Steps to an Ecology of Mind*, New York, NY, Ballentine, 1972, p. 272.

17. T. Andersen, *The Reflecting Team: Dialogues and Dialogues about the Dialogues*, New York, NY, W.W. Norton, 1991, p. 33.

18. McNamee – Gergen, *Relational Responsibility* (n. 13).

becomes, I believe, fertile soil within which to craft generative transformation.

5. *Imagine Possibilities*

Another resource that orients us toward dialogic potentials can be called the imaginative. Here, I find it useful to engage in conversations where we allow ourselves and invite our conversational partners to talk "as if"[19]. Can we talk "as if" we are the other in this situation? Can we talk "as if" we were a spouse, rather than a professional? How might we invite the other to speak "as if" he or she were curious about alternative views? These questions open dialogic possibilities by encouraging participants to move beyond sedimented images of self and other.

Along with "as if" conversations, we might engage in "what if" talk. As with "as if" conversations, when we play with potential scenarios beyond the expected, we have a stronger chance of inviting our relational partners into the crafting of new scenarios. Often, both "as if" and "what if" conversations can be usefully positioned within a broader dialogue about the future. When we speak from certainty about abstract positions, we tend to focus our attention on the past and why things have emerged as they have. However, when we engage in talk about the future and our idealized hopes for how we might jointly craft that future, our focus shifts from "why" to "how" our views and practices are in conflict. This shift to "how" suggests a final resource we might use to encourage dialogue.

When we focus on how we differ (or even how we manage to coordinate our activities together so well), we attend to our joint activities. How do *we* do this *together*? My actions alone are not wholly mine. They are *ours*. They are responsive to the situated moment, to our traditions of discourse, and to our imagined futures. We should not be concerned with asking, "How did we get here?" but rather be interested in asking, "How can *we* get *there*?". These pragmatic resources can enhance our potential for inviting others and ourselves into the openness of dialogue.

As we can see, when our attention is focused on coordinating a multiplicity of voices within a context where the notion of absolute truth is suspended, we invite a relationally sensitive ethic. This relational ethic moves beyond right and wrong, judgment and assessment. Instead, a relational ethic is attentive to the very unique ways in which participants, in their situated contexts, craft a sense of value in their lives. Appreciating

19. H. ANDERSON, *Conversation, Language, and Possibilities: A Postmodern Approach to Therapy*, New York, NY, Basic Books, 1997.

these nuanced values and beliefs on their own terms, opens the possibility for further coordinations that often might include alternative beliefs and values. In sum, transformation is the likely by-product of appreciation, respect, and relational engagement. This is what a relational ethic offers.

III. Some Concluding Remarks

Clearly, there is more to be said about dialogue and relational ethics. My hope is that these reflections open further possibilities. Dialogue is a joint performance wherein participants are responsive to each other and to their environment. Such responsivity renders dialogue unusual and unexpected. Yet, entering into dialogue so as to invite the unexpected requires preparation. It requires us to give up our desire to explain the present by pointing to the past. It requires us to replace our abstract positions with our lived stories – the richly textured, relational scenarios we engage in with others. It requires us to listen for, to provide the space for, and to invite difference – for ourselves and for our dialogic partners. This unusual aspect of dialogue opens possibilities for engaging with others relationally.

We live in a relational world. Cultures are thrown into ever increasing contact. And yet, for the most part, we operate within an ideology that privileges the thinking, acting, feeling individual. There is both pragmatic and theoretical demand for forms of practice that emphasize our relational interdependence because it is from our relations that all we take as valuable emerges.

Department of Communication
University of New Hamsphire
20 Academic Way, Durham, NH 03 824
U.S.A.
sheila.mcnamee@unh.edu

Sheila McNamee

THE VOCATION OF LISTENING

THE OTHER SIDE OF DIALOGUE

As a topic of study with roots in many disciplines – be they in Plato's dialogues, Bakhtin's literary theory, Buber's religious existentialism or Levinas's ethics, or be they in Vygotsky's psycholinguistics, Rogers's clinical psychology or Freire's pedagogy, to name but a few domains – it does not seem terribly unfair to say that the study of dialogue has tended, by and large, to pass over listening in favor of speaking[1]. Even in quotidian parlance, it would appear that *dialogue* is about *talking*. The Oxford English Dictionary (OED), for example, defines dialogue as "a conversation carried on between two or more persons; a colloquy, talk together", and, circularly, it defines conversation as the "interchange of thoughts and words; familiar discourse or talk". Thus among the various domains of dialogical study, there is, for the most part, a remarkable silence when it comes to listening. Whichever way it is glossed – as rhetoric, dialogue, language, or argumentation – the western conception of *the logos* emphasizes speech at the expense of listening[2]. And the problem with conceiving of language in terms of speech and speaking is not only that it obscures and minimizes the importance of listening, but also, as I shall argue below, that it conceals the ways in which listening is the event, occurrence, and performance of the ethical relation. Without it, no ethical relation can exist.

I. Philosophical Foundations

The writings of Martin Buber and Emmanuel Levinas represent two important strands of dialogical philosophy that focus on the relationship between ethics and dialogue. Yet in spite of their mutual emphasis on the face-to-face relation, both Levinas and Buber posit an ethical encounter that *presupposes yet underestimates* the importance of

1. Some important exceptions exist in areas of educational, clinical and therapeutic research where listening is understood to be of fundamental importance to dialogue.

2. For a thorough philosophical explication of this problematic, see G. Corradi Fiumara, *The Other Side of Language: A Philosophy of Listening*, trans. Charles Lambert, New York, NY, Routledge, 1990.

listening. As scholars, Buber and Levinas drew from similar religious, existentialist and phenomenological intellectual traditions. But they also differed in significant ways, and their work is to be distinguished by the dimensions and scope of their projects. Buber was principally a philosopher of religion, and although his work on dialogical philosophy was perhaps his most well known, it did not comprise the bulk of his bibliography. Further, his work tends to be poetic and aphoristic in style, lending itself more readily to theology and psychology than to philosophical argumentation. Levinas, in contrast, produced a voluminous bibliography of work that generated his philosophy of ethics and the other. Like Buber, Levinas also wrote Jewish philosophy, but unlike Buber, he intentionally kept the two projects of Judaism and philosophy separate.

As individuals with different historical experiences and religious affiliations, there are also some important distinctions to be made between the two scholars. Buber, born in Vienna in 1878, wrote as a non-statist Zionist Jew, steeped in both German Romanticism and Hasidic folk traditions of mysticism and Kabbalah. Buber moved to Israel in 1938 and lived out the Shoah within the Jewish community there serving as a critic of Israeli nationalism and a proponent of a joint Arab-Jewish state. He died in 1965 at age 87. Unlike Levinas, Buber rejected a Halakahic interpretation of Torah and saw the Bible instead as a dialogical encounter between man and God. Buber's rejection of traditional Judaism apparently began early. For example, Avnon describes how Buber, when called to read from the Torah during his Bar Mitzvah, instead read and interpreted a poem by the German romantic poet and philosopher Schiller[3]. Further, according to Katz, "Buber's understanding of revelation as relation is one of his most fundamental and radical claims ... Revelation, argues Buber, is never objective content. Rather, in revelation one comes 'face to face' with the Eternal Thou"[4]. Buber's interest thus begins with the immanent God of everyday life and the relations of embodied, historical human beings in the ethical possibilities of the dialogical encounter. His concerns, while ontological, are not about being in an abstract or metaphysical sense, but in a rooted relational being-in-the-world sense. Thus Buber's dialogical philosophy is deeply intertwined with his religious scholarship.

3. D. AVNON, *Martin Buber: The Hidden Dialogue*, Lanham, MD, Rowman and Littlefield, 1998.

4. S. KATZ, *Jewish Philosophers*, New York, NY, Bloch, 1975, pp. 193-194.

Levinas was born in 1905 (December 30)[5] in Lithuania and settled in France in 1923. Upon spending a year in Germany studying with Husserl and Heidegger in 1928-1929, Levinas steadily engaged his philosophical project regarding ethics and the other and also wrote Jewish commentary steeped in the orthodoxies of Talmud and Halakah. After surviving the war and the Shoah in a prison camp as a military prisoner in the French army while his wife and child were hidden in the French countryside, Levinas settled in France for the rest of his life. His entire Lithuanian family, however, was murdered by Nazis during the war. He died in 1995 at the age of 89. In his ethical philosophy Levinas is not attempting to sketch a normative ethics or define principles, but to locate the origin of being in its own transcendence in the relation of responsibility. His view of God, moreover, is "wholly other" and thereby rooted in imagery of transcendence. Although Levinas says that he considers his philosophical writing to be distinctly secular and therefore separate from his religious writings, there are nevertheless clear affinities between the two and much of his biblical commentary resonates with ideas from his philosophy. For example, in a commentary on temptation and the Tractact Shabbath Levinas writes that "The Torah is given in Light of a face. The epiphany of the other person is *ipso facto* my responsibility toward him: seeing the other is already an obligation toward him. A direct optics – without the mediation of any idea – can only be accomplished as ethics. Integral knowledge or Revelation (the receiving of the Torah) is ethical behavior"[6].

Philosophically, two overlapping but different dimensions of Levinas and Buber's work provide the scaffolding needed to reframe the face-to-face from a speech-centered to a listening-centered phenomenon. The first dimension pertains to ontology and the origins of the self. Buber's perspective takes ontology to be fundamentally dialogical, wherein the self arises in relational, intersubjective space of the dialogical encounter. This is expressed in Buber's pronominal words "I and Thou" and "I and It", which cannot be reduced simply to two pairs of pronouns; each figure is itself a full and complete "word". In his classic 1923 book *I and Thou*, Buber describes how subjectivity begins, is born, in the encounter with another. He writes, "I become through my relation to Thou" and "in the beginning is relation"[7]. Thus to Buber, subjectivity is itself

5. According to the Julian calendar; or: January 12, 1906 according to the Gregorian calendar.

6. E. LEVINAS, *Nine Talmudic Readings*, trans. Annette Aronowicz, Bloomington, IN – Indianapolis, IN, Indiana University Press, 1994, p. 47.

7. M. BUBER, *I and Thou*, trans. Roland Gregor Smith, New York, NY, Scribner, 1958, p. 18. A brief note on translation: Although Walter Kaufmann's translation of *I and Thou*

dialogical and emerges from interpersonal interaction. The second scaffold pertains to ethics and its place in philosophy. From Levinas, we learn the ways in which ethics is first philosophy – that is, what comes first in philosophical inquiry is not an ontological question about being, but an ethical question about our relation to the other. As Levinas describes it, "preexisting the plane of ontology is the ethical plane"[8]. Thus first philosophy asks not the ontological question of whether to be or not to be, but the ethical question of whether the relation of my being to others is justified. In short, it means "to fear injustice more than death, to prefer to suffer than to commit injustice"[9]. To Levinas, the self is always accompanied by the "bad conscience" about whether I have usurped the place of the other. Thus in contrast to their teachers and existentialist contemporaries such as Husserl, Merleau-Ponty, and Sartre who focus on the consciousness and ideation of the self, the Buber and Levinas subject of the self is not a self-same-subject, but a relational intersubjective subject. To Levinas subjectivity is not for itself, but for the other. To Buber subjectivity only arises in and through relation to the other. Thus it might be said that the face-to-face encounter exemplifies a kind of simultaneous dimensionality between the ethical and the dialogical, for it facilitates the co-constitution of selves in relation and is organized around fundamentally ethical questions of goodness and well-being.

II. Dialogical Ethics

This essay draws upon three central ideas in Buber and Levinas's dialogical philosophy to build the case for listening as the nascence of the ethical relation[10]. The three concepts – alterity, intersubjectivity, and

is the only American English version currently in print, I generally prefer Smith's translation. For example, Smith's use of *Thou* conveys a sense of the other's distance and alterity in a manner less apparent in Kaufmann's *You*. Similarly, Smith's rendering "All real living is meeting" is more evocative and participatory than Kaufman's nominalized "All actual life is encounter".

8. E. Levinas, *Totality and Infinity: An Essay on Exteriority*, trans. Alphonso Lingis, Pittsburgh, PA, Duquesne University Press, 1969, p. 201.

9. E. Levinas, *Ethics as First Philosophy*, in S. Hand (ed.), *The Levinas Reader*, trans. Alphonso Lingis, Oxford, Blackwell, 1989, 75-87, p. 85.

10. Much has been written regarding the differences between Levinas and Buber's approach to dialogical ethics. For a range of perspectives on these differences, see R. Bernasconi, *'Failure of Communication' as a Surplus: Dialogue and Lack of Dialogue Between Buber and Levinas*, in R. Bernasconi – D. Wood (eds.), *The Provocation of Levinas: Rethinking the Other*, New York, NY, Routledge, 1988; D. Casey, *Levinas and Buber: Transcendence and Society*, in *Sophia* 38 (1999) 69-92; M. Friedman, *Martin*

responsibility – comprise essential foundations from which dialogical ethics spring. When speaking of dialogue and ethics, we are not speaking of two separate things, but two dimensions of the same thing: *being* human together with other humans. That is, *being* in relationship with others. From Buber we will build upon the idea that the ontological ground of dialogical ethics is an intersubjectively grounded self that is called into being by the relational encounter with the other, the face-to-face. From Levinas, we will build on the idea that the philosophical ground of dialogical ethics begins from the face-to-face relational encounter with the other that calls the self's "right to be" into question. And everything begins with awareness, acceptance, and acknowledgment of the infinite exteriority of others.

1. *Alterity*

In both Levinas's and Buber's view of dialogue, we are called upon to never lose sight of the *radical alterity*, or *otherness*, of the other. That is, we are asked to never mistake *our* understanding of the other for the *other herself*, never to impose our meaning and understanding upon him, never to attempt to absorb/assimilate/appropriate the other into ourselves. We are enjoined by Buber to relate to the other across a "narrow ridge" and by Levinas to avoid absorbing the other's *difference* into my own *same*. In writing of the relation to the other, for example, Levinas observes how the other is always more than she appears: "The face of the other at each moment destroys and overflows the plastic image it leaves me"[11]. Similarly, Buber points to the importance of my interlocutor's alterity when he writes that "Genuine conversation, and therefore every actual fulfillment of relation between men, means acceptance of otherness ... Everything depends so far as human life is concerned, on

Buber and Emmanuel Levinas: An Ethical Query, in *Philosophy Today* 45 (2001) 3-11; N. GORDON, *Ethics as Reciprocity: An Analysis of Levinas's Reading of Buber*, in *International Studies in Philosophy* 31 (1999) 91-109; A. KELLY, *Reciprocity and the Height of God: A Defense of Buber against Levinas*, in *Sophia* 34 (1995) 65-73; P. LAWTON, *Love and Justice: Levinas' Reading of Buber*, in *Philosophy Today* 20 (1976) 77-83; L. LIPARI, *Listening for the Other: Ethical Implications of the Buber-Levinas Encounter*, in *Communication Theory* 14 (2004) 122-141; S. LUMSDEN, *Absolute Difference and Social Ontology: Levinas Face to Face with Buber and Fichte*, in *Human Studies* 23 (2000) 227-241; J.W. MURRAY, *Face to Face in Dialogue: Emmanuel Levinas and (the) Communication (of) Ethics*, Lanham, MD, University Press of America, 2003; A. TALLON, *Intentionality, Intersubjectivity, and the Between: Buber and Levinas on Affectivity and the Dialogical Principle*, in *Thought* 53 (1978) 292-309.

11. LEVINAS, *Totality and Infinity* (n. 8), p. 51.

whether each thinks of the other as the one he is"[12]. As with the irreducible otherness of the Levinasian face, Buber describes the I-Thou relation as an encounter with alterity – the other is unknown and unimagined. Moreover, the I-Thou relation is without goal and arrives on the scene serendipitously as if by "will and grace". To Buber, dialogue arises not from prior intentions or future aims, but from the present moment, and he describes the relation of dialogue as one of "turning towards the other"[13]. Buber theorizes the ways in which both separation *and* relation occur simultaneously in dialogue: "Neither needs to give up his point of view ... they enter a realm where the point of view no longer holds"[14].

In dialogical ethics, the acknowledgment of alterity enables speakers to acknowledge, if not honor, radical differences in thought, belief, political and social location, communicative, symbolic, and social capital, and so forth. Thus, unlike a Habermasian discourse ethics of the ideal speech situation, where interlocutors are instructed to "bracket status differentials and deliberate as if they were social equals", or a Rawlsian theory of justice, which asks interlocutors to deliberate behind a "veil of ignorance" with respect to social location, dialogical ethics deliberately invites and acknowledges difference. Thus, rather than viewing misunderstanding, conflict, or disagreement as a failure of communication, dialogical ethics offers a view of difference and difficulty as not just inevitable, but as foundational dimensions of language and social interaction. From this perspective, difference and misunderstanding are a kind of ringing bell whose reverberations remind us, again and again, that other persons are, in fact, truly *other* than us and that each of us arrive "on the scene" of communication with different histories, traditions, experiences, and perspectives.

2. *Intersubjectivity and the Face*

Intersubjectivity describes the space between persons who collaboratively create and share meaning. Originally central to the philosophy of phenomenology, the concept of intersubjectivity is employed in a number of other fields where it points to the constitutive dimensions of communication in which understandings, meanings and identities are produced

12. M. BUBER, *The Knowledge of Man: Selected Essays*, ed. Maurice FRIEDMAN, trans. Maurice Friedman and Roland Gregor Smith, Amherst, NY, Humanity Books, 1998, p. 59.

13. M. BUBER, *Between Man and Man*, trans. Roland Gregor Smith, New York, NY, Macmillan, 1975, p. 22.

14. *Ibid.*, p. 6.

not by individual subjects but rather by interacting social subjects who abide collectively within communities of discourse. Buber's notion of the relation as central to personhood and Levinas's idea of ethics as first philosophy both place intersubjectivity, rather than egocentric or monologic subjectivity, at the center of dialogical philosophy. The intersubjective engagement manifests for both Buber and Levinas in the face-to-face of the dialogical encounter where *the face* of the other transcends social categories of identity and dialogical ethics emerges from the intersubjective interaction among faces, in all their otherness.

To Levinas, the face is the manifestation of the ethical exigency that is woven into the very structure of human being. The face is neither figurative nor literal, but is the expression of the demand of the other, which calls my being into question. Thus the face, like the face-to-face, is always dual. It is a relational and not an absolute term. "The facing position, opposition par excellence, can only be as a moral summons"[15]. As an absolute and infinite exteriority, the face can never be grasped, possessed, or absorbed into the familiar and already known homogeneities that Levinas calls "the same". Ethics "begins in the face of the exteriority of the other, in the face of the other – that face which enlists my responsibility by its human expression … an ethic of heteronomy"[16]. Although not a central metaphor in Buber, the face makes an important appearance in *I and Thou*. As with Levinas, Buber's face evokes an ethical response. But whereas Levinas's face expresses the irreducible alterity of the other person as a human being, Buber's face represents the ultimate Thou of God immanent in all things. He writes: "He who has approached the Face has indeed surpassed duty and obligation – but not because he is now remote from the world; rather because he has truly drawn closer to it … The world, lit by eternity, becomes fully present to him who approaches the Face, and to the Being of beings he can in a single response say Thou"[17].

Both Levinas and Buber conceptualize a self that does not fully exist prior to its encounter with the face of other. Because the Levinasian self is always already responsible for the other, it owes its basic existence to the call of the other. In Levinas, the self is called to responsibility for the other before it is free. It is, in his words, a 'hostage' perpetually 'accused' and 'persecuted' by the other's call. "The uniqueness of the responsible

15. LEVINAS, *Totality and Infinity* (n. 8), p. 196.
16. ID., *Martin Buber, Gabriel Marcel and Philosophy*, in H. GORDON – J. BLOCH (eds.), *Martin Buber: A Centenary Volume*, Negev, Israel, KTAV Publishing House, 1984, p. 317.
17. BUBER, *I and Thou* (n. 7), pp. 108-109.

ego is possible only *in* being obsessed by another, in the trauma suffered prior to any auto-identification, in an unrepresentable before"[18]. Similarly, to Buber, the person *becomes* by saying Thou: "I become through my relation to the Thou; as I become *I*, I say *Thou*"[19]. By saying *Thou*, one is unyoked from the imperialism of the egocentric self. For Buber "real living is meeting" and in meeting one suspends egocentricity for an opening to intersubjectivity, the unpredictable and foreign land he names the 'between'. As Friedman describes it, in the I-Thou relation, one is liberated from the strong hold of the ego, which awakens "in the other the need of help and in yourself the capacity to help; it means coming from behind the fortress of your spirit in which you have enclosed yourself"[20].

3. *Response and Responsibility*

Responsibility in dialogical ethics derives directly from the ability-to-respond to the other – both communicatively and otherwise. That is to say that the ethical response is not a mere utterance or reply, but it is both a condition and manifestation of *being* in relation. Thus to Buber, responsibility derives from *Thou saying* and to Levinas, from subordination of myself to the other. To Buber therefore, "Genuine responsibility exists only when there is real responding"[21] and for Levinas, the self's responsibility to respond to the face of the other is infinite, unlimited. Levinas grounds the response in the subjugation of the self to the other, the substitution of the self-for-the other. This substitution *requires* "divesting the ego of its imperialism ... the self *gnawing away at oneself* in responsibility"[22]. But quietly embedded in these questions of response a hidden but presupposed prior action endures – that of listening –about which the philosophy of dialogue falls, ironically, silent. The idea of *the response* as related to ideas of reply, answer, and reaction as well as its etymological derivation from the Latin *spondere* 'to pledge' (promise, offer, sacrifice) stresses only the speaking of an ethical actor. The act of listening is itself concealed and rendered invisible. Thus the ethical response presupposes the hidden entailments of *listening*. For in order to

18. E. LEVINAS, *Otherwise than Being or Beyond Essence*, trans. Alphonso Lingis, Pittsburgh, PA, Duquesne University Press, 1998, p. 123.
19. BUBER, *I and Thou* (n. 7), p. 11.
20. M. FRIEDMAN, *Martin Buber's Life and Work: The Early Years 1878-1923*, New York, NY, E.P. Dutton, 1981, p. 243.
21. BUBER, *I and Thou* (n. 7), p. 16.
22. LEVINAS, *Otherwise than Being* (n. 18), p. 121.

respond I must first listen – that is attend, observe, attune – and in doing so receive the otherness of the other. Without this listening there simply can be no response. There may be speaking, and there may be acting, but there can be no genuine engagement. As I will explore below, dialogical ethics is empty without listening.

III. Listening, Embodiment and Voice[23]

In spite of their warnings about the dangers of the failure to make strange and see the other as wholly other, neither Levinas nor Buber highlight dialogue's other – listening – and as a result both leave the relation between *listening* and *responsibility* somewhat in the shadows. Thus despite the import of Levinas's distinction between *the saying* and *the said* and of Buber's differentiation between *I-It* and *I-Thou dialogue,* these distinctions, perhaps inadvertently, seem to place too much emphasis on speaking and not enough on listening. In the English language, we have two words for the auditory process: hearing and listening. The verb *to hear* derives from the Middle English *heren*, Old High German *hOren*, and Latin *cavEre*. Webster's (n.d.) defines *to hear* as (1): to perceive or apprehend by ear and (2): to gain knowledge of by hearing. Similarly, the Oxford English Dictionary (n.d) defines *to hear* as "To perceive, or have the sensation of, sound; to possess or exercise the faculty of audition of which the specific organ is the ear". The verb *to listen*, in contrast, is derived from Middle English as *listnen* and is defined by the idea of *attention* to sound. The OED (n.d.) defines *listen* as "to hear attentively; to give ear to; to pay attention". The OED derives *listen* from the Sanskrit *crusti* (meaning obedience) and relates it to words associated with audition (audit, auditorium, audio, etc.) that stem from the Latin *Audire* (obedience).

This etymology illustrates that *listen* and *hear* are not simply synonyms, but are inflected with different meanings that suggest different ways of being in the world. Etymologically, *listening* comes from a root that emphasizes *attention* and *giving to others,* while *hearing* comes from a root that emphasizes *perception* and *receiving from others*. Indeed, the ideas of "gaining" and "possessing" found in *hearing* foreground the

23. Section III, IV & V of this essay contain portions of material previously published by the author in the following venues: *Listening Otherwise: The Voice of Ethics*, in *International Journal of Listening* 23 (2009) 44-59; *Listening, Thinking, Being*, in *Communication Theory* 20 (2010) 348-362; *Rhetoric's Other: Levinas, Listening, and the Ethical Responce*, in *Philosophy and Rhetoric* 45 (2012) 227-245.

self's experience, while the ideas of attention and obedience found in *listening* focus on the other. Unfortunately, these two distinctions are often lost in both philosophical and everyday usages. For example, while Gadamer considers *hearing* to be "the basis of the hermeneutical phenomenon" he nevertheless fails to distinguish hearing from listening when he writes "when you look at something you can also look away from it by looking in another direction, but you cannot 'hear away'"[24]. While it is certainly true that we can literally shut out visual but not auditory stimuli, it is also true that we can *hear* but fail to *listen*. For just as *seeing* can occur in the absence of *looking*, so can *hearing* occur without *listening*, and both the communication literature and everyday life are filled with examples (ranging from "turning a deaf ear", to "selective listening") that convey the idea of what Gadamer calls "*hearing away*". That is, hearing without listening is response without responsibility; it is a form of pseudo-dialogue without ethics. This connection between listening and responding is revealed in the etymology of the words *obedience* and *obey*. The Latin root of *obey* is *oboedire* – combined from the intensifier *ob* and the verb *audire*, which means *to hear*. Obedience is thus a form of listening – a listening for and toward the other.

1. *The Listening and the Heard*

The distinction between listening and hearing raises another possible distinction which, echoing Levinas's distinction between *the saying* and *the said*, we might call *the listening* and *the heard*. If *the saying*, to Levinas, expresses an infinite surplus of responsibility and vulnerability that precedes signification, then *the listening* enacts an infinite surplus of welcoming invitation and reception, no matter what is said or heard. As Levinas writes of the saying, it "opens me to the other before saying what is said, before the said uttered in this sincerity forms a screen between me and the other. This saying without a word is thus like silence. It is without words, but not with hands empty"[25]. Thus *the listening,* in contrast to *the heard,* is an enactment of responsibility made manifest through a posture of receptivity, a passivity of receiving the other into oneself without assimilation or appropriation. *The listening* is a process of contraction, of stepping back and creating a void into which the other

24. H.-G. GADAMER, *Truth and Method*, trans. Joel Weinsheimer and Donald G. Marshall, New York, NY, Continuum, 2003, p. 462.

25. E. LEVINAS, *God and Philosophy*, in ID., *Collected Philosophical Papers*, trans. Alphonso Lingis, Dordrecht – Boston, MA – Lancaster, Martinus Nijhoff, 1987, p. 170.

may enter. It is the distance I create so that you may come forward. In *the listening* I create a space to receive you, letting your speech enter me, flow through me. To listen without judgment or making your words or meanings mine means that I stand close, but at a distance. Receptive but unattached. 'Disinter-ested' as Levinas would write.

The heard, in contrast to *the listening*, involves taking in your words and making them mine. It involves judgment and distinction – seeking certainty using cognitive structures, schemas, familiar ways of seeing and doing. *The heard* is when I fix your words over and against mine – there may be contest, disagreement, discord. I may try to assimilate, appropriate, convince, or seek a kind of communion. Or we may stand on opposite ends of what Buber calls the "narrow ridge" looking down at the shear drop, the dizzying height, with no common goal in sight. Without attending to the significance of listening, our ethical inquiries tend to focus too much on *the heard* and miss the fact that *the listening*, like *the saying*, has its own meaning, if not priority. As both Buber and Levinas enjoin, to make the stranger a familiar is to somehow do violence to the otherness of the other, to leave some part of the stranger outside of the dwelling place of our presence. Listening, as opposed to the heard, is not to place the other in conformity with ourselves, what Levinas calls "self-coinciding" but is instead to create space to receive the alterity of the other and let it resonate.

2. *Embodiment and Voice*

We humans are embodied beings. That is, we live in and with and from our bodies. But as many artists, thinkers, and scholars note, we, in the west, tend to live from the neck up, "between the ears", as it were. But do we? The philosophical tradition in the west has tended to separate mind and body, thought and emotion, but as recent advances in neuroscience and biology are demonstrating, such separation is an illusion – mind and body are deeply interconnected, if they are even two things at all. So, following this idea, what if our ears aren't really in our heads, but are our whole body? What if our entire body were one giant listening organ, one great resonating chamber? What if we were *all ears*?

Perhaps it is not too farfetched to think this way. Sound waves can travel in any medium – air, water, bone, skin, stone. Sound waves are an expression of energy with the power to shape matter. Sound waves travel through air, then through the skin of the timpanic membrane (our ear 'drum') and then along the bones of our inner ear (the malleus, incus, and stapes), and then into the mysterious cochlea, a fluid-filled membrane lined with tiny hairs that are each tuned to a different vibration, which in turn trigger auditory neurons that fire up the auditory nerve and travel into the brain. So one thing about listening is that it takes place in time and in the body. And one of its key elements is rhythm, which, as George Leonard has pointed out, is the pulse of life.

The voice, the organ of speech, literally testifies to our embodiment as speaking and listening beings. Levinas frequently invokes the Biblical phrase "here I am" (*Hineni* in Hebrew), which is spoken both by Moses and Isaiah upon encountering God. This "here I am" is a posture of receptivity – a readiness to listen to the Other who is God. By bringing the voice more fully into our conception of the face-to-face, we can bring in the listening upon which the ethical relation depends. In Levinas, the speech of the face contains both language and non-language elements and can convey meaning without words. But unlike the face, speech is disembodied and detached. So in place of speech, I will here introduce the notion of *the voice* as the face's counterpart. While voice and face are both elements of the human body that can signify and express, the voice brings the *temporal* embodiment of human *being* into sharper relief. The voice moves rhythmically through time as an event, not an object, through the medium of the breath and its rhythm of inhalation and exhalation. The voice of the other, unlike the face of the other, is invisible and cannot be seen. It has not one but many surfaces, and reverberates with the echoes of all the other voices past and present, heard and unheard. As sound, the voice of the other is a wave of energy that surrounds me, enters me. But unlike the exteriority of the face, which preserves the subject/object dualism of *the seeing* and *the seen*, the voice of the other mingles inextricably, crossing through semi-permeable boundaries between inner and outer[26]. Like light, sound has a horizon that animates space, but unlike light, sound blurs the boundaries between interior and exterior. When sound waves of speech enter me, they become me, by vibrating my eardrums so that I am, as deaf percussionist Evelyn Glennie says, a "participator" of sound. Sound is thus embodied in its reception, rippling through skin, muscle, bone and synapse. Most significantly, perhaps, *the voice* invokes a *listening ear* grounded in the intersubjectivity of the relation rather than a *seeing eye* born through the subjectivity of objectification and domination. As Levinas writes, "To put speech at the origin of truth is to abandon the thesis that … the solitude of vision is

26. For an exploration of the priority of voice in both dialogical and cognitive processes, see M.-C. BERTAU, *Voice: A Pathway to Consciousness as 'Social Contact to Oneself'*, in *Integrative Psychological and Behavioral Science* 42 (2008) 92-113.

the first work of truth"[27]. But might we not go still further, and put *listening*, rather than speech, at the origin of truth? That is, perhaps my encounter with the voice of the other is made manifest in neither the separation of vision nor the invocation of the other, but in the receptive relation of listening – my attentive attunement to the speech of the other. But, importantly, this must be a listening and not a hearing, it must not be an assimilation or a unification, but must preserve the others' alterity at each moment. Levinas states the problem quite directly when he writes, "if communication bears the mark of failure or inauthenticity in this way, it is because it is sought as a fusion. One begins with the idea that the duality must be transformed into a unity, and that social relations must culminate in communion"[28]. Thus whereas the face points to the alterity of the unsaid and unsayable, to the inexhaustible infinite ineffability of *the saying*, the voice resounds with the echoes the unheard and unhearable, with the inexorable infinite responsibility of *the listening*.

IV. The Vocation of Listening

The voice calls, but do I listen? And when the face of the other calls me into question, what do I hear? What, we might ask, does this Levinasian invocation, this call, evoke? In contemporary English, the word vocation has become nearly synonymous with occupation, work, labor, career, or profession. We have vocational training and vocational rehabilitation, vocational services and vocational-technical schools. Still lingering, however, is the sense of the religious vocation as something closer to a call, to being summoned. We think of the religious vocation as being "called" or "summoned" by God. Thomas Merton describes how the religious vocation requires one "to deliver oneself up, to hand oneself over, entrust oneself completely"[29] to the call. But what is a call without an ear to listen? Might we say that it is not quite, not yet, a vocation? The English etymology of the word "vocation" comes by way of the Latin *Voc* for voice, originally from the Sanskrit *Vak* or *Vac*, "an early Vedic term for the absolute word"[30] and for the goddess of speech.

27. Levinas, *Totality and Infinity* (n. 8), p. 99.

28. Id., *The Other in Proust*, in Hand (ed.), *The Levinas Reader* (n. 9), 160-165, p. 164.

29. T. Merton, *Thoughts in Solitude*, New York, NY, Farrar, Straus & Giroux, 1956, p. 101.

30. For an extraordinary in-depth study into the role of sound in Hindu Theology, see G.L. Beck, *Sonic Sound: Hinduism and Sacred Sound*, Columbia, SC, University of South Carolina Press, 1993, p. 251.

The word *vocation* also echoes in its cognates such as *invocation* and *evocation*, which imply something more, something beyond a call or a summons. According to the OED, *to evoke* is "to draw out something hidden" and *to invoke* is to perform "a form of conjuring". Thus we might say that in dialogical ethics, listening is my vocation, my calling. And this vocation of listening requires me to evoke or invoke an encounter with the unknown; a listening that draws forth something hidden, bringing something new into the world. But an implict question still hangs in the air: does the vocation of listening precede, rather than follow, the call?

1. *The Perils of Language*

A great deal of why we don't listen has to do with the nature of knowledge and understanding and the role of language, cognition, and belief. In brief, the problem is that we habituate to already existing linguistic categories, structures and schemas and mistake these conceptual formations as the truth of the way things are. And although our linguistic categories, structures and schemas enable us to make worlds – both wonderful and hideous – Gurevitch describes how when our perceptions become "securely encrusted around some conviction, justification, identity, cause or the like, [we deny] the legitimacy of the other"[31]. The cognitive structures of language are particularly dangerous when we become habituated to them such that they are automatic and invisible to us. They distort our perceptions and point us to see what we expect to see and ignore everything else. As Merton describes it, "The human dilemma of communication is that we cannot communicate ordinarily without words and signs, but even ordinary experience tends to be falsified by our habits of verbalization and rationalization. The convenient tools of language enable us to decided beforehand what we think things mean, and tempt us all too easily to see things only in a way that fits our logical preconceptions and our verbal formulas"[32].

In short, dialogical ethics is not about what we already know or think we know about the other or his point of view. It is instead about process and presence as much or more than it is about content. Buber calls this communicative opening to the other "presence" and Levinas calls it

31. Z.D. GUREVITCH, *The Power of Not Understanding: The Meeting of Conflicting Identities*, in P.K. CHEW (ed), *The Conflict and Culture Reader*, New York, NY, New York University Press, 2001, 241-248, p. 244.

32. T. MERTON, *Thoughts on the East*, New York, NY, New Directions, 1995, p. 38.

"saying". To Levinas, "*the said* [le dit] does not count as much as *the saying* [le dire] itself"[33].

Thus dialogical ethics privileges not the content of signification per se, but the process of opening to the other. Levinas writes: "Communication is not a modality of cognition ... it is irreducible to the circulation of information which presupposes it"[34]. Similarly, in describing the I – Thou encounter, Buber writes that "Man receives, and he receives not a specific 'content' but a Presence"[35]. Thus both Buber and Levinas conceptualize communication as more than a system of signs and symbols used to convey information. Rather, dialogue is understood to be an emergent, generative praxis that brings new worlds into being[36]. As we will see below, the ethical significance of listening becomes apparent when language and communication are considered to be more than structured symbolic forms that represent or transmit content.

2. *Listening Otherwise*

Among the innumerable ways one can fail ethically, the communicative subjection of the other to one's self is perhaps among the most hidden. This is where one holds fast to cognitive preconceptions and assimilates the words of the other into what one already knows, or thinks one knows. To resist these habitual and often invisible interpretive routines, the ethical response requires what we might call a process of *listening otherwise* – that is, listening not merely for an exchange of signs or receipt of information, but for the emergent self-transcendence that involves opening and vulnerability[37]. In this form of open listening we give up our attachment to our familiar and already understood certainties and cognitions about the world in order to fully receive the other. Gurevitch describes this as an "interpersonal Copernican discovery [in which] one's sense of centrality is lost and with it the taken-for-granted meaning of all that this centrality entailed"[38]. This opening to the other is a

33. E. LEVINAS, *Ethics and Infinity*, trans. Richard A. Cohen, Pittsburgh, PA, Duquesne University Press, 1985, p. 42.

34. LEVINAS, *Otherwise than Being* (n. 18), p. 48.

35. BUBER, *I and Thou* (n. 7), p. 110.

36. For a thorough exploration of this distinction, see J. STEWART, *The Symbol Model vs. Language as Constitutive Articulate Contact*, in ID. (ed.), *Beyond the Symbol Model: Reflections on the Representational Nature of Language*, Albany, NY, State University of New York, 2002.

37. For a fuller explication of this idea, see LIPARI, *Listening Otherwise* (n. 23).

38. Z.D. GUREVITCH, *The Other Side of Dialogue: On Making the Other Strange and the Experience of Otherness*, in *American Journal of Sociology* 93 (1988) 1179-1199, p. 1188.

process of de-familiarization in which we renounce the familiar and embrace the strange. "When the other is perceived as strange, he or she is liberated from the image that one has projected onto the other's experience from the center of one's self. The other emerges as an independent and 'distant' phenomenon"[39].

In ethical dialogue, *listening otherwise* is where communicative acrobatics take place, where one steps off the cliff of self-certainty and flies toward the other without the safety of ground and into a space of groundless self-transcendence. It must be stressed here that the self-transcendence of ethical listening is not to be confused with an unquestioned universalization of self or subject position. Postmodern theories have clearly called into question the supposition of a universalized a-historical, and/or value-neutral subject position that transcends culture and sociality. In contrast, the self-transcendence of *listening otherwise* is not a disavowal or denial of self, historicity, or of contingency. *Listening otherwise* takes us beyond the self and out into the groundlessness and ambiguity of the radical alterity of the other. As Noddings describes care ethics, "We are not attempting to transform the world, but we are allowing ourselves to be transformed"[40]. This openness to letting ourselves be transformed in the face of the other is difficult, because it involves to a certain degree, the disruption and at times renunciation of self and what it already knows and understands. As an ethical stance, *listening otherwise* requires a willingness to suspend already familiar conceptions, beliefs and understandings. Because language is one of the most powerful means by which our conceptual habits are shaped, *listening otherwise* requires a steady simultaneity of presence, awareness and emptiness. When we become habituated to the familiar, we hear only what we already know, or expect, to hear. *Listening otherwise* requires both an awareness of our habitual categories and a willingness to go beyond them. In *listening otherwise*, the listener's emptiness is a form of inner silence that has suspended the noise of inner discursive thought. This form of inner emptiness facilitates a focus and attention that enables one to really absorb the other's words beyond the confines of what one has already thought, believed, or understood. That is, in *listening otherwise* one comes to the conversation empty – not empty of experience or history – but empty of the belief that one's experience or history defines the limits of possible meaning and experience. By *listening otherwise*,

39. GUREVITCH, *The Power of Not Understanding* (n. 31), p. 242.

40. N. NODDINGS, *Caring: A Feminine Approach to Ethics and Moral Education*, Berkeley, CA, University of California Press, 1984, p. 34.

I empty myself of all intentions other than the intention of engagement with you – as Kaplan describes it, "When I am really talking to you, I *have* nothing to say"[41]. In this way, listening otherwise is not unlike the listening of improvisational jazz where players begin with a shared context of a "tune" – a familiar melodic and harmonic structure – and then, one by one, or perhaps in tandem, push beyond the boundaries of rhythmic, harmonic, and/or melodic structure. Truly gifted players take the melody and bend it around the key or time signature, lifting it beyond what they already know. When they are *really* playing – really improvising – they "have nothing to say". Each player abides entirely in the present – *listening otherwise*.

A similar analogy is found in religious traditions with a process often called *bearing witness* – a refusal to turn away from suffering and instead to look at it unflinchingly. It is a kind of looking and listening without objectification or appropriation, but with a kind of awareness that makes space for the unthinkable, unimaginable, other. This kind of presence is described by Zen Roshi Bernie Glassman, who conducts interfaith international retreats in Auschwitz aimed at bearing witness to the sufferings of the Holocaust. Glassman describes how in the first days of the retreat the overwhelming pain of Auschwitz leaves people speechless and everything they thought they knew and understood fails them. Glassman describes how the interfaith group of Jews and Germans and Poles, Tutsi's and Hutus, Zen and Catholic priests react: "They were in shock. Their usual concepts and ideas failed them. They didn't know what to think. They'd lost control. They were in a space of unknowing"[42]. It is only when we have lost our sense of mastery, conviction and certainty that we are able to truly *listen otherwise*. When we are strong enough to bear witness and *listen otherwise*, we can listen from the space of unknowing where the ethical response emerges. It is a listening that does not resort to what is easy, what I already know, or what we have in common. It means that I listen for and make space for the difficult, the different, and the radically strange. I turn toward you with fearless acceptance and openness to what is, right now, here, before us. To *listen otherwise* is to listen with all the presence of our being and is similar to what Levinas calls "proximity" and "beyond dialogue", and what Buber calls "the personal making present"[43] which is not about merging,

41. A. KAPLAN, *The Life of Dialogue*, in R. ANDERSON – K.N. CISSNA – R.C. ARNETT (eds.), *The Reach of Dialogue*, Cresskill, NJ, Hampton Press, 1994, 34-46, p. 40.

42. B. GLASSMAN, *Bearing Witness: A Zen Master's Lessons in Making Peace*, New York, NY, Bell Tower, 1998, p. 16.

43. BUBER, *The Knowledge of Man* (n. 12), p. 70.

absorption, or unification, but about the fundamental intersubjectivity of the dialogical relation.

V. Giving Birth to Speech by Listening

When Levinas contends that the communicative action of *saying* takes priority over the substance of *the said*, it is not just a matter of situating speech in the intersubjective occurrence of dialogical address to an interlocutor. With this claim, Levinas is also, as Heidegger did with the word *being*, privileging the verb form over the noun form. *Saying* precedes *the said* just as *being* precedes *the being*. As I have previously discussed, what is missing from this formulation is the way that *the listening* precedes *the heard*. But now we are faced with another question regarding yet another grammatical distinction; whether the verb *listening* is transitive or intransitive. The transitivity of verbs expresses a form of agentive action – a subject does something to or with an object, as in, the phrase *she speaks the words*. Transitive verbs transfer some form of energy or action from the subject to the object. Intransitive verbs, in contrast, can only express the agency of a subject directionally in relation to an object, but not directly upon it. Thus, the intransitive verb form either stands alone, as in *he wept*, or requires a preposition, as in *he wept before her*, but it cannot take a direct object as in *he wept her*. In English, many verbs have both transitive and intransitive uses as in the phrase *she speaks to him* (intransitive) or *she speaks the words* (transitive). In English, the verb *hear* has both transitive and intransitive uses – we can say the phrase *she hears the words* or simply the phrase *she hears*. The verb listen, however, has only an intransitive use in contemporary English[44]. Thus we can say *we heard the words* but not *we listened the words*. Similarly, we can say *she listens* or *she listens to the others*, but not *she listens the others*. The question of why the transitive form of *listen* has disappeared from English is beyond the scope of this essay, but it is worth examining the previously undisclosed meanings that emerge when we employ the verb *to listen* in a transitive form.

The feminist theologian Nelle Morton provides a clue when she examines the ways in which *listening others to speech* is itself political. She writes that "we empower one another by hearing the other to speech. We

44. According to the Oxford English Dictionary, an archaic transitive form of the verb listen existed until the early 19th century.

empower the disinherited, the outsider..."[45]. How resonant Morton's phrasing is with Levinas's ethical directive that we respond to the face the "widow, the orphan, and the stranger" who "commands me as Master" from "a dimension of height"[46]. The empowerment of *listening others to speech* is thus both political and ethical, in that it reverses authoritative normative social arrangements that silence and/or refuse *to listen the voices* of the oppressed. And, as with Buber's I – Thou relation, *listening others to speech* is not a strategic or tactical practice aimed at achieving a predetermined goal because doing so would be to cease to obey the demands of the present moment. Buber's observation that true dialogue is "a matter of renouncing the pantechnical mania or habit with its easy 'mastery' of every situation"[47], is echoed by Levinas's insistence on the mastery of the other and on Morton's reflection that "clever techniques seen as positive agents for creation and change are not good for the kind of hearing that brings forth speech"[48].

Transitive uses of the verb *listening* thus convey a sense of listening as constitutive of and prior to speaking – that listening is an invocation, a calling forth of speech. The (in)vocation of dialogical ethics is thus a giving birth to speech by listening, it is a *dwelling place* from where we offer our hospitality, to the other and the world. But it is not only that the voice of the other calling requires a listener to be complete; it is that, more radically, without a listener the speaking simply may not occur. Morton describes how Carl Gustav Jung, as a young doctor, worked with women who were not willing, or able, to speak to their doctors, who, in turn, assumed the women had no language. With patience and perseverance Jung found a way to connect with the women by imitating their gestures and movements until finally they began to speak. Morton writes how Jung "had touched the place where the connection had been broken. But he did this through their language and not the language of the doctors. He had heard them to speech"[49]. Another example of the constitutive power of listening can be seen in the work of therapist Dori Laub, who describes the process of psychoanalytic work with holocaust survivors. Through the process of listening to untold and repressed stories, therapists and survivors were able to co-create "a record that is

45. N. MORTON, *The Journey Is Home*, Boston, MA, Beacon Press, 1985, p. 128.
46. LEVINAS, *Totality and Infinity* (n. 8), pp. 213, 214.
47. BUBER, *The Knowledge of Man* (n. 12), p. 39.
48. MORTON, *The Journey Is Home* (n. 44), p. 206.
49. *Ibid.*, p. 209.

yet to be made"[50]. Laub writes: "The emergence of the narrative which is being listened to – and heard – is, therefore, the process and the place wherein the cognizance, the 'knowing' of the event is given birth to. The listener, therefore, is a party to the creation of knowledge de novo"[51].

VI. CONCLUSION

When communication and language are understood only to represent, depict, or stand for non-linguistic objects and events, we lose track of the ways in which *listening, as well as speaking,* brings new worlds into being[52]. In other words, language constitutes worlds not only through *speaking*, but perhaps more importantly, through *listening*. These constitutive dimensions of speaking and listening happen not only within and between individuals sitting face to face, but among large collectivities gathered side by side as well. One need only consider the power of public orators to constitute large groups of people into previously nonexistent communities and solidarities. It is not simply the voice of a Rev. Dr. Martin Luther King, Jr., a Mohandas Gandhi, or an Adolph Hitler, that creates new worlds for good or ill, but it is what "comes to presence" in the those assembled collectivities through the processes of listening. We become when we listen together – to the voice of God, to a singer, to a speaker, to the wind blowing through the trees. This is what is meant in Quakerism as the "gathered meeting"[53] and, perhaps, what Heidegger, frighteningly, implies by *gathered hearkening*[54].

Beyond the constitutive dimensions of listening, this essay has also argued that listening constitutes the nascent origin of the ethical relation. That is, listening is neither a secondary subordinate process that follows and flows from speech, nor is it a futile gesture of "the feeble-minded

50. D. LAUB, *Bearing Witness*, in S. FELDMAN – D. LAUB (eds.), *Testimony: Crises of Witnessing in Literature, Psychoanalysis, and History*, New York, NY, Routledge, 1992, 57-92.

51. *Ibid.*, p. 57.

52. For a fuller explication of this idea, see LIPARI, *Listening, Thinking, Being* (n. 23).

53. H.E. COLLIER, *The Quaker Meeting*, Wallingford, PA, Pendle Hill Pamphlets, 1944/2003 (Retrieved 1/18/05, 2005, from http://www.pendlehill.org/pendle_hill_pamphlets.htm).

54. M. HEIDEGGER, *Early Greek Thinking*, trans. D.F. Krell, F.A. Capuzzi, New York, NY, Harper and Row, 1975, p. 65. I am of course here referring to Heidegger's endorsement of and participation in Nazi ideology – the shadow side of dialogical ethics.

[who attempt] to douse the worldwide conflagration with a syringe"[55]. Rather, listening is the invisible and inaudible enactment of the ethical relation itself; upon it, everything depends. This privileged aspect of listening is perhaps best described by the poet Kuusisto, who describes "the difference between speaking and being. This is what listening is, true listening, the lonely but open mind … the soul's path is in the ear – not in the mirror"[56].

Finally, this essay has argued that the (in)vocation of dialogical ethics is a communicative process that *listens others to speech*, thus giving voice to the voiceless and conjuring "the idea of a possibility in which the impossible may be sleeping"[57]. As Heidegger has observed, "Mortals speak insofar as they listen"[58]. When we *listen others to speech* in dialogue we create the conditions for ethical worlds and possibilities yet to be imagined. And it begins with a posture of receptivity to and responsibility for the other, with the simple but tremendously difficult "*Après Vous*, Monsieur!"[59].

Department of Communication Lisbeth LIPARI
Denison University
Granville, OH 43023
U.S.A.
lipari@denison.edu

55. This is from Levinas's paraphrase of Vasily Grossman's *Life and Fate*, in E. LEVINAS, *Alterity and Transcendence*, trans. Michael B. Smith, New York, NY, Columbia University Press, 1999, p. 108.

56. S. KUUSISTO, *Eavesdropping: A Life By Ear*, New York, NY, W.W. Norton, 2006, p. 50.

57. LEVINAS, *Alterity and Transcendence* (n. 55), p. 89.

58. M. HEIDEGGER, *Poetry, Language, Thought*, trans. A. Hofstadter, New York, NY, Perennial Classics, 1971, pp. 206-207. For more elaboration on the place of language see also *On the Way to Language*, trans. P.D. Hertz, New York, NY, Harper and Row, 1971.

59. J. ROBBINS (ed.), *Is It Righteous to Be? Interviews with Emmanuel Levinas*, Stanford, CA, Stanford University Press, 2001, p. 106: "(…) the human – this is extraordinary – cedes its first place. *Après vous, Monsieur!* Ontological courtesey, being-for-the-other".

VOICES OF OTHERS UNTO THE SELF, VOICES OF OTHERS IN THE SELF

POLYPHONY AS MEANS AND RESOURCE FOR CONSTRUCTING AND RECONSTRUCTING SOCIAL REALITY

Addressing forms of interiorizing the voice of others in the course of self-development, our contribution will follow two strands, corresponding different moments in this development. After a brief introduction to the core term of polyphony exploring its metaphorical and its literal understandings, the first strand of arguments will be described, which concerns interiorization in ontogenetic development. It will become clear how the infant and child is driven into its specific culture with corresponding meanings and evaluations, and into other-self-structures through coordinated, dialogic and voiced patterns of exchanges. The psychological polyphony will be explained as the ability to shape and perform different social, meaningful, addressing and being-addressed positions. In this development, the voice of the care-giver functions as a meaningful and sensitive means for interiorization permitting non-communicative (though still social) language usages leading to cognitive kills as well as to complex social behavior. This comes to state alterity as the grounding of the self in the other.

The second strand addresses the multiplicity of speech in adult language use, the pervasiveness of different voices integrated in speaker's utterances, and explores the continuation of interiorization processes in adulthood. It will become clear how the social language activity of adults is drawn through by *multivocal speaking*, manifesting but also constructing different social positions, intentions and meanings, different forms of 'addressivity'[1], promoting thus not only communicative efficiency, but also social complexity. Also the phenomenon of the *inner voice*, a specific continuation of earlier interiorization, will be explored. The *inner speech* will be stated to involve a partly dialogic structure, and different

1. According to Mikhail Bakthin, addressivity is a constitutive and inherent factor of every utterance. It refers to the quality of being both addressed and addressive – be it utterances or human subjects. In Bakhtin's world-view, addressivity expresses the fact that, as existence is shared, it manifests itself "as the condition of being addressed". See M. HOLQUIST, *Dialogism: Bakhtin and His World*, London – New York, Routledge, 1999, p. 27.

voice positions as manifestation of specific dialogic and addressivity experiences. Starting from the experienced voices of others, the self becomes able to stimulate these voices, setting up dialogues and exploring different points of view. It will be proposed that adults' interiorization is taking place as internal integration and simulation of voices. This simulation opens a protected space which functions as a resource for the self, and possibly – through the integration of new significant others – contributes to the construction of a new voice.

I. Prerequisites

1. *Alterity and Affected Subjects*

I would like to start with some basic ideas about language and speaking/listening subjects, themselves derived from the notion of fundamental human alterity. These prerequisites account for the specific conception of voice I here propose.

Alterity is in my understanding to be conceived as developmental *and* relational movement. This movement follows the socio-historical development of the individual self, which sets very clearly the origin of individual psyche and consciousness in the other[2]. As the human way of being and acting in the world is mediated by specific cultural means and especially by language, it is assumed that language plays a deeply formative and generating role within the developmental movement growing into a socialized, individual self. It is the language-mediated relationship *to others*, which acts as means to become oneself. It is the word of the other which acts as a means to the formation of individual psychological functions and consciousness.

Alterity is thus a movement, constituting related positions and negating a primeval, self-contained *ego* by setting a clear direction, a starting point which is not located in the *ego* but in the other *as related to the ego*. This is to say that the other is in no sense the powerful one determining the helpless *ego*; as the other is an *ego* her/himself and thus in relation to a different other, i.e., just because of the very reciprocity of their positions, the other and the *ego*, the self, are interdependent. Each is the giving one

2. M.-C. Bertau, *Anreden, Erwidern, Verstehen: Elemente einer Psycholinguistik der Alterität*, Berlin, Lehmanns Media, 2011; L.S. Vygotsky, *Consciousness as a Problem in the Psychology of Behavior*, in N. Veresov, *Undiscovered Vygotsky: Etudes on the Pre-History of Cultural-Historical Psychology*, Frankfurt am Main, Peter Lang, 1999, 256-281, p. 285.

for the other, her/his starting point, and at the same time a recipient of the given. This simultaneity reflects the specificity of human activity as "logical medium between activity and passivity", so it is no pure and self-controlled activity, and nor is it possible for the *ego* alone, but only for two, for a relationship[3]. This topic is found in Feuerbach, to which Vygotsky refers when writing at the end of his reflections on thought and word: "In consciousness, the word is what [...] is absolutely impossible for one person but possible for two. The word is the most direct manifestation of the historical nature of human consciousness"[4].

In this conception, although any self-formation is regarded as originating in the other, individual uniqueness is acknowledged within the movement and as its result. It is thus a necessary movement, inevitable for human beings in the process of becoming human beings. Further, the movement manifests itself as concrete, i.e., vividly experienced dynamics, as addressivity. Addressivity adopts specific, sensible forms in time, and gives shape to the relationship and its positions: you to me and me to you within a space-time-realm we jointly mould through the performance of a common means, namely spoken language.

Thus, the source of the self lies in the other, and this other is a speaking, listening, and addressing one. The movement just named entails *performed* language, vividly experienced through tones and rhythms, psycho-physically touching the subjects – *affecting* them. The jointly moulded space-time is a space of language[5].

Hence, the basic position of the subject can be thought of as addressed and affected by the other. At the moment of birth (even with conception) the subject enters into the world of others. It enters into a world constituted in language and constituted by the language of others, performed again and again, presented, and made meaningful in these performances. The ways of speaking and listening to the newborn is faced with are ways of making sense of the world. They are meanings, given and affirmed in the act of giving and transmitting them.

The fact that the newborn has not yet acquired language does not mean that she is outside and will one day make a step and come into language:

3. See V. SCHÜRMANN, *Prozess und Tätigkeit: Zur Spezifik der Tätigkeitstheorie*, in *Behindertenpädagogik* 47 (2008) 21-30. I refer to "das autonome freie Tun des Menschen ist eben nicht reine Aktivität, sondern ein logisch Mittleres von Aktiv und Passiv" (*ibid.*, p. 28).

4. L.S. VYGOTSKY, *Thinking and Speech*, in R.W. RIEBER – A.S. CARTON (eds.), *The Collected Works of L.S. Vygotsky*. Volume 1: *Problems of General Psychology*, New York – London, Plenum Press, 1987, 39-285, p. 285.

5. "Sprachraum": see BERTAU, *Anreden* (n. 2), pp. 219-227.

in human existence, there is no language-free place. At least at the moment when the unborn baby develops hearing (around the 5th month of pregnancy) she is 'in' language, listening to the voice of her mother and her specific language: both will be preferred by the newborn baby. The newborn herself is already producing language-specific cries, i.e., her cry melodies are shaped by her native language, I would add: by her *listening*[6]. The newborn has listened to that language for approximately four months, and one could see her shaped cries as *response* to this situation, a response to the heard voice of the mother: coming into her own life is thus coupled with a responsive act.

So, language experience starts with listening to the mother's voice, and this is what it means to be affected by the other, by her voice and ways of speaking which are deeply corporeal and moreover neatly coupled with bodily touches, ways of handling the newborn[7]. Leaving the womb means to gain distance and clarity in regard to this voice, but it is still a touch, a vivid experience of degrees of proximity, an experience shaped in time and form[8]. This basic position will not change during life. As human beings we are affected and addressed and it is on these grounds that we act and think, that we experience others, our self and the world.

So far, my prerequisites include a notion of alterity as relational and developmental movement, whose origin lies in the other; it includes further the means of that movement which is language as spoken and performed, vividly experienced dynamics: addressivity. The basic position of subjects is to be affected and addressed through the means of performed language that takes basically a dialogical form. From this developmental-relational point of view the speaking, touching voice comes to play a central role. As it is bound to a language specific expression, to a certain language, the voice always manifests cultural and social, as well as individual meanings and value accents. A voice is always a socioculturally specific gesture giving dialogues a specific vivid relief.

6. See A.J. De Casper – W.P. Fifer, *Of Human Bonding: Newborns Prefer Their Mother's Voices*, in *Science* 208 (1980) 1174-1176; B. Mampe – A.D. Friederici – A. Christophe – K. Wermke, *Newborn's Cry Melody Is Shaped by Their Native Language*, in *Current Biology* 19 (2009) 1994-1997.

7. See the "techniques of the body" as described by M. Mauss, *Les techniques du corps*, in Id., *Sociologie et anthropologie*, Paris, Quadrige – PUF, 1999, 365-386.

8. Didier Anzieu relates voice and psychological development from a psychoanalytical point of view, thus going beyond Lacan's mirror stage and the hereby given privilege of vision. See D. Anzieu, *L'enveloppe sonore du soi*, in *Nouvelle Revue de Psychanalyse* 13 (1976) 161-179; Id., *Le Moi-peau*, Paris, Dunod, 1995.

2. *'De-veloping' Dialogue*

Going now a step further, I would like to add an idea of development and voice, throwing a certain light on the notion of dialogue.

Looking at Bakhtin's analysis of Dostojevsky's work and his theory of discourse types, it appears that the reciprocal relationship between the positions of the other (alien voice) and *ego* (own voice) is not a harmonious, egalitarian one[9]. For Bakhtin, dialogicality emerges at the very moment of opening to the other, where the alien voice interferes with the own one, a risky moment and full of tension, resounding in the bivocal word[10]. Further, this moment of opening is not controlled by the *ego*, it resembles more a battle between the other's and the *ego*'s voice than a friendly encounter.

The Italian philosopher Augusto Ponzio elaborates this aspect, writing that for Bakhtin a dialogue is not something one can undertake but something which is suffered. According to Ponzio, it is for that reason that a dialogue is not conceivable as the *result* of an opening to the other but rather as an impossibility of closure[11]. This comes near to the above stated notion of subjects as addressed and affected ones. Highlighting the constraining aspect of addressivity, the inevitability of being addressed, opens in my opinion the way to a sense of development as a process of shaping and moulding the openness to the other, both in a joint communicative activity with other and in a detached one – detached from the real, actual other. In this twofold process dialogue comes to play a key role.

Dialogue is suffered, but at the same time it can be shaped and formed by both partners in regard to proximity and distance as ways of being related to one another. This work of physical and psychological space management is done in distinguishing voices and positions, in distinguishing *as whom* one is addressed and addresses others, and *as whom* one may reply, is supposed to reply etc. "As whom" includes "how", i.e., the position implies a form, a way of vocalizing and of speaking (gently, angry, loudly, staccato, with certain words in a certain order) as connected to a certain position.

Distinguishing is constructing sameness and difference through practices and experiencing these conditions. A good illustration for this

9. M. BAKHTIN, *Problems of Dostoevsky's Poetics*, trans. and edit. by C. EMERSON, Minneapolis, MN, University of Minnesota Press, 1984, chapter 5.

10. *Ibid.*, p. 194.

11. A. PONZIO, *Presentazione: Dialogo e polifonia in Dostoevskij: Como è stato frainteso il pensiero di Bachtin*, in M. BACHTIN, *Problemi dell'opera di Dostoevskij (1929)*, Bari, Edizioni dal Sud, 1980, 5-30, p. 12.

distinguishing process is to be found in vocalizations practiced by mothers and infants in alternation as well as in unison[12]. Vocalizing in unison means coordination in terms of synchronized and 'syn-formed' activity, joint corporeality, a momentary fusion often related to a high level of affectively positive arousal, where the partners obviously derive much enjoyment from their coactive vocalization. On the other hand alternation – more manifest at a midlevel of arousal – means coordination in terms of successivity, of rhythmically distributed activity, ordered in time as well as in form according to principles of coherence. This mode of communication seems to be connected to the mother's "teaching" of her infant[13]. These two modes reflect different ways of relating to one another and are coupled with different functions in regard to attachment and to language acquisition[14].

In this brief glance at the beginning of development, incipient dialogue can be seen as dynamics taking different forms, a dynamics that partners construct and enact jointly. Being affected is a starting point to this construction through which the partners develop as partners, as differently positioned individuals acting in regard to each other. Dialogue comes to be the means of reciprocal development, meaning detachment as well as attachment, for the positions make sense only in relation to each other and function only with enough distance and enough proximity.

The gain of Bakhtin's notion of voice lies in this: it enables a differentiation of the speaking subjects in regard to the position they take and suffer in relation to each other – to their mutual voices. The self and the other are then not monolithic blocks but always positioned in a concrete socio-cultural and psycho-linguistical space – and thus absolutely not a mere sender and receiver. For Bakhtin, utterances address the voice(s) of the other as present in the uttered words, and not simply the bodily person sitting there. There is always an "as" playing its role: my utterance is spoken as your mother, angry for the moment, addressing you as disobedient child, and you can reply in addressing another voice of myself, namely the voice of the child who also enjoyed being disobedient.

12. For the first investigation highlighting both practices, see D.N. STERN – J. JAFFE – B. BEEBE – S.L. BENNETT, *Vocalizing in Unison and in Alternation: Two Modes of Communication Within the Mother-Infant Dyad*, in D. AARONSON – R.W. RIEBER (eds.), *Developmental Psycholinguistics and Communication Disorders*, New York, NY, Annals of the New York Academy of Sciences, 1975, 89-100.

13. *Ibid.*, p. 97.

14. Different practices of reprise and repetition observable during language acquisition between adults and children can be seen as continuation of this basic pattern of fusion and detachment. See BERTAU, *Anreden* (n. 2), pp. 254-268; see also C. MARTINOT (ed.), *Langages: Acquisition et reformulation*, Paris, Larousse, 2000.

Turning away from the monolithic speaker and her addressee entails two aspects, already alluded to. First, it means – with Bakhtin – turning to the utterance and to its interrelatedness with other spoken, i.e., addressed and replied utterances. In this perspective any speaking is a reply, taking up already spoken utterances and words, used again and again and to which the speaking subject has to take a stance:

> The desire to make one's speech understood is only an abstract aspect of the speaker's concrete and total speech plan. Moreover, any speaker is himself a respondent to a greater or lesser degree. He is not, after all, the first speaker, the one who disturbs the eternal silence of the universe. And he presupposes not only the existence of the language system he is using, but also the existence of preceding utterances – his own and other's – with which his given utterance enters into a kind of relation or another (builds on them, polemicizes with them, or simply presumes that they are already known to the listener). Any utterance is a link in a very complex organized chain of other utterances[15].

According to this perspective, no neutral speaking is possible, and moreover no self-controlled, self-contained speaking. What emerges here is a *texture of utterances, a texture of voices* we are immersed in and with which we form our actual utterance, our present and presented voice.

Second, it means to refrain from a Cartesian monolithical and monolingual *ego* and to assume an internally structured, manifold self, a multi-voiced self[16]. This self manifests itself for others as well as for itself *in performing language*, in uttering words to somebody. I suspect that the spoken, positioned word is more than a mere manifestation of internal multiplicity. I will come back to this further.

Taking affectedness of subjects as the starting point for their development, dialogue is here seen as its locus, which is jointly shaped and refined regarding form and content. This corresponds to one of the two above-mentioned processes at work in shaping the openness to the other.

In this first process partners are working together as subjects who are actually present using language socially, within an actual social space. They shape conjointly their language space, creating patterns of communication they can rely on and refer to, re-enact, vary, and transfer in other

15. M. Bakhtin, *Speech Genres and Other Late Essays*, Austin, TX, University of Texas Press, 2006, p. 69.

16. This is the basic idea of the dialogical self, a notion developed by Hermans and colleagues, see e.g. H.J.M. Hermans, *Voicing the Self: From Information Processing to Dialogical Interchange*, in *Psychological Bulletin* 119 (1996) 31-50; Id., *The Dialogical Self: Toward a Theory of Personal and Cultural Positioning*, in *Culture and Psychology* 7 (2001) 243-281; Id. – A. Hermans Konopka, *Dialogical Self Theory*, Cambridge, Cambridge University Press, 2009.

language spaces with other partners[17]. Dialogue is shaped by the partners, and in doing so the partners actively come to an understanding with their affectedness by the other. Especially infants and children come to 'developing' through the other by means of giving a form to their affectedness. This form is a specific kind of relationship which generally entails the distinction between the other and the self and allows the creation of an attitude towards the world[18]. Thus, dialogue is coupled with an activity of distinguishing and relating which comes to be 'de-veloping' in the sense of stepping out of a diffuse envelope enclosing different subjects. This stepping out gives them addressable positions and has thus an individualizing effect.

The second process at work in coming to an understanding with affectedness is accomplished solitarily by an individual in an act of 'de-coupling'. The individual turns away from an actual other. In children, this can be done in the presence of this other, but not more addressing the child explicitly. In this process, the subject uses language for her/his own purposes, within a psychological space (which can be exterior as well as interior), and with addressees who are not actually present, who can be fictitious characters or imagined real others. The dialogues taking place here are turned away, are 'de-coupled' from actual reality and from others and unfold their power on this ground.

In order to grasp the quality of the 'de-coupled' dialogues I propose to think of Winnicott's transitional object enabling the child to detach herself from the first significant other, the first object in the psychoanalytical sense[19]. This transitional, material object offers a bridge for the passage into independence from the mother and renders possible mature relationships to other actual others. Two functions are related to this object. First, the transitional object is a substitute for the mother insofar as it is always accessible to the child, in its possession, although not being part of the child herself. Thus it is – secondly – the prototype of any object (Winnicott speaks of "not-me possession"). Especially the first function is interesting: the transitional object is under the control of the child who may even be aggressive against it without consequences for the primary object, the mother. Transitional objects offer the child a

17. For early pattern construction where reciprocal forms as abbreviations and their variations play a key role, see M.C.P.D. LYRA – M.-C. BERTAU, *Dialogical Practices as Basis for Self*, in *Studia Psychologica* 6 (2008) 173-193.

18. This holds for healthy development, pathological variations affect one of the three basic relationships we need to live as human beings: to the other, oneself, and the world.

19. D.W. WINNICOTT, *Transitional Objects and Transitional Phenomena – A Study of the First Not-Me Possession*, in *International Journal of Psychoanalysis* 34 (1953) 89-97.

neutral experiential space, which is not called into question. It is worth noting that these experiences belong to the domain of illusion appearing throughout life in any intense experience as made in religion, the arts, imaginative life and science[20].

The power of decoupled dialogues lies similarly in the fact that the addressee is not a real one and the dialogues thus can be conducted in the way the subject wishes and needs, without fearing communicative consequences. They open up a domain of activity in which the subject can elaborate a language space on its own, continuing the work on positions and voices which began in the social and shared language space. In this individual space, simulation of the other and the self, of their voices and positions, plays an important role, allowing to practise and vary the known voices, to test position reversals and to play on voice interference. In this process of decoupling, the voice of the other is used to turn away from this very other by simultaneously retaining a significant aspect of her/his addressing activity, of her/his presence: as vividly, psycho-physically manifested way of being attuned, turned to oneself. The specific quality of the other's presence is related to her/his voice in an indissoluble way. The self can remember and retrieve the experience of that voice, what leads back to that presence and evokes it, thus corresponding to a displacement realized in imagination[21].

From that point of view, the voice of the other is used, or – in a (positive, constructive) sense – abused. As a further step in distancing and relating this use-abuse corresponds again to a de-velopment of the (dialogical) self. It is part of the relational construction to actual significant others.

3. *Polyphony: Where Voices Meet but Do not Unify*

The last piece in my prerequisites is the notion of polyphony, which needs a little explanation in regard to its oscillation between metaphorical and literal understanding. Together with that notion, the core concept of voice is given in a certain way.

Almost all actual linguistic and psychological investigations based on a dialogic approach refer to the work of Bakhtin, and, actually, the terms "polyphony" and the ensuing "voice" have their point of departure as root metaphors in Bakhtin's work, namely in his analysis of Dostojevsky's

20. J. LAPLANCHE – J.-B. PONTALIS, *Das Vokabular der Psychoanalyse. Zweiter Band*, Frankfurt am Main, Suhrkamp, 1972, p. 549.

21. With the term of displacement I refer to Bühler's "Versetzung", a core notion in his theory of language. See K. BÜHLER, *Sprachtheorie: Zur Darstellungsfunktion der Sprache*, Stuttgart – New York, Gustav Fischer, 1982.

literary technique. It is interesting to observe how Bakhtin himself comes to the term of polyphony, accompanied by the notion of voice. According to Bakhtin, it was Komarovič who introduced the analogy to polyphony and to the counterpoint of fugue to explain Dostojevsky's technique of "harmonization of voices" as different voices of a fugue developing contrapuntally[22]. But, according to Bakhtin, Komarovič has not well understood the essence of polyphony lying firstly in the *autonomy* of voices, and secondly in that this autonomy becomes unified into a "unity of a higher order than in homophony"[23]. Concluding, Bakhtin underscores that the comparison with polyphony is only an illustrating analogy and that one has to bear in mind the metaphorical source of his term "polyphonous novel". Thus, Bakhtin is using "polyphony" and "voice" in an explicitly metaphorical way, stressing the difference between music and novels[24].

As a remark to this pronounced metaphorical understanding, I would like to point out the fact that occidental polyphonic music developed in the Middle Ages and the Renaissance within the *vocal* domain (e.g., Gregorian chorus, school of Notre Dame). Hence, speaking about polyphony and voice with regard to instrumental music is itself a metaphor. Bearing in mind that Bakhtin's focus was literacy, his use of the musical metaphor shows at the end more affinity between written texts and instrumental music than difference – the affinity lying in a certain distancing from body experience. Thus, the Bakhtinian metaphor speaks of an abstraction, and it may well be that it is this very use that allows Bakhtin to think of voice not only in terms of acting and speaking characters but in terms of utterances, and lastly of consciousness. His metaphor applies to a quality of language as well as to the nature of consciousness[25].

This simultaneity reflects in my opinion the two-fold-ness of voice as psychophysical phenomenon, bound to both body and psyche of speaking individuals. Detaching it from one or the other dimension of the human being would mean to lose its substance and at the same time to lose any comprehensible notion of what language is for other-self-related individuals. Thus, the metaphor can be seen as a sign of the voice's relevance

22. BAKHTIN, *Problems of Dostoevsky's Poetics* (n. 9), p. 21.

23. *Ibid.*

24. *Ibid.*, p. 22.

25. I address the relationship of voice and consciousness in M.-C. BERTAU, *Voice: A Pathway to Consciousness as 'Social Contact to Oneself'*, in *Integrative Psychological and Behavioral Science* 42 (2008) 92-113.

for intrapsychological processes[26]; but this reading needs to be lead back to the voice's vivid materiality as experienced by speaking and listening subjects. Similarly, a material, auditive understanding of voice needs a continuation in the psychological dimension in order to grasp its meaning for these speaking and listening subjects, to grasp its functioning for the subjects' shaping of the language space they share and dynamically co-construct.

Coming back to Bakhtin's critique, it is the aspect of the voice's independence which he puts forth in contradiction to Komarovič. "True polyphony" is for Bakhtin the manifoldness of autonomous voices, coexisting and reciprocating. This is what Bakhtin acknowledges in Dostojevsky: "In every voice he could hear two contending voices, in every expression a crack [...] he perceived the profound ambiguity, even multiple ambiguity, of every phenomenon"[27]. Dostojevsky's particular ability to hear several voices *at once* thus enables him to develop the polyphonic novel. This complexity, which frequently entails contradictions, has its locus in the consciousness of the novel's characters, a reflection of the general nature of man's consciousness. Further, man's consciousness is never self-sufficient but exists within a tension to other consciousnesses. Thus, each thought is to be conceived as a reply in "an unfinalized dialogue"[28].

Hence, polyphony represents complexity of voices not in succession, but in simultaneity. With that point of departure it becomes clear that voice is not defined as belonging to one body in a one-to-one correspondence, but as a multitude happening in one person and seeking for the other person's multitude in order to continue the dialogue. This step from the simple correspondence between voice and uttering person-body is also accomplished by the above-mentioned shift to the utterance itself.

The polyphonic structure Bakhtin builds up with Dostojevsky is thus "dialogic through and through", all elements are related dialogically, and they are organized in a contrapuntal way to each other[29]. Simultaneity and juxtaposition, coexistence and contact are the leading notions, resulting in an internal differentiation of voice: more then the auditive event, it is a psychological principle of organization. As psychosocial, evaluative phenomenon the voice appertains to socially organized and

26. See HERMANS, *The Dialogical Self* (n. 16); K. OSATUKE – A. GREY – M.J. GLICK – W.B. STILES – M. BARKHAM, *Hearing Voices: Methodological Issues in Measuring Internal Multiplicity*, in H.J.M. HERMANS – G. DIMAGGIO (eds.), *The Dialogical Self in Psychotherapy*, Hove – New York, NY, Brunner – Routledge, 2004, 237-254.

27. BAKHTIN, *Problems of Dostoevsky's Poetics* (n. 9), p. 30.

28. *Ibid.*, p. 32.

29. *Ibid.*, p. 40.

positioned speakers, it carries and manifests necessary manifoldness, inherent to vivid language. Individual manifoldness of voices is rooted in social manifoldness, for as social individuals we are in different positions, differently related to others – as well as to ourselves[30].

II. Interiorization

With the notions of dialogue and polyphony developed in the prerequisites, an approach to the voice's psychosocial dynamics, i.e., to its work in the interpsychological as well as in the intrapsychological domain of activity, can become more transparent. This work of the voice – a process altering psychological functions, social attitudes and behaviours – is deeply related to the other, to her/his voice so that one can speak of voices of others *unto the* self and *in* the self. This is to say that the other's voice is a means in the development and construction of the self. A space of activity emerges hereby that is withdrawn and detached from communication with actual others, although necessarily related to it. This leads to the issue of interiorization of voices and to its role for processes of understanding and change. In the following, I will first develop the notion of interiorization in its ontogenetic dimension, exploring secondly forms of interiorizing the voices of others in adulthood.

1. *Ontogeny*

Vygotsky can be called the theorist of interiorization, a process based on social semiotic means necessary to human activity. As said at the start, this activity is conceived as a mediated one. In that sociocultural frame interiorization is *not* simply the same as internalization because in interiorization it is the role of the *sign*, which is stressed – and this is foremost language. Interiorization is thus a process rooted in semiotic societal practices and in the relationships between individuals as actors of these practices. This, in turn, means that the resulting individual psychological processes *remain* social, regarding their organization as well

30. The connection of socially organized individuals acting verbally through evaluative (ideological) signs is proper to the notion of language as developed by the Bakhtin – Medvedev – Vološhinov Circle. See especially V.N. Vološhinov, *Marxism and the Philosophy of Language*, trans. L. Matejka – I.R. Titunik, Cambridge, MA, – London, Seminar Press, 1986; J. Friedrich, *Der Gehalt der Sprachform: Paradigmen von Bachtin bis Vygotskij*, Berlin, Akademie Verlag, 1993; Bertau, *Anreden* (n. 2), pp. 70-133.

as regarding their means, the verbal sign. This is what Vygotsky formulates in his well-known general law of cultural development:

> Every function in the child's cultural development appears twice: first, on the social level, and later, on the individual level; first, *between* people (*interpsychological*), and then *inside* the child (*intrapsychological*). This applies equally to voluntary attention, to logical memory, and to the formation of concepts. All the higher functions originate as actual relations between human individuals[31].

In this transfer from interpsychological and common activity to intrapsychological, individual activity, language is of critical importance. It is understood by Vygotsky as a means of influence, first of acting on the other and then – by interiorization – of acting on oneself[32]. This is what permits Vygotsky to write: "Through others, we become ourselves"[33].

Analyzing the regulatory activity ("acting on") Vygotsky observes an important step for the transfer: the child takes the role of the mother toward her/himself and comes through that role integration and reversion to control her/his own behaviour. Hence, it is a turning movement leading away from the other, which leads to a self-determined regulatory activity, a movement with a clear social origin. The child's activity remains social insofar as it replicates the other's activity *toward* herself *for* herself. The formerly socially distributed activity, performed by two persons in two different positions with different competences, is now synthesized within the child's psyche[34]. As Vygotsky underscores, this unified process remains distributed on a psychological plane, preserved in the act of *as if:* as if done by two persons. Doing this, the child is able to move from outer use of means to an inner one.

Tharp and Gallimore give an illustration of the kind of process here addressed:

> A 6-year-old child has lost a toy and asks her father for help. The father asks where she saw the toy; the child says "I can't remember". He asks a series of questions: Did you have it in your room? Outside? Next door?

31. L.S. VYGOTSKY, *Internalization of Higher Psychological Functions*, in ID., *Mind in Society: The Development of Higher Psychological Processes*, ed. M. COLE – V. JOHN-STEINER – S. SCRIBNER – E. SOUBERMAN, Cambridge, MA – London, 1978, 52-57, p. 57, emphasizes in the orginal.

32. For a detailed analysis see P. KEILER, *Lev Vygotskij – ein Leben für die Psychologie*, Weinheim – Basel, Beltz, 2002, p. 201; and BERTAU, *Voice: A Pathway* (n. 25), pp. 104-107.

33. L.S. VYGOTSKY, *Child Psychology,* in R.W. RIEBER (ed.), *The Collected Works of L.S. Vygotsky*. Vol. 5, New York – London, Plenum Press, 1998, p. 170.

34. See *ibid.*, p. 104.

> To each question, the child answers "no". When he says "in the car?" she says: "I think so" and goes to retrieve the toy[35].

The mental function of remembering is distributed between two persons, and this is reflected in their speaking roles: asking and answering questions which, in turn, are related to clear positions, namely the competent and helpful one and the less competent one letting herself to lead through thinking (remembering). This "social memorization" can be interiorized so that the child can manage remembering for herself, synthesizing the two roles and their means for herself. As Wertsch points out, it is a dyad that has carried out the function of remembering, this mental function is not attributable to only one person and to her, so to speak, inner and private mind[36].

As-if and psychological use of means – that is where the role of performed and addressed language comes in. The integration of the other's way of speaking to oneself, the other's way of wording and addressing oneself corresponds to a differentiation of the self as a kind of multiplication: becoming multiple positions and voices, coupled with their psychological, cognitive, and affective possibilities of acting. Developing psychologically and socially means thus to integrate others, to interiorize especially their semiotic activity – it means to multiply oneself in order to become an individual. Seemingly a paradox, this relationship between multiplicity and oneness (or unity) is at the base of human beings – at least within the theoretical frames of both sociocultural and dialogical psychology[37].

In this view the means of activity comes to play a central role. As already pointed out, the means is foremost language as performed; it is first a sensible means with meaning and form. *Meaning* is to be seen as

35. R.G. THARP – R. GALLIMORE, *Rousing Minds to Life: Teaching, Learning, and Schooling in Social Context*, New York, NY, Cambridge University Press, 1988, p. 7. Collaborative problem solving as forerunner of individual problem solving is analysed within the sociocultural paradigm. See as one of the first works in Western psychology: D. WOOD – J.S. BRUNER – G. ROSS, *The Role of Tutoring in Problem Solving*, in *Journal of Child Psychology and Psychiatry* 17 (1976) 89-100.

36. J.V. WERTSCH, *Voices of the Mind: A Sociocultural Approach to Mediated Action*, Cambridge, MA, Harvard University Press, 1993, p. 28.

37. Sociocultural psychology is situated in the Vygotskyan tradition, see e.g. M. COLE, *Cultural Psychology: A Once and Future Discipline*, Cambridge,MA – London, The Belknap Press of Harvard University Press, 2000; WERTSCH, *Voices of the Mind* (n. 36); Y. CLOT (ed.), *Avec Vygotski*, Paris, La Dispute, 2002. Dialogical psychology corresponds to the approach of Hermans and colleagues. See e.g. H.J.M. HERMANS, *Culture and the Dialogical Self: Theory, Method and Practice Theory*, in *Culture and Psychology (Special Issue)* 7 (2001); ID. – T. GIESER, *Handbook of Dialogical Self Theory*, Cambridge, Cambridge University Press, 2012.

given and deeply social both because of the other-self-relationship, but social also in its quality, its volume. The verbal sign represents social meanings, produced and reproduced in a certain speech community, understandable within social space and not detachable from this context[38]. *Form*, on the other hand, is to be seen as performed, a sensible event enacted by communicating partners in the language space, including not only certain words in a certain word order, but also intonational qualities. These three aspects of verbal form are conventional, their performance is coupled with positioned speakers and listeners in certain social situations. Thus form is not accidental, but speaks of the partners' relationship within their sociality[39]. Thus, not only what is said verbally but also how it is said, which sensible form is enacted, matters: the way of voicing in speaking. Voices matter, manifesting both the social as well as the individual dimension of speaking subjects.

Leading back "semiotical means" to performed language and then to voice means to re-state the role of the here-and-now performed language, bound to individuals addressing each other in a certain way, with certain affects and a particular quality of presence. Putting forward voice means in the end to acknowledge its role for the Vygotskyan process of interiorization. In my prerequisites, I introduced the term of decoupled dialogue as dialogue performed without the actual other facing the self. This is a variation of the Vygotskyan interiorization with its dialogic dimension highlighted. As said, the voice of the other is used to turn away from her or him, simultaneously retaining her/his addressing quality. Hence, in interiorization the voice of the other plays the role of a means leading the activity from social to individual.

It is worth noting that the child experiences within social language the practices, which will serve the de-coupling, and the transformation of social to individual activity. Thus, specific social practices prepare and enable the child to detach herself from actual others. These practices occur during ontogenesis between several partners in multiple repetitions involving variations and transfer to more abstract (more body-detached) forms of voicing and positioning. This commonly and socially constructed ground is important as forerunner and enabler of interiorization – conferring it also a specific quality in the affective dimension as well as

38. For a detailed analysis see D. PAPADOPOULOS, *Lew Wygostki – Werk und Wirkung*, Frankfurt am Main – New York, Campus, 1998, pp. 175-197.

39. This notion of form is developed in BERTAU, *Anreden* (n. 2), pp. 232-245. The three form aspects are derived from VOLOŠHINOV, *Marxism* (n. 30).

in regard to range (diversity of voices and positions allowed, made possible)[40].

Diverse voice plays are thus to be seen as such forerunners and enablers, naturally involving role reversals and the multiplication of positions and voices. I already hinted at the practice of vocalizations in unison and alternation, a practice, which takes place before the child is able to speak. It underlines the importance of the third aspect of form, intonation, and with it rhythmicity and timing[41].

The structure of imitation – a pervasive phenomenon of interactions during ontogenesis – entails also the important ingredients, which are taking the other's performance and enacting it *as other's* and also *as one's own*. In reciprocal imitation chains this is fused, fusions are then varied, distributed in roles, again fused in one position or voice performed by both[42]. Repetitions – another pervasive phenomenon in ontogenesis – are akin to imitations, they play with time delay as well as with expansions and/or variations of the first given form. Not the least is the voicing of pets and other toys by adults and children, a powerful means in creating new and fictitious voices and positions, in demonstrating to each other the polyphonic possibilities given with voice as social, meaningful phenomenon.

A beautiful illustration of the role pets and toys play in developing voice and position is found in Fogel, de Koyer, Bellagamba and Bell[43].

40. Because of their sociocultural nature the practices are of course performed very differently in different cultures, social groups, families. A high diversification (and its positive valuation) is surely a feature of middle-class families in Western culture. A hint to the cultural specificity of practices can be the sociocultural stance taken toward imaginery role play and imaginary companions in children, see S.M. CARLSON – M. TAYLOR – G. LEVIN, *The Influence of Culture on Pretend Play: The Case of Mennonite Children*, in *Merril-Palmer Quarterly* 44 (1998) 538-656; see also E. KLAUSSEN – R.H. PASSMAN, *Prentend Companions (Imaginery Playmates): The Emergence of a Field*, in *The Journal of Genetic Psychology* 167 (2007) 349-364, pointing to the fact of culturallly specific living conditions of children possibly leading to a development of imaginery companions (being left alone or not, individualistic versus collectivistic societies).

41. STERN, *et al.*, *Vocalizing in Unison and in Alternation* (n. 12).

42. See e.g. M. PAPOUŠEK – H. PAPOUŠEK, *Stimmliche Kommunikation im Säuglingsalter als Wegbereiter der Sprachentwicklung*, in H. KELLER (ed.), *Handbuch der Kleinkindforschung*, Bern, Huber, 2003, 927-963. See also the analysis in BERTAU, *Anreden* (n. 2), pp. 285-290. Barbara Lang analyses a case of two young children performing sound-dialogues where sensitivity for timing, reciprocal reprises, imitations and variations are well seen; B. LANG, *Lautspieldialoge in der Kind-Kind-Interaktion*, in M.-C. BERTAU – A. WERANI – G. KEGEL (eds.), *Psycholinguistische Studien 2*, Aachen, Shaker, 2005, 103-124. Thus, voicing practices are not constrained to adult-child interactions.

43. A. FOGEL – I. DE KOYER – F. BELLAGAMBA – H. BELL, *The Dialogical Self in the First Two Years of Life: Embarking on a Journey of Discovery*, in *Theory and Psychology* 12 (2002) 191-205. See also M.-C. BERTAU, *Developmental Origins of the Dialogical Self: Some Significant Moments*, in HERMANS – DIMAGGIO (eds.), *The Dialogical Self in Psychotherapy* (n. 26), 29-42.

The mother's voice works as a supporting structure for the child's "voicing in" the common dialogue as individual voice, and also for the demonstration of the possibility to perform not only the two actual roles embodied by the dialogue partners, but to perform multiple and embedded voices. Mother and child (17 months, 2 weeks) have played the lion game with a lion puppet many times with clear roles, the mother always being the lion. Then a change comes in as the child puts the puppet on her own hand and acts with the voice of the lion, as she previously experienced the mother doing it. The child aligns with the voice of the mother *as lion*, nevertheless belonging to the mother, thus a reflection of the mother's perspective (on lions, on playfulness, on her child, on herself as playmate, on their mother-daughter-relationship). Hence, the mother's voice leads the child into a new position and at the same time conveys the perspective, meaning and form of that position. As the authors point out,

> [d]uring this episode, Susan is experimenting and playing with new I-positions and their corresponding emotions: being frightened if you are followed by a lion, being frightening if you are playing the lion. She explores them as she physically embodies the lion with her hand. [...] In this way, she traverses from the role of the child to the role of the lion-adult, and vice versa. Susan is now able to imagine and act in both roles [...] A new voice exchanges information with the old one, resulting in a more complex and narratively structured self[44].

I think it is important to add that Susan is not only exploring the new role via her hand but also via *her voice*, i.e., via the actual performance of a differently sounding vocal event (a roar). This sensible experience is accompanied by the role's emotions (frightening versus being frightened) and actions (moving the puppet in a specific way). The new voice Fogel *et al.* are speaking of is then a psychological phenomenon, derived from the actual experience. Worth noting, the new voice enters into a relationship to Susan's "old" voice. This means that new voices are not simply added but come to form a structure in the self (which can be more or less coherent)[45]. Thus, as soon as a multiplicity of voices and positions is assumed, it becomes necessary to model their relationship as system as well as their dynamics over time.

44. FOGEL, *et al.*, *The Dialogical Self in the First Two Years* (n. 43), p. 201.

45. Cf. W.B. STILES – K. OSATUKE – M.J. GLICK – H. MACKAY, *Encounters Between Internal Voices Generate Emotion: An Elaboration of the Assimilation Model*, in HERMANS – DIMAGGIO (eds.), *The Dialogical Self in Psychotherapy* (n. 26), 91-107: coherently related voices are called communities or constellations of voices; they can in turn speak with one voice.

Regarding the social origin of this voice acquisition, Fogel *et al.* stress also the importance of the mother in respect to two narrowly related aspects:

> The *presence* and the *voice* of the mother constitute a fundamental pole of the dialogue. In the absence of the mother and of her voice, Susan may not have been able to go through this process of self-exploration[46].

Practices of voice and position diversification are coupled with language acquisition, as Goffman (1981) points out:

> So even when the child learns to speak, it learns to speak for, learns to speak in the name of figures that will never be, or at least aren't yet, the self. George Herbert Mead notwithstanding, the child does not merely learn to refer to itself through a name for itself that others had first chosen; it learns just as early to embed the statements and mannerisms of a zoo-full of beings in its own verbal behavior[47].

What turns out is a multiplicity of voices and positions performed in the social language space, as well as the competence to vary, to switch between them for playful as well as for communicative purposes.

Interiorization is, as said, grounded in such practices because it continues and deepens the positional manifoldness of social language activity in the individual domain. It takes the voice of the other as it means for individual psychological purposes such as remembering, problem solving, and self-regulation.

But in interiorization, language is not only present as a semiotic means, as a tool for a psychological, merely cognitive activity. It is also present as an addressed performance, which is coupled with the performance of voices and positions. Interiorization thus also takes in experienced multiplicity as demonstrated in performed voices. Interiorization takes in and works with the experience of possibilities in positioning and voicing, in shifting positions and voices, in inventing new ones within dialogical activities.

To say that the voice is a transitional object is to underline its autonomy from the actual speaking other – although related to her/him. This autonomy permits steps into self-development *as* self, *as* individual by simultaneously retaining bonds to the social space and to significant others. Voice is in social language performance already not tied and constrained to one body, it rather transgresses the speaking person, thus

46. FOGEL, *et al.*, *The Dialogical Self in the First Two Years* (n. 43), p. 201, emphasizes by the author.

47. E. GOFFMAN, *Footing*, in ID., *Forms of Talk*, Philadelphia, PA, University of Pennsylvania Press, 1981, 124-159, p. 151.

manifesting her as social person. Voice is coupled with utterance, and is as such in dialogic relations with other utterances and voices heard there. In ontogenesis, the infant and child participates actively in the social language space and learns to unfold – with the support of significant others – different voices, and enhances her possibilities of acting as social person. Thus, voice can be said to have a multiplying effect, both within the social and within the individual language space. Hence, voice has a core function for the development of social complexity – meaning always complexity of individual selves, too.

2. *Adulthood*

In adulthood, manifoldness of voices is developed to a certain extent, performed in social as well as in individual language activities. Thus, the person facing us in a social encounter has a story of specific interactional, voice and position bounded experiences, and speaks and listens on this grounds. And so do we ourself.

In order to understand what I called the work of voice in adults, a look at the continuation and further differentiation voice multiplicity in the social space will first be taken. The underlying argument is – according to the theoretical frame chosen – that practices in the social language space are deeply related to those in the individual one. This means also that we need to take into account *both* movements and their reciprocal influencing: interiorization continues into exteriorization, where voices and positions are submitted to the social space, to actual others, and where they are experienced in their actual relatedness. These experiences, in turn, affect inner activities; they may deepen some position and differentiate the voice(s) coupled with it, or may question a position and alter the voice(s). It may be that the whole system of voices and positions is transformed, resulting in a new configuration allowing for different stances toward the other, the self and the world. Thus, a first resource of self-development in adulthood can be seen in the relatedness of the social and the individual language space itself, which is a movement of to and fro. This resource is particularly effective when enacted in dialogues permitting and supporting the experience of the partner's multivoicedness – pretend play is thus to be seen as a powerful and naturally occurring means of this experience.

In this perspective, it becomes important to observe the voicing practices at hand in the social language space for an individual as well as for a specific speech community. The second look to be taken will regard inner voice and inner speech. Here, in so-called decoupled and inner dialogues, lies a specific resource of self-development, contributing to the construction of social reality.

a) *Voicing Practices in the Social Language Space: Diversification and Concentration*

Sociological and ethnographical conversation analysis investigates the complexity in processes of addressing and positioning within the social language space. One of the key elements to this complexity is the different conversational positions speakers and hearers can take. This is what Goffman's deconstruction of both conversational roles demonstrates[48]. Following Goffman, a speaker may be a sole *animator* of the spoken words, producing utterances as the "sounding box in use". As *author* the speaker selects the sentiments and the words to express them, and is experienced as individual. The social identity of a speaker and with it a commitment to the words said, is related to the *principal*: "someone whose position is established by the words that are spoken"[49]. Thus, speakers are not always committed to their words in the same way, and they are not always speaking their own words. These cases are for Goffman not exceptions but rather the rule, notably in spontaneous daily dialogues[50].

Here, one may think of several situations. We animate the words of others in reading aloud, in reciting a poem, delivering a joke or reproducing something learned for an exam. We *speak for* someone who is no more or not yet able to speak for his own (aphasics, children), whom we paraphrase, e.g., to make understanding sure; and we *speak as* someone, *in* his words in reported talk. This can be done embedding our own (past or fictitious) utterances in actual ones, or in embedding somebody else's utterances in one's own actual utterance.

Goffman addresses the issue of embedding in regard to the speaker roles he analysed. A more radical, and in my opinion more fruitful way of looking at reported talk puts to the fore the relationships the *utterances* undergo to each other. Doing this, the dialogical relationships of the utterances and of their voices, the dynamics of voices in polyphony and counterpoint will become clear. This leads again back to the Bakhtin-Medvedev-Vološhinov Circle mentioned above, and especially to Vološhinov and his detailed analysis of reported speech: "Reported speech is speech within speech, utterance within utterance, and at the same time also *speech about speech, utterance about utterance*". And Vološhinov

48. *Ibid.*
49. *Ibid.*, p. 144.
50. *Ibid.*, p. 146.

is quite clear about the constructive process at work in this kind of *about*-relation: "Thus, what is expressed in the forms employed for reporting speech is an *active relation* of one message to another [...] We are dealing here with words reacting on words"[51].

Vološhinov's approach is actually taken up by conversational analysts as Tannen and Goodwin[52]. In line with Vološhinov, Tannen argues that when speech is reported, it is fundamentally changed – "even if 'reported' accurately", just because of the fact that it is spoken by someone else in another context in space and time; besides, "most [...] material represented as dialogue was never spoken by anyone else in a form resembling that constructed, if at all"[53]. On this ground, Tannen takes the stance that reported speech should be understood as "constructed dialogue" – a term reflecting the dynamics at work between utterances Vološhinov addresses.

Taking together these considerations and investigations concerned with ways of voicing and uttering, one can observe that speakers can speak for themselves as well as for others, that they can also talk as others, up to the point of presenting several voices in their own utterance. Several voices are thus intertwined in the performance of a speaker. I suggest to call this process in which a speaker realizes diverse positions and voices *diversification*. The corresponding movement of *concentration* means that several speakers are realizing together one voice and position. Speakers may do this to support someone who is not able to speak himself, this is the case in Goodwin's illustration of a couple speaking with and for an aphasic man. Speakers may also adopt this technique not in order to speak for someone but *as one* person, as one voice, this is the case of choral speaking[54].

As seen, these movements occur early in ontogeny. The mother-infant communication technique of vocalizing in unison and alternation shows beautifully the movement of concentration, leading to a momentary fusion of voices, replaced then by distinguishable voices in dialogical relationship[55]. At the beginning this serves grounding intersubjectivity

51. VOLOŠHINOV, *Marxism* (n. 30), pp. 115, 116 (emphasizes in the original).

52. D. TANNEN, *Talking Voices: Repetition, Dialogue, and Imagery in Conversational Discourse*, Cambridge, MA, Cambridge University Press, 1989; C. GOODWIN, *Interactive Footing*, in E. HOLT – R. CLIFT (eds.), *Reporting Talk: Reported Speech in Interaction*, Cambridge, MA, Cambridge University Press, 2007, 16-46.

53. TANNEN, *Talking Voices* (n. 52), p. 110.

54. Choral speaking occurs not only in ritual contexts, as Schwitalla demonstrates with dialogues between women in a club; see J. SCHWITALLA, *Über einige Weisen des gemeinsamen Sprechens*, in *Zeitschrift für Sprachwissenschaft* 11 (1993) 68-98.

55. STERN, *et al.*, *Vocalizing in Unison and in Alternation* (n. 12).

and attachment. The case of Susan and the lion puppet shows the movement of diversification, the discovery of new voices, coupled with role and position reversal of actual dialogue partners and endorsement of a fictitious position with the corresponding voice. At the same time, this shows a move from the actual voice of a significant other to possible, imaginable voices, presented in utterances obviously not constrained to a specific speaker. This development shows in turn social and self-complexification, serving the specific meaning making activities of a speech community, thus opening the way to symbolic activity. It further turns out that the developmental point of view confirms the Russian move from speakers to utterances and to *their* dialogic interrelatedness.

Hence, early and rapidly evolving positional moves are smoothly followed by adult practices of voicing, easy switches between and moves within voices. As adults, our social language activity is drawn through by multivocal speaking; our utterances are full of tones and echoes (Bakhtin). Performed language activities as manifested in voiced utterances allow the dialogical self to develop – not as a ventriloquist of other's voices, but as a polyphonic performer of utterances, experienced in other's and subsequently in self's multivoiced uttering. Other's voices are thus always themselves multiple, showing their multiplicity the more the child comes into socio-symbolic activities with language acquisition.

The very easiness of switches and moves pervasive in adult speech is in my opinion a sign of their powerful functionality for both social and individual language practices. They construct different social positions, intentions and meanings, different forms of addressivity, promoting thus not only communicative efficiency[56], but also social and symbolic complexity. Functionality of diversification and concentration shows also that these techniques are the spring-board for individual language activity, where one makes use of the practised unification of voices in one's inner dialogues, e.g., for cognitive and emotional problem solving.

Within the plane of social language activity, the practices of diversification and concentration are to be seen as types of voice integration. The great diversity of positioned and voiced utterances an individual experiences in communication is taken into own voicing-uttering. This process is to be thought of as occurring within what I call the dialectics of own and alien. Both poles are appropriated, varied and transformed by individuals in their common communicative activities and leading to the formation, affirmation and transformation of self-other relations – within voicing, through voicing.

56. TANNEN, *Talking Voices* (n. 52).

b) *Inner Speech and Inner Voice*

In individual language activity developed from the social experience, the individual performs and uses language for own purposes, i.e., purposes which are no more constrained by actual others and an actual language space. Thus, a certain detachment from the social space is given, allowing the individual to put forth her/his own psychological needs and aims. It also can be assumed that it allows a deepening of the dialogicality *of utterances*, detaching them a step further from real speaking individuals and this means detaching them also from the constraints of the physical and temporal world we live in. Thus, in psychological usage of voices, polyphony will be more pronounced, as well as simultaneity, temporary fusion and other forms of superposition of voices can be expected.

Inner speech in adults is a process assumed foremost in socioculturally oriented psychology as a result of the interiorization of social language, through the intermediary step of egocentric or private speech in children, which is still heard[57]. Inner speech is traced in speaking-aloud protocols of problem-solving adults acting on their own, it is assumed to involve at least partly a dialogic structure. Thus, verbal thinking can be realized in distinguishable dialogic voices and positions[58]. The following example of an adult solving one of Raven's Matrices shows a dialogue between positions which can be assigned to two positions, one belonging to a competent and helpful other (CHO), the other one to the problem-solver (PS). This assignment is made on the grounds of interiorization theory[59]:

(1) C8/ [task number]
(2) aha/
(3) …./

57. See, e.g., G. ZIVIN (ed.), *The Development of Self-Regulation Through Private Speech*, New York, NY, John Wiley and Sons, 1979; R.M. DIAZ – L.E. BERK (eds.), *Private Speech: From Social Interaction to Self-Regulation*, Hillsdale, NJ, Lawrence Erlbaum, 1992; B. VAN OERS – W. WARDEKKER – E. ELBERS – R. VAN DER VEER (eds.), *The Transformation of Learning: Advances in Cultural-Historical Activity Theory*, New York, NY, Cambridge University Press, 2008.

58. See e.g. C. BARTL – D. DÖRNER, *Sprachlos beim Denken – zum Einfluß von Sprache auf die Problemlöse- und Gedächtnisleistung bei der Bearbeitung eines nicht-sprachlichen Problems*, in *Sprache & Kognition* 17 (1998) 224-238; M.-C. BERTAU, *Spuren des Gesprächs in innerer Sprache: Versuch einer Analyse der dialogischen Anteile des lauten Denkens*, in *Sprache & Kognition* 18 (1999) 4-19; A. WERANI, *Inneres Sprechen: Ergebnisse einer Indiziensuche*, Berlin, Lehmanns Media, 2011.

59. The steps from other-regulation by a competent other (the mother) to self-regulation by an individual having interiorized this other is demonstrated with clarity in J.V. WERTSCH, *From Social Interaction to Higher Psychological Processes*, in *Human Development* 22 (1979) 1-22.

(4) this must be hatched obliquely/
(5) aha/
(6) obliquely to the left or obliquely to the right?/ [CHO turn]
(7) therefore/ [PS tries to answer]
(8) completely hatched/ [PS answers]
(9) where's this?/ [CHO turn]
(10) ../ [PS is looking for the answer]
(11) that is/ [PS begins to answer with an objection]
(12) that's not/ [continuing (11)]
(13) not so logical/ [PS finishing objection]
(14) nevertheless/ [CHO counters objection]
(15) now I see the figure/ [PS understands and answers (9)]
(16) this is number one C8[60].

Two aspects in adult verbal thinking – as indexed in thinking aloud – can be inferred from investigations and are worthy of note. First, its realization as dialogic form is coupled with the difficulty of the task, that is, the more difficult an individual experiences the task to be, the more dialogic will be her/his verbal thinking[61]. Second, the *quality* of the verbal expression plays a key role for the efficiency of the problem-solving process, not mere verbalization. Thus, sole statements, stuck to the present time, not much related to each other and hence not opening thinking through imagining and formulating possibilities are not efficient. On the contrary, inner speech using questions and replies, future tense and conditional mode together with different conjunctions in order to relate ideas, proves to be efficient for problem-solving[62].

These observations lead to understand efficient verbalization as the ability to form a coherent dialogue between voices, leading and permitting thinking. Inner speech is to be conceived as the manifestation of specific dialogic and addressivity experiences and as such it implies, in turn, the notion of inner voice. The approach offered by Steels (2003) points to the importance of an inner voice to different regards[63].

Starting from the observation that normal people, including deaf people, report hearing almost constantly a silent voice when not overtly speaking, Steels introduces the notion of inner voice and links it closely to the self, and asks for the conditions of producing an inner voice; he then turns to its functions in looking for the reasons it has arisen in

60. Example translated from BERTAU, *Spuren des Gesprächs in innerer Sprache* (n. 58), pp. 9f.

61. *Ibid.*

62. BARTL – DÖRNER, *Sprachlos beim Denken* (n. 58).

63. L. STEELS, *Language Re-Entrance and the 'Inner Voice'*, in *Journal of Consciousness Studies* 10 (2003) 173-185.

evolution, and for the benefits once such an inner voice is established. His answers focus on two aspects, language and self, the last one leading Steels to reflect on consciousness.

Regarding language, the inner voice helps to explain the emergence of grammatical complexity, where so-called re-entrance is the central mechanism. In short, a re-entrant system applied to language builds on the idea that a speaker applies his own language processing system to his/her own utterances, and this re-entrant mapping is, according to Steels, "necessary for bootstrapping a lexical language into a grammatical one"[64]. Once this re-entrant system is established, it can be used for purposes outside communication. Firstly, to verbalize thoughts without communicating them only in order to test "how they sound". It thus becomes possible to reflect own thoughts, which is for Steels the foundation for the creation of a sense of self[65]. Secondly, in using different bodies of grammatical conventions, one becomes able to simulate the way *somebody else would speak*: "As a consequence, we are able to simulate the voice of somebody else, and thus set up an internal dialogue which explores different points of view"[66].

Hence, the way language is processed through a re-entrant system leads to the kind of deviation already described and consisting in using the means of spoken language not for others but for oneself. It is precisely this detour and de-coupling from others, which makes conceiving both (as sides of the same coin) a self and an imagination of others possible.

Two points should be highlighted. First, internal language, and therefore inner voice, is for Steels a side effect of being able to learn and use *external* language: it is social communication which matters, and its interiorization. Second, the "inner voice mechanism" can be used in order to understand one's own experiences, enabling a *simulation* of the verbal thought processes of others, thus providing the foundation for complex social behaviour[67].

Here, it should be noted that simulation within *external* communication is found in children's pretend role play, quite important to theory of mind, to the imagination of other's perspective and thinking[68]. And children's role-play is exactly that: enacting different roles and positions,

64. *Ibid.*, p. 182.
65. *Ibid.*, p. 183.
66. *Ibid.*
67. *Ibid.*, p. 175.
68. A.P. LILLARD, *Pretend Play as Twin Earth: A Social-Cognitive Analysis*, in *Developmental Review* 21 (2001) 495-531, p. 20.

often performed with differently sounding voices[69]. Hence, social language activities prepare us well for the inner work of voice.

Simulation of uttering voices is in my opinion a powerful resource to the self in its work on affectedness of the other. The self gets the possibility to gain distance in regard to the other's addressivity and speaking. This distancing leads to availability of voices and to the possibility of exploring own and other's voices as positioned ones. To this belongs the enhanced possibility of any role reversal, often not possible with actual others.

Further, simulation allows conceptualization and verbalization of thoughts without communicating them, only in order to test "how they sound", which leads to a reflection of the self's own thoughts. This can be done in the sense of rehearsing future dialogues before entering the social language space, of submitting thoughts to self-criticism, or to "conceptualize and re-affirm a memory of past experiences"[70]. It can also be understood in the sense of a working-through of experiences[71].

In terms of structure, internal (psychological) simulation of voices makes use of one of the main advantages of spoken language: successivity, the transformation of simultaneity into linear order. At the same time, inner simulation allows freedom from actual successivity conditioned by physical and temporal limitations of the actual speaking activity. The structure is at the same time linear and highly polyphonic, because each turn, each utterance can involve much more overtones and echoes, can change much more rapidly in position and possibly entail more that one position then in the actual, physical world.

Summing up, the following processes can be identified in adult multivocal speaking and thinking. First, in everyday talk there is great diversity in voiced utterances, showing the multivoicedness of our speaking (Goffman, Tannen, Goodwin). This multivoicedness can take the forms of diversification and of concentration, leading thus clearly beyond the speaking individual. This takes place in relation to established interiorization and a developed dialogical self with different voices and positions: it is this self who is acting and speaking/listening at an actual moment. This self with multiple positions and voices is structured in a certain way to form the "landscape" of the self (Hermans). Between the pragmatic

69. P. MILLER – C. GARVEY, *Mother-Baby Role Play: Its Origins in Social Support*, in I. BRETHERTON (ed.), *Symbolic Play*, Orlando, FL, Academic Press, 1984, 101-130; J. COOK-GUMPERZ, *Reproducing the Discourse of Mothering: How Gendered Talk Makes Gendered Lives*, in K. HALL – M. BUCHHOLTZ (eds.), *Gender Articulated*, Boston, MA – London, Routledge, 1995, 401-419.

70. STEELS, *Language Re-Entrance and the 'Inner Voice'* (n. 63), p. 183.

71. This is also hinted to by STEELS, *ibid.*, p. 175: "The 'inner voice mechanism' [...] can also be used to come to terms with our experiences".

activities of this self and its psychological ones, one must assume exchange and reciprocal influence, and it is in this relation – nothing but a movement between interiorization and exteriorization – that lies in my opinion one of the main resources of self-development.

The argument is, that the acquisition of language is the acquisition of ways of speaking: utterances coupled with voices and positions. Hence, pragmatics is acquired in the first place, from which syntactical, lexical, grammatical acquisition derives – from where it is *motivated*. The multivocal way of speaking is genuine part of interiorization, leading to the development of higher psychological functions (Vygotsky), and is also at the base of dialogical self-development in the sense that a self experiences others addressing the self in different ways, with different voices. That acquired multivoicedness is practised in the social as well as in the individual space, and in correspondence to the development of both social and individual language space, the multivocal activities will diverge in structure and function[72].

Thus, secondly, it is this *bidirectionality of voices*, their enactment in the social as well as in the individual language space that offers the resource of creative development and changes in the self. This comes to say that a voice is not only the "endowment of a position with a voice" (Hermans), where the direction of construction is only from inner space to outer. It is also the creation of positions never experienced, but accessible through simulation of actual and fictitious voices (lions, so to speak), role reversal, and availability of voices in turning away from the actual other (voice as transitional object).

In acknowledging both directions, the very movement of interiorization-exteriorization, one must acknowledge the formative aspect of the voice. Vivid language, voiced utterances have a formative aspect. They not only re-trace and affirm experienced positions (experienced in uttering to someone), without which the self-experience would be lost. This can be done by oneself in speaking to oneself in some way, but it *has to be done* in the sense of performed, it is not just "there". Beside re-tracing, there is also the possibility to form new positions in speaking, through the very performance of voiced utterances, to make a trace in the space of language which the self can re-trace in other situations, with others and itself.

72. This corresponds to the moment where speaking and thinking cross in child development: speech becomes intellectual and thinking becomes verbal. See VYGOTSKY, *Thinking and Speech* (n. 4), p. 112. After the crossing, different structure and function ensue for both, regarding especially the feature of predicativity. See *ibid.*, chapter 7.

III. Conclusion

In this essay, the speaking and listening subject is thought to be in a position of being affected by addressing the other. This addressivity is the vivid experience of the principle of alterity, grounding and defining the relationship of individuals and their being in the world. Thus, alterity is a movement, constituting the other and the self, without privilege for either of them. This relational movement is also developmental insofar as it originates in ontogeny, driving the newborn – and even the foetus – into a position towards an addressing and speaking/listening person. Self-formation is hence regarded as originating with the other, and language as the mediational means of human beings is the formative means to this process.

As spoken language is at issue in addressivity, the touching voice of the other comes to play a central role for the conception of the self, of its development as social as well as psychological being. Further, spoken language means dialogue, the very locus of affectedness with which individuals must come to an understanding. In regard to affectedness, dialogue is suffered in the sense that it is inescapable for human beings who are inevitably addressed (however friendly or not), i.e., put into a position (an address), and *need* to be addressed in order to survive. At the same moment, dialogue shows itself to be the means of developing *from* the other's constraining addressivity in offering itself the possibilities to shape and mould openness to the other. These possibilities are given in dialogic tools for positional distinctions and distancing, which will become more and more refined with language acquisition (imitation, role reversal, polyphonic practices); further, in the form of decoupled dialogues as tool for a withdraw from the other. In this last step, the voice of the other is used as means for the self's own needs and aims, it may serve as transitional object as well as ground for explorations not constrained by actual communication with actual others. Simulation of other's voices is here certainly a major resource, the more as it is coupled with role reversal and enactment of fictitious voices.

Development is thus understood as occurring in and through dialogue, the enactment of multiple and polyphonous voices. Multiple in the sense that every speaking individual is able to move and switch between several voices – own, other's, fictitious ones. Polyphonous in the sense that dialogic language does not only relate speaking persons, but spoken utterances. In opening dialogicality to utterances and their relationship, dialogicality of language as used and re-used (spoken, listened to, reported, transformed) thousands and thousands of time becomes obvious, leading to a kind of thickness, of density which is *not* mere reference of signs. On this speakers rely, as Bakhtin writes[73]. They connect themselves to these worn utterances in order to gain access to understanding (of the other, of the self, of the world). And in the very moment speakers perform utterances, they not only add an element to the complex chain of utterances, they also deliver a fresh one: never spoken precisely like that, any time a "constructed utterance" (in analogy to Tannen's constructed dialogues). Utterances are the form and meaning bridges between partners in the language space, unique and worn at the same time. Performing an utterance, one can explore its voice, nevertheless remaining this unique speaking subject. Thus, it is the *form*, the vivid and sensible form of spoken language in time, with its specific wording, tones and echoes, which acts as a carrier into new positions (and thus: meanings). And in this very performance, something else becomes visible: The dialogicality of the speaking person herself, her dialogical self in action.

Thus, dialogue is always a dialogue of voices – even when we do not easily or consciously perceive distinctions. Voices belonging to speakers, to the persons actually encountering each other and as such already formed by their culture, by their social and individual life forms, by their common social situation and relationship. But also voices belonging to the multiplicity of the human self, not constrained to its body, but from early age on able to perform – and I think also to perceive – several voices and polyphonious ones.

One of the challenges in any supportive work with others is to refrain from the conception of the unified, monolithical and monophonic individual. The other challenge is in my opinion to acknowledge that we cannot control dialogue from a self-contained *ego*-position, but that we have to accept this specific medial state between activity and passivity, characteristic of human activity. This would lead to work, i.e., speak and listen within *kairós*: a situation to which we can open ourselves, but not construct deliberately.

Ludwig-Maximilians-Universität München — Marie-Cécile BERTAU
Institut für Phonetik und Sprachverarbeitung
Schellingstrasse 3
D-80799 München
Germany
bertau@lmu.de

73. See the quote given in I.2, BAKHTIN, *Speech Genres and Other Late Essays* (n. 15), p. 69.

THE CLIENT'S "NO"

THE CHALLENGE OF CREATING DIALOGICAL SPACE FOR BOTH PARTNERS IN MARITAL THERAPY

There is ample scientific evidence that marital and family therapy (MFT) works for a wide range of problems[1], and as in other kinds of therapy probably the most potent factors in MFT are so called *common factors*[2]. These are therapeutic factors that MFT shares with other kinds of therapy. However, besides these common factors there is also the specificity of MFT[3] that has to do more with the specificity of the setting, than with the underlying theoretical model. Dialogue in MFT is by definition a multi-actor dialogue: in marital therapy it is a dialogue of the therapist with two partners of the same generation, and in family therapy it is a dialogue with at least two family members of at least two different generations. The fact that sessions of marital and family therapists are essentially multi-actor dialogues raises important challenges for therapists. For instance, while the therapeutic relationship is one of the most potent factors in all therapies, the therapeutic relationship in MFT is more complex than in individual therapy as the family members bring their differences and their conflicts in the consultation room. Furthermore, the MFT session is not just a transitional space[4], in which people can free-associate. Often the tension is high in MFT sessions as the other family members hear everything that is said. Furthermore, real-life consequences are often the result of decisions made in MFT sessions, such as the decision to file for divorce, the decision to place a child in residential care, or the decision to report family violence. Within such a high-tension context, it is not easy for the therapist to form an effective therapeutic

1. A. CARR, *The Effectiveness of Family Therapy and Systemic Intervention for Child-Focused Problems*, in *Journal of Family Therapy* 31 (2009) 3-45; ID, *The Effectiveness of Family Therapy and Systemic Intervention for Adult-Focused Problems*, in *Journal of Family Therapy* 31 (2009) 46-74.

2. D.H. SPRENKLE – S.D. DAVIS – J.L. LEBOW, *Common Factors in Couple and Family Therapy: The Overlooked Foundation for Effective Practice*, New York, NY, Guilford, 2009.

3. D.H. SPRENKLE – A.J. BLOW, *Common Factors and Our Sacred Models*, in *Journal of Marital and Family Therapy* 30 (2004) 113-129.

4. D.W. WINICOTT, *Collected Papers: Through Paediatrics to Psycho-Analysis*, London, Tavistock Publications, 1958.

alliance with each of the family members, as well as with the family as a whole.

In this essay we will reflect on the complexity of therapeutic relationship in a multi-actor dialogue, and we will focus especially on the way a therapist can deal with the tensions and differences that are so often present in such a context. In the first part of the essay we will develop a conceptual frame in which we will rely on the MFT literature on the subject as well as on the conceptual discussion in the field around the concept of not-knowing. Furthermore, we will especially highlight the validity of some of the concepts of Mikhail Bahktin[5] to address the specific complexities of the MFT encounter. Then we will present a case study. In this case study we will limit ourselves to a micro-analysis of the first minutes of a first session of a marital therapy. In the third part of the essay we will discuss what we learned from the case-study against the background of some of the central concepts and ideas we developed in the first part.

I. Conceptual Frame

1. *The Therapeutic Relationship in Marital and Family Therapy*

In the MFT field there has been a fierce debate on the characteristics of an effective therapy and therapeutic relationship. When the cybernetic perspective still reigned in the field, the debate focused on the epistemology of strategy and control, and the importance of the therapist as a directive interventionist[6]. Although there were a lot of discussions about the therapeutic relationship, often the family therapist was seen as an outsider to the family who could intervene on the family structure in order to optimise its functioning. Since the narrative turn in MFT, the focus is more on the ethical aspects of the therapeutic relationship. The influence of social constructionism[7] on the MFT field was vast, and the suspicion towards the notion of objective knowledge highlighted the importance of ethical values in the therapist's decision making.

5. M.M. Bakhtin, *The Dialogic Imagination*, Austin, TX, University of Texas Press, 1981; Id., *Problems of Dostoevsky's Poetics*, Minneapolis, MN, University of Minnesota Press, 1984; Id., *Speech Genres and Other Late Essays*, Austin, TX, University of Texas Press, 1986.

6. L. Hoffman, *Foundations of Family Therapy*, New York, NY, Basic Books, 1981.

7. K.J. Gergen, *An Invitation to Social Construction*, London, Sage, 1999; S. McNamee – K.J. Gergen (eds.), *Therapy as Social Construction*, London, Sage, 1992.

In their struggles with the ethical aspects of the therapeutic relationship in MFT practice, the concept of not-knowing became very important in the field. The concept was originally described as a general attitude in which the therapist's actions communicate a genuine curiosity[8]. In order to really listen to the client's story, and to really understand what the client means, the therapist needs to be not-knowing in the sense that he/she has to suspend his/her own assumptions and preconceptions, and be open to what the client wants to convey[9]. It is not the therapist but the client who is the real expert is[10].

The notion of the client as an expert does not deny that a therapist has expertise. The concept doesn't dispute that therapists have pre-learned knowledge – theoretical and experiential, professional and personal: "A therapist cannot be a blank screen, void of ideas, opinions, and prejudices ... To the contrary, we each take who we are, and all that entails – personal and professional experiences, values, biases, and convictions-with us in the therapy room"[11]. Clearly, according to Anderson, the therapist's mind is not empty. He/she has opinions, ideas, and feelings, just as the client does. However, in contrast to the client who is the expert of his/her own life, the therapist's expertise is in the area of process, instead of the area of the content of the conversation: "... [A] therapist is the expert in engaging and participating with a client in a dialogical process of first-person storytelling"[12]. Explaining what she means by this, Anderson highlights the importance of the receptive aspect of the therapist's expertise: to "invite, respect, hear and be engaged in a client's story"[13].

In the field, however, there is a lot of controversy over the concept of not-knowing. For one thing, some authors have argued that the concept insufficiently addresses therapy as a dialogical phenomenon. David Paré, for instance, maintains that by one-sidedly stressing the expertise of the clients, the concept of not-knowing betrays an underlying individualistic perspective on the therapeutic relationship[14]. As Paré remarks, "[t]he notion of client as expert ... failed to capture the tenor of an intersubjective relationship. It does not dismantle the notion of individualistic expertise:

8. H. ANDERSON – H. GOOLISHIAN, *The Client Is the Expert: A Not-Knowing Approach to Therapy*, in MCNAMEE – GERGEN (eds.), *Therapy as Social Construction* (n. 7), 25-39.

9. H. ANDERSON, *Conversation, Language and Possibilities: A Postmodern Approach to Therapy*, New York, NY, Basic Books, 1997.

10. ANDERSON – GOOLISHIAN, *The Client Is the Expert* (n. 8).

11. ANDERSON, *Conversation, Language and Possibilities* (n. 9), p. 137.

12. *Ibid.*, p. 95.

13. *Ibid.*

14. D.A. PARÉ, *Discursive Wisdom: Reflections on Ethics and Therapeutic Knowledge*, in *International Journal of Critical Psychology* 7 (2002) 30-52.

it merely shifts it from the therapist to the client"[15]. According to Paré, the not-knowing concept doesn't capture the mutuality and shared activity of a therapeutic relationship, as the therapist's lived experience in the encounter with the family is not valued.

Another interesting objection to the uncritical use of the concept of not-knowing has to do with its denial of power issues in relationships. Guilfoyle explores the relationship between dialogue and power in the practice of not-knowing forms of therapy[16]. According to Guilfoyle, therapists relying on the not-knowing concept associate power with authority, domination and control, and implicitly propose that the removal of power from therapy is an ethical imperative for dialogical therapies. These therapists also seem to suppose that removing power from the therapeutic relationship, in and of itself, would lead to therapeutic change. In that way power is considered an obstruction to dialogue as it limits the dialogical space for the client. However, introducing Foucault's concept of power, Guilfoyle argues that power relations can infuse dialogue, without compromising the dialogical status of the interaction: Power and resistance work together to produce a dialogical encounter[17].

Notwithstanding the controversy in the field about the concept of not-knowing, hardly any family therapist denies the importance of the concept for marital and family therapy practice[18], and the not-knowing concept has become one of the central concepts in MFT reflection on the therapeutic relationship. The immense influence of the concept in the MFT field is emblematic of the way family therapists have tried to deal with the ethical challenge of being in a therapeutic relationship with clients. The concept of not-knowing is just one example of the different ways in which family therapists have emphasized the importance of otherness in the therapeutic relationship. These family therapists have often found their inspiration in the philosophic work of philosophers like Derrida[19], Levinas[20] and

15. *Ibid.*, p. 32.

16. M. GUILFOYLE, *Dialogue and Power: A Critical Analysis of Power in Dialogical Therapy*, in *Family Process* 42 (2003) 331-343.

17. *Ibid.*

18. P. ROBER, *The Therapist's Self in Dialogical Family Therapy: Some Ideas about Not-Knowing and the Therapist's Inner Conversation*, in *Family Process* 44 (2005) 477-495.

19. G. LARNER, *Derrida and the Deconstruction of Power as Context and Topic in Therapy*, in I. PARKER (ed.), *Deconstructing Psychotherapy*, London, Sage, 1999, 39-53.

20. G. LARNER, *Levinas: Therapy as Discourse Ethics*, in T. STRONG – D. PARÉ (eds.), *Furthering Talk: Advances in Discursive Therapies*, New York, NY, KluwerAcademic – Plenum Publishers, 2004, 15-32; G. LARNER, *Exploring Levinas: The Ethical Self in Family Therapy*, in *Journal of Family Therapy* 30 (2008) 351-360.

Foucault[21]. More recently, Mikhail Bakhtin has also been an inspiration for some family therapists who have conceptualised MFT as a dialogue[22]. Referring to some of these sources of inspiration we will reflect in this essay on the complexity of creating dialogical space in MFT practice.

2. *Dialogue*

While Bakhtin's dialogical concepts have become very important in contemporary family therapeutic reflection, in the MFT literature the concept of dialogue is often used in an idealizing way. Usually it is rather simplistically opposed to monologue, implicitly suggesting that good therapy is dialogical, while bad therapy is monological; or arguing that clients enter therapy with fixed, monologic stories, and that therapy consists of dialogizing these stories[23]. Some authors have used dialogical concepts mainly as a way to legitimate the rejection the therapist's expert position and describe the therapist's task as listening empathically to the client's story from a not-knowing position[24]. However, the concept of dialogue in Bakhtin's work is complex[25] and it cannot be simply described as the opposite of monologue. Indeed, in a sense monologue can be understood as a part of dialogism, and we can speak of dialogical dialogues and monological dialogues[26]. In every conversation there is a dynamic tension between the monological and the dialogical functions[27]. This illustrates something of the complexity of Bakhtin's concept of dialogue, of which Bakhtin scholar Caryl Emerson writes: "Dialogue is by no means a safe or secure relation. Yes, a 'thou' is always potentially there, but it is exceptionally fragile; the 'I' must create it (and be created by it) in a

21. M. White – D. Epston, *Narrative Means to Therapeutic Ends*, New York, NY, Norton, 1990.

22. J. Seikula – M. Olson, *The Open Dialogue Approach to Acute Psychosis: Its Poetics and Micropolitics*, in *Family Process* 42 (2003) 403-418; W. Seltzer – M. Seltzer, *Tales Full of Sound and Fury: A Cultural Approach to Family Therapeutic Work and Research in Rural Scandinavia*, in *Family Process* 39 (2000) 285-306; P. Rober, *Constructive Hypothesizing, Dialogic Understanding, and the Therapist's Inner Conversation: Some Ideas about Knowing and Not-Knowing in the Family Therapy Session*, in *Journal of Marital and Family Therapy* 28 (2002) 467-478; Id., *The Therapist's Self in Dialogical Family Therapy* (n. 18); Id., *Family Therapy as a Dialogue of Living Persons*, in *Journal of Marital and Family Therapy* 31 (2005) 385-397.

23. P. Penn – M. Frankfurt, *Creating a Participant Text: Writing, Multiple Voices, Narrative Multiplicity*, in *Family Process* 33 (1994) 217-231.

24. Anderson, *Conversation, Language and Possibilities* (n. 9).

25. S. Vice, *Introducing Bakhtin*, Manchester, Manchester University Press, 1997.

26. G.L. Morson – C. Emerson, *Mikhail Bakhtin: Creation of a Prosaics*, Stanford, CA, Stanford University Press, 1990.

27. J. Shotter, *Conversational Realities*, London, Sage, 1993.

simultaneously mutual gesture, over and over again, and it comes with no special authority or promise of constancy ... Imbalance is the norm"[28]. According to Bakhtin, life is an ongoing, unfinalisable dialogue continually taking place[29]. There is a constant tension in dialogues between what is said and what is not said, as language is the product of dynamic, tension filled processes in which two tendencies are involved: the centripetal (centralising, unifying) forces and centrifugal (decentralising, differentiating) forces[30]. Contrary to Hegelian dialectics that prescribes the finalisation of dialectic tensions in a synthesis, according to Bakhtin these dialogical processes are unfinalisable: the tension between the two opposing forces never finds a final solution. As Baxter writes, "This view stands in sharp contrast to dominant approaches to relational communication ... [that] ... have articulated the grand narratives of connection, certainty and openness"[31]. In such approaches autonomy is linked with distance and secrecy between partners. Intimacy is linked with openness, and closedness is viewed as problematic and unhealthy. From a dialectical perspective, however, these approaches underestimate the importance of the continuous dynamic interplay of centripetal and centrifugal forces, as well as the uniqueness of every moment and the shaping force of the time and place of the dialogical exchange. In other words, there is a constant tension between expression and non-expression in relationships, and what is actually said or not said in relationships is not the final outcome of a process, but rather is a momentary freeze frame of the tension, uniquely shaped by the dialogical context.

3. *Otherness and Dialogical Space*

One of the most interesting contributions of Bakhtin's thinking to the field of MFT is that his concepts allow family therapists to reflect on some of the complexities of the family therapeutic encounter like multiplicity (e.g. dealing with the different stories about the same events), identity (e.g. the therapist's becoming part of the family while remaining

28. C. EMERSON, *The First Hundred Years of Mikhail Bakhtin*, Princeton, NJ, Princeton University Press, 1997, pp. 229-230.

29. MORSON – EMERSON, *Mikhail Bakhtin* (n. 26), p. 59.

30. BAKHTIN, *The Dialogic Imagination* (n. 5); L.A. BAXTER – B.M. MONTGOMERY, *Relating: Dialogues and Dialectics*, New York, NY, Guilford Press, 1996; L.A. BAXTER, *Dialogues of Relating*, in R. ANDERSON – L.A. BAXTER – K.N. CISSNA (eds.), *Dialogue: Theorizing Difference in Communication Studies*, London, Sage, 2004, 107-124.

31. BAXTER, *Dialogues of Relating* (n. 30), p. 144.

an outsider), and power (e.g. the therapist leading the session by making dialogical space for the clients).

Being a scholar of literary theory and studying novels of Dostojevski, Rabelais and others, Bakhtin often thought in terms of Authors and Heros. In Bakhtin's psychology, authoring is a central concept[32]: I (the author) take shape in dialogue with the other (the hero). I can only start to get to know myself through the other's outsideness. Through the continual dialogical process with others, my self – distinct from the others – is in a constant state of becoming: I am different from others and it is exactly by this constant and ever-changing dialogue with otherness that I continuously become the distinct centre of experience that I am[33].

The other is central in Bakhtin's thinking, not only in his thinking about the self, but also in his theory on the speech act. Dialogue is not possible without the other[34]. According to Bakhtin, my speech is never my speech as it is addressed to the other (addressivity), and a response from the other is anticipated[35]. What I say is always a response to what has been said before, and in addressing the other, my utterance is not only shaped by the anticipated response of the other, it also invites a response from the other (responsivity)[36].

4. *Positioning*

While addressivity and responsivity refer to the fundamental dialogical nature of our being, these concepts also touch upon challenges for the therapist, as, according to Bakhtin, no speech is value free[37]. As a therapist, I cannot be *positionless*, as in each utterance I take up a position revealing my evaluation of what has been said before. Taking a position, I invite the other to also take a position by proposing his/her position and waiting for his/her response: to accept or reject the position I proposed.

32. MORSON – EMERSON, *Mikhail Bakhtin* (n. 26).

33. J. SALGADO, *The Feeling of a Dialogical Self: Affectivity, Agency and Otherness*, in L.M. SIMÃO – J. VALSINER (eds.), *Otherness in Question: Labyrinths of the Self*, Charlotte, NC, Information Age Publishing, 2007, 53-71; J. SALGADO – M. GONÇALVES, *The Dialogical Self: Social, Personal, and (Un)Conscious*, in A. ROSA – J. VALSINER (eds.), *The Cambridge Handbook of Social Cultural Psychology*, Cambridge, Cambridge University Press, 2007, 608-621.

34. I. MARKOVÁ, *Dialogicality and Social Representations: The Dynamics of Mind*, Cambridge, Cambridge University Press, 2003.

35. BAKHTIN, *Speech Genres and Other Late Essays* (n. 5).

36. *Ibid.*

37. MORSON – EMERSON, *Mikhail Bakhtin* (n. 26).

Positioning theory[38] is an important enrichment of therapeutic reflection in the field of MFT as it opens space to talk about the rhetorical aspect of the encounter[39]. Positioning implies a spatial metaphor linking a voice with a point of view from which one observes reality. Each point of view gives one a perspective, but at the same time it has inherent limitations: from each point of view some things can be seen, while others remain out of focus, in the shadows or out of sight. Dialogue consists of the meeting of different points of view, in which each voice expresses something from its perspective, activating another voice speaking from another point of view in a continuous game of agreement/disagreement (content), or identification/differentiation (process).

Since a distinction can be made between story (content) and storytelling (process) in dialogue, we can also distinguish between representational positioning and interactional positioning[40]. Representational positioning refers to the positions of the protagonists in the story (content), while interactional positioning refers to the positioning of the speaker, the addressee and the audience in the storytelling situation (process). In family therapy, more than in individual therapies, interactional positioning – how the family members position themselves in the here-and-now of the session – needs careful consideration. As family members contrast their perspectives to the positions that they attribute to the other interlocutors, conflict and disagreement are interesting phenomena to observe in family session. They refer to the continuous dance of changing positions in the session, giving the therapist some sense of what is at stake for the family members. However, the therapist is also part of the dialogue. This means that he/she is also invited to take positions in the family's performance[41]. The task for the family therapist is to remain sensitive for the family's invitations and to guard his/her mental space to reflect on this positioning: do these invitations open space for stories untold? Do they add to the security in the session? Do they leave enough space for other family members to move flexibly in the family performance?

38. B. DAVIES – R. HARRÉ, *Positioning: The Discursive Production of Selves*, 1990. Paper downloaded from the internet: http://www.massey.ac.nz/~alock/position/position.htm on January 4th 2006; R. HARRÉ – L. VAN LANGENHOVE (eds.), *Positioning Theory*, Oxford, Blackwell, 1999.

39. M. BILLIG, *Arguing and Thinking: A Rhetorical Approach to Social Psychology*, Cambridge, MA, Cambridge University Press, 1996 (2nd ed.).

40. S. WORTHAM, *Narratives in Action: Strategy for Research and Analysis*, New York, NY, Teachers College Press, Colombia University, 2001.

41. ROBER, *The Therapist's Self in Dialogical Family Therapy* (n. 18); ID. – M. SELTZER, *Avoiding Colonizer Positions in the Therapy Room*, in *Family Process* 49 (2010) 123-137.

5. *Dialogue in Marital and Family Therapy*

The concept of positioning can help us to address the specific challenges for the marital and family therapist, as it sets the stage for addressing tension, coercion, conflict and violence, as inherent potentialities of dialogue. Often in dialogue others are forced to speak, to listen, or to act. Or they may be silenced by intimidation, or threatened to abstain from acting. Free and spontaneous dialogue is the exception rather than the rule in our world[42].

Free and spontaneous dialogue, in which mutual understanding and intimacy can grow, is what most therapists aim at. The challenge for me as a couple therapist and a family therapists is; how to position myself in the session, in such a way that the chances of a constructive conversation are increased and the risk of violence, repression and coercion are lifted as much as possible from the dialogue. Or, in other words, how can dialogical space be created in the therapy session, in such a way that there is room for growth and understanding? This is a challenge, because family therapeutic conversations so often are explicitly or implicitly tension filled and rich in conflicts that have long and painful histories.

In this essay, I will address this challenge of creating dialogical space in a therapeutic encounter, and I will focus on a marital therapy encounter. However, before I shift to therapy practice, a remark should be made. In talking about therapeutic practice, I will take the perspective of the therapist (what Bakhtin would call the *I-for-myself* and the *other-for-me* positions), and address some of the issues that are raised for the therapist in dealing with otherness. For some readers this might come as a surprise, because it seems antithetical to the dialogical framework I have outlined in this essay so far. However, as a therapist I cannot really speak from the client's perspective, if I want to respect the client's otherness. So ethically the therapist's perspective is the only perspective I can speak from. Furthermore, there is also a practical reason why I speak from the perspective of the therapist: as a MFT supervisor and trainer I am always looking for ways in which I can teach young therapists how to survive in therapy practice, and if possible do a good job. Efforts of therapists to do a good job, in my opinion, always have to start from their own perspective and what they can change in themselves or in their positioning, in order to create space for the clients to tell their stories and to gain some kind of

42. A. FOGEL, *Coercion to Speak, Conrad's Poetics of Dialogue*, Cambridge, MA, Harvard University Press, 1985; ID., *Coerced Speech and the Oedipus Dialogue Complex*, in G.L. MORSON – C. EMERSON (eds.), *Rethinking Mikhail Bakhtin*, New York, NY, Vintage Books, 1989, 173-196.

understanding and agency in their lives. It is important to realise, however, that no image created from Bakhtin's *I-for-myself* and the *other-for-me* positions is ever finalised. It is at best partial as it misses the surplus that a *me-for-another* perspective can offer[43].

II. The Case-Study

1. *Marital Therapy Practice*

When the marital therapist meets a family for the first time, he/she is faced with a big challenge. The clients come to him/her as a couple, not as individuals. This is expressed in their talking in the beginning of the first session in which they almost always start to talk in terms of we, referring to the couple. The division is between *we* (couple) – *you* (therapist): at that moment the therapist is the couple's other, and the couple is the therapist's other.

But very soon in the session (sometimes already after a few seconds), when the therapist and the clients exchange their first words, a relationship starts to build in which gradually differentiation in the couple will appear. Otherness within the couple system starts to emerge. In the beginning of the first session this very often has to do with the difference between the partners in terms of commitment to therapy. While both partners come in therapy usually one has the most outspoken concern about the relationship, and took the initiative to make the appointment with the therapist. The other had to be asked to come along, or even stronger, he/she had to be convinced, talked into, coerced or seduced into going to the marital therapist. In this dynamic, the couple's ambivalence towards therapy surfaces: one partner says "yes" to therapy in one form or another, another partner says "no". The "no" can be expressed in a myriad of ways: it can be a sigh, a hesitation, an open rejection of therapy, a reluctance to speak, and so on. However it is expressed, most often therapists sense who in the couple is ready to start to tell their stories, and who is reluctant. Here lies a first big challenge for the marital therapist: how to create out of this context of ambivalence a dialogical space in which the multiple voices can be heard, also those of the more reluctant partner.

43. Morson – Emerson, *Mikhail Bakhtin* (n. 26).

2. *The Case of John and Tina*

> John and Tina come to therapy for the first time. I meet them in the waiting room. Tina looks sad and withdrawn, but she comes to me to shake my hand. In a subdued way she seems pleased to see me as if she has been waiting long for this moment. John however is more reluctant to stand up and shake hands.
>
> We go to the therapy room and I introduce myself. I feel that Tina is interested in what I'm saying, while John remains distant and aloof. When I ask them who took the initiative to contact me, Tina says, "I did". I hear her eagerness to answer and I sense that she is poised to start to explain why she thinks therapy is needed.

In the vignette, the therapist senses John's "no" in his reluctance to stand up, to shake hands and to follow the therapist to the consultation room. The therapist can also sense it in the way John listens to the therapist when he introduces himself. Tina on the other hand, in a restrained way seems to be eager to start with the therapy. It seems that she has a lot on her mind and that she wants to share it with the therapist.

For the therapist, it would be very easy to open dialogical space for Tina's story. She is eager to explain why she thinks therapy is necessary for the couple and to reveal some of the ways in which the couple has struggled to survive. The telling of Tina's story would legitimate the meeting as a therapeutic meeting: A dialogical space would be created in which Tina is positioned as the client in need of a listening ear, and the therapist is positioned as a professional listener open for her story. Needles to say that for the therapist, this is a comfortable positioning, as it offers the therapist the possibility to assume his preferred identity in the therapy context: that of benevolent and skilled helper. In both Tina's and the therapist's inner conversations a picture is beginning to take shape of a fruitful therapeutic encounter. There, however, lies the trap. In this picture there is no place for John and his otherness. Such a dialogical space would exclude him. Ethically this is unacceptable but also therapeutically there is a problem. Indeed, if John is already reluctant to come into therapy (as he seems to be at that moment), the chances are that Tina's telling of her story will only increase his reluctance as she might start giving her account of all that went wrong in their marriage for so many years, and share things with the therapist about their intimate relationship before John has had a chance to choose this exchange for himself. Chances are that if that were to happen, he would feel more or less subtly exposed or even violated by Tina's story. He might feel pinned down in an identity that he doesn't recognise as his own. This might only push him in a more defensive position, increasing his reluctance to choose for therapy and decreasing the chances of an effective couples therapy.

> The therapist then asks who took the initiative to make an appointment.
> Tina says: "I did", and she glances at John. The therapist wonders if there is a reproach in that glance.
> The therapist then turns to John and asks him: "Was it difficult for your wife to convince you that therapy might be a good idea for you?"
> "Well no, ... I mean yes ... at first I did not want to come", replies John.

This is an important moment, because these questions of the therapist offer him the opportunity to move closer to what otherness means in practice. John's hesitations about therapy expresses his otherness in comparison with his wife (who really wants therapy). However, it also expresses his otherness from the therapist. As John does not seem eager to take the position of a help-seeker, he denies the therapist the position of a potential helper. This is very delicate, because if the therapist is not positioned as a helper, how is he positioned? How does John see the therapist? This illustrates that making room for the otherness of John might be threatening for the therapist's identity within the therapeutic dialogue. No wonder it feels uncomfortable for the therapist when he tries to open space in which John's otherness can be expressed.

> "Can you help me to understand your hesitation to come?" the therapist asks.
> John looks at his wife. Then he says: "Therapy is just not for me. We should find a solution for our problems ourselves. And also, therapy doesn't help".
> "It doesn't help?"
> "Well, that's my experience anyway. We went to a couples therapist two years ago and it did not do us any good".

This is what often happens in therapy. Behind the client's hesitations towards therapy there are stories about earlier attempts to find help or to find relief that turn out to be disappointing. This can be about previous conversations between the partners that only lead to more conflict or pain, but it can also be about conversations with professional helpers (GP, counsellor, priest, pastor, therapist, ...). Acknowledging the client's hesitations and making room to talk about these disappointing experiences can create room for new experiences.

> The therapist asks John to talk about the previous therapy.
> John talks about the therapy with a female therapist and he says: "All she did was listen. She didn't say anything. We had to pay her and she did not do anything".
> "You would expect more from your therapist?"

> "Yes, I would at least want to hear what my therapist is thinking. But that was not the only thing. Even more important was that she sided with my wife against me. My wife felt understood by her, but I could feel her becoming irritated with me".
> "So you want your therapist to share his ideas with you and you don't want him to side with your wife against you. You want to be understood too?"
> "Yes. I think she thought of me as being very rational and she wanted me to share my feelings. And that is what my wife has been saying all the time".

The exploration of John's previous experiences with therapy positions him as someone with legitimate feelings and preferences. Through his recounting of his experiences he becomes someone in the session. Furthermore, this sequence of the conversation, while acknowledging John's reluctance, positions the therapist as potentially different from the previous therapist: it opens space for the possibility that some therapist might share his ideas and that some therapist might understand him too (and not only his wife).

While we can easily see the advantages of making room for John's reluctance towards therapy for the positioning of John, the therapist has to be aware that this is a test of Tina's patience. From the beginning of the session, she is eager to start to talk about what brings her to therapy, and John's talking about his experiences in the previous therapy may only provide evidence for her of his unwillingness to talk about the real issues in the relationship. So it is important that the therapist brings equilibrium by giving space to Tina to tell her story.

III. Discussion

1. *Alliance Building in Marital Therapy*

Psychotherapy research suggests that alliance building may be one of the most important therapeutic tasks of the first session of marital therapy[44]. In marital therapy alliance building has its complications however[45]. When a couple comes in therapy, there is usually one partner who took the initiative, and the other partner who hesitates more, or says "no" more or less explicitly. The danger, as the case of Tina and John illustrates, is

44. L. Knobloch-Fedders – W.M. Pinsof – B.J. Mann, *The Formation of the Therapeutic Alliance in Couple Therapy*, in *Family Process* 43 (2004) 425-442.

45. E.g. S.E.G. Thomas – R.J. Werner-Wilson – M.J. Murphy, *Influence of Therapist and Client Behaviors on Therapy Alliance*, in *Contemporary Family Therapy* 27 (2005) 19-35; J. Moynehan – J. Adams, *What's the Problem? A Look at Men in Marital Therapy*, in *The American Journal of Family Therapy* 35 (2007) 41-51.

that the therapist would start to build a therapeutic alliance with one partner by going into the problem description and thereby neglecting the otherness of the one who is more reluctant to go into therapy. In that way the more reluctant partner is neglected and the power dimension that is so central in troubled human relationships, is not acknowledged. This is in sync with the analysis of Guilfoyle about power and dialogue in family therapeutic relationships[46]. According to Guilfoyle, the not-knowing concept suggests that power is a threat to dialogue, and as a consequence, therapists relying on the not-knowing concept deny the presence of power in their encounter with the client. However, in denying a place to power in the therapeutic relationship, and assuming a virginal ethical position, the possibility of the client's resistance is denied: "Dialogue, in other words, does not require the removal of power operations or rhetoric. It does however require resistance to the exercise of power"[47]. It is only by acknowledging the importance of power, and opening space for the client's resistance (for the client's "no") that a dialogical meeting can be obtained. In addition to Guilfoyle's objections to the way the not-knowing concept is used as a disavowal of power in the therapeutic encounter, our analysis suggests that the concept also insufficiently addresses the specificity of the MFT meeting, as a tension filled meeting, in which the therapist is emotionally pushed and pulled by the different family members to take certain positions and to acknowledge certain truths. The therapist can not afford the ethical innocence of a passive receptive stance, because such a stance would only perpetuate the differences and unbalances already present in the relationship.

2. *Husbands and Wives*

Studies show that husbands are more reluctant to seek therapy than wives[48], and it seems that this gender difference in the seeking of marital therapy is a complex issue. Three factors are involved[49]: 1. Men are generally more reluctant to commit in therapy and women are more psychologically minded[50]; 2. Women make more use of external support;

46. GUILFOYLE, *Dialogue and Power* (n. 16).
47. *Ibid.*, p. 335.
48. E.g. B.D. DOSS – D.C. ATKINS – A. CHRISTENSEN, *Who's Dragging Their Feet? Husbands and Wives Seeking Marital Therapy*, in *Journal of Marital and Family Therapy* 29 (2003) 165-177.
49. *Ibid.*
50. M.A. SHILL – M.A. LUMLEY, *The Psychological-Mindedness Scale: Factor Structure, Convergent Validity and Gender in a Non-Psychiatric Sample*, in *Psychology and Psychotherapy: Theory, Research and Practice* 75 (2002) 131-150.

and 3. Women expect more from their intimate relationships, and they are barometers of the relationship. While some studies suggest that for men family-of-origin distress might play a critical role in their reluctance to build an alliance in the beginning of therapy[51], other studies point out that the husband's reluctance for therapy is not attributable to their lack of problem awareness[52]. Rather, it seems that husbands might have concerns about discretion, shame and embarrassment:

> Men acknowledge problems but prefer to keep them to themselves. They are culturally conditioned to solve their problems on their own. If men then are reluctant to discuss emotional difficulties or ask for help from close friends, the activity of therapy which requires disclosure to a complete stranger (most often a woman) is likely to meet with stiff resistance. Men may know they are unhappy but they will be dragged kicking and screaming to treatment where they are required to disclose and discuss problems[53].

Because of this complexity and the sensitive issues involved, some researchers have recommended marital therapists to examine how the decision was made to come to therapy before embarking on a description of the couples' problems[54]. Such an examination can create room for the story of the husband: his worry that his perspective will not get a fair hearing, his feeling a failure now that they have to ask for help, and his negative experiences with talking about sensitive issues in the relationship. Starting therapy in such a way enhances men's commitment in the early stages of therapy, enhances the therapeutic alliances and prevents his prematurely ending the therapy[55].

3. *Empathic Connection with Both Partners*

However, the husbands are not always the most reluctant partner to commit to marital therapy, and besides, this essay is not about gender differences. Rather, it is about differences in couples in terms of motivation for therapy and initiative to make a first appointment, and about the importance of creating dialogical space in which also the more reluctant partner gets a place. This is all the more important as research seems to suggest that the spouse who is the more reluctant to seek therapy might

51. KNOBLOCH-FEDDERS – PINSOF – MANN, *The Formation of the Therapeutic Alliance in Couple Therapy* (n. 44).
52. MOYNEHAN – ADAMS, *What's the Problem?* (n. 45).
53. *Ibid.*, pp. 42-43.
54. *Ibid.*
55. DOSS – ATKINS – CHRISTENSEN, *Who's Dragging Their Feet?* (n. 48).

be the most distressed[56]. One way to deal with this challenge is taking a shortcut towards a safe and comfortable therapeutic alliance with the willing partner by listening empathically to his/her problem story and taking a not-knowing position. In this essay, however, we propose that the therapist would take the longer and more difficult route of first making dialogical space for the otherness of the more reluctant partner. This may lead to a therapeutic alliance in which the therapist has an empathic connection with both partners.

In the case of Tina and John a crucial moment was when the therapist asked *who took the initiative to make an appointment* for marital therapy. This question may be counterintuitive for some as it is not focused on the problem that brings the couple to therapy. Some textbooks suggest that the first question in a couple therapy should be: "What brings you in today and how might you want me to help?"[57]. Let's hypothesize for a moment that the therapist would have asked that question. For sure, it would have opened space for Tina's story and it would have offered right away the chance to the therapist to take a receptive listening stance. However, if the therapist had asked this question he would have immediately aligned with Tina by implicitly agreeing with her that it was a good idea to go into therapy. Tina would be positioned as the seeker of help, and the therapist as the provider of help. Here we see Bakhtin's authoring process in practice: the therapist is the author of a client as his hero, and the client is author of the therapist as her hero. However, how would John have been authored? As the one who does not want help? As the one who does not understand that something is wrong in the relationship? ... It seems that while the question "What brings you in today and how might you want me to help?" at that moment in the session would create a dialogical space for Tina, it would only do so via an act of exclusion of John. And this is what often happens in marital therapy: the therapist succeeds in building an alliance with the partner who is most motivated for therapy. The one who hesitates to commit to therapy or says 'no' is then referred to as being 'negative', 'rigid' or 'unreasonable', and sometimes he/she is given a psychopathological label that provides the act of exclusion with scientific legitimacy. In that way, however, otherness is neglected and the specificity of the therapeutic relationship in MFT, as a tension filled and unstable multi-actor dialogue, is not acknowledged[58].

56. *Ibid.*

57. See e.g. J. PATTERSON – L. WILLIAMS – T.M. EDWARDS – L. CHAMOV – C. GRAUF-GROUNDS, *Essential Skills in Family Therapy: From the First Interview to Termination*, New York, NY, Guilford, 2009.

58. PARÉ, *Discursive Wisdom* (n. 14).

4. *Major Difficulties*

In my experience as a clinician and as a trainer, there are two major difficulties for therapists in making space for the 'no' of the client. First there is the bearing of the growing frustration of the partner who is most committed to therapy. Often in the beginning of the first session, when the therapist is exploring the reluctant partner's good reasons for hesitating to go in therapy[59], the other partner becomes more impatient and shows this in his/her behavior (e.g. sighs, looks away, ...). The therapist has to bear this for the time being until a first alliance is made with the reluctant partner, in such a way that he/she will not turn away from therapy further when the problem story is told. Secondly, there is the difficulty for the therapist of resisting the temptation to be a good therapist for the partner who is most committed to therapy and who is more than ready to acknowledge the therapist in his/her position as a therapist by telling his/her story of pain and suffering. Both difficulties connect with our fantasies as therapists of being the benevolent healer (denying our own power and self-interest), and with our professional ideology of testimony as healing[60]. We present ourselves as accepting and non-judgmental helpers and we are bent on creating a relationship that will make everything better[61]. Also, we want our clients to testify about their experiences, as we think that may free them of their suffering and pain. However, our invitation to testify can unwillingly represent an act of violence. Sometimes our insisting that our client should articulate what has remained unexpressed until then is not done so much for the sake of the testifier or his/her partner, but because it is necessary to acknowledge our identity as professional helpers. Feeling acknowledged as professional helpers, we turn a blind eye to the contextual suffering (e.g. exclusion, pathologizing, ...) such a testimony may contribute to.

5. *Other Kinds of Settings*

While in this essay we focused on differences in the couple about commitment in therapy, the same dynamics can be found in other kinds of therapy setting, albeit in a slightly different guise. In individual therapy a similar dynamic can be observed in a client's ambivalence towards

59. P. ROBER, *Hesitations and their Non-Verbal Expression in the Family Therapy Session*, in *Journal of Family Therapy* 24 (2002) 187-204.
60. ROBER – SELTZER, *Avoiding Colonizer Positions in the Therapy Room* (n. 41).
61. J.C. NORCROSS – B.A. FARBER, *Choosing Psychotherapy as a Career: Beyond "I Want to Help People"*, in *Journal of Clinical Psychology* 61 (2005) 939-943.

therapy as it may surface in the transference relationship with the therapist: "I want therapy because..., but I don't want therapy because..."[62]. In family therapy, most of the time, the parents have taken the initiative to phone the therapist for a first appointment, and usually the children come along with some measure of reluctance. The children are there, not because they want to come, nor because they think therapy is necessary or could be potentially useful, but because they have to. In this family dynamic, the family's ambivalence towards therapy surfaces in a split between parents and children: one parent (or both parents) says "yes" to therapy in one form or another, while one of the children (or several children) say "no", or are at least hesitant towards it. Like in couple therapy, also in individual and family therapy it is probably recommendable to postpone exploration of the problem story, and first make dialogical space for the voices of reluctance and hesitation.

IV. Conclusion

Psychotherapy research has consistently pointed out that therapists differ in their effectiveness to affect change[63]. Miller, Hubble & Duncan found that superior therapeutic performance stems from an attitude of openness towards the client's corrective feedback about the therapy, which is then used to guide the therapy[64]. This is also what researchers found when they examined the effect of providing systematic feedback to therapists about the client's progress in therapy: therapy became much more effective[65]. An open attitude towards the client's feedback supposes

62. D.E. Engle – H. Arkowitz, *Ambivalence in Psychotherapy*, New York, NY, Guilford, 2006.

63. E.g. B.E. Wampold, *The Great Psychotherapy Debate: Models, Methods, and Findings*, Mahwah, NJ, Erlbaum, 2001; Id., *The Psychotherapist*, in J.C. Norcross – LE. Beutler – R.F. Levant (eds.), *Evidence-Based Practices in Mental Health: Debate and Dialogue on the Fundamental Questions*, Washington, DC, American Psychological Association, 2006, 200-208; L.E. Beutler – M.L. Malik – S. Alimohamed – T.M. Harwood – H. Talebi – S. Noble – E. Wong, *Therapist Variables*, in M.J. Lambert (ed.), *Bergin and Garfield's Handbook of Psychotherapy and Behavior Change*, New York, NY, Wiley, 2004, 227-306.

64. S.L. Miller – M. Hubble – B.L. Duncan, *Supershrinks, What's the Secret of Their Success?*, in *Psychotherapy in Australia* 14 (2008) 14-22.

65. E.g. M.J. Lambert – C. Harmon – K. Slade – J.L. Whipple – E.J. Hawkins, *Providing Feedback to Psychotherapists on Their Patients' Progress: Clinical Results and Practice Suggestions*, in *Journal of Clinical Psychology* 61 (2005) 165-174; M.J. Lambert – J.L. Whipple – D.W. Smart – D.A. Vermeersch – S.L. Nielsen – E.J. Hawkins, *The Effects of Providing Therapists with Feedback on Patient Progress during Psychotherapy: Are Outcomes Enhanced?*, in *Psychotherapy Research* 11 (2001) 49-68.

an active interest of the therapist in the client's otherness and the continued commitment to creating a dialogical space in which the client feels legitimated to say "no" to the therapist, and in which the therapist values this "no" and uses it to guide his/her actions in therapy by the feedback he/she receives from the clients.

In this essay we have concentrated on the complexity of the specific setting of MFT and we zoomed in on one instance in which the otherness of the client surfaces in marital and family therapy: the client's "no" to therapy in the first meeting, expressed as reluctance, hesitation or resistance, and how this can be observed in the differences between the partners about commitment in marital therapy. A microanalysis of the first minutes in the first session of the marital therapy with Tina and John illustrated the challenges for the couple therapist and some of the ways in which these challenges can be dealt with. The microanalysis shows that a receptive stance of the therapist too early in the first marital therapy session can reinforce an already existing imbalance in the couple: one partner is more motivated for therapy, while the other is more reluctant to commit to therapy. To deal with this imbalance in the couple, the therapist has to position in such a way that the otherness of the more reluctant partner is acknowledged and room is made for him/her as a another human being with a rich inner life filled with personal stories and a meaningful experience of life.

Dealing with the challenge of the otherness of the partners is a project throughout the whole therapy. It is never finished as a tension between expression and non-expression is always there. In this essay we claim however, that dealing with this challenge presents itself already in the first minutes of the first meeting, and that acknowledging the otherness of the other at that moment can lead to a therapeutic alliance in which the therapist has an empathic connection with both partners. Conversely, it is also possible that making room for the otherness of the partners would uncover insurmountable differences between both partners (or between one of the partners and the therapist). As explained above, in marital and family therapy tension and conflict come with the territory, and sometimes the instability and nervousness can be so overpowering that a constructive dialogue is not likely.

For Bakthin, disorder is a given, and wholeness is a project. For him, the natural state of things is mess[66]. This is often forgotten by marital and family therapists who use Bakhtin's ideas to support an idealistic view of dialogue as natural state of equilibrium that can be found whenever the

66. MORSON – EMERSON, *Mikhail Bakhtin* (n. 26).

therapists doesn't interfere with the system from an expert position, and merely listens receptively to the client's stories. In this essay, starting from the specificity of the MFT setting we have affirmed that the domain of human relationships is one where we should always expect antagonism and discord. While, as we have claimed in this essay, acknowledging the antagonistic dimension of intimate human relationships may be a pre-requisite for dialogue, consensus and understanding, we have to bear in mind the possibility that sometimes the outcome of a therapeutic conversation may not be consensus, or some kind of understanding. Sometimes we have to be content with the outcome of a mere recognition of the fundamental otherness of the other, without the relief of a compromise or a solution.

Stating this, I am taking a big risk as this touches upon our very identity as therapists. We all want to be helpers[67], and we all want to relieve our clients of their pain and suffering. Questioning the therapeutic effectiveness of egalitarian intentions and stripping away the idealistic view of the naturally healing dialogue, may confront us with our uncertainty and powerlessness as therapists. It may confront us with the fact that our individual well-meaning intentions don't transcend the pervasive power balances at play in the broader context. Furthermore, it confronts us with our ethical duty as therapists. It puts us in the uncomfortable position of having a responsibility to find ways to actively contribute to a fruitful dialogue that is not a natural given at all, but rather a project.

Interfaculty Institute
for Family and Sexuality Studies
Faculty of Medicine KU Leuven
Kapucijnenvoer 33 blok i - box 7001
3000 Leuven
Belgium
peter.rober@med.kuleuven.be

Peter ROBER

67. NORCROSS – FARBER, *Choosing Psychotherapy as a Career* (n. 61).

QUICKENING PRACTICE

THE ETHICAL SPACE OF ACTION[1]

I. Introduction: The Space between People is not Empty[2]

On the first page of Roger Poole's 1972 book, *Towards Deep Subjectivity*, a photo shows three Russian soldiers and four Czech citizens sitting on park benches. It is late summer in Prague, 1968. The three Russians sit in a row, staring in front of them. One soldier has a weapon leaning against his knee. Two Czech citizens sit next to the soldiers, bent forward, staring at the ground. On benches at right angles, a young man and woman look furtively at the Russians, both immobile and reflective. According to Poole the space spread out in front of, between, and including all the people in this photo is ethical space – a moral geography where meaning and interpretation belong together. Each and every person in the picture and even the observer invest meaning into the space depending on their moral presuppositions, the partial vision seen and the position they occupy. In ethical space, interpretation is immediate (a moment) yet can always be changed (a process).

Poole pointed out that in the Prague photo the space between people is not empty, but rather filled with ethical possibilities. With each person is a whole set of intentions, feelings, experiences, family and community history, religious beliefs, cultural, social, economic, and political systems – including institutions. Poole's photographic depiction of ethical space shows the differing intentions that are evident; the Russian soldiers represent the dominant and occupying force, while the Czech citizens represent the 'occupied' and also dominant force (it is their land, after all) – a space where the ethical is set up instantaneously.

1. Dedicated to the memory of Ford Riley Lakowski Couture, May 12, 2009 – July 5, 2010.

2. Throughout this essay, I use ideas presented in other works: V. Bergum – J. Dossetor. *Relational Ethics: The Full Meaning of Respect*, Hagerstown, MD, University Publishing Group, 2005; V. Bergum, *Relational Ethics for Nursing*, in J.L. Storch – P. Rodney – R. Starzomski (eds.), *Toward a Moral Horizon: Nursing Ethics in Leadership and Practice*, Toronto, Pearson Education Canada, 2004, 485-503; V. Bergum, *Relational Pedagogy: Embodiment, Improvisation, and Interdependence*, in *Nursing Philosophy* 4 (2003) 121-128.

Acts in ethical space are embodied: "It is sensitive bodies in proximity that are the space of ethics, the fields of meeting"[3], and it is in these fields of meeting that it is possible to hold and enact what Poole says is the prime ethical principle, that of *total respect of the personhood of each person* in the situation. "Any action is morally right if it promotes a personal relation of persons", said Jeffko[4], who also reminds that the self is a person like any other so how we treat the self has moral significance.

In embodied space, where ethical action is quickened, one is touched by the needs and situation of another person. One meaning of the word *quickening* refers to that moment when a pregnant woman feels the movement of her unborn baby in her belly. She touches and is touched by this new person in her life, and she is quickened to her own new life as well, her life of a mother. In any moment of touching another one is touched, one recognizes both self and other. The embodied experience of quickening can be seen as a moral moment, a moment of touching and recognizing the other, so that the on going process of listening and talking (dialogue) can continue. Again, it is the ethical space where interpretation is immediate (a moment) yet can always be changed and developed (a process).

In his 2007 paper, The *Ethical Space of Engagement*[5], Willie Ermine proposed a framework for dialogue as a way to respond to the moments when one recognizes the differing intentions between individuals and communities. Exploring the disparate worldviews of Canadian Indigenous peoples and Western institutions, Ermine proposed rules of engagement that would facilitate constructive dialogue between diverse people. Ermine reminded us that when two such communities and/or individuals respectfully meet (touch) each other with their unique intentions and experiences an ethical space is set up instantaneously, and from that moment dialogue (process) can occur.

In this essay I take on two central tasks.

The first, already begun, is to show that relational or ethical space offers a unique perspective for ethical quickening, deliberation and practice. By attending to the relational space between people, not only can new knowledge grow – knowledge that comes alive – but, more importantly,

3. J.H. Olthuis, *Face-to-Face: Ethical Asymmetry or the Symmetry of Mutuality?*, in Id. (ed.), *Knowing Other-wise: Philosophy at the Threshold of Spirituality*, New York, NY, Fordham University Press, 1997, 121-158, p. 138.

4. W. Jeffko, *Contemporary Ethical Issues: A Personalistic Perspective*, Amherst, NY, Humanity Books, 1999, p. 22.

5. W. Ermine, *The Ethical Space of Engagement*, in *Indigenous Law Journal* 6 (2007) 193-203.

new understanding of people in the relationship can grow. Such understanding is a quickening, an awakening to the shared nature of our humanity, a mutuality, a love of the other or as Olthuis says, "love is the quickening, the quivering which evokes life and permeates life"[6].

The second task is to explore how to quicken ethical practice by encouraging engagement with one another in helpful rather than harmful ways. In this paper I attend to ethical space found in the classroom (the teaching/learning situation) using the clinic (professional/patient/client) as the backdrop.

Knowing ethical principles, laws and rules, theories of virtue or definitions of compassion are not enough to prepare for the challenges of the ethical space. With concern for action, attention will be paid to how to engage with others without losing or effacing ourselves. Through engagement with other, through touch and dialogue there arises the possibility of coming to know oneself and the other better. From this perspective, to live ethics is seen as the nature of life itself, not an afterthought to be fitted in later.

II. Ethical Space

The ethical space and its quickening provides the basis for a partnership model where new currents of thought can flow in different directions and overrun the old ways of thinking. It is a space in which the most precious of all human rights can flourish and that, Ermine says, is "the freedom to be ourselves"[7]. This sounds very much like the principle of autonomy, yet there is something stimulating in the words 'the freedom to be ourselves' that goes beyond the individualistic focus of the principle of autonomy. Ermine, says 'ourselves' rather than 'myself'. He discusses how *community*, in his case the Canadian indigenous community, is where the "forming of the heart and face of the individual as one of the people is most fully expressed"[8]. The bioethical principle of autonomy as a universal principle undermines the reality of human interdependence and tends to ignore the influence of history, family, culture and community on every individual. Wendy Austin, who holds a Canada Research Chair in Relational Ethics in Health Care, writes that the dominant bioethics approach – principlism – is "grounded in the belief that ethical

6. Olthuis, *Face-to-Face* (n. 3), p. 139.
7. *Ibid.*, p. 199.
8. *Ibid.*, p. 200.

reasoning should be objective (unemotional) and independent of context … and for the most part remains formalistic, procedural, disembodied and universalistic"[9]. She goes on to say that the emphasis of individualism "negates the reality that ethics is fundamentally about our collective life". The notion of ethic space holds as central the principle of respect for personhood (of all parties in the ethical space). All relationships have to do with ethics or morality for how to treat each other is the ethical bottom line and, as such, there is need to consider the quality of all relationships, whether it is professional and client, teacher and student or people sitting together on park benches.

Exploration of ethical space demonstrates a shift from focus on the person as an individual (as a bearer of rights) to the person as an interdependent agent (engaged in activity for one's own flourishing, both as individuals and part of the local and world community). Even children are realizing the need for such a change. The "Me to We" Canadian Campaign[10] motivates children and young people to change the world by developing attitudes of compassion, courage, and commitment to community. Other shifts are also needed: the shift from a focus on the mind (developing theory and facts) to a focus on the mind and body (how to act); the shift from solving the ethical problem to asking the ethical question (that requires openness, deliberation, self-questioning, uncertainty and contemplation)[11]; and the shift in focus from paternalistic rules to collaborative discovery[12]. With these shifts it is clear that ethical knowledge for specific situations cannot be known ahead of time, rather ethical knowledge must be developed in relationship with the particular. Of course, it does not mean that nothing is known ahead of time: we do know ethical theory and principles, clinical expertise, communication skills, and so forth. The expectation that ethical knowledge can be secured once and for all time or can be held as 'expert' knowledge by a privileged few (bioethicists, clinicians, philosophers, lawyers) is under attack. The post-modern challenge of many truths is not to say that there is no truth, but that what is true is found within the history and the current configurations through which people live out their lives.

9. W. AUSTIN, *Ethics in a Time of Contagion: A Relational Perspective*, in *Canadian Journal of Nursing Research* 40 (2008), no. 4, p. 17.

10. C. KIELBURGER – M. KIELBURGER – S. PAGE, *The World Needs Your Kid: How to Raise Children Who Care and Contribute*, Toronto, Me to We Books and Greystone Publishing, 2009.

11. V. BERGUM, *Ethics as Question*, in T. KOHN (ed.), *Extending the Boundaries of Care: Medical Ethics and Caring Practices*, New York, NY, Berg Publishers, 1999.

12. V. BERGUM, *Knowledge for Ethical Care*, in *Nursing Ethics: An International Journal for Health Care Professionals* 1 (1994), no. 2, June, 72-79.

In practice, ethical action often takes place without anyone being absolutely sure of the right thing to do. "We act not on the basis of unshakable grounds but in order to do what we can, taking what action as seems wise, and not without misgivings ... We act because something has to be done"[13]. In the space of ethical action, certainty is rarely attainable, as is seen in the following examples. Instead of certainty, ethical clarity is quickened through the process of dialogue in the living experiences. Responses to the questions – 'How should I act?' 'What is the right and good thing for me to do?' or 'What is fitting for this situation and people?' – are discovered within concrete and practical relationships.

Foundational knowledge for a relational ethic, thus, is not found in the search for more scientific facts, more technological advancement, or from universal principles. Rather foundational knowledge for assisting in acting in ethical space is found in a different direction where many kinds of knowledge (personal, theoretical, scientific, embodied, narrative) are valued. In ethical space understanding another's situation (individuality, experience, and culture) is given equal measure to knowledge of ethical theory and principles. A relational or ethical space is where continual learning occurs, learning "who one is (what values make a person who she or he is), who one wants to become (what values are worth cultivating) and how best to facilitate others in the process of becoming"[14]. In the moral geography of ethical space interdependence of self and other is realized.

The following two examples, one from the end of life (Allison's story) and one from the beginning of life (the story of baby Ford), show the importance of considering ethical space. The use of story opens ethical imagination to the experiences of others and is one way to make ethical spaces more habitable.

1. *Allison's Story*

> Allison Brown was a young active woman when her car slipped off the road one rainy night just outside of Vancouver. After three months of intensive care during which Allison did not show any signs of response or improvement in her consciousness, the neurosurgeon told Allison's family to put her in an institution and "get on with their lives". The family did not do

13. J. CAPUTO, *Disseminating Originary Ethics and the Ethics of Dissemination*, in A.B. DALLERY – C.E. SCOTT (eds.), *The Question of the Other: Essays in Contemporary Continental Philosophy*, Albany, NY, State University of New York Press, 1989, 55-62, p. 59.

14. A.W. FRANK, *Ethics in Medicine, Ethics as Process and Practice*, in *Internal Medicine Journal* (2004), no. 34, p. 357.

that. Instead they had her transferred to a long-term care facility in her home community, which made it possible for her to have frequent weekend and vacation visits to her parent's home and with her family. Because there was no treatment available in the facility, the family recruited and trained volunteers to provide Allison with a consistent program of physical exercise and mental stimulation thought useful for her improvement. Over the next four years, Allison did not improve[15].

Allison's father and two sisters who shared Allison's story said that the first ethical decision was for the family to remain part of Allison's life. "We became engrossed in her life", they said. Another ethical decision was to simply treat Allison as another member of the family, as an equal, different now than she was before her accident, but still a member of the family. They always spoke to her as if she understood, and they believed that there was some meaning to her erratic movements. They acted on Poole's point of view that total respect be given what is due to a person in their embodied subjectivity[16].

The family said that their ethics evolved out of the practicalities of what they were facing everyday. The final ethical decision was made four years after Allison's accident, after much discussion with all members of the family, professional staff, care-givers, and ethicists. At this time the family decided to remove the feeding tube that was keeping Allison's body alive.

This is a decision that people should not have to make, said Arthur Frank[17] – that is, to make a decision that would end someone else's life. The family made that decision and did not leave it to someone else. They stayed engaged and acted out their ethics by initiating a process – a slow process of four years – to come to feel that how they acted was as good as it could be, given the impossibility of the situation. This family knew that they would live with their decision for the rest of their lives and needed to attend to "*who I become* as a result of making such a decision"[18].

The family said that their ethics emerged out of a family consciousness. They felt that Allison was caught in a kind of death, yet, at the same time,

15. V. BERGUM – J. DOSSETOR, *Relational Ethics: The Full Meaning of Respect*, Hagerstown, MD, University Publishing Group, 2005. Excerpts (italicized) were taken from Chapter 5: *Bringing Knowledge Back to Life* (pp. 137-163).

16. R. POOLE, *Towards Deep Subjectivity*, London, Harper and Row, 1972, p. 151: "It is ... in philosophical space that ethical space can be retained, preserved and understood. And it is only in philosophical space that the other is accorded that total respect which is due to him (or her) as an embodied subjectivity. And since that is the fundamental principle of all ethics, the preservation of that fundamental principle depends on the preservation of philosophical space".

17. FRANK, *Ethics in Medicine* (n. 14).

18. *Ibid.*, p. 357.

she could not die as the feeding tube provided the nutrition needed to keep her breathing. Her body gave an anchor to life but she wasn't really in it. Another factor that they considered was that in the hospital, in a time of extensive cutbacks in health care, there would be very little interaction and meaningful activities in Allison's life (only time to turn, feed, bath – asking staff to get Allison into a chair was just too much). As the family had to cut back on their extensive involvement in the daily care that Allison needed, they were concerned that Allison would be left alone. The family considered the ethical space, the moral geography, of all people (family, staff, volunteers and Allison herself) engaged in the process of ethical decision-making. Each person had to live his or her own life, and yet each person was a significant part of Allison's life.

> This was a very big issue for our family. We felt that removing Allison's feeding tube was a spiritual act. Every member struggled with their conscience and then we came together many times to express our thoughts and feelings on how we could reconcile our intentions and Allison's wishes, within our own spirituality. We felt that it was the most difficult decision that we would ever have to make in our lives and we asked for spiritual guidance, not only from ministers and priests, but most importantly from within ourselves.

Individual family members had developed different belief systems over the years yet they felt that their divergent beliefs converged in a general agreement about the meaning of Allison's life until now and the act of her death. After talking and talking and talking about it, they finally all agreed. They felt that their decision was correct based on who they were and what they knew of Allison. They faced the fact, which they had avoided to think about until this point, that before her accident Allison had asked them to promise to 'pull the tube' if she should ever be in a state like Karen Ann Quinlan, a young American woman who lived in a deep coma for ten years before she died. While the family still had hope that Allison could improve they did not contemplate acting on Allison's previously stated wishes.

The day the family asked to have the tube removed, they told Allison what was being done. They told her about their doubts and said that they asked for spiritual help to make the right decision. They discussed their decision and their questions with a large circle of people (nurses, doctors, ethicists, ministers, priests, extended family, care-givers and volunteers). "It was this small community that gave us support and encouragement", the family said. "They knew what Allison's life was like for the last four years and they were there for her when she passed away". Allison did not die alone.

As Allison's family experienced it, the relational ethical space is not an easy place to be. We hear the demands of staying engaged (years of daily visiting, feeding, getting Allison into a chair, doing the exercises), showing respect for the needs of everyone in the process (meetings with all the family as well as Allison) and the reality of the environment (with cutbacks that left Allison with minimal care) – the complete moral geography. Staying engaged means embodying the reality of being a father, sister, or friend and all that means ethically. One sister, the primary family care-giver, talked of her own need to continue her education which meant less day-to-day involvement with Allison, which raises the question of what *being for the other* really means. While Allison's sister has been eagerly willing to give her life to her sister, the reality of being responsible for her own life was also strongly felt. It might seem that convenience was the factor that brought the family to the decision to remove the feeding tube. James Olthuis faces such a concern in his notion of the ethics of mutuality. "I want to suggest", said Olthuis, "an ethics of mutuality in which self-sacrifice is seen not as the heart of ethics, but as an emergency compromise ethic because of the breakdown of mutuality"[19]. As an alternative to Levinas's model of the priority of the other, Olthuis's ethics of mutuality promotes the recognition that there is an equal responsibility to care for the self and the needs of the self. What do we do when a fellow human is reaching the end of life, through loss of cognition, through loss of cellular function? Bauman[20] suggests that *all* we have is the "moral party of two" – the quality of our relationships.

2. *The Story of Baby Ford*

The second story comes from the beginning of life.

A young couple found out four months before the birth that their baby had a complex congenital health defect called hypoplastic left heart syndrome (HLHS). Because the systemic or left ventricle and left-side mitral and aortic valves are not adequately developed, this condition is uniformly lethal without immediate diagnosis and intervention following birth. At the present time babies who survive a three-stage surgical approach – to establish systemic blood flow using the right ventricle as the pump instead of the hypoplastic, non-functional left ventricle – have a chance to live.

19. OLTHUIS, *Face-to-Face* (n. 3), p. 132.
20. Z. BAUMAN, *Postmodern Ethics*, Oxford, Blackwell, 1993.

The first ethical decision these young parents made was to take that chance and move 800 kilometres so their baby could have the best possible treatment and care. The first operation was the Norwood procedure, which occurred within the first few days of the baby's life and the second surgery, the Glenn, occurred at about the fourth month. The third surgery, the Fontan, is done after the child is three years old. While health care and scientific communities have applauded the advance in medical technology that enhances the length and quality of life in spite of the uncertain outcomes and incredible costs, little attention has been given to what these processes mean to the lives of the family members throughout the process. Gwen Rempel and Margaret Harrison[21] describe research that explored the experience of parents, and found extraordinary parenting of babies that have the three-stage surgical approach. These extraordinary parents learned to apply extensive assessment and problem solving knowledge as they took charge of complex tasks such as tube feeding, medication administration, oxygen therapy, and wound care.

Baby Ford, born in a highly specialized hospital with expert clinicians, is now over eight months old. He has recovered from the second of the three surgeries to repair his heart but is still not thriving so has been placed on the list for a heart transplant. Since his birth, his parents have taken, at times, the full daily care of their baby, sharing a small hospital room with him with the support of medical and nursing staff and even took him home for a few days. After the latest surgery, the Glenn, when their baby was once again in the intensive care unit (ICU), the parents faced various changing rules about access to their baby boy. The father writes on his blog that they are:

> ... struggling again with the ICU's inconsistent 'confidentiality' policy which frequently has us barred from entering the ICU or thrown out when they want to talk about someone else near us. We've had to argue and push our way into the ward at some point every day this week and are really starting to resent having to do it. In spite of having many sympathetic and understanding nurses who have gone out of their way to impress upon the doctors and administrative staff that we 'really' want to be there when big decisions about Ford's care are being deliberated, yet as soon as these nurses go off shift their impressions trail out the door behind them. There seems to be a big shift in attitude around a family's participation in their child's care on different wards and with different professionals. ... here (and I know I've complained about this before) we are made to feel at best like our presence is irrelevant to Ford and his treatment and at worst like

21. G. Rempel – M. Harrison, *Safeguarding Precarious Survival: Parenting Children Who Have Life-Threatening Heart Disease*, in *Qualitative Health Research* 17 (2007) 824-837.

> we are a nuisance to him and an impediment to his recovery. The daily experience of having to fight with someone on the phone to get permission to come in and see our baby is exhausting, humiliating, and incredibly disempowering. But then tonight, after a horrible day, we had an amazing nurse who went out of her way to make sure Ford was comfortable, who made us feel welcomed and involved, and who listened to and answered all my obscure and unnecessary questions. I left feeling happy. What a difference a nurse makes[22].

Some staff did not engage with the parents nor were they respectful of their need to be part of the decision-making for their baby. The staff did not recognize the baby's need to have daily contact with his parents, to hear their voices and feel their touch, or that the family unit must be held together during all stages of the baby's treatment. The ICU environment became one of control and technological competence and both parents and baby experienced the results of disengagement. As a result parents were harmed – exhausted, humiliated, and disempowered. In this scenario attention to the ethical space between baby, parents and staff was neglected. One person, though, could make a difference.

The ethical task is more than procedures such as consent from patients for treatments or to maintain confidentiality, although both are important. Focussing on a set of procedures and rules removes the active subject and ethics becomes another intellectual specialty that some (experts) do, and therefore can be left to them. But one can never become an expert in the ongoing work of *being* ethical "being ethical (possessing a greater measure of practical wisdom) is never anything one *has* … it is a commitment to a form of life, not a fixed quality of competence"[23]. As a way of being it is always under construction.

III. Ethical Action as Process

Ethics is a process, often a slow process, like the decision-making of Allison's family. With ethics as process, taking place in the space between people, we recognize that one action is based on another, like the parent's commitment to care for Baby Ford during the tough precarious times as well as the times when his care involved only one tube rather than a baby connected to a whole array of machines.

22. Sesame Mucho, *What a Difference a Nurse Makes*. http://lilsesame.blogspot.com/, Friday, September 25, 2009 (accessed October 14, 2009). (Excerpt used with permission).
23. Frank, *Ethics and Medicine* (n. 14), p. 356.

Arthur Frank says that attention to an ethic of process is needed especially when one group of actors claims to represent an interest that trumps all others, such as 'preserving life'. For we know now that the notion of life, itself, is no longer self evident for "disputes over the criterion 'dead' underscore society's increasing lack of consensus about what constitutes life"[24].

The book title, *After You*, is evocative in its desire to recognize the other person's self – and world – understanding. We often say, 'after you', as we wait for a person to go through the door ahead of us but soon we walk side-by-side to the next destination, or as Ermine says, we find a common meeting place of ethical space "which offers a venue to step out of our allegiances, to detach from the cages of our mental worlds and assume a position where human-to-human dialogue can occur … where notions of universality are replaced by concepts of equality"[25]. The uniqueness of ethical space invites mutuality – an opening to understand the self and not only attention to the other.

The ethical space and its inherent process must be open to questioning and doubt because participants need to listen to and examine ideas from all who are involved. For a space to be respectful and open, there can be no trumps. But it doesn't mean that there can be no debate. In fact, said a lawyer, Robert Burt[26], it is entirely appropriate and essential for people with different perspectives to disagree. In conversation with Dax Cowart, a severely burned man, who wanted his doctors to stop all life-saving treatment and that it was his own and nobody else's business that he make such a decision, Burt disagreed. Burt said, "I think it is both permissible and essential for the doctor to say, 'No, no, it is my business', and not because I'm a doctor (or chaplain, psychologist or nurse), but because I am another human being who is necessarily involved in your life. We define one another in important kinds of ways, and while, of course, I can't define you, we have to negotiate together what our shared meanings are about, what it is that you want me to do and not to do (brackets added)". There needs to be a commitment on the part of both participants (professional and client), to stay together, to have the time – respectable, extensive time – to be able to consider all that is at stake. This process can be enormously burdensome but, as Robert Burt said, burden might be at the heart of attention to this ethical space.

24. *Ibid.*

25. ERMINE, *Ethical Space of Engagement* (n. 5), p. 202.

26. D. COWART – R. BURT, *Confronting Death: Who Chooses, Who Controls. A Dialogue Between Dax Cowart and Robert Burt*, in *Hastings Center Report* 28 (1998) 14-24, p. 15.

IV. The Classroom as an Ethical Space

> In the classroom space … students and teachers *all* play a role in an interdependent community, with everyone's well-being tied to one another. Such interdependence does not mean dependence *upon* one another, but rather connection *to* one another for the better of the community as a whole[27].

The classroom, like the clinic, can be enhanced and invigorated (quickened) by attention to the electrifying notion of ethical space. The teacher has to imagine the work/world the student is to be prepared for, and be respectful of that work. The pedagogical (not limited to the teaching of children) space – the relation of teacher and student(s) – attends to the relational themes of *being* the teaching, *doing* the teaching through engagement with each other. Ted Aoki, an inspiring educator, once said that it is urgent to understand that teaching is a realization that what we do as teachers is "harboured within the pedagogical presence of our beings, that is, of who we *are* as teachers", so that we will be able to "savour … the elusively true, the mystery of what teaching essentially is"[28]. The focus of teaching ethics is not only on what is taught, the content. Rather the focus of teaching ethics has to be on who teachers are and how the interdependence of teacher and student can be realized. Embodiment, the lived reality of *who* teachers are, is what opens the possibility of relation between teacher and student where teaching is understood as a watchfulness, trust of the student and letting the student learn.

1. *Curriculum as Planned versus Curriculum as Lived*

The following tale, attributed to Friedrich Schleiermacher, a theologian and hermeneutic scholar of the early19th century, shows how a people relate to the world in multiple ways.

> Three people, an architect, a carpenter, and a worshipper visit a Gothic cathedral. The architect (as a theoretician) experiences a cathedral conceptually classifying it by its shape (pointed arch, clustered columns), its style (hammer-beam roofs, pitched brick vaulting), its materials (limestone, sandstone, marble), in order to discover when it was built. As a scholar, the architect would use a broad intellect and theoretical ability to analyze the cathedral and as an object, the cathedral could be subordinated to this intellect. The carpenter who walked into the cathedral would see what needs

27. J.J. Ryoo – J. Crawford – D. Moreno – P. McLaren, *Critical Spiritual Pedagogy: Reclaiming Humanity through a Pedagogy of Integrity, Community, and Love*, in *Power and Education* 1 (2009) 132-146, p. 138.

28. T. Aoki, *Inspiriting Curriculum and Pedagogy: Talks to Teachers*, Edmonton, AB (Canada), University of Alberta Faculty of Education, 1991, pp. 5, 6.

> fixing and mending. As a technician, the carpenter would be intent on being practical and making the cathedral serviceable (fixing window or roofs) to the needs of people entering. The interest of the carpenter or builder would be functional. When a worshipper entered the cathedral, it becomes a spiritual dwelling place, where the worshipper would feel the might and glory of God and the institution that God represents. The interest of the worshiper would be the meaning of the place in its wholeness, its silence, divinity and humanness.

In planning curricula for teaching ethics the differing interests exemplified by the three perspectives of the people visiting the cathedral is explored. To understand the world theoretically and practically (where the interest is efficiency, effectiveness, certainty and predictability), the curriculum would reflect that interest, with didactic lectures, analytical reasoning, and explanation. In this empirical-analytic (technical) discourse, evaluation would occur through objective testing and goal-based evaluation.

However, if classes explore the meaning of the experiences in the world, to understand the world we live in (a world that wraps itself around us) the curricula would be planned so that life experiences are valued and shared. In such a curricula there would be a commitment to listening to individual patient's stories or life narratives about their journey through health and illness. There would be an insistence on understanding the complexity of the moral situation as it is revealed in consideration of the contextual particulars and through this understanding students realize that rules and principles, while helpful, cannot always provide adequate solutions to dilemmas. A curriculum based on understanding the meaning in lived experiences, of human being and becoming, the root activity is authentic dialogue. Evaluation in such a curriculum would be a concern for the quality of lived experience of teachers and students. In teaching ethics there is room for all approaches. In this essay, however, the interest is to explore issues of meaning, of being and becoming human, which occurs in the intersubjective ethical space of self and others.

Even as we plan curriculum for ethics courses what actually happens is what Aoki[29] calls the other curriculum, the curriculum-as-lived, curriculum that teachers, in their practical wisdom, know. Especially within our world of multiplicity in which classed are filled with diversity and difference, such a curriculum would accommodate the lived meanings – legitimating thoughtful everyday stories and narratives – in and by which

29. *Ibid.*, pp. 7-10.

students live their daily lives. In the lived curriculum there is a move away from faceless others (the generalized other imagined in the course outline) toward the faces (the touch) of others, in their embodiment.

When clinical or teaching practice is quickened, where one feels as well as sees the other person (student or client), one is faced again with the moral responsibility of being a teacher or a chaplain. I am the teacher. I am the chaplain. If we lose ability to touch one another we become disengaged from our own bodies and theirs as well, "making of us disembodied, dehumanized beings, indifferent to the nihilistic drying out of inspiritedness"[30]. How do students and professionals, who are surrounded by technology (strength of modern education and health care), keep "inspirited", and not fall into technological traps that separate knowledge from human experience and let technology direct human action? With such technological traps there is danger of cultivating insensitivity, which is experienced as clinical detachment, with a deadening of emotions that can lead to becoming less human.

Two situations suggest a need for quickening in our educational practices. The first is reported by Austin[31] and describes a study in the moral education of health professionals, where one of the participants described how he learned to become detached and to cultivate a 'remote' demeanour. This second-year medical student said that his lesson in detachment from patients began in his first year. In trying to find a drink of water for a patient lying on a stretcher in the hospital corridor, this student was teased (perhaps for being too gullible or naïve) by the staff of the emergency room staff. He quickly learned to pass patients while averting his eyes so that he could not see them as people and be stopped by their needs. In this situation the education of professionals whose work is to care for others, primary attention is given to theoretical and scientific content and practical skills and no recognition is given to the ethical space of the hospital corridor. The seeds of compassion (love for another) that lived in the young student at the beginning of his studies must be quickened in order to flourish.

The second example comes out a column written by Mark Kingwell, a University of Toronto philosopher, in Canada's *Globe and Mail* daily newspaper. In a column called *Let's not cheat our students*, Kingwell argued that if we don't treat students as individuals when it comes to ethics, they won't take responsibility for themselves. He wrote that we

30. *Ibid.*, p. 30.
31. W. AUSTIN, *Engagement in Contemporary Practice: A Relational Ethics Perspective*, in *Texto & Contexto* 15 (2006) 135-141, p. 139.

must establish mechanisms that would 'reindividuate' students so that they will feel a strong connection to their own work and not be so ready to cheat. Kingwell was responding to the major problem of cheating that is occurring in many universities and colleges. One way to connect with students is to have smaller classes and office hours where the sea of faces is broken down so the professor comes face-to-face with students. Other ways to connect student to their actions and ideas is to have personal assessments without a grade attached; feedback and the chance to revise work; and self-devised essay topics. It would be time-consuming and costly, Kingwell admitted, but there is no other way or "we (professors) will be the ones doing the cheating"[32].

2. *Teaching Approaches*

The printed word is not the best way to come to understand ethical space. Other approaches such as listening to personal stories, sharing talk together (narrative), images (photographs and art) and drama need to be used. Visual and literary approaches sharpen senses and feelings, generate new insights and understandings, and promote ethical awareness[33]. In consideration of ethical commitments and decisions, both the heart and the mind must be stimulated as neither emotion nor rationality alone is adequate.

a) *Building on Student's Own Experience*

During the first week of an interdisciplinary graduate-level class (IntD 570. Health Care Ethics) taught at the University of Alberta, both face-to-face and on-line, the question was asked: "What ethical questions (dilemmas, disappointments, residue) do you have from your own practice or life experience"? Students often have situations that they cannot forget even many years later. For doctoral student Dianne Godkin, one moment that occurred early in her career left her with residue that led to her continued research and subsequent work as a clinical ethicist. Here is her story.

> Very early one morning as I worked the night shift on a haematology and cardiology unit, an urgent plea for assistance penetrated the quiet stillness of the floor. I was the first to arrive to help. When I entered the room, I saw

32. M. KINGWELL, *Let's Not Cheat Our Students*, in *The Globe and Mail* (2009), August 21. http://www.theglobeandmail.com/news/opinions/lets-not-cheat-our-students/article1260436/ (Accessed October 19, 2009).

33. P. DARBYSHIRE, *Understanding Caring Through Photography*, in N.L. DIEKELMANN – M.L. RATHER (eds.), *Transforming RN Education: Dialogue and Debate*, New York, NY, National League for Nursing Press, 1993, 275-290.

> a frail, emaciated, elderly woman – breathless and pulseless – lying prostate on the bed. In accordance with hospital policy, I began cardiopulmonary resuscitation (CPR) efforts. As I attempted to breath life into her limp body, my lips came into contact with hers – blue, clammy, cool and lifeless. The code team arrived shortly thereafter and without a moment's hesitation, sprang into action, doing precisely what they were expertly trained to do. Over the next 15 to 20 minutes, the inert woman was stabbed with large bore needles, zapped with electricity, and physically battered with chest compressions by a roomful of strangers. After an 'acceptable period' of time had passed, the resuscitation efforts ceased, and the elderly woman was pronounced, simply and efficiently, dead[34].

Following this experience Godkin described how she felt physically ill and emotionally distraught with a residual sense of anger, guilt and despair regarding the suffering of the 82-year-old widow dying from leukaemia. The woman's condition was spiralling downward and the goal of care for her was to be kept comfortable for the remainder of her days. Godkin's questions following the administration of the code team's life saving treatment: did we do harm? where did we go wrong? and how can we prevent this experience happening again? These questions led Godkin to explore end-of-life decision-making in her doctoral research.

The emotion that is often experienced in such ethical moments (moments of moral distress) is not incidental, rather is knowledge that gives credibility to 'gut' reaction. Building on experience, the teacher needs to help students to reflect on what emotional reactions suggest, what can be done with them, and how they relate to ethical care. Emotion cannot be left to smoulder. Rather emotion suggests a need of further communication and dialogue.

Although Godkin states that she has participated in CPR that resulted in individuals to recover and lead productive lives, she wants to make sure that emergency end-of-life codes are done appropriately.

b) *Theatre and Drama*

To inspire connection to another's experience theatre or role-playing can be used. In the play, *A Child on Her Mind*[35], based partially on research[36] on the experiences of women coming to motherhood in various

34. M.D. Godkin, *Living Will, Living Well*, Edmonton, AB (Canada), University of Alberta Press, 2008, p. 2.

35. J. Nisker – V. Bergum, *A Child on Her Mind: A Play*, in Id. – J. Vanderzalm (eds.), *Motherlife: Studies of Mothering Experience*, Edmonton, AB (Canada), Pedagon Publishing, 2007, 364-398.

36. V. Bergum, *A Child on Her Mind: The Experience of Becoming Mother through Birthing, Adopting and Placing a Child*, Westport, CT, Bergin and Garvey, 1997.

ways: birth, adoption and with the use of reproductive technologies, university students acted the parts of the various characters. When a student took the role of a single mother who struggled with the decision of whether or not to place her baby for adoption, she needed to be attentive to feelings, attitudes, and the voice of the character. The student described how the experience of playing a role changed the way she attends to the single pregnant woman she sees on the street or meets on an obstetrical unit. She now wonders what the young woman is going through rather than either judging or pitying. She enters the ethical space and considers the subjective question about the young mother's particular experience and does not just apply generalized and theoretical knowledge learned from the social, medical, and ethical narratives.

Instead of seeing the pregnant young single woman as a 'problem to be solved', as a nurse she might ask further questions, 'what is your experience?' or 'what is it like for you'? From this open position the nurse is ready to engage in a relationship with a young teen mother – to improvise – without an already prepared script. In lived life there is never any experience that is exactly like the other so that individual persons must forge their own understanding of life.

The teacher has to have knowledge of the subject matter, yet without the ability to connect the information to the lived life of students the information is merely technical or mechanistic rather than whole. In theatre, audience/students can engage with experiences of others from their own experience. The goal is to open space for the student to 'come into one's own'. Teachers let go of the need to control the outcome. Teachers listen – "heart to heart" – responding in ways that are appropriate to the rhythm of the other person and what is needed in the moment – unexpected, exciting. Teachers realize that the opposite of believing that 'my way is the best and only way', is not 'freedom to do as I please' but through relationships with others we can listen for some new tones, new ideas, new music.

c) *Dialogue*

Willie Ermine puts forward the argument that ethical space offers a "refuge of possibility"[37] for persons to come to a firmer understanding of their own moral beliefs through respectful dialogue with others. Embodied dialogue is a multifaceted process that explores the wide range of our human nature – from closely-held values to the nature and intensities of emotions, and from patterns of thought processes to the function of

37. ERMINE, *Ethical Space of Engagement* (n. 5), p. 203.

memory. Embodied dialogue offers the opportunity to explore the manner in which thought is generated and sustained. It questions deeply-held assumptions about culture, meaning, and identity.

David Jopling[38] identified six characteristics of a dialogic encounter that are useful for this discussion:

1. Dialogue is open textured, not goal oriented. One does not know what will come of it. One does not know how each partner in the dialogue will be changed; how own self-understandings will be expanded. In genuine dialogue nothing is predetermined as there may be unexpected outcomes.
2. In dialogue there is mutual respect in order to encounter the other as other. It is otherness, rather than sameness (like-mindedness), that needs to be respected. If one consistently puts what is said into one's own terms to fit one's own point of view, one cannot learn from the other. In mutual respect one regards the other as a responsible partner within established norms of trustworthiness.
3. In dialogue one addresses the other with forthrightness and therefore responds with forthrightness. One is present to the other's company. "One of the most common events of everyday life is the act of addressing and responding to another person face-to-face, engaging the other in a way that is frank and unrehearsed in order to establish a commonly understood meaning. Language would be a rootless and impersonal system of signs if it were not anchored in the face-to-face confrontation"[39].
4. Feelings give body to words – and bring back words to the body. When dialogue is embodied with evocative components, one recognizes that feelings and emotion are not accompaniment to careful responses to questions. Rather feelings (such as compassion, anger, sympathy, shame, desire) themselves constitute the response.
5. Dialogue signals mutual recognition by addressing the other as *you*. The pronoun "you" is personal, and calls forth the personal in "me" as well.
6. Dialogue is found in the ethical space – when one is present *with* and *for* someone – not merely thinking about them. Here the person is not an object of observation but is "called into conversation" with an actual other bringing about an understanding of moral and social identity.

38. D.A. Jopling, *Self-Knowledge and the Self*, New York, NY, Routledge, 2002, pp. 152-157.

39. *Ibid.*, p. 156.

The potential of ethical space is that it can be filled with dialogue, embodied dialogue, which includes silence as well as speech. Through dialogue, which could be in the actual words, in the silences or in touch, people with differing history, culture, beliefs, and intentions find the way to be ethical.

The power imbalance found in professional relationship is of concern as the professional holds the power – the power of knowledge, the power of position, and the power of privilege. This is certainly felt in teaching and learning with the teacher holding the evaluative final point. In the ethical space, teacher and student strive for power-with rather than power-over where mutual recognition, attunement, and empowerment is the desire.

> In giving to the other, I, paradoxically, in being received, am enlarged and enhanced – receiving, in the words of Levinas, "inspiration" … Instead of power-over (with the corollary of power-under), or power-held-in-abeyance (to avoid domination), there is power-with and the dance of mutual empowerment"[40].

Instead of power-over (and its worrisome implications – control, domination, coercion), we find words like listening, initiative, creativity, example, appropriate moment, leadership, letting be, and respect. Of course, the teacher has the responsibility to evaluate the student. Yet, it is primarily how the teacher approaches the problem within the shared space with the student, an approach that includes the student in exploring the possible outcomes. Such relationship allows for "pedagogic creativity, a coming into being of a clearing that is vibrant with pedagogic possibilities"[41]. Teaching and learning is not delegating or sharing power as a commodity, but rather understanding authority in terms of the wisdom that comes from sharing the lived life. It is about "engaging in dialogue that renegotiates narrative and social power"[42].

David Smith[43] says that teaching must first and foremost involve the practice of truth which has three *aspects:* personal truth as it arises in experience, shared truth as something between us, and finding truth as finding home. "The labour of finding truth as home is ultimately the labour of overcoming our primal sense of estrangement from the world". Smith says, "this is at once a religious task (<L. religere, to tie together

40. OLTHUIS, *Face-to-Face* (n. 3), p. 146.

41. AOKI, *Inspiriting Curriculum and Pedagogy* (n. 28), p. 45.

42. C.A. TAYLOR, *Positioning Subjects and Objects: Agency, Narration, Relationality*, in *Hypatia* 8 (1993) 55-80, p. 70.

43. D.G. SMITH, *Teaching in Global Times*, Edmonton, AB (Canada), Pedagon Press, 2002, pp. 39-40.

again), which in the age of globalization means addressing the specifically religious roots of contemporary economic theory, as well as the pedagogical one, in the agogical sense of taking responsibility for guiding others (<L. agogos, guide)"[44]. Interpretations are constructed and, as such, are alterable which provides the opportunity and freedom for new interpretations. The possibility of new interpretations is the possibility of freedom.

Teaching and learning has to do with touching, listening, dialogue, and "inspiriting" – lessons learned through experience of many teachers. Such an ethical responsiveness occurs as we come face-to-face with patients and students and in so doing we come face-to-face with ourselves.

V. Conclusion

The ethical space of engagement with others, whether between chaplain [or pastor] and client or between student and teacher, is a place of invention to fashion something different, even unexpected. The engaged voice is never fixed or absolute rather is changing and evolving through dialogue between those within the ethical space. Sacks described the ethical space where he, as physician, met his patients[45]. He says that he has to become a fellow traveler, a fellow explorer, continually moving *with* his patients to discover the language that would bring them together. To be a fellow traveler, instead of seeing the journey as planned on a map (curricula as planned) the professional must travel with the patient or student along the bumpy road through illness and learning together taking the turns and valleys, together viewing the scenery, together deciding on other companions, and together choosing where to go – perhaps even sharing the job of driver (curricula as lived). Such a journey and its search for common language blurred the distinction of separate individuals. It recognized the connections and interdependence.

The ethical space should introduce doubt in the expectation that there are distinctive personal boundaries when one is in an empathic ethical relation. In such a relation boundaries tend to become diffuse and flexible. Sharing experiences, sharing feelings and thoughts, using imagination to understand another's pain leads to a relation that blurs the sharp distinction between people. Rather, in spite of the confusion, through honest effort to keep conversation open each may come to experience self more clearly.

44. *Ibid.*
45. O. Sacks, *Awakenings*, New York, NY, HarpersCollins, 1973 (1st ed.), 1990 (rev. ed.).

The ethical space is not merely a means to an end. Such a relation uses forms of knowledge that are not abstract but rather immediate, local, intuitive, emotive, informal, and embodied. Subjectively experienced, interaction acknowledges the vulnerability of both and holds onto what it means to be human and to remain human in the face of unimaginable adversities and threats. The ethical space is a relation that moves and changes like dance partners sensitive and quickened to the movement and rhythm of the other.

The significance of this concern for the ethical space in which love is possible comes at a time in our history where words like individualism, autonomy, human rights, justice, and personhood have become the grounding of ethical/moral stance. The current emphasis on personal autonomy, on individual rights, on life defined in terms of brain-death criteria, and on health care bound by technological or instrumental reasoning brings with it the danger of losing the capacity to care deeply for each other. As interdependent (both dependent yet independent), autonomous yet connected to others, we live in a world of possibility – responsible for others as well as ourselves.

Attention to ethical space, and its quickening, is not a panacea for easy ethical action. Rather the focus on relationship and engagement with others may make ethical considerations even more complex and burdensome. Within a concept of ethical space healthcare professionals, counsellors, chaplains and teachers continue to learn more about the self and in that self-knowledge and openness they are able to care for and know others better.

John Dossetor Health Ethics Centre
& Faculty of Nursing
University of Alberta
5-16 University Terrace
8303 – 112 Street
Edmonton, Alberta
Canada, T6G 2T4
Vangie.bergum@ualberta.ca

Vangie BERGUM

THE INDIVIDUAL, RELATIONAL AND SOCIAL NEUROBIOLOGICAL DEVELOPMENT OF MORALITY

A discussion of moral development often begins with questions philosophers ask: Is morality innate (Emerson, Rousseau, Thoreau) or is human nature evil (Augustine, Hobbes, Machiavelli)? Can morality be taught explicitly through reason (Plato), or is it a matter of learning from experience (Aristotle)? These are empirical questions that require an interdisciplinary and empirical approach. It may be best to begin with Socrates' (or the Oracle of Delphi's) insight, *Know thyself*. What do we know about human evolution and human nature, that is, what is innate, and what is "plastic" (malleable), or developed from experience? Can experience influence human moral nature? Are there sensitive periods for learning that is fundamental to moral functioning? After examining the current state of knowledge about the evolution and ontogeny of morality, the essay concludes with suggestions for how to cultivate compassionate morality.

I. The Evolution of Morality

In *Descent of Man* (1871)[1], Charles Darwin identified characteristics that evolved to culminate in humanity's 'moral sense' which he considered the greater propellant, over natural selection, of human evolution. He noted the phylogenetic changes of the moral sense through the Tree of Life, reaching its pinnacle in humans. In his definition of the moral sense, Darwin included these characteristics: sympathy for others; the ability to remember the past and compare it to the present; language; conversation and concern for social opinion; and the ability to form habits and shape one's behavior in response to social preferences. Darwin ascribed these characteristics to humans, yet several of these characteristics seem to be absent or nearly so in some individuals, particularly, those who come from backgrounds of early neglect, abuse or trauma[2]. When

1. C. Darwin, *The Descent of Man*, Princeton, NJ, Princeton University Press, 1871 (1st ed.), 1981.

2. E.g.: M.M. Sanchez – C.O. Ladd – P.M. Plotsky, *Early Adverse Experience as a Developmental Risk Factor for Later Psychopathology*, in *Development and Psychopathology* 13 (2001) 419-449.

the environment is able to have such a powerful effect, it suggests that the characteristics are facultative (malleable) rather than inherited adaptations[3]. Supportive experience early in life appears to be fundamental to the development of the moral sense[4].

Unlike all other animals, humans are born with 75% of the brain yet to develop. As a result of this rapid development after birth, children's initial brain and body formation is highly influenced by those who care for them, especially in the first five years of life. The foundations of the brain develop in concert with care-giver treatment[5]. Later functioning is influenced by these early foundations, including moral functioning. What kind of early caregiving does the human brain require for later optimal functioning? We can answer this question by looking at human evolution and data on what happens when it is violated.

Our ancestors spent 99% of their existence in simple foraging communities (small-band hunter gatherers or SBHG)[6]. This ancestral context represents what Bowlby[7] (after Hartmann[8]) called "the environment of evolutionary adaptedness" (EEA), when human parenting and infant needs co-evolved[9]. Our ancestors appear to have had a consistent set of child caregiving practices that anthropologists have inferred and summarized from extant SBHG communities[10]. A child's life in this EEA-like context is characterized not only by natural childbirth (without imposed painful procedures) but by being "nursed frequently; held, touched, or kept near others almost constantly; frequently cared for by individuals other than their mothers (fathers and grandmothers, in particular) though

3. G.C. WILLIAMS, *Adaptation and Natural Selection: A Critique of Some Current Evolutionary Thought*, Princeton, NJ, Princeton University Press, 1966.

4. D. NARVAEZ – T. GLEASON, *Developmental Optimization*, in D. NARVAEZ – J. PANKSEPP – A. SCHORE – T. GLEASON (eds.), *Evolution, Early Experience and Human Development: From Research to Practice and Policy*, New York, NY, Oxford University Press, 2013, 307-325.

5. D.J. SIEGEL, *The Developing Mind: How Relationships and the Brain Interact to Shape Who We Are*, New York, NY, Guilford Press, 1999.

6. D.P. FRY, *The Human Potential for Peace: An Anthropological Challenge to Assumptions about War and Violence*, New York, NY, Oxford University Press, 2006.

7. J. BOWLBY, *Maternal Care and Mental Health*, New York, NY, Schocken, 1951; ID., *Attachment and Loss*, New York, NY, Basic Books, 1969; ID., *A Secure Base: Parent-Child Attachment and Healthy Human Development*, New York, NY, Basic Books, 1988.

8. H. HARTMANN, *Ego Psychology and the Problem of Adaptation*, New York, NY, International University Press, 1939.

9. W. TREVATHAN, *Human Childbirth: An Evolutionary Perspective*, New Brunswick, NJ, Aldine, 2011.

10. B.S. HEWLETT – M.E. LAMB, *Hunter-Gatherer Childhoods: Evolutionary, Developmental and Cultural Perspectives*, New Brunswick, NJ, Aldine, 2005.

seldom by older siblings; [they] experience prompt responses to their fusses and cries; and [they] enjoy multiage play groups in early childhood"[11]. These early life characteristics largely match up with the emergence of social mammals over 30 million years ago[12]. Douglas Fry, James Prescott and others link childcare practices like these to peaceful character and societies that do not go to war[13].

Narvaez and colleagues[14] review the effects of EEA-consistent parenting on child outcomes, finding each to be vital for short-term and long-term well-being and noting that traditional practices have become uncommon in the USA. Indeed, children's well-being overall in the USA is worse than 50 years ago[15]. Child neglect and abuse which used to be limited to a subset of the population is becoming mainstream and affecting child outcomes[16]. Children seem to be receiving less and less optimal care. For example, children are arriving at school with poor social skills, poor emotion regulation, and sets of poor habits, all of which do not lend themselves to prosocial behavior[17]. One of four USA teenagers is at risk for a poor life outcome[18]. Moreover, the USA has epidemics of anxiety and depression among all age groups[19]. The negative trajectories in

11. *Ibid.*, p. 15.

12. M. Konner, *The Evolution of Childhood*, Cambridge, MA, Belknap Press, 2010.

13. D.P. Fry, *The Human Potential for Peace*, New York, NY, Oxford University Press; J.W. Prescott, *The Origins of Human Love and Violence*, in *Pre- and Perinatal Psychology Journal* 10 (1996) 143-188.

14. D. Narvaez – J. Panksepp – A.N. Schore – T. Gleason, *The Value of the Environment of Evolutionary Adaptedness for Gauging Children's Well-being*, in Narvaez – Panksepp – Schore – Gleason (eds.), *Evolution, Early Experience and Human Development* (n. 4), 3-30.

15. J. Heckman, *Schools, Skills and Synapses*, Bonn (Germany), Institute for the Study of Labor, IZA DP No. 3515, 2008.

16. United Nations Children's Fund, *Child Poverty in Perspective: An Overview of Child Well-Being in Rich Countries, a Comprehensive Assessment of the Lives and Well-Being of Children and Adolescents in the Economically Advanced Nations*, Report Card 7, Florence (Italy), United Nations Children's Fund Innocenti Research Centre, 2007.

17. W.S. Gilliam, *Prekindergarteners Left Behind: Expulsion Rates in State Prekindergarten Systems*, New Haven, CT, Yale University Child Study Center, 2005; D. Powell – D. Fixsen – G. Dunlap – B. Smith – L. Fox, *A Synthesis of Knowledge Relevant to Service Utilization and Delivery for Young Children with or at Risk of Challenging Behavior*, in *Journal of Early Intervention* 29 (2007) 81-106; J. Zito – D. Safer – S. dosReis – J. Gardener – M. Boles – F. Lynch, *Trends in Prescribing Psychotropic Medications to Preschoolers*, in *Journal of the American Medical Association* (2000), no. 282, 1025-1030.

18. J. Eccles – J.A. Gootman, *Community Programs to Promote Youth Development*, Washington, DC, Committee on Community-Level Programs for Youth. Board on Children, Youth, and Families, Commission on Behavioral and Social Sciences Education, National Research Council and Institute of Medicine, 2002.

19. U.S. Department of Health and Human Services, *Substance Abuse and Mental Health Services Administration*, in *Mental Health: A Report of the Surgeon General*,

well-being among children (and adults) in the USA suggest that a re-examination of cultural practices is needed.

Missing support in childhood influences not only cognitive, emotional, and psychological outcomes but also moral outcomes. The position taken here is that experience during sensitive periods is critical for moral sensibilities to develop. Sensitive periods occur not only during development, but include moments of crisis and therapy. Moral sensibilities are rooted in emotion and cognitive systems. When these have a poor start, moral functioning can be negatively affected. Multi-Ethics Theory[20], described below, specifies how early child care practices can influence personality and moral development. Later, methods for modifying less-than-optimal moral functioning are suggested.

II. The Social Neurobiological Development of Morality: Multi-Ethics Theory

Morality, like intelligence generally, is rooted in the emotion structures of the brain. Emotions have evolved as "psychobehavioral potentials" and "evolutionary operants" that help animals behave adaptively[21]. Our basic emotions are formed in early life from "elemental units of visceral-autonomic experiences that accompany certain behavior patterns"[22]. Caregiving practices affect the development of emotion systems and, including the ability to regulate anxiety[23]. Early care affects personality formation[24], for example, bringing about more or less agreeableness

Rockville, MD, Center for Mental Health Services, National Institutes of Health, National Institute of Mental Health, 1999; World Health Organiztion/Wonca, *Integrating Mental Health into Primary Care: A Global Perspective*, Geneva & London, World Health Organization and World Organization of Family Doctors, 2008.

20. D. Narvaez, *Triune Ethics: The Neurobiological Roots of Our Multiple Moralities*, in *New Ideas in Psychology* 26 (2008) 95-119: Id., *Triune Ethics Theory and Moral Personality*, in Id. – D. Lapsley (eds.), *Moral Personality, Identity and Character: An Interdisciplinary Future*, New York, NY, Cambridge University Press, 2009, 136-158.

21. J. Panksepp, *Affective Neuroscience: The Foundations of Human and Animal Emotions*, New York, NY, Oxford University Press, 1988, p. 55.

22. *Ibid.*, pp. 44-45.

23. F.A. Champagne – M.J. Meaney, *Stress during Gestation Alters Maternal Care and the Development of Offspring in a Rodent Model*, in *Biological Psychology* 59 (2006) 1227-1235.

24. E.g. A. Schore, *Affect Regulation and the Repair of the Self*, New York, NY, Norton, 2003; Id., *Affect Dysregulation and Disorders of the Self*, New York, NY, Norton, 2003.

which is linked to prosocial behavior[25]. Early care influences cognitive capabilities, including the ability to imagine[26]. Especially important for social and moral functioning is proper development of the right brain, which occurs with attentive, sensitive parenting[27]. Parents who support an infant with a "good enough holding environment" assist the infant in maintaining 'relational presence' with the care-giver, a factor related to later mental health[28] and social functioning[29]. Early experience forms "ideo-affective postures" (cognitive-emotional orientations) the child takes into adulthood[30]. In adults, emotion systems interact with cognitive structures and physiological and motor outputs, powerfully influencing sensory, perceptual and cognitive processing[31]. Multi-Ethics Theory postulates three basic moral orientations (see Table 1).

Multi-Ethics Theory (MET)[32] is a moral psychology theory that integrates neurobiological and other human sciences to describe early moral development and suggest types of moral personality. MET identifies three neurobiologically-rooted orientations or central motives that drive moral functioning[33]: the Safety ethic (self-protection), the Engagement ethic (relational presence), and the Imagination ethic (reflective abstraction). See Figure 1. These ethics and their subtypes draw on different parts of the brain. Each ethic represents a particular set of activated emotion and physiological systems that influence cognition and action. Each orientation influences the prioritization of values that, when acted upon, trumps other values and becomes an ethic. An ethic can be dispositional (more deeply embedded in personality) but also triggered by situations (e.g., threat triggers self-protection whereas emotional safety promotes engagement).

25. G. KOCHANSKA, *Mutually Responsive Orientation between Mothers and Their Young Children: A Context for the Early Development of Conscience*, in *Current Directios in Psychological Science* 11 (2002) 191-195.

26. S.I. GREENSPAN – S.I. SHANKER, *The First Idea*, Cambridge, MA, Da Capo Press, 2004.

27. A. SCHORE, *Affect Regulation*, Hillsdale, NJ, Erlbaum, 1994.

28. D.W. WINNICOTT, *Mother and Child: A Primer of First Relationships*, New York, NY, Basic Books, 1975.

29. SIEGEL, *The Developing Mind* (n. 5).

30. S.S. TOMKINS, *Affect and the Psychology of Knowledge*, in S.S. TOMKINS – C.E. IZARD (eds.), *Affect, Cognition, and Personality*, New York, NY, Springer, 1965.

31. SIEGEL, *The Developing Mind* (n. 5).

32. NARVAEZ, *Triune Ethics* (n. 20).

33. J. MOLL – R. ZAHN – R. DE OLIVERA-SOUZA – F. KRUEGER – J. GRAFMAN, *The Neural Basis of Human Moral Cognition*, in *Nature Reviews: Neuroscience* 6 (2005) 799-809.

Experiences during sensitive periods in life (early childhood, early adolescence, emerging adulthood, therapy, crises) influence the formation of emotion systems that underlie and influence the three ethics. When parenting is inconsistent with what our ancestors experienced in the EEA (e.g., minimal social interaction; physical isolation; allowing a baby to become distressed before a response is undertaken), the systems underlying the Safety Ethic are strengthened and those underlying the Engagement Ethic are weakened. Imagination Ethic systems can also be weakened by poor social support or harmful experiences during sensitive periods (e.g., violent media immersion or binge drinking during late adolescence and emerging adulthood)[34].

Table 1. Multi-Ethics Theory Mindsets

Mindsets and Sub-Types
Mindful Morality (The "Moral Zone")
Engagement Calm and Communal Imagination
Imagination
Detached Imagination (Intellectualized Morality)
Vicious Imagination (Righteous Morality)
Communal Imagination (Agape Morality)
Engagement
Engagement Calm (Harmony Morality)
Engagement Distress (Co-Dependent Morality)
Safety
Wallflower Mindset (Submissive Morality)
Bunker Mindset (Aggressive Morality)

1. *Safety Ethic*

The extrapyramidal action nervous system[35] fosters basic survival and relates to territoriality, imitation, deception, struggles for power,

34. A. BECHARA, *Decision Making, Impulse Control and Loss of Willpower to Resist Drugs: A Neurocognitive Perspective*, in *Nature Neuroscience* 8 (2005) 1458-1463; V.P. MATHEWS – W.G. KRONENBERGER – L. WANG – J.T. YANG – M.J. LOWE – D.W. DUNN, *Media Violence Exposure and Frontal Lobe Activation Measured by Functional Magnetic Resonance Imaging in Aggressive and Nonaggressive Adolescents*, in *Journal of Computer Assisted Tomography* 29 (2005) 287-292.

35. PANKSEPP, *Affective Neuroscience* (n. 21).

maintenance of routine and following precedent[36]. When threat arises, the Safety ethic tends to take charge, seeing what is advantageous for the self to adapt to and survive intact. The Safety Ethic is the default system for the organism when all else fails. It was useful for our ancestors when temporarily facing predators or other dangers. However, it is not the best long-term orientation for moral functioning because of its self-centered nature. It is a self-protective morality, rooted in instincts for survival. When people are fearful for their own safety or their self-beliefs, they are less responsive to helping others and more focused on self-preservation[37]. When competition is the norm, the safety ethic can become dominant among members of a group[38]. It can become an uphill battle to calm the self down in a world where one is confronted constantly with the unfamiliar (people, actions, things). Ongoing change can keep people in a state of alarm, especially when the right brain has been underdeveloped[39].

If the emotion systems underlying other ethics are damaged by trauma or suboptimal from poor care, the safety ethic will dominate the personality. It can dominate personality in two ways. First, the safety ethic can manifest itself as an overcontrolled disposition – a withdrawn, depressive *wallflower mindset* – that tends towards freezing, flight or submissive response as a moral habit. One can see this most easily in those who are chronically abused. For centuries, a wallflower mindset was expected from wives, slaves and children. Second, the safety ethic can reflect a resistant *bunker mindset*, which is an undercontrolled aggressive disposition, as the means of self-protection (physical or psychological, i.e., ego). These two personality orientations can develop from neglectful care or trauma in early life[40] and can combine in a unique person-by-context hybrid in which the person oscillates from one to the other. Suggestions for calming the safety ethic are offered below.

36. P.D. MacLean, *A Triune Concept of the Brain and Behavior*, Toronto, University of Toronto Press, 1973; Id., *The Triune Brain in Evolution: Role in Paleocerebral Functions*. New York, NY, Plenum, 1990.

37. E.g. M. Mikulincer – P.R. Shaver – O. Gillath – R.A. Nitzberg, *Attachment, Caregiving, and Altruism: Boosting Attachment Security Increases Compassion and Helping*, in *Journal of Personality and Social Psychology* 89 (2005) 817-839.

38. E.g. M. Mikulincer – P.R. Shaver, *Attachment Theory and Intergroup Bias: Evidence that Priming the Secure Base Schema Attenuates Negative Reactions to Out-Groups*, in *Journal of Personality and Social Psychology* 81 (2001) 97-115.

39. Schore, *Affect Regulation* (n. 24).

40. J.P. Henry – S. Wang, *Effects of Early Stress on Adult Affiliative Behavior*, in *Psychoneuroendocrinology* 23 (1998) 863-875; Siegel, *The Developing Mind* (n. 5).

2. *Engagement Ethic*

The Engagement ethic is rooted primarily in a well-functioning visceral-emotional nervous system on the hypothalamic-limbic axis[41] and a well-developed right brain[42]. These brain formations allow for here-and-now emotional signaling both internally (learning) and externally (sociality)[43]. The engagement ethic concerns the emotions of intimacy and interpersonal harmony in the present moment, which means the right brain is dominating experience. Engagement as a "harmony morality" is about love/care/attachment, enhancement, and elevation. The engagement ethic embraces the notions of worship and community feeling. Engagement is "here and now", it is experiencing full presence in the flow of life, connecting to others in the moment.

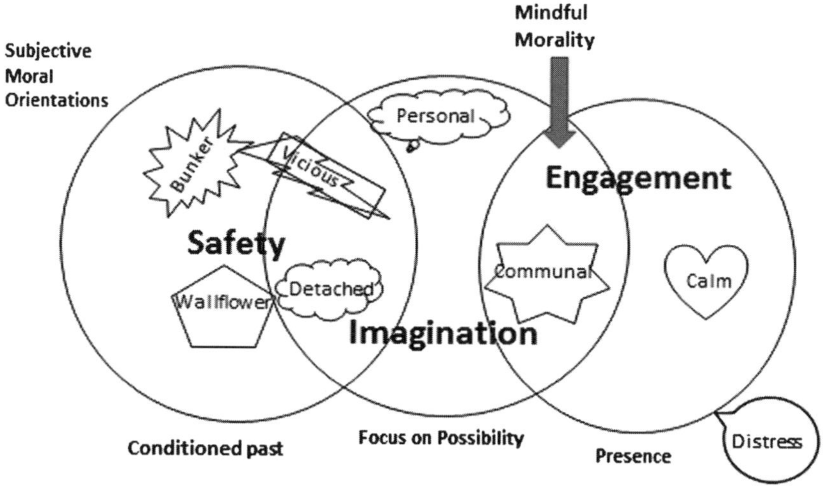

Figure 1. Graphic of Different Moral Mindsets and their subtypes

The Engagement Ethic is dependent for its full development on supportive emotional experience during sensitive periods. For example, the functionality of the hypothalamic-pituitary-adrenal axis (HPA) is co-constructed by care-givers and shaped during sensitive periods early in life,

41. PANKSEPP, *Affective Neuroscience* (n. 21).
42. SCHORE, *Affect Regulation* (n. 24).
43. M. KONNER, *The Tangled Wing*, New York, NY, Owl Books, 2000.

as described by Bowlby's ethological theory of attachment[44]. Mammalian brains do not self-assemble. The process of attachment and relating to primary care-givers sculpts the particular ways an individual brain's emotion and cognitive systems function. Mammalian nervous systems depend on interactive coordination with other in-tune mammals for their stability. When caregiving is poor, the adaptive nature of emotion systems is disrupted, and when it is traumatic, cognition is undermined. Mammalian brains shift into physiological chaos when isolated[45]. Inadequate care leads to deficiencies in the brain wiring, hormonal regulation and system integration that lead to sociality[46]. Insufficient development of self-regulatory systems can lead to *engagement distress*, a co-dependent reflexive orientation to social functioning. In contrast, ideal caregiving involves "*limbic resonance* – a symphony of mutual exchange and internal adaptation whereby two mammals become attuned to each other's inner states"[47]. Limbic resonance "tunes up" empathy and puts the child in hormonal states that are linked to prosociality. The ability to maintain these states in moral situations becomes an *engagement calm* ethic. Suggestions for fostering the Engagement ethic are below.

3. *Imagination Ethic*

The Imagination ethic ideally is grounded in a well-functioning somatic-cognitive nervous system on the thalamic-neocortical axis[48], relying on the more recently evolved frontal lobes and especially the prefrontal cortex. Areas in the prefrontal cortex comprise executive functions such as planning, foreseeing consequences, stopping and starting actions, and taking the perspective of others. These capacities allow for a broader view of action possibilities. When these are used for personal gain without thinking of others, the individual is operating from *personal*

44. BOWLBY, *A Secure Base* (n. 7); ID., *Attachment and Loss* (n. 7); SCHORE, *Affect Regulation* (n. 24).

45. M.A. HOFER, *Early Social Relationships as Regulators of Infant Physiology and Behavior*, in *Child Development* 58 (1987) 633-647; A. GAWANDE, *Hellhole*, in *The New Yorker* 2009, March 30.

46. E.g. S.D. POLLAK – B. PERRY, *Early Neglect Can Hinder Child's Relationships*, in *Proceedings of the National Academy of Sciences* 2005, November, 21-25; I.C. WEAVER – M. SZYF – M.J. MEANEY, *From Maternal Care to Gene Expression: DNA Methylation and the Maternal Programming of Stress Responses*, in *Endocrine Research* 28 (2002), p. 699.

47. T. LEWIS – F. AMINI – R. LANNON, *A General Theory of Love*, New York, NY, Vintage, 2000, p. 63.

48. PANKSEPP, *Affective Neuroscience* (n. 21).

imagination. No moral considerations are involved although an individual's actions always have moral side effects.

Multi-Ethics Theory proposes that the Imagination Ethic has three forms. When imagination is detached from emotion and presence in the here-and-now, which means it is dominated by the left brain[49], the imagination ethic can lead to a *detached* or *heartless imagination*. This is intellectualized morality that sees life in discrete pieces, solves abstracted moral problems without attending to the rich context, using rational logic to make social and moral decisions. Morality can become narrowly focused and degrades into a set of procedures.

If neglect is sufficiently profound, the visceral-emotion nervous system is unable to "resonate" with others. The result is a "functionally reptilian organism armed with the cunning of the neocortical brain" – a psychopath[50]. The left brain becomes dominant but is additionally fueled by the primitive emotions of anger, forming *vicious imagination*, driven by a clever seeking of power. Ruthlessness is considered necessary for control. This is an ego-centered morality that is more sophisticated and reflective than the bunker mindset (which is more reflexively aggressive). It is the sophisticated reptile. Ridicule of right-brain holistic views, destruction of anything that gets in the way of maintaining power, including for example, life forms that impede economic progress, can be viewed as moral imperatives. Vicious imagination can also include "pathological altruism" where an individual forces their will on others, "for their own good"[51].

Although humans have evolved to favor face-to-face relationships and have difficulty imagining those not present (such as future generations), *communal imagination* is the capacity for a sense of connection that extends beyond immediate relations. It uses the capabilities of the mind in a manner that is deeply prosocial such as imagining the consequences of one's actions on future generations, foreseeing possible social ramifications. Using the fullest capabilities of executive functions, it is able to make plans and monitor the execution of action. It is also dependent on embodied experience in the domain of concern. Only those with deep experience will be able to accurately and fully imagine future possibilities. Those without deep experience will likely operate from detached imagination.

49. I. McGilchrist, *The Master and His Emissary: The Divided Brain and the Making of the Western World*, New Haven, CT, Yale University Press, 2009. McGilchrist offers a detailed description of left-brain functions and the consequences of left-brain dominance.

50. Lewis – Amini – Lannon, *A General Theory of Love* (n. 47), p. 218.

51. B. Oakley – A. Knafo – G. Madhavan – D.S. Wilson, *Pathological Altruism: An Introduction*, New York, NY, Oxford University Press, 2011.

In the ideal – when communal imagination accesses the whole brain and partners with the Engagement ethic, to being present in the moment, emotionally open but able to use higher abstract thinking as a partner – we have *mindful morality*. Mindful morality coordinates the right and left parts of the brain, intuition and conscious reason. Mindful morality includes full presence (engagement) in the moment – intersubjectivity and resonance with the other. It also includes the use of abstraction capabilities grounded in experience to solve moral problems based in deep ethical know how for the particular situation (communal imagination). Mindful morality allows the individual to deliberate about moral situations: imagine multiple options, action choices and outcomes; consider consequences and outcomes; weigh principles, situational uniqueness, goals and opportunities. This is moral wisdom. The moral imagination allows reflection on virtue and vice, which comes from knowledgeable experience. As part of the deliberative mind, mindful morality can countermand emotional reactions in the older parts of the brain, stopping what would otherwise be an instinctive response. It can also select the environments in which intuitions (and character) will be shaped[52].

MET suggests that one's ethical stance can shift from moment to moment. A particular ethic can be evoked by the situation. Or better said, the experiencing of particular emotion (or not) influences the type of moral identity one adopts in the context. If one is personally distressed (fearful, anxious, depressed), one will more often make decisions based on the safety ethic: what is morally right is perceived to be that which protects oneself and one's own. In contrast, if one feels positive relational emotions such as sympathy, one is more likely to act from the engagement ethic. Or, if one has shut down the right brain and becomes focused on the abstract, one may act from a detached imagination ethic. Ideally in situations of moral import, one maintains emotional calm, fully engages the right brain, uses the abstract skills of the left brain and takes action from a mindful morality stance.

Dispositional tendencies, shaped from experience since the earliest of life, interact with the power of the situation to influence individual behavior. That is, although particular environments may press individuals to activate one or another ethic, personality disposition also plays a role. Personality dispositions interact with situations to evoke different moral identities in different situations for different people. A person might be habitually kind and compassionate in one situation, for example, operating

52. R.M. HOGARTH, *Educating Intuition*, Chicago, IL, University of Chicago Press, 2001.

from the engagement ethic at home, but ruthless in another, or operating with heartless imagination at work.

III. Human Moral Nature

What then is humanity's moral nature? Since human brains and minds are constructed in interaction with the environment, the answer is: *it depends*. If according to anthropologists, 99% of human genus history was spent in small-band foraging hunter-gatherer groups[53], we perhaps should be more attentive to human nature in these environments. Current members of such communities are deeply cooperative and find a great deal of enjoyment in social relations (laughing, singing, dancing, touching). Their basic social needs are met (trust, belonging, autonomy, competence/effectance, meaningfulness/purpose, self enhancement)[54]. Like most organisms, humans thrive when basic needs are met but act out in frustration when basic needs are thwarted[55]. From what we can tell, basic needs were typically met in these settings.

Small-band hunter gatherer societies in circumstances similar to those of our ancestors are largely peaceful. However, if one looks at other types of societies (tribes, chiefdoms, industrial nations), as complexity increases one finds corresponding increases in violence and aggression. As inequality and complexity increases, so does social discontent, aggression and poor health[56]. Further, modern societies often undermine basic needs, including for social support, increasing stress on families and children, undermining peaceful development. And so the social well-being and peaceableness fairly ubiquitous among hunter gatherers are less certain and sometimes missing in complex modern societies (like the USA).

Human emotion systems underlie human psyches and are shaped by embodied experience, particularly early experience. Real-life experiences

53. E.g. Fry, *The Human Potential for Peace* (n. 13).

54. E.L. Deci – M.R. Ryan, *Intrinsic Motivation and Self-Determination in Human Behavior*, New York, NY, Academic Press, 1985; S.T. Fiske, *Social Beings: A Core Motives Approach to Social Psychology*, New York, NY, Wiley, 2004; E. Staub, *Positive Bocial Behavior and Morality*, Vol. 1: *Social and Personal Influences*, New York, NY, Academic Press, 1978; Id., *The Roots of Evil*, Cambridge (England), Cambridge University Press, 1992: Id., *The Psychology of Good and Evil: Why Children, Adults, and Groups Help and Harm Others*, New York, NY, Cambridge University Press, 2003.

55. E.g. Deci – Ryan, *Intrinsic Motivation and Self-Determination in Human Behavior* (n. 54).

56. Fry, *The Human Potential for Peace* (n. 13); D.P. Fry, *Beyond War: The Human Potential for Peace*, New York, NY, Oxford University Press, 2009.

"train up" certain emotion systems, hormones, patterned responses and behavioral tendencies. Affective cognitive science is demonstrating what our ancestors long knew, that contrary to perhaps 2000 years of dualistic thought, human minds are not separable from their bodies. Humans are deeply embodied creatures who think with body metaphors and who think better about a topic after actual embodied experience[57]. Our embodiment means we learn most of our beingness as bodies, not as minds. We learn what it means to love and be loved from our care-givers in the early months of life. We learn about justice from the reciprocity we experience in early life[58]. Our personalities are shaped around what we learn to find rewarding – responsive, sensitive relationships or escape from intrusive or hurtful relationships. The human brain gravitates towards whatever brings more pleasure. For a neglected or abused child, the social pleasure systems will be underdeveloped, so pleasure may be sought elsewhere such as in illicit drug use.

We can surmise that our ancestors experienced a supportive and pleasurable social life which included: (1) high social embeddedness (mostly with kin), with little or no social isolation; (2) virtuous role models; (3) socially purposeful living; (4) deep social enjoyment including actions that promote social bonding hormones (e.g., oxytocin)[59]; (5) extensive freedom, leisure, and space (1 person per 4 or 8 miles)[60]; (6) egalitarianism; and (7) partnership with the natural world rather than exploitation. We are just learning how important each of these characteristics is for personal and societal cooperation[61]. Most of these diminished over the 20th century in the USA[62] (see Table 2).

As human beings are profoundly social creatures, human well-being relies on deeply felt social support from birth if not before. Cultures and families vary in the kind of support they provide and influences which

57. G. Lakoff – M. Johnson, *Philosophy in the Flesh: The Embodied Mind and Its Challenge to Western Thought*, New York, NY, Harper Collins Publishers, 1999.

58. M. Lerner, *Pursuing the Justice Motive*, in M. Ross – D.T. Miller (eds.), *The Justice Motive in Everyday Life*, Cambridge, MA, Cambridge University Press, 2002.

59. See S. Taylor, *Tend and Befriend: Biobehavioral Bases of Affiliation Under Stress*, in *Current Directions in Psychological Science* 15 (2006), no. 6, 273-277.

60. L.R. Binford, *Constructing Frames of Reference: An Analytical Method for Archeological Theory Building Using Hunter-Gatherer and Environmental Data Sets*, Berkeley, CA, University of California Press, 2001; J.B. Birdsell, *Australia: Ecology, Spacing Mechanisms and Adaptive Behaviour in Aboriginal Land Tenure*, in R. Crocombe (ed.), *Land Tenure in the Pacific*, New York, NY, Oxford University Press, 1971, 334-361.

61. Narvaez – Gleason, *Developmental Optimization* (n. 4).

62. Of course there were negative features like high infant mortality, shorter lifespans, physical duress including regular fasting. But these were mostly physical negatives, not social ones.

emotion systems are promoted. In cultures that are responsive to child needs and "indulgent" with young children, touch is predominant, leading to (it is assumed) social satisfaction through the elevation of bonding hormones such as oxytocin. These cultures tend to raise people of "sweet" disposition who are cooperative, empathic and emotionally present with others[63]. Cultures that are wary of "spoiling" babies are less responsive to the needs of young children, fostering stressed brains (e.g., poor vagal tone) and promoting more primitive emotion systems (e.g., dominance/submission) that focus on self-concern[64]. In these cultures, people are less agreeable and cooperative, and less sensitive to the needs of others.

Table 2. Adult Life Comparison

Adult Ancestral Life (Small Band Hunter Gatherers)	**Modern Adult Life (Economically Developed Societies)**
(1) High social embeddedness and support (mostly with kin) and absence of social isolation	(1) Social isolation and lack of social support
(2) Virtuous (not vicious) role models	(2) Vicious role models in media and public life
(3) Socially purposeful living	(3) Self-oriented life purpose
(4) Deep social enjoyment including actions that promote social bonding hormones	(4) Minimal social enjoyment, increasing preference for isolation or mediated social experience (e.g., TV, internet)
(5) Extensive freedom, leisure, and space	(5) Minimal freedom, leisure and space
(6) Egalitarian relationships	(6) Hierarchical relationships
(7) Partnership with the natural world rather than exploitation	(7) Exploitation of natural world is normative
(8) Considerable physical contact with others (sleeping, resting)	(8) Little physical touch
(9) Multi-age group living day and night	(9) Age-group isolation in school, work, leisure activities

63. See PRESCOTT, *The Origins of Human Love and Violence* (n. 13).
64. See HENRY – WANG, *Effects of Early Stress on Adult Affiliative Behavior* (n. 40).

We can surmise how the ancestral context supported the moral sense. In our ancestors' context, morality is linked with survival. Our ancestors were immersed in actions that were considered both virtuous and causally linked to surviving and thriving (e.g., being socially responsive). What was virtuous was responsive, cooperative sociality, and it was enjoyable. There was no isolation and little desire for it. Behavior most typically had immediate social consequences. Without group trust and support, an individual would be in mortal peril. In these circumstances, the band was united for survival but also thrived in community. There was little need to control individual autonomy because morality was deeply internalized from early and ongoing lived experience. The moral sense was built from the ground up.

Thus, in my reading of simple hunter-gatherer communities that are not pressured by the modern world, the bunker mindset was a rarity with other humans, but useful for threats from predators. In reports from anthropologists, members of bands who became psychotic (harmful to others) were killed. Detached imagination would have been virtually unseen because it reflects the underdevelopment of the right brain and overuse of the left brain found primarily in Western society[65]. Good caregiving and social support foster the positive social emotions (care, play, joy in relationship, empathy) and the regular and deep social pleasures found among hunter-gatherers would facilitate the right brain and the engagement ethic.

Many modern Western societies have eliminated the supports for virtue development that our ancestors experienced at all ages. These supports were the locus of pleasure as well. In the USA, social supports have been decreasing among all age groups for over 50 years[66]. With neglectful or harmful child care now common in USA practices[67], the right brain and the social emotions are not cultivated with much intensity or are thwarted entirely. So the view presented here is that the USA is more likely to raise people with dispositions toward detached and vicious imagination among the privileged and wallflower or bunker mindset among the poor. These are conclusions I have drawn from looking at a range of data and findings from across disciplines. The culture influences not only childrearing practices but moral functioning generally.

65. See McGilchrist, *The Master and the Emissary* (n. 49).
66. See Narvaez – Gleason, *Developmental Optimization* (n. 4).
67. V.J. Felitti – R.F. Anda, *The Adverse Childhood Experiences (ACE) Study*, Atlanta, GA, Centers for Disease Control and Kaiser Permanente, 2005.

IV. The Influence of Cultural Identity on Moral Functioning

Cultural practices that shape brains are highly influenced by the culture's narratives. Cultural practices, such as child rearing, promote particular brain sets and emotion systems. But cultural narratives themselves establish what is considered normal and can influence how much social support the mother and other care-givers receive. The layers of meaning and meaning-making that surround the child affect him or her holistically – brain and body development, personality, goals and preferences. Moral identities also are shaped by immersion in culture and family; cultural and family narratives and practices are the landscape on which the child constructs him or herself. Such narratives explain the past, one's role in life, and marshal one's energy to fulfill the preferred narrative. Three types of morality are examined in light of cultural influence, vicious imagination, detached imagination and mindful morality.

1. *Encouraging Bunker Mindset and Vicious Imagination*

Religious narratives play a role similar to that of cultural narratives. Like cultures, religions can promote different ethics depending on their discourse and practices. Some religious narratives are more conducive to peaceful coexistence and respect than are others. For example, when religions emphasize suspicion of outsiders, an "us-against-them" orientation or a sense of ongoing threat, they promote a bunker mindset ethic or even a vicious imagination ethic. Eidelson and Eidelson[68] found five "dangerous ideas", any one of which can drive groups into conflict: a sense of vulnerability, distrust, a sense of helplessness, the belief that injustice has been done against the self or group, and a sense of superiority. Fundamentalist theologies typically emphasize these types of dangerous ideas. Constantly focused on threat (e.g., modernity, Satan), fundamentalists envision themselves as part of a cosmic struggle of good against evil and demonize those outside the group[69]. An other-negating orientation strengthens bunker mindset and encourages a vicious imagination, as exhibited by Al Qaeda and similar groups. But these inclinations are also found among presumably normal members of society. For example, in an evangelical congregation that traditionally emphasized exclusivity,

68. R.J. Eidelson – J.I. Eidelson, *Dangerous Ideas: Five Beliefs that Propel Groups toward Conflict*, in *American Psychologist* 58 (2003) 182-192.

69. M.E. Marty – R.S. Appleby (eds.), *Fundamentalisms Observed*, Chicago, IL, University of Chicago Press, 1995.

90% of members left after the minister began to preach that the whole world would be saved and not just those of their brand of faith[70]. As Allport[71] wrote:

> The role of religion is paradoxical. It makes prejudice, and it unmakes prejudice. While the creeds of the great religions are universalistic, stressing brotherhood, the practice of these creeds is frequently divisive and brutal. The sublimity of religious ideals is offset by the horrors of persecution in the name of the same ideal.

The evangelical church example shows the interaction between the individual and the culture. Believers can interpret religious doctrine and guidance according to different ethics depending on their own personal narrative frameworks and dispositions. In examining the "evolution of God", Wright shows how the view of God in the Old Testament greatly fluctuated based on the Israelites' sense of security[72]. When under threat, the "word of the Lord" was interpreted intolerantly. When resources were sufficient and there was a lack of threat, the word was interpreted benignly. This supports the view that people shift in ethical identity (i.e., safety, engagement, imagination) based on circumstance, and according to which emotions the context triggers.

2. *Detached Morality in Western Civilization*

Derrick Jensen condemns Western philosophy for emphasizing a mindless approach to life[73]. Jensen, like others, argues that the current capitalist system is rooted in Western rationality divorced from presence – the embodied emotionality that is vital for the engagement ethic. The Western world has for so long divorced body from mind, emotion from reason, absenting itself from the present moment of being, that it cannot feel the trauma it has and is causing to life and lives throughout all ecosystems. It is based on a hierarchical, dominator model of relationships rather than on a cooperator model that is documented across simple small-band hunter gatherer communities[74]. The dominator model assumes

70. NATIONAL CATHOLIC REPORTER, *Membership Plummets after Pastor Preaches Whole World Will Be Saved*, in *National Catholic Reporter* 42 (2005), no. 7, p. 3.

71. G.W. ALLPORT, *The Nature of Prejudice*, New York, NY, Doubleday Anchor, 1958.

72. R. WRIGHT, *The Evolution of God*, New York, NY, Little, Brown and Co, 2009.

73. D. JENSEN, *A Language Older Than Words*, White River Junction, VT, Chelsea Green Publishing, 2004.

74. D. KORTEN, *The Great Turning: From Empire to Earth Community*, San Francisco, CA, Kumarian – Berrett-Koehler, 2006.

that one must coerce others for one's survival, that your group is superior, and that only humans (or, *some* humans) are worthwhile keeping alive. The rest of the earth and its life forms can be used at will. This is the left brain approach of vicious imagination.

As Jared Diamond has pointed out in his book, *Collapse*, across the centuries in hierarchical societies the wealthy race one another to consume more and then *all* resources, thereby undermining their and their children's futures[75]. We seem to be rapidly heading in this direction but on a global scale. As Jensen points out, the powerful in science, religion and business are collaborating to destroy indigenous ways of life that for centuries coexisted in ecologically sustainable ways[76]. Characteristics once construed as vices – greed, lust, envy – were converted to virtues in modern capitalism[77]. The safety ethic is powerful and so are the left-brain driven ethics. All these forces are driven by the focus on primitive survival/dominance mechanisms that are the human default when an affectionate upbringing or supportive culture is missing, or when competition fever is lit. These destructive forces can be contrasted with the type of moral functioning that may be optimal for guaranteeing humanity's future.

3. *Mindful Morality*

The great religions of the world, at their best emphasize compassion and love and concern for strangers and future generations, in other words, mindful morality. Mindful morality gives a full sense of humanity's Imago Dei. Mindful morality promotes our embodied moral sense. Our moral sense informs us that we are created for deep fellowship with others and with the natural world. Mindful morality is about turning around (*metanoia*), away from the focus on self, ego-identity, having, and getting. It is letting go of I/me/they/you dichotomies and the fracturing of life and becoming one with the Spirit. The New Testament Jesus condemned those who focused on safety ethic concerns (who is up, who is down, who is better/worse), and detached imagination concerns (keeping the rules, following procedures) both of which harden the heart. Instead, Jesus emphasized being present with others in the here-and-now. How can we foster a mindful morality orientation?

75. J. DIAMOND, *Collapse: How Societies Choose to Succeed or Fail*, New York, NY, Viking Press, 2005.

76. JENSEN, *A Language Older Than Words* (n. 73).

77. J.Z. MULLER, *The Mind and the Market: Capitalism in Modern European Thought*, New York, NY, Knopf, 2002.

V. Fostering Peaceable Moral Natures

Have humans lost their way? We seem to be off the path of love and pleasure that corresponds to our evolved nature[78]. The view here is that we have lost our sense of how to foster virtue because we have neglected to develop intuitions for being present in the here and now, interdependently engaged with one another and deeply related to the natural ecosystem in which we live. Among religious scholars of the past, there was an understanding of how a person's character is shaped by experience. Thomas Aquinas theorized that "virtue's cognitive elements join with appropriately developed dispositions to determine a person's character, actions, and emotional responses"[79]. It is never too late to shape character (although it becomes much more difficult with age). Pastoral counsellors can play a role in what types of moral functioning a client adopts, practices or employs.

The recommendations here are based on what we know leads to human flourishing, both individually and communally. Some ways of being are better than others. For example, prosocial behavior facilitates flourishing in individuals and communities whereas violence does not. Developmental moral psychology identifies exemplarity and developmental trajectories and suggests ways to facilitate and improve moral functioning towards optimality[80].

Because Mindful Morality uses humanity's fullest moral capacities, we examine some characteristics of ways to foster it. Ethical know-how or virtue, seems to best describe mindful moral functioning[81]. Mindful moral character is a set of skills or capacities or ethical know-how that can be cultivated to high levels of expertise.

Expertise development has gained prominence in education where intellectual abilities are forms of expertise. Children develop along a continuum from novice to expert in each area of study, including moral character[82]. Expert knowledge includes both deliberative and intuitive systems[83]: knowing "that" and knowing how, when, and how much.

78. Lewis – Amini – Lannon, *A General Theory of Love* (n. 47).

79. L.H. Yearley. *Mencius and Aquinas: Theories of Virtue and Conceptions of Courage*, Albany, NY, State University of New York Press, 1990, p. 58.

80. L.P. Nucci – D. Narvaez (eds.), *Handbook of Moral and Character Education*, New York, NY, Routledge, 2008.

81. W.D. Casebeer, *Natural Ethical Facts: Evolution, Connectionism, and Moral Cognition*, Cambridge, MA, The MIT Press, 2003.

82. D. Narvaez, *Integrative Ethical Education*, in M. Killen – J. Smetana (eds.), *Handbook of Moral Development*, Mahwah, NJ, Erlbaum, 2006, 703-733.

83. Hogarth, *Educating Intuition* (n. 52).

Expertise is situated, embodied, dynamic. Mind development is inextricably linked to embodied experience[84]. We think in terms of physical metaphors (e.g., "up against the wall;" "see eye-to-eye"). Cognition is ultimately represented in multiple biological systems[85]. Biochemical responses to situations signal "good/bad" action (based on prior experience). Because cognition is "situated" or contextualized, in unfamiliar domains, we have to learn effective ways of thinking and acting. In unfamiliar domains, we have to learn the ethical constructs, landscape, and actions for that domain.

Experts in training, in any field, are educated holistically. Good training fosters *good intuitions* (right brain) through immersion and appropriate feedback. Perceptions and sensibilities are fine tuned and developed into chronically used constructs and actions[86]. Good training also fosters *deliberative understanding* (theoretical grounding and meta-cognitive guidance) (mostly left brain). Interpretive frameworks are learned and, with practice, applied automatically for information processing, judging action, taking action.

Moral psychology research examines "moral exemplars", those that exhibit extraordinary moral action. Moral exemplars exhibit at the same time higher *affiliation* with others (communion and compassion) and *higher self efficacy or agency*[87]. For example, a clear agency distinction is found among rescuers and non-rescuers in WWII. The rescuers often said "What else could I do? – They were human beings like you and me". On the other hand, non-rescuers were more likely to say things like: "What could I do? – I was one person alone against the Nazis".

Adaptive ethical expertise is deep "ethical know how"[88]. *Adaptive* ethical expertise (unlike *routine* expertise) allows flexible, innovative response in the situation. How do we educate ethical know-how? Experts-

84. LAKOFF – JOHNSON, *Philosophy in the Flesh* (n. 57); GREENSPAN – SHANKER, *The First Idea* (n. 26).

85. A. DAMASIO, *The Feeling of What Happens*, London, Heineman, 1999.

86. D. LAPSLEY – D. NARVAEZ, *A Social-Cognitive View of Moral Character*, in D. LAPSLEY – D. NARVAEZ (eds.), *Moral Development: Self and Identity*, Mahwah, NJ, Erlbaum, 2004, 189-212.

87. L.J. WALKER – J.A. FRIMER, *Being Good for Goodness' Sake: Transcendence in the Lives of Moral Heros*, in F.K. OSER – W.M.M.H. VEUGELERS (eds.), *Getting Involved: Global Citizenship Development and Sources of Moral Values*, Rotterdam (Netherlands), Sense Publishers, 2008, 309-326; L.J. WALKER, *Moral Personality Exemplified*, in NARVAEZ – LAPSLEY (eds.), *Moral Personality, Identity, and Character* (n. 20), 232-255.

88. D. NARVAEZ, *The Neo-Kohlbergian Tradition and Beyond: Schemas, Expertise and Character*, in G. CARLO – C. POPE-EDWARDS (eds.), *Nebraska Symposium on Motivation. Vol. 51: Oral Motivation through the Lifespan*, Lincoln, NE, University of Nebraska Press, 2005, 119-163.

in-training experience practice that is focused, extensive, and coached. Know how is contextualized or situation-specific[89]. Ethical know-how is relational, situational capacities for moral relations in the moment. What kinds of capacities are needed for mindful morality? Ethical expertise can be mapped into several sets of individual capacities: (1) Ethical Sensitivity (perception, imagination, feeling); (2) Ethical Judgment (reasoning, reflection); (3) Ethical Focus (attention, motivation, identity); (4) Ethical Action (effectivities, steadfastness). Action schemas in each of these components are honed to high levels of automaticity[90]. Like other kinds of intelligence, moral intelligence is embodied in *action*[91]. It is not enough to *feel* empathy or sympathy or to *reason* well and make a good moral judgment or to be *motivated* to take a moral action. In the end, it is the *action* that counts (but which relies on these other processes of sensitivity, reasoning and motivation).

VI. Fostering Moral Transformation

How do we foster moral virtue in ourselves and our clients? How can we cultivate more peaceable moral identities? How do we help individuals develop at least an engagement ethic if not mindful morality, especially in a world of constant change? The Integrative Ethical Education model[92] has been developed to guide educators in classrooms to cultivate moral personhood. It is possible to use the same steps in a counsellor-client situation. There are five proposals in the original model. See Table 3 for the full list.

Table 3. The Steps of the Integrative Ethical Education Model

Integrative Ethical Education
1. Form a caring and secure relationship.
2. Provide a supportive climate for ethics and excellence.
3. Cultivate ethical skills using a novice to expert approach.
4. Foster self-authorship.
5. Restore the village of support.

89. Hogarth, *Educating Intuition* (n. 52).

90. *Ibid.*

91. F.J. Varela, *Present Time Consciousness*, in *Journal of Consciousness Studies* 6 (1999) 111-140.

92. Narvaez, *Integrative Ethical Education* (n. 82).

1. *Form a Caring and Secure Relationship*

First, it is vital to establish a caring relationship with the client, one that fosters a secure attachment[93]. Although things can be learned from insecure relationships, the purpose here is to provide an "immersion in care" that the client may have lacked in family life. A caring relationship can release or build up the emotion systems that lead to mindful morality. Marinating the mind in emotional support and encouragement (and the hormones that go with them) is the first step towards modifying old ways into new, or helping the individual grow and change. (More specifics about this are included in step 3 below.) Sometimes (e.g., crisis situations), a supportive relationship means providing a shoulder to cry on. Ultimately for the counsellor, it means practicing engagement (being "here-and-now") and communal imagination (taking into account the moral landscape of the client and the counsellor-client relationship).

2. *Provide a Supportive Climate for Ethics and Excellence*

Second, the general climate of support usually involves more than a pair of people but here refers to the culture that the counsellor brings to the situation. This includes the expectations for growth and ethical excellence and expected efforts towards change. Climate also refers to the counsellor practices that foster these endeavors. Does the counsellor expect the client to grow in a positive direction? Does the counsellor expect efforts towards change to be beneficial? Does the counsellor express patience as the client attempts new forms of being and expression? A supportive climate provides affirmative answers to questions like these. Sometimes a supportive climate is one that challenges the client to remember his or her moral responsibilities (e.g., to talk to an estranged family member before death).

3. *Cultivate Ethical Skills Using a Novice to Expert Approach*

Step three is about remembering how people learn best: with immersion in experience accompanied by a mentor who offers explanation and guides understanding of what is being experienced. This is a novice-to-expert instructional approach (see previous discussion), or an apprenticeship model[94]. In applying this to moral development,

93. SIEGEL, *The Developing Mind* (n. 5).

94. B. ROGOFF, *Apprenticeship in Thinking: Cognitive Development in Social Context*, New York, NY, Oxford University Press, 1990.

Narvaez[95] identified four levels of guidance or instruction that lead the client through knowledge acquisition, understanding and execution.

> (1) *Immersion in examples and opportunities* in which the client develops a sense of 'the big picture' in an embodied manner. Here, the counsellor draws attention to examples of the skill or orientation to be learned, demonstrating how it is practiced and honed. So if the topic is relaxation, then different ways to relax are demonstrated, discussed and practiced.
> (2) *Attention to facts and skills.* Here the counsellor helps the client learn to make distinctions within the domain. The client might learn how relaxation can be triggered with deep breathing, by focusing on positive emotion, or by touch from a loved one. Different skills are practiced until they become second nature.
> (3) *Practice procedures,* The learner puts together several skills. In terms of learning to relax, this might include paying attention to particular types of body tension and applying appropriate relaxation techniques or learning to recognize a tight jaw at different times during the day.
> (4) *Integrate across contexts.* Here the learner applies the skill in different contexts. For relaxation skills, this involves learning to use different relaxation techniques, for example, at work with the boss, at home with the children, or during commuting.

Step three is also about selecting activities that foster particular emotions and character dispositions, specifically, positive emotions and imaginative response, which are related to mindful morality. Although moral personality is best built beginning in early life from the ground up, there are some things that adults can do to increase moral personality. Here are two capacities that counsellors can help clients develop.

Foster Emotional "Presence in the Moment". Those who focus on the present are happier than those who worry about the past or future[96]. Our ancestors lived in the moment. Many mystical aspects of major religions focus on feeling God's presence "here and now" at least once in a while (e.g., worship, ecstatic rituals) or even in an ongoing way (meditation, prayer). One similar intervention that an individual can adopt alone or with guidance is learning mindfulness. Mindfulness training typically begins with deep breathing and attention to sensory and perceptual input. It means pulling oneself out of automatic responses to familiar contexts and paying attention to the newness in the situation. Mindfulness is related to savoring. Savoring is the ability to pay attention to the positive

95. D. NARVAEZ – T.S. BOCK – L. ENDICOTT – J. LIES, *Minnesota's Community Voices and Character Education Project*, in *Journal of Research in Character Education* 2 (2004) 89-112; NARVAEZ, *Integrative Ethical Education* (n. 82).

96. E. LANGER, *Mindfulness*, New York, NY, Da Capo Press, 1999.

feelings that one experiences in life[97]. One can increase savoring by writing about negative life experiences. This can create a logical narrative that provides insight into personal suffering. Writing to explain one's joys can also enhance savoring as does thinking about how much worse things could have been. Social support generally or through spiritual or religious affiliations also can contribute to savoring. Savoring can be noticing the uniqueness and beauty of a living creature (e.g., tree, animal, person), including a loved one.

Learning everyday emotional presence may require not only learning how to pay attention to "now" but also dealing with past history that has frozen one's emotions in place. It may require uncovering and reconstructing deeply buried emotions or convoluted painful memory through psychotherapy or spiritual regeneration. It may also require awakening the right brain systems that were never adequately stimulated for prosocial emotion or were shut down by traumatic experience[98]. This will typically happen within a caring relationship. The counsellor, as Sills suggested[99], can provide the "holding environment" of emotional security that was missed in early life. Initially, there needs to be immersion in responsive, caring relationships in order to "retrain" the attachment system. Secure attachment is mediated by "emotionally involving, elaborative, and contingent communication with others"[100]. "Earned secure/ autonomous attachment" occurs when an individual with insecure or poor attachment from early life relearns to attach through a close friend, partner or therapist. In therapy, clients are helped to explore their emotional life, current relationships, the relationship with the counsellor, and imagine and act on better relational choices[101]. The client can learn *social* mindfulness, the ability to attend to the relational context and the person with whom one is speaking or interacting.

Mindfulness is important for moral functioning in part because *mindlessness* can lead to harmful outcomes. Detachment from emotional response to others can lead to cruelty and destructiveness. John Kekes calls these *unintentional* evil actions because they occur from a lack of

97. F.B. BRYANT – J. VEROFF, *Savoring: A New Model of Positive Experience*, Mahwah, NJ, Erlbaum, 2007.

98. A. SCHORE, *The Effects of Early Relational Trauma on Right Brain Development, Affect Regulation, and Infant Mental Health*, in *Infant Mental Health Journal* 22 (2001) 201-269; ID., *Affect Regulation and the Repair of the Self*; ID., *Affect Dysregulation and Disorders of the Self* (n. 24).

99. F. SILLS, *Being and Becoming: Psychodynamics, Buddhism, and the Origins of Selfhood*, Berkeley, CA, North Atlantic Books, 2009.

100. SIEGEL, *The Developing Mind* (n. 5), p. 97.

101. BOWLBY, *A Secure Base* (n. 7).

reflection and shaped automatic responses[102]. Mindlessness! If character morality comes about from the choices one makes and the actions one takes, Kekes suggests that vices can be formed from *not* making a choice, by falling into characteristic, unchosen behaviors that bring about evil. According to Kekes, these 'accidental' behaviors are the source of most evil in the world, resulting from failing to develop appropriate sensibilities and habits, perhaps as a result of one or more of the three types of vices he names: malevolence (blaming), insufficiency (not reflecting critically) and expediency (harming others when they get in your way). These are characteristics of defective characters and, in his view, being dominated by these vices represents evil.

Increase Positive Emotions and Attitudes Towards Others. Positive social emotions such as gratitude, sympathy and compassion provide fertile ground for mindful morality. Like mindfulness training, open-heart meditations can facilitate sympathy development in the present moment. The Heartmath Institute has studied the effects of heart-centered meditation and visualizations on alleviating stress, re-balancing the body, and increasing empathy and positive action towards others[103]. They have developed several techniques that individuals can practice. One is called the "heart lock-in". In this exercise, the individual focuses on the heart in a meditative way for five to fifteen minutes and remembers a feeling of care or appreciation for someone easy to love. The individual imagines gently sending the feeling of love or appreciation to self and others. The neurobiology of the heart influences the functioning of body and brain, facilitating moral mindfulness. With greater practice, the individual can expand the heart lock-in to persons that are difficult to love.

Individuals can expand understanding of others by becoming acquainted with people from outgroups through face to face relationships, long-distant or online relationships or through reading rich descriptions of other people's lives. They can participate in activities where participants are of equal status working towards a common goal (i.e., social contact theory[104]) which increases empathy and understanding.

102. J. KEKES, *The Roots of Evil*, Ithaca, NY, Cornell University Press, 1990.

103. D. CHILDRE, *The HeartMath Solution: The Institute of HeartMath's Revolutionary Program for Engaging the Power of the Heart's Intelligence*, New York, NY, Harper One, 2000.

104. ALLPORT, *The Nature of Prejudice* (n. 71).

4. *Foster Self-Authorship*

Increasing self awareness is also a route to mindful morality. Sometimes the counsellor can ask a simple question that brings the client back to a focus on self-becoming (e.g., "is your anger more important than a peaceful death"?). Self-awareness increases through attention to one's emotions. If one has little sense of one's own feelings, one have difficulty recognizing them in others. Individuals can restore and revitalize the emotional parts of the brain, particularly the soft emotions through self-awareness activities such as journaling, paying attention to likes and dislikes and spending more time doing things that bring joy. Siegel[105] describes the opening of the right brain emotion systems through artistic, musical, and playful endeavors. Playful activity is also a good way to learn to stay in the present (e.g., rough-and-tumble play, being silly, making up music and songs, making up stories). Brown[106] suggests that when people don't play, they are more likely to be depressed.

5. *Restore the Village of Support*

Support groups, new friends or revised relationships are important for maintaining the changes that come about from immersion in therapy or similar experiences. These changes can fall away if the person returns to old environments and relationships, or becomes isolated. Perhaps the best place for support in a religious setting is attending worship services with supportive others. Active, full body experiences such as singing, playing, dancing, and laughing are ways to feel an embodied, positive sense of community. Sometimes clients are lonely and isolated. The counsellor can check to make sure the client is feeling connected to and supported by the community in a way that brings the client joy.

VII. Conclusion: Supportive Relationships

The human "moral sense" is not innate but is shaped by experience. When individuals have not experienced the sustaining and encouraging relationships from a young age that are necessary for optimal brain and moral functioning, there are several interventions that can facilitate the growth of mindful morality. Although morality is a matter of self-authorship, it can be fostered through guided apprenticeship and a village of

105. Siegel, *The Developing Mind* (n. 5).

106. S. Brown – C. Vaughan, *Play: How It Shapes the Brain, Opens the Imagination, and Invigorates the Soul*, New York, NY, Avery-Penguin, 2009.

support. It requires supportive relationships and a conducive climate for its unfolding, both of which can be provided by pastoral care-givers.

Darcia NARVAEZ

Department of Psychology
University of Notre Dame
100 Haggar Hall
Notre Dame, IN 46556
U.S.A.
dnarvaez@nd.edu

PART II

THE PASTORAL COUNSELLING PROCESS AS ETHICAL EVENT

ASYMMETRIC RECIPROCITY IN PASTORAL DIALOGUE

REFLECTIONS ON EFFECTIVE PASTORAL COUNSELLING INSPIRED BY THE THOUGHT OF LEVINAS AND BUBER

What is the correct approach to use in professional pastoral counselling? What does a pastor owe a counselling partner in the context of a pastoral relationship? In this essay we aim to find out what is correct in pastoral counselling and what is 'against doing justice' to the counselling partner. For Levinas doing justice has to do with giving priority to the counselling partner and to suffer with the suffering of the other: "after You". For Buber it means that the pastor and the counselling partner build up an authentic person to person relationship. This essay discusses and compares the philosophy of Levinas and Buber for use in pastoral counselling[1].

Because terminology is important to understand correctly what is discussed, I want to introduce immediately my definition of pastoral counselling, namely: *pastoral counselling is any counselling in which a pastor has a wordy contact with a counselling partner*. 'Counselling' is limited to a dialogue[2], 'pastor' implies all authorised pastoral professionals[3], 'counselling partner' means all persons who are contacted by pastors

1. A research team of two ethicists engaged in pastoral and moral theology (Prof. A. Liégeois and Prof. R. Burggraeve), a psychologist (Prof. J. Corveleyn) and a hospital chaplain and CPE supervisor (MA M. Riemslagh) investigated the ethics of pastoral discourses. They worked out a research project on 'The ethics of the pastoral counselling process'. This project contained a fundamental and empirical research part. The research was conducted in Leuven, at the KU Leuven (Catholic University of Leuven), Department of Pastoral Theology of the Faculty of Theology and Religious Studies, supported by the Flemish Fund for Scientific Research. In this essay we focus on the philosophical part of the research project. The research project led to the PhD of Marina Riemslagh, '(In)Correct Counselling: Fundamental and Empirical Research into the Ethics of the Pastoral Counselling Process': M. Riemslagh, *(In) Correcte Gespreksvoering I: Fundamenteel onderzoek naar de ethiek van het pastorale gespreksproces*, Puurs, Unibind, 2011; Id., *(In)Correcte Gespreksvoering II: Empirisch onderzoek naar de ethiek van het pastorale gespreksproces*, Puurs, Unibind, 2011.

2. Describing counselling with several counselling partners at the same time complicates matters so that the focus from which I look at counselling, namely ethics, threatens to be overlooked.

3. With 'authorised' I mean all professionally employed pastors, 'professionals', whether they are paid or not. Volunteers in pastoral counselling are ideally instructed in doing so. But, as the word itself suggests, they are volunteers, not professionals; they do not do this job professionally.

during the practice of their function[4]. By the term 'counselling process' we express the practice of the pastor[5]. For the ethics of the counselling process we use 'ethically correct behaviour' or 'ethically correct conduct'[6]. We try to express that the interests of the persons involved are taken into account (individually and socially) and are respected as important[7]. Taking into consideration the interest of everyone involved requires what Krasner and Joyce call 'ethical imagination', a creative process that stems from the double imperative of 'being both just and free'.

I. Levinas: Pastoral Counselling as Ethical Asymmetry

In present literature on pastoral care and especially pastoral counselling references to the philosophy of Levinas are not rare[8]. This is quite understandable because no author has so explicitly put the other in the centre, which also belongs to the objective of pastorate. Levinas does not only stress the ethical attitude with which the pastor has to approach the other, as his/her counselling partners. He also founds this attitude religiously, namely in the transcendence of the other. If the other suffers, I, as pastor, find myself confronted with the ethical demand for compassion (co-suffering). Therefore, in the first part of this essay I want to check to what degree Levinas's philosophy can found the ethics of pastoral counselling. First I will describe pastoral counselling as face-to-face (1) and then I will examine the ethics of compassion (2). In the second

4. Regardless of their age, living condition, relationship to the pastor, ... people with whom the pastor enters into counselling as a result of his/her function, are called 'counselling partners'.

5. The process is the whole of successive, closely connected activities and operations on the spiritual, psychic and social levels; it is the procedure in action.

6. 'Ethically correct behaviour' is no norm that has come into being externally, on the basis of theological and philosophical literature. The criteria for ethically correct behaviour have here equally been developed on the basis of what 12 pastors, in in-depth interviews, have called characteristic of correct procedures.

7. B. Krasner – A. Joyce, *Truth, Trust, and Relationships: Healing Interventions in Contextual Therapy*, New York, NY, Brunner – Mazel, 1995, p. 44.

8. Cf. for instance: P. Cooper-White, *Many Voices: Pastoral Psychotherapy in Relational and Theological Perspective*, Minneapolis, MN, Augsburg Fortress Press, 2011; N.J. Ramsay, *Pastoral Diagnosis: A Resource for Ministries of Care and Counseling*, Minneapolis, MN, Augsburg Fortress Press, 1998; N.A. Kirkwood, *Pastoral Care in Hospitals*, Harrisburg, PA, Morehouse Publishing, 2005; G. Lynch, *Pastoral Care & Counselling*, London, Sage Publications, 2002; A. Dillen – A. Vandenhoeck (eds.), *Prophetic Witness in World Christianities: Rethinking Pastoral Care and Counseling*, Wien, Lit Verlag, 2011.

part of this essay I will focus on Buber's philosophy, explaining the necessity of building reciprocity with the other in pastoral counselling.

1. *Counselling as Face-to-Face*

Levinas (1905-1995)[9] has written 'about' the dialogue as the founding dynamic of our inter-human relationships than actually 'described' the dialogue in action[10]. This does not exclude that his phenomenology implies some basic elements of the concrete discourse between two people. He writes about the face-to-face, the responsibility that I have for the other. Writing as such 'about' the face-to-face, he takes a meta-position, namely the position of 'ethics before ethics'. He tries to make clear how we are relational beings and how the basic dynamics of this relationality (interhumanity) is the dialogue of face-to-face, preceding every concrete ethical and dialogical practice. When he 'describes' the face-to-face dialogue, he reasons 'from' face-to-face speaking, from within the dialogue. This positioning has direct consequences for what he ascribes to the I and the other. 'About' the dialogue he follows the aforementioned train of thought concerning the other (TI 79-81). The dialogue with anyone about anything is immanent while the dialogue with the other touches the transcendent[11]. The dialogue only becomes ethical in the asymmetry present, where I am at the service of the other. The stress is then on the asymmetry, albeit a changing asymmetry: a dissymmetry, in which the position of the I and the other oscillate; yet remain distinguished and asymmetric (GCM 150-151). When Levinas 'describes' the face-to-face the positions do not change; they are fixed. As a consequence, face-to-face speech, in order to be respectful, needs reciprocity. Levinas has explored aspects of the face-to-face as an actual experience in two early

9. For the references to the works of Levinas, the following abbreviations will be used throughout the essay: **EN**: *Entre Nous: Thinking-of-the-Other*, London – New York, Continuum, 2006; **ES:** *Une éthique de la souffrance*, in J.-M. KAENEL – B. AJCHENBAUM-BOFFETY (eds.), *Souffrances: Corps et âme, épreuves partagées*, Paris, Éditions Autrement, 1994, 127-137; **OS**: *Outside the Subject*, London, The Athlone Press, 1993; **OB**: *Otherwise than Being or Beyond Essence*, The Hague – Boston, MA – London, Martinus Nijhoff Publishers, 1981; **GCM**: *Of God Who Comes to Mind*, Stanford, CA, Stanford University Press, 2000; **TI**: *Totality and Infinity: An Essay on Exteriority*, The Hague – Boston, MA – London, Martinus Nijhoff Publishers, 1979.

10. M. RIEMSLAGH, *The Face-to-Face as Asymmetrical and Reciprocal Revelation: Founding the Ethics of the Process of Pastoral Counselling in the Footsteps of Levinas*, in R. BURGGRAEVE (ed.), *The Awakening to the Other: A Provocative Dialogue with Emmanuel Levinas*, Leuven – Dudley, MA, Peeters, 2008, 191-214.

11. Cf. GCM 139: "Dialogue of Immanence" and GCM 143: "Dialogue of Transcendence".

articles that serve as the basis for my subsequent thinking[12]. I will analyse this direct dialogue as if analysing a slow-motion film, where one moment passes after the other: *showing understanding for the other*, *addressing*, *meeting* and *speaking to one another as showing respect.*

For Levinas, meeting is looking the other right in the eyes: face-to-face. This is only possible within a relation in which there is no talking 'about' or if need be 'to', but 'with' one another. In talking with one another we turn into one another's fellow human being (EN 8). To give a better insight, I will bring his description of the meeting as contrasted to the rhetorical argument. I start with the meeting between two people, which for Levinas is a respectful, reciprocal face-to-face between two just persons[13].

Showing understanding of the other is not yet what Levinas means by speaking. Showing understanding of the other is trying to see the person with respect for his/her history, his/her context and his/her way of doing things; in short, it is trying to understand him/her as s/he is, in his/her way of being (EN 8). Levinas's intent is for us to approach the other as a being in proximity to me, a being who I am commanded not to kill: "At the very moment when my power to kill is realised, the other has escaped. (...) To be in relation with the other face-to-face – is to be unable to kill. This is also the situation of discourse" (EN 8-9).

By speaking with the other and trying to understand him/her, *I address him/her*, I call out to his/her face (*invocation*). I address the other (OB 5-6). Speaking begins with proximity and seeking approach. Then I speak 'about something', about one or another thing. It is an attempt to approach (OB 6-7)[14]. I address the other 'with something'. By addressing him/her

12. "L'ontologie est-elle fondamentale?" (1951); "Le moi et la totalité" (1954). See EN 13-24, 25-52. In his later writings (TI, OB, GCM) Levinas not only describes 'from' within the dialogue as experience, but he philosophises primarily 'about' the relationship of the I and the other as a foundational structure: "The face-to-face remains an ultimate situation" (TI 81). From this transcendental meta-position, in search of the conditions of possibility for the real dialogue between people, the idea of reciprocity remains in the background, and the idea of asymmetric and ethical otherness comes to the front. The idea of reciprocity re-emerges on the level of the "third party" (*le tiers*), paradigm of the plurality and of the absence of others (cf. supra). Through the presence of a third, appealing to comparison, measure, knowing, organisation and justice, I am approached as an other by the others, that is to say, their equal. We are fellows to one another. With the appearance of the third party, symmetry enters the asymmetric proximity: togetherness as synchrony, reciprocity as correction of the original asymmetry (OB 157-160).

13. Levinas seldom uses the word 'reciprocal' (cf. the preceding footnote), unless in his direct description of the actual face-to-face experience. Reciprocity can be wrongly understood as symmetry. By reciprocal, though, I only denote the 'to-and-from', 'there and back', from the other to me and from me to the other' in the dialogue.

14. Levinas calls such speaking 'about something' the inevitable treason that goes together with the approach to the other (OB 6). Because speaking 'about' is so intertwined

'about something' the face can show itself in its nakedness (EN 28). Addressing the other 'about something', in accordance with the expression *autrui*, has as its aim the irreducible in the other. It assumes to approach a person by recognising his/her in this beforehand. This explains the need for ultimate respect both for this other, as for third persons about whom something might be said. Without this fundamental respect, the other does not receive any space to show him/herself. That is why Levinas can rightly pose that responsibility for the other already presents itself before the revelation of the face. Believing in the other and trusting him/her precedes being together with him/her. "S/he is not affirmed as a truth, but is believed. Faith or trust does not mean here a second source of knowledge, but which is assumed by every theoretical statement" (EN 28). Believing in the other as *autrui* is seeing him/her as a human being. *Autrui* is being a human being oneself, i.e. being called to responsibility for the other. *Autrui* is being a bearer of one's own uniqueness and being called to reach the destination according to the dictates of responsibility. In calling to his/her face, I address him/her 'beyond being', calling upon the promise 'who s/he has to become'.

I can, nevertheless, walk past the transcendence of the other, or try to trample it; *autrui* is therefore vulnerable. The other is transcendent insofar as s/he stands in front of me, facing me: "Dialogue is not merely a way of speaking. Its significance has a general reach. It is transcendence. The saying involved in dialogue would not be one of the possible forms of transcendence but its original mode. Transcendence has no meaning except by way of a person addressing another person, an "I" saying "You". It is the *dia* of the dialogue" (GCM 147). The language indicates this transcendence because it presupposes the other. This transcendence does not oppress, but rather, it obliges, it makes me responsible to speak. It obliges me to respect the other through words: 'being responsible is speaking' (EN 28). I am responsible to recognise the other as an interlocutor, so that s/he can speak his/her own language (EN 28-29).

So far, the discourse has not yet been a meeting. After all, I can speak with the other and in doing so, leave him/her as s/he is (EN 5). Moreover, I can speak with the other as if s/he were a third person, whose confidence I try to win in order to gain influence over him/her (EN 29).

I can only really *meet* the other in his/her real transcendence, in his/her face, when I, from the understanding I show, recognise that s/he is

with the real speaking with the other, Levinas restricts the 'saying' (*le Dire*) to the diachronic, i.e. to these moments when the other suddenly breaks through the usual experience of time.

strange to me and at the same time believe in him/her as irreducible (EN 29). "Transcendence is what turns its face towards us. The face breaks the system. The ontology of being and truth may not ignore this face-to-face structure, that is, the structure of faith. The condition for propositional truth resides not in the revelation of a being or of the being of beings, but in the expression of the interlocutor to whom I say both the being he/she is and the being of his/her being. One must be face to face with a person as myself. The interlocutor appears as without a history, as outside the system. I can neither fail nor vindicate him; he remains transcendent in expression" (EN 30). Showing solidarity with him/her, seeing him/her, recognising him/her and believing in his/her transcendence, this is at all times my responsibility.

By *showing respect for the other by speaking with her/him*, the other will in turn confirm me. When coming face-to-face with the other, the denial of the other is mutually impossible. Looking one another in the eye is therefore a compulsion to recognition. By speaking with one another in this way, two people are being built. "Speech, then, is a relationship between freedoms who neither limit nor deny one another, but reciprocally affirm one another. They are transcendent in relation to one another" (EN 30). Levinas uses the word respect for such a meeting. Respect is the condition for ethics. "The reciprocity of this respect is not an indifferent relationship, such as a serene contemplation, it is language; that is, responsibility" (EN 30). This is the essence of Levinas's concept of responsibility: I always owe the other absolute respect, and in the face-to-face speech, this mutual respect is shown in words (TI 73). In our respectful speaking with one another, the sense of everyone's existence is disclosed (EN 22).

In order to prevent a situation in which respecting the other humiliates the 'I', I must be able to respect the other as a person of worth (EN 30-31). I must be able to experience him/her as a person deserving of respect. That is why in my address I call on him/her to behave as a noble, respectable human being, in order to do justice to his/her transcendence. In this sense, both of us are willingly submitted to the commandment that we – through the epiphany of our face – address to one another. "Respect thus described is not the result of justice, since the commanded man is outside the realm of justice and injustice. The respected one is not the one to whom, but with whom justice is done. Respect is a relationship between equals" (EN 31). By showing reciprocal respect, the other and I are a 'we'. Both of us are at the service of justice[15], both of us face the transcendence that commands us.

15. This does not imply a dividing justice towards third persons, but 'doing justice to the other', which is much wider than the content that is usually assigned to justice (TI 99).

In contrast to the respectful face-to-face dialogue, in which both approach one another in their transcendence, rhetoric is revealed as impersonal speech[16]. Levinas calls this rhetoric a "discourse without interlocutors" (EN 21). In this, the alterity of the one I am speaking with is indeed removed. The other, as a transcendent person, remains unseen. S/he could have been replaced by anyone else with whom a conversation is held. With this other a respectful relation is not being built, s/he is rather to be approached as known, to be diagnosed as an 'idealised object to be served', as an anonymous 'anyone'. Levinas believes that in every discourse rhetoric is present. Not only in political, but also in pedagogical, psychological and pastoral situations discourses are often rhetorical. They imply nicely presented arguments, intended to extract from the other what one finds desirable. By appraisal, diplomacy, flattery, propaganda, argumentation *ad hominem*, intimidation, impressing, speaking nicely and attractively or convincingly, the other is overwhelmed (TI 70). In doing so, I 'address' the other, but at the same time I reduce her to someone who has to follow my orders. Here the other is not approached face-to-face, it does not concern him/her, but myself. Because I am 'in conversation' with him/her, it seems as if s/he is not objectified. But because I do not have any concern for his/her being in and of him/herself and rather only desire her assent, I corrupt his/her freedom, I deny him/her as irreducibly other to myself (HS 135; OS 138-139, 143). Levinas insists that not only does the other lose his/her alterity in such an interaction, but also I lose contact with my transcendence as such: "The transcendence of the interlocutor and the access to the other through language show that man is a singularity" (EN 22). But, "impersonal discourse is a necrological discourse" (EN 22). The rhetorical argument kills. The face is not addressed, the other is not recognised nor confirmed as other. In this respect rhetoric is especially unjust: ruse, emprise, and exploitation (TI 72). The recognition of the other is indeed directed to my own interest, by which the recognition itself is perverted. It is exactly by persuading the other that I try to corrupt him/her such that s/he becomes a function of the rhetorical I rather than a self-expression of his/her own alterity. Here the discourse results in alienation, fear and resistance of not being allowed to be other. Often there is no recognition (or only subconscious and repressed recognition) that this alienating process is taking place. Here the trace of the Infinite is washed away, obscured and rendered opaque.

16. For a deeper understanding of the rhetorical, see in this book the contribution of Roger BURGGRAEVE, *From 'Good Morning' to the Responsibility for the Responsibility of the Other*, section 5. *The Temptation of Rhetoric*.

Levinas demonstrates two ways out of the inherent dangers of rhetoric. On the one hand, he poses that I must deny all rhetoric in favour of an ethically authentic face-to-face dialogue. I am called upon to criticise all manners of demagogy and attempts to persuade the other and instead take seriously my responsibility to respect the other as transcendent – even if she or he would not require this in any way (TI 71). On the other hand, I must always give the other the opportunity to actively reply. By way of the 'and you?', I must ask him/her how my approach reaches him/her and how s/he him/herself thinks about this (EN, 28). I have to transcend rhetoric always again by rendering to the other the mastery of him/herself, by revealing the freedom of his/her otherness towards me and thus being my master who teaches me through his/her otherness (TI 100-101). Respecting his/her transcendence is possible only by calling upon him/her as a unique person and subsequently engaging him/her in mutual exchange, face-to-face.

It is essential as a criterion for authentic pastoral counselling, that Levinas means by responsibility respect and that this respect is shown by giving the other the possibility to reply in his/her own way. Seen from within the 'descriptive' face-to-face speech, this respect, especially when things matter, is realised as a reciprocal dissymmetric address. Seen from outside, 'about' the dialogue, it is fundamentally an asymmetric obligation from I towards the other. That is to say, the ethical norm not to kill the other, formulated as responsibility for the other that precedes the relationship, becomes most visible in the face-to-face dialogue of two persons, whereby both *show understanding for the other*, *address each other*, *really meet each other* and *speak to one another by showing absolute respect*.

2. *An Ethics of Compassion*

At the end of his life Levinas gave an interview in which he designed an ethics of suffering (ES)[17]. Because this ethics is extremely relevant to pastors who deal with suffering people, I will follow below the logic of his contribution.

Levinas states that the experience of pain differs from all our other experiences, like for instance colour or sound (ES 130-131). Specific to a sensation of pain is that it is the consciousness of something we do not

17. See also the shorter article by E. LEVINAS, *Useless Suffering*, in ID., *Entre Nous: Thinking-of-the-Other*, London – New York, Continuum, 2006, 78-87, pp. 78-81: *1. Phenomenology* and pp. 86-87: *4. The Interhuman Order*.

want to be conscious of, something our consciousness opposes (ES 127). Pain is a border experience of the consciousness, a 'no', a wish to draw away from the consciousness. In that sense pain is the refusal of the experience that imposes itself. Pain is not to be integrated into the consciousness. The person who experiences pain does not want to know him/herself like this, nor will s/he be known in this way (ES 129). The refusal of pain becomes in this way the rejection of the self and of the other. The normal way of the 'I' with itself is breached by pain (ES 130). Suffering thus breaks the pleasant relationship that the person has built with him/herself. The pain causes the consciousness not to bear itself, as a result the person experiences him/herself as unbearable (ES 131).

Suffering is passive, the person does not experience reality, he/she undergoes, cannot but endure the unbearable. In pain one does not know peace. Suffering is always going against, even against those who have accepted suffering (ES 132). The person is torn by it, s/he has to suffer. Suffering is a 'no' to any possible interpretation of it, for Levinas it is the most explicit articulation of absurdity.

On the one hand suffering locks the person inside him/herself, on the other hand it calls one as a cry out of him/herself. From the abyss of his/her consciousness, the essence of the person moans, begs for help, s/he appeals to the other (ES 133). In the working situation of the pastorate the other is the pastor. S/he can refer him/herself only partly, but not completely, to the suffering of the other, s/he can substitute him/herself with the sufferer to participate in his/her suffering. However, a pastor can only realise this proximity insofar as s/he recognises the unbearable that s/he carries him/herself. The least thing is that s/he should not be indifferent to it[18]. This is decisive for his/her being human (ES 133)[19]. Being moved by the other and by his/her suffering is essential. It is both carrying responsibility for the well-being of the other and the ground of this responsibility. Sympathy is the foundation of communal life. Being moved by the need of the other precedes living together, it is its ultimate ground. The pain the pastor feels when s/he dares to go along with the suffering of the counselling partner, can be meaningful as long as suffering because of another is involved (ES 134). In other words, the pain

18. What Levinas calls indifference becomes concrete in the transcripts of pastoral counselling when a pastor loses contact with the counselling partner. Among other things this becomes visible when s/he limits the counselling partner, when s/he refuses recognition, minimalizes, labels the counselling partner intra-psychically, cannot stand the theme of the counselling partner.

19. ES 136-137. For Levinas encountering the other in his/her suffering is the justification of the existence of man on earth.

from the own life of the pastor, incited by the suffering (in the story) of the counselling partner, is worth facing, accepting and transforming. It does after all decide his/her quality as a human being and the quality of the pastoral service.

For Levinas this is the core of ethics: suffering in order to diminish the suffering of the other (ES 134). Although such behaviour goes against the normal affair of matters, it is the only justification of any suffering (ES 135). Levinas is quite aware of the fact that the task of loving the other in his/her suffering requires the investment of the whole person. If the pastor does not go along the spiritual way of such compassion, this directly affects the quality of his/her pastoral counselling. If the pastor does his/her homework by going into the suffering that s/he experiences in the counselling of his/her counselling partners, s/he takes a risk. S/he is confronted with unknown depths in his/her own history of life. If s/he wants to be or become a professional pastor, s/he cannot but take this road. This risk is necessary in order to become or remain a sensitive, intelligent pastor (ES 136).

In this first point the responsibility of the pastor in listening to the counselling partner in his/her destination, in whom s/he here and now essentially is, has been brought to the fore. Otherwise directed pastoral conduct is not evident, especially not when the being different of the counselling partner interrupts the pastor in his/her evident perspective. A real encounter even becomes impossible when the Other is being met as well-known and the pastor is being seduced into diagnostic reduction, rhetoric and/or dominance[20].

In the second point we followed Levinas in his 'ethics of suffering'. If a pastor is closely associated with the suffering of the counselling partner, this awakens painful moments in his/her own history. In order to be or become a sensitive and intelligent pastor, capable of true compassion/co-suffering, pastors need to have contact with their own pain.

II. Buber: Pastoral Counselling as Ethical Reciprocity

As far as the philosophical foundation of the ethics of the counselling process is concerned, we first entered into the assymmetry of counselling partners as stressed by Levinas. This is of course relevant: relational ethics is based on this assymmetry. In this paragraph we discuss Buber's

20. For a further elaboration of the violence of diagnostic reduction and dominance, cf. Burggraeve's contribution.

philosophy of reciprocity[21]. In order to build relationships assymmetry between counselling partners precedes, while the quality of the relationship is largely determined by building collectivity. In Buber the assymmetry is pretended in the independence of the persons who relate to one another. In his phenomenology the cultivation of the encounter between persons is central. For the reciprocal building of mutual commitment it is necessary to invest in the building of reciprocity.

We disregard the discussion in which Levinas and Buber got entangled. Often Buber, with respect to content, is judged from the reading of Levinas[22]. Lipari writes that neither of them were able to listen to each other well; she approaches their dispute in the course of the process[23]. We approach Buber in himself, because of the added value of his dialogical philosophy on the success or otherwise of the pastoral encounter[24].

For Buber encounter is the contact between two people, in which both become aware of their *uniqueness*. They realise their *uniqueness* because they address each other in their *being a person* and because they let themselves *be touched* by the *being different* of the other in such a way that both *know themselves accepted* as *this* human being. An encounter, therefore, is not just a discourse, which one can have with no matter whom about no matter what. Man is present in another way in an encounter than in a loose contact (DDP 9). If I speak from I-You to you,

21. In English literature on pastorate and especially pastoral counselling, there are regular references to the philosophy of Buber: H. CLINEBELL, *Basic Types of Pastoral Counseling*, Nashville, TN, Abingdon Press, 1966; P. COOPER-WHITE, *Shared Wisdom: Use of the Self in Pastoral Care and Counseling*, Minneapolis, MN, Fortress Press, 2004; E. GRIFFIN, *A First Look at Communication Theory*, New York, NY, Mc Graw Hill, 2006 (6th ed.); D. MEARNS – M. COOPER, *Working at Relational Depth in Counselling and Psychotherapy*, London – New Delhi – Thousand Oaks, Sage, 2005; A. MONTEIRO DOS SANTOS, *Miracle Moments: The Nature of the Mind's Power in Relationships and Psychotherapy*, Lincoln, NE, iUniverse, 2003; W. OATES – T.W. CHAPMAN (eds.), *A Practical Handbook for Ministry: From the Writings of Wayne E. Oates*, Westminster, MD, John Knox Press, 1992; P. SENGE, *et al.*, *Presence: Human Purpose and the Field of the Future*, New York, NY, Doubleday, 2004.

22. P. ATTERTON – M. CALARCO – M. FRIEDMAN (eds.), *Levinas and Buber: Dialogue and Difference*, Pittsburgh, PA, Dusquesne University Press, 2004.

23. L. LIPARI, *Listening for the Other: Ethical Implications of the Buber-Levinas Encounter*, in *Communication Theory* 14 (2004), no. 2, 122-141. Cf. also Lipari's contribution in this book.

24. For the references to the work of M. BUBER, *Das Dialogische Prinzip*, Gütersloh, Gütersloher Verlagshaus, 2002 (9th ed.), the following abbreviation will be used throughout the essay: DDP. The writings of Buber contained in *Das Dialogische Prinzip* are: *Ich und Du*, pp. 5-136; *Zwiesprache*, pp. 137-196; *Die Frage an den Einzelnen*, pp. 199-267; *Elemente des Zwischenmenschlichen*, pp. 269-298.

I realise with all my being that I speak to you and with you[25]; I approach you in your being, while I at the same time realise that this relationship is about me, at this very moment. It is a meeting between my whole being and your whole being. If I speak from I-It, I talk 'about' you and 'about' others; I am only half present and I do not realise that I do really say something to you and that You with your history and condition of life hear this. In an I-It contact I do not realise that I matter in this discourse, that I am important. I-You is quality of discourse. (DDP 8).

When Buber talks about encounter, he uses the term 'person' or 'man'. When he talks about 'individual', he has in mind someone unique and developed, who does not really live together with others. A man is someone who lives consciously in reciprocal contact with reality. Buber says about himself that he is "against individuals and for men"[26].

1. *Characteristics of Dialogical Encounter*

Das dialogische Prinzip defines the characteristics of dialogical encounter, as Buber discusses phenomenologically, explained and explored in a spiral way. I will summarise them as follows.

Encounter is *building the human person.* "Der Mensch wird am Du zum Ich" (DDP 32). Here Buber describes the *process character* of the encounter. A man has to go a long way before s/he can enter into a relationship 'as I'. A lot of You's have invested in this I before s/he, 'released' as a unique person, can encounter others. The *independence of the person* precedes and makes possible conditions for the dialogical meeting. The complete dialogue implies adult people who can encounter each other in an equal way. In order to freely go towards the other, one needs a place of departure, one needs to have been with oneself, in other words, one needs to be someone, a person (DDP 169). Being a person implies that one can recognise one's own reality, so that one can meet the reality of the other (DDP 62). One's own contribution is important, just like the belief that mutual solidarity is possible. Both are crucial to encounter.

In "Das Du begegnet mir von Gnaden" (DDP 15), *You* come towards me with kindness. *You* are there and *come to me as a gift to me*. Moreover,

25. In accordance with Buber's thinking, the universal 'I' and the universal 'You' are written with capital letters and we, as authors of this contribution, without a capital.

26. M. BUBER – C.R. ROGERS – R. ANDERSON – K. CISSNA, *The Martin Buber – Carl Rogers Dialogue: A New Transcript with Commentary*, Albany, NY, State University of New York Press, 1997. Cf. M. FRIEDMAN, *Reflections on the Buber-Rogers Dialogue*, in *Journal of Humanistic Psychology* 34 (1994), no. 1, Winter, 46-65.

when You approach me as a person, this is remarkable, *unexpected*: a merciful presence.

The first movement in the dialogue is *turning towards the other*, then it is necessary to *perceive the other as a person*. There are three ways to approach the other: observing (interest in the other), contemplating (as if meeting someone strange) and perceiving that this person concerns me (I am concerned about him or her). Only in this last way does allow a person to develop him or herself and claim me as an answering person (DDP 152).

The dialogical basic attitude is therefore the *turning towards* (DDP 170). It seems to be something common and selfless: one looks at someone, addresses him/her, turns to him/her bodily, prepares oneself with heart and soul for him/her and directs one's *attention* to him/her. The turning towards can be so complete that one allows the other one *to be present* in his/her independence, enclosing him/her in such a way that one can experience the common situation also *from him/her*, and *experience* from the other *how it is* (DDP 173).

The possible borders of the dialogical are the borders of *perceiving*. What exactly does it mean 'to perceive a person'? Buber uses several words: perceive: imagine bodily and interiorise. Imagine a person bodily means that I observe him/her completely and concretely, that I observe him/her *in his/her potency and destination*, that I surmise the *dynamic core* from which s/he externalises him/herself and acts. In short, that I imagine myself in his/her concrete *uniqueness*. Such an imagination is impossible as long as the other is the object of my longing or is perceived as such. Seeing him/her really becomes only possible when s/he as another person can really be present and I imagine him/her from within (DDP 284). Perceiving is *no intuition*. Buber proposes to call this 'Realphantasie', 'real phantasy'. When this interiorisation happens mutually, the inter-human dimension can blossom in a real discourse (DDP 286-287).

Dealing with the other in such a way has also consequences for my thinking. It is not enough to think *about* the other as subject. I have to think *with* him/her, *from* him/her, as *if from his/her own body*. It is not correct to live across the concrete other. We have to focus our thinking on the person who belongs to the energy of thinking (DDP 179-180).

Buber expresses the process of encounter as follows. In a real discourse the *turning towards* the partner happens in all truth, one turns towards his/her essence, his/her personal existence. The senses of experience and the 'real phantasy' work together to *represent* the other as only and unique being. The other is *confirmed* and *accepted* as unique person, I say 'Yes' to whom s/he is. Then one will *introduce oneself*, i.e.

that one wants to speak for and towards the other the own word, *faithful to oneself* and *faithfully answering the other*. A real encounter exists when whatever I have to say is really put on the table. So both are listening under the word that addresses (is spoken). It is not a matter of just talking loosely, but speaking in a manner that legitimizes what I have to say. On top of that all appearance, all 'doing as if' should be overcome. Wherever such a discourse is had, common fertility comes into being. The inter-human dimension discloses whatever has not yet been disclosed. In this one can discover that whatever is being said, has never been heard before and that it presents itself as the call of the Spirit (DDP 293-296).

Buber also underlines that in another encounter the inter-human dimension manifests itself in an own way. He states that it is appropriate *to thank the inter-human dimension*, which sets us free (DDP 298).

I will summarize the previous characteristics of the dialogue. Prior to the encounter I have been developed into an independent person and You are present here and now. The first movement is that I turn towards you with attention. Then I open all my senses and imagination in order to perceive you, not only as You are now, but also in your potency and destination. I think with you as if from your own body. In a third movement I answer you, faithful to myself and to you. What I want to say I put in words. The encounter is closed down in thankfulness.

2. *What Impedes Authentic Encounter*

Successively I discuss the characteristics of the encounter and I study what can impede the dialogue. The encounter that Buber proposes is quite an exigent happening, which requires high demands from the counselling partners.

First of all the encounter is only possible between 'independent' persons. It is typical of such persons that they know their own history and feel comfortable in their own body, in short, that they have reasonably integrated body and spirit, past and present. Personal freedom and living with limitations are linked to his/her fate. If a person is not consistent with his/her own history, old mechanisms restrict the encounter where neither I nor the other are allowed to exist as we really are (DDP 55-56). Who from a dualistic attitude humiliates the body and so to speak cultivates the soul, harms the dialogical: not the other nor oneself is taken seriously. In the bodily aspect, though, the other comes to me as a concrete and contingent person. "Only he who promotes the other man completely because of the wellbeing of the other, receives the whole world" (DDP 183).

There are three kinds of dialogue. The *real* one is the one in which every participant really takes him/herself and the other in his/her being-there and being-so seriously, turns himself towards the other with full intention and creates the living reciprocity between him/herself and the other. The *technical* dialogue is only inspired by the need for practical understanding. In a *monologue disguised as dialogue* several people are in the same space, everyone is busy with him/herself and tries to get rid of the pain of being left to one's own devices (DDP 166). Living dialogically does not just exist when people are together, it comes into being when I am concerned about *this* person (DDP 167).

Instead of *turning towards* the other, one can also stay with oneself, the other then becomes one-of-the people (DDP 171). Then the dialogue becomes appearance, the secret interaction between people degenerates and the essence of reality is devalued (DDP 173). Approaching the other as other with attention and interest is typical of dialogical behaviour. Buber sees *two basic attitudes* from which acting is careless. In a first basic attitude *one sinks into ecstasy because of the other person*, in the other basic attitude *one drops out and falls into indifference and routine*. The consequences are clear. In the first situation one experiences the other so closely that the distinction between 'You' and 'I' becomes non-existent. In the second situation the distance is so big that every person becomes one of the many people with whom one can barely have a relationship. In dialogue one touches the other as other and allows him/herself to be touched and the confrontation with the strangeness (peculiarity) of the other happens. Not in ecstasy nor in indifference the uniqueness of the partners in dialogue is respected. (DDP 235-237).

The characteristic of real encounter is that people *want to communicate themselves to each other* and to apply themselves to the other as particular other. Appearance is a major problem in the inter-human contact. Buber shows this by distinguishing between *two ways of inter-human presence*, *being* and *resembling*. The one (being) can be designated as living from the essence, the other (resembling) as living from the image, living as one would like to be seen. In general they occur in a mingled way (DDP 277).

"Let us take a situation in which the one looks at the other and in which both belong to the different basic types. The one looks at the other, like one looks at someone with whom one has a personal relationship. It is a spontaneous, open-minded look, which is of course influenced by the other to whom he wants to make himself understood. He is not influenced by thinking of the image that his look causes in the other. It is different with the second one, who cares more about the image, the first appearance. Because his look is the most expressive part of his appearance, he produces, 'makes', this look. In doing so he will, more or less apt, show a certain quality in his look, so that his look will work as spontaneous expression often effectively works. In the externity of this look an appropriated image appears, which presents itself to the other" (DDP 278). When the appearance comes from a lie and is maintained from the person him/herself, one essentially deceives the inter-human dimension. This is worse than telling a lie in which a matter is wrongly presented. The untruth that is shown here does not concern words or deeds, but existence itself, and it attacks the inter-human dimension itself. In this way someone wastes the possibility of the actual happening between You and I, purely and solely in order to caress his/her poor vanity (DDP 279). It is pernicious in such a diversion that it undermines the reliability of the person and of the encounter as such. Because the encounter is existentially important, appearance may damage the reliability of life itself.

The next important element in the dialogical is *perceiving the other*. This is absent when just 'talking'. In general people do not really talk to one another, although both are turned towards one another, in reality they are talking to a fictive person, whose "being there exists in just listening" (DDP 282). Our language respects this distinction. We talk *against*, *about* or *to* someone, rather than *with* someone. Only talking *with* someone can lead to encounter.

It is typical of the dialogical that one is prepared to feel through the *influence* that the other exerts and at the same time to exert influence on the other. Buber distinguishes between *two basis ways in which the other can be influenced*. In the first way one wants to affect the other and move him to something of which one thinks it is good for him/her. The second basic way of influencing tries to find and promote in the soul of the other what has been discovered in the own soul. The other has only to be disclosed in his/her potency, certainly not by pedantic teaching, but by kindness, by existential communication between someone who is and someone who can become (DDP 287). The one who forces, looks at the individual, the one who leaves space, believes in the basic power that has been sown in every person and that can grow to its own shape by interhuman kindness (DDP 288-290). The one who forces, thinks he/she knows what has to be changed in the other, the one who leaves space, believes that the destination lives in every person and that disclosing this is an act of creation. The work of disclosure leads both the one who gives as who receives to God (DDP 291-292).

Because of the clarity the monological is often presented as a dialogue. When encounter happens between several persons, this is considered community as communicative happening. Where the dialogical is no longer practised in society, dehumanisation of collectivity is imminent. "There is no connection between people, just clustering: compressed individual next to individual, commonly equipped, commonly trained, from man to man just as much life as is triggered. Community on the other hand, growing community is no longer being next to one another, but with one another, is jointly moving towards a goal, everywhere a going towards one another, a dynamic face-to-face, experienced influence from I to You. Community is where community happens. The collectivity is based on the organised reduction of the personality, the community facilitates personalities in promoting one another" (DDP 185).

Concretely applied to pastoral counselling. Buber draws attention to the fact that ethically correct pastoral counselling is impeded by the lack of 'independence', and by the dualistic attitude in the life of the pastor. Contact between pastor and counselling partner does not come into being as a practical link nor as a monologue disguised as a dialogue. In order to really encounter the counselling partner the pastor has to go out to the other as other. This does not happen when one loses oneself in the other of when one treats the other as 'everyone'. Diversion or just pretending is pernicious in pastoral counselling. Talking against, about or to someone is not the true discourse with a person. Thinking that one knows what the other has to do, and/or forcing the person to do so, is pastorally vain. When pastoral counselling is made impossible as a dialogue, society degenerates for the persons involved, its foundations are shaken.

III. Conclusion: Pastoral Counselling as Asymmetric Reciprocity

In the research into the way in which one can speak 'about' as well as 'with' the other, the distinction between the other as alter-ego and the transcendent other who appeals to me, who at times can be identified with the divine Other, presented itself. Using the language of Levinas, it is typical of pastoral care to approach the other as *autrui*. Whether this approach in counselling is also effectively realised depends on the way in which different moments in the process of counselling are handled. It is therefore a matter of repeatedly recognising the transcendence of the other. Going into the question of the relevance of Levinas's philosophy to pastoral care, I want to stress the importance that Levinas attaches to the answering, listening and speaking respect of the I for the other as *autrui*, applied to the pastor and his/her counselling partner.

For Levinas respect is not a principal starting point or a position of the 'I'; rather, respect is something that must be realised where the other appears in his/her otherness. No matter what his/her factual characteristics or problems may be, the other always has the right to be respected for who s/he was and is and can be, a human being with his/her own pathway of taking up responsibility. That is why speaking face-to-face with one another is the opportunity to endorse the transcendence of both. The dialogue is the place *par excellence* to realise this absolute respect in a mutual way, on the condition of a lasting and repeated focus on the appealing face of the other, whom I do not know but in whom I believe. I discovered Levinas's notion of dissymmetry, of reciprocal asymmetry by looking for some texts in which Levinas philosophises 'in' or 'from' the discourse. In his principal, major writings there are far more indications of philosophising 'about' the dialogue, which is a meta-viewpoint from which Levinas consequently only thinks from the other facing the 'I'. Only when he describes the experience of the face-to-face dialogue, we find both asymmetry and reciprocity.

From a standpoint of once and forever being touched (vocation) and recognised in their capacities and engagement (appointment), pastors have professionally chosen to commit themselves to the other(s) and to be there for the other(s). It is not evident whether they also effectively realise this commitment. The real possibility of violence through rhetorical indifference, assimilation, reduction, overpowering, etc., is a serious issue in pastoral counselling. Pastors nevertheless have a service-rooted task towards the other(s). For Levinas, this is a task for every human being; for the Church, it is also the pastor's job. In accordance with the working areas in which pastors are active, they enter into relation with marginal people especially, people who struggle with their contingent existence, and people with questions of faith. Within these relations pastors are committed to the faithful and/or spiritual well-being of the other. To this end, they make themselves familiar with this working area and the response to the otherness of the other becomes part of their life project. So far, pastoral care has been characterised by the initiative and the effort of the pastor. This, nevertheless, only serves to make room for the essence of it: to do justice to the other as a dignified human being, as a trace of the Infinite. Here the contribution of Levinas becomes crucial, here the focus is reversed and the other receives here his/her own language and story. Here the commitment of the pastor to the other turns into flesh and blood, the word becomes incarnated. In the pastoral dialogue, where the other appears to me face-to-face, the faith in the Infinite becomes concrete in the respect for *autrui*. Allowing oneself to be effectively and repeatedly 'here and now' disturbed by the otherness of this other allowing oneself to be determined by him/her and to commit oneself to him/her because of his/her face, defines the quality of the ethical attitude of the pastor. Here faith and ethics are intertwined. If indeed the other receives the opportunity to meet the pastor as a human being (beyond his 'being') and if the pastor is allowed to confirm the other in his/her becoming (as *autrui*), then their transcendence is mutually recognised and they both come to responsibility. Then both are who they are essentially 'beyond being': image of the Living God. And even if Levinas does not formulate his concept of the 'beyond being' as just described above, from a specifically Christian perspective of pastoral care, the Infinite surely is in their midst.

Buber lays different stresses than Levinas. He pays more attention to the distinction between authentic and inauthentic counselling. He tries to find the possible conditions for a real discourse. The pastor should develop 'independence' and be averse to a dualistic attitude to life. Buber also looks for the atmosphere that creates space for encounter. This is not practical but personal. Next he stresses the dialogical character of 'personal counselling'. One-way communication cannot create personal encounter. To pastors 'dialogical' means that they should be as a whole person concerned about the counselling partner. When they try the adventure of really setting off with the counselling partner, their own history, their own well-being and suffering vibrate too. Here Levinas and Buber encounter each other. What Buber calls 'bodily imagination' of the other, is for Levinas, in case of suffering, compassion (co-suffering).

The basis of the encounter is approaching the other as a unique person to whom the pastor himself in his/her unique pastorship makes him/herself available. Not the affected-friendly encounter but true concern should support the quality of pastoral counselling. By talking against, about or to someone the pastor and the counselling partner do not truly get into contact with each other. Thinking that one knows how life is for the counselling partner, what s/he has to do and making the counselling partner do what the pastor has in mind for him/her, damage the transcendence of the other.

Pastors also have a religious ground to be dialogically concerned about counselling partners: dialogical behaviour creates community. When a pastor believes that only God is God, we as humans, as children of God depend on one another as brothers and sisters. 'Building community' therefore is a secular expression for the fundamentally theological concept 'One God'. Where community is lacking, people remain behind as orphans. True discourse, dialogue from person to person, is the foundation of broader community building. By truly seeing the other and by showing oneself 'as pastor', people can taste something of the safety of God, a security from which they themselves can again go to others.

Levinas and Buber show us what our being human can constitute: truly speaking with the counselling partner, face-to-face, in which the pastor to the 'peculiar – unique' counselling partner from the bottom of his/her essence says: "After You".

Puursesteenweg 10
B-2880 Bornem
Belgium
Marina.Riemslagh@gmail.com

Marina RIEMSLAGH

THE PRACTICE OF RELATIONAL-ETHICAL PASTORAL CARE

AN INTERCULTURAL APPROACH

The purpose of this essay is to outline an intercultural approach to pastoral care[1] based on the relational ethics of Emmanuel Levinas. I will describe this intercultural approach as a three-part process. First, pastoral counsellors must be able to use a comparative approach to religion that highlights what is different about each person's religious faith – the "strangeness of the Other, his irreducibility to the I, to my thoughts and possessions"[2], such that "the absolutely foreign [aspects of those seeking care] can instruct us"[3]. Second, pastoral counsellors must cultivate a critical self-awareness of who they are spiritually and theologically, so that they do not unwittingly impose their religious meaning-making and practices on those seeking care. Such self-reflexivity and other-awareness will de-center pastoral counsellors and reveal the care-seeker as stranger and "other" in the *infini* (infinity), such that "the epiphany of the face as face opens up humanity"[4]. When this remarkable relational space opens up, the third and culminating moment of intercultural care is possible. This is when pastoral counsellors and care-seekers co-create contextual provisional meanings and ways of experiencing holiness[5]. As I elaborate this process, I will highlight how the relational ethics of Emmanuel Levinas[6] informs this intercultural approach to pastoral care.

1. Lartey's proposal (see E. LARTEY, *Pastoral Theology in an Intercultural World*, Cleveland, OH, Pilgrim, 2006) for an intercultural paradigm of pastoral care provides a framework that utilizes postmodern approaches to knowledge.

2. E. LEVINAS, *Totality and Infinity: An Essay on Exteriority*, trans. A. Lingis, London, Kluwer, 1988, p. 43.

3. ID., *Otherwise than Being or Beyond Essence*, trans. A. Lingis, The Hague, Martinus Nijhoff, 1979, p. 207.

4. ID., *The Temptation of Temptation*, in ID., *Nine Talmudic Readings*, trans. A. Aronowicz, Bloomington, IN – Indianapolis, IN, Indiana University Press, 1990, p. 234.

5. This opening up of oneself to the other arises from a radical recognition that this obligation to and responsibility for the other comes first. See R.A. COHEN, *Maternal Psyche*, in E. GANTT – R. WILLIAMS (eds.), *Psychology for the Other: Levinas, Ethics and the Practice of Psychology*, Pittsburgh, PA, Duquesne University Press, 2002, 32-64, p. 42: "To say 'the self is for-the-other' does not mean that first there is a self and then this self becomes 'for-the-other' but rather that insofar as the self is for-the-other it is itself. Its original way of being is moral".

6. Levinas, in a conversation with Derrida: J. DERRIDA, *Adieu to Emmanuel Levinas*, trans. P. Brault – M. Nass, Stanford, CA, Stanford University Press, 1999, p. 4: "You

I. Using a Phenomenological Comparative Approach that Respects Differences

Levinas's description of Western philosophy can be transposed upon Western theologies, to highlight how pastoral counsellors unwittingly impose religious meanings and interpretations on others: "Western philosophy has most often been an ontology: a reduction of the other to the same by interposition of a middle and neutral term that ensures comprehension of being"[7]. Ontology is used as a way of "apprehending the individual (which alone exists) not in its individuality but in its generality"[8]. The temptation of knowledge, described by Levinas as the temptation of temptation, "will no longer leave the other in its otherness but always include it in its whole ... From this stems the inability to recognize the other person as other person, as outside all calculation, as neighbor, as first come"[9].

One of the ways in which pastoral counsellors and, more generally, members of religious communities have "reduced the other to the same" is in the theological or universalistic comparative approach they take to religions other than their own. Pastoral counsellors who simply use their theology to interpret the care-seeker's narrative, practices, and meaning systems may believe in an exclusivist way that their meaning system is the only true meaning system. In an inclusivist theological approach that seemingly embraces the "truth" of all religious faiths, pastoral counsellors assume that all other meaning systems can be translated into their meaning system; for example, that everyone is an unconscious Christian whether they realize it or not.

When pastoral counsellors use this comparative approach covertly (without conscious awareness) they can easily end up submerging the other person's religious faith within their own. Paden notes, "Spiritual caregivers all tend naturally to reduce areas of [a care receiver's] life to certain uses that fit their own worldview"[10]. Given the coercive and violent history of Christianity's participation in colonialism, pastoral counsellors need to be aware of the implicit comparative method underlying their practices of care, lest they colonize the religious or spiritual

know, one often speaks of ethics to describe what I do, but what really interests me in the end is not ethics, not ethics alone, but the holy, the holiness of the holy".

7. Levinas, *Totality and Infinity* (n. 2), p. 43.

8. *Ibid.*, p. 44.

9. Id., *The Temptation of Temptation* (n. 4), p. 35.

10. W.E. Paden, *Religious Worlds: The Comparative Study of Religion*, Boston, MA, Beacon Press, 1994 (2nd ed.), p. 2.

world of those who are not Christians. Levinas's experience of anti-Semitism made him acutely aware of the potential for violence when differences are not acknowledged: "According to Levinas, the core of racism consists not in the denial of, or failure to appreciate, similarities between people, but in the denial of, or better said, failure to appreciate and value, people's differences, or better still, the fundamental and irreducible otherness by which they fall outside of every genre and are thus 'unique'"[11]. Levinas's use of the ethical imperative, "Thou shalt not kill" continually reminds pastoral counsellors that failure to value difference can and has been part of insidious and horrifically overt webs of violence that desecrate that which is holy: the 'other' that pastoral counsellors encounter when they recognize the differences between their religious faith and a care-seeker's.

Pastoral counsellors using a universalistic comparative approach believe that all religions of the world have a common core. Like the Christian theological approach this universalistic approach has a long history dating back to antiquity. When used by Christians, this approach often resembles a Christian theological comparative method, in that the common core is invariably most like Christian religious traditions. This tendency can be seen among Western scholars creating taxonomies of the religions of the world from the 17th century onwards. Initially they came up with four classifications: Jewish, Christian, Muslim, and pagan. By the middle of the 19th century a longer list of ten to twelve "world religions" was created, which is still used today. Masuzawa demonstrates that these 19th century scholars used a theological approach that assumed the universality of Christianity. She argues that

> ... the new discourse of pluralism and diversity of religions, when it finally broke out into the open and became an established practice in the first half of the twentieth century, neither displaced nor disabled the logic of European hegemony – formerly couched in the language of the universality of Christianity – but, in a way, gave it a new lease[12].

In other words, a Christian theological method often is embedded in the ways in which world religions are categorized and taught in comparative methods courses and textbooks. The insidious myopia that sees all religions of the world through the lens of Christianity can be corrected

11. R. BURGGRAEVE, *Violence and the Vulnerable Face of the Other: The Vision of Emmanuel Levinas on Moral Evil and Our Responsibility*, in *Journal of Social Philosophy* 30 (1999) 29-45, p. 29.

12. T. MASUZAWA, *The Invention of World Religions: Or, How European Universalism Was Preserved in the Language of Pluralism*, Chicago, IL, University of Chicago Press, 2005, p. xiv.

with Levinas's insistence that pastoral counsellors not "kill" the otherness of care-seekers' religious faith by covertly using a Christian theological or universalizing comparative approach.

Another instance of how religious difference is insidiously obliterated and a Christian theological approach extinguishes the uniqueness of the other's tradition can be found among health professionals who develop spiritually-oriented approaches to healthcare and who do not draw upon current debates in the comparative study of religion. For example, psychologists often rely on the work of a single scholar of world religions, a practice that would be considered psychologically naïve if they were only relying upon one psychologist to represent the field of psychological studies[13]. They "assume one god, 'God' – with a capital G – to be the reality behind all worlds and religions"[14].

In order to offer care that respects and does not erase the otherness of a care-seeker's religious faith, pastoral counsellors need to use a phenomenological approach that pays attention to the differences between the unique religious, spiritual, and existential meaning systems and practices that each person constructs out of her or his various relational matrices. The term religious world, coined by William Paden in his comparative studies of religion, can be used to describe each person's religious faith as a habitat, "a system of language and practice that organizes the world in terms of what is deemed sacred"[15]. From a relational perspective, we can understand each person's religious world as a syncretistic compilation of multiple religious and spiritual symbols, beliefs, and schema, all generated out of the web of relationships in which they are embedded. Bourdieu's concept of *habitus* as "embodied history, internalized as a second nature"[16] can be used to describe such religious practices[17]. Often the only way to identify what is in one's

13. See, for example, T.G. Plante, *Spiritual Practices in Psychotherapy: Thirteen Tools for Enhancing Psychological Health*, Washington, DC, American Psychological Association, 2009. Plante bases his comparative understanding of religions of the world on H. Smith, *The World's Religions: Our Great Wisdom Traditions*, San Francisco, CA, HarperSanFrancisco, 1991, which is a revised and expanded edition of H. Smith, *The Religions of Man*, San Francisco, CA, HarperSanFrancisco, 1958. Similarly, P.S. Richards – A.E. Bergin, *A Spiritual Strategy for Counseling and Psychotherapy* (Washington, DC, American Psychological Association, 2005, 2nd ed.) rely upon one comparative scholar: N. Smart, *Religions of the West*, Englewood Cliffs, NJ, Prentice Hall, 1994.

14. *Ibid.*, p. 121.

15. Paden, *Religiuous Worlds* (n. 10), p. 10.

16. P. Bourdieu, *The Logic of Practice*, Cambridge, MA, Polity Press, 1992, p. 56.

17. See E. Graham – H. Walton – F. Ward, *Theological Reflection: Methods*, London, SCM Press, 2007, p. 194: "Bourdieu is presenting a model of tradition and continuity by which the values of the past are encoded in social life yet continually evolve

religious world is to dialogue with others (through reading and conversations) about one's practices[18].

For those of us raised in individualistic Western cultures, we experience our religious world as a bounded set of beliefs, values, practices, and stories. When someone asks us to describe our spiritual journey, it is as if they have invited themselves into our spiritual or religious home. To us it feels as if there is a clear boundary demarking this highly personal religious world we have constructed over time. However, it is often the outsider who can see how much the various relational matrices in which we are embedded (our family of origin, formative relationships generated in life-giving, life-limiting, and life-threatening encounters, relationships within communities of faith, etc.) continually engage us in an ongoing process of world-making. As Paden notes, "To the inhabitant, the world is a singular experience and has an absoluteness; to the observer, it is an instance of common processes of construction and function"[19]. What we identify as self-contained meaning systems are, in Paden's words, "Worlds [that] are the ever-changing precipitates of process of selection and transmission by which individuals chose imagined continuities from the past and versions of the past that applied to the present"[20]. While the term religious world helps us visualize the uniqueness of each person's religious faith and spirituality, it doesn't help us appreciate how religious worlds are continually constructed and reconstructed within relational matrices, and not "within" a person's mind. For this reason, I prefer a related somewhat cumbersome term coined by Paden[21] – religious world-making – to describe this ongoing process of putting into practice the religious and spiritual meanings and values formed out of these relational matrices.

… [Similarly] Christians [can be described] as participating in and reshaping a living faith through their contemporary practices of worship, care, and social concern".

18. Here religion, spirituality, and theology are understood as performative knowledge rather than propositional knowledge, and praxis as the way in which communities and persons embody and enact their beliefs. The intercultural spiritual care process I describe follows Elaine Graham's inductive method of critical phenomenology (E. GRAHAM, *Transforming Practice: Pastoral Theology in an Age of Uncertainty*, New York, NY, Mowbray, 1996). This method begins with dialogue that identifies the concrete experiential theology that persons and communities enact in their practices. Intercultural spiritual care becomes an occasion for constructing a public critical account of the faith claims embedded in practices.

19. W.E. PADEN, *Theaters of Worldmaking Behaviors: Panhuman Contexts for Comparative Religion*, in T.A. IDINOPULOS – B.C. WILSON – J.C. HANGES (eds.), *Comparing Religions: Possibilities and Perils?*, Boston, MA, Brill, 2006, 59-74, p. 62.

20. *Ibid.*, p. 63.

21. *Ibid.*

A phenomenological approach to comparing the religious world-making of pastoral counsellors and care-seekers utilizes various aspects of postmodern approaches to knowledge:

- a perspectival understanding of religious knowledge as socially constructed[22];
- reflexivity that allows one to deliberate "on a given construction of the world from multiple, diverging standpoints"[23];
- an appreciation for the performative[24] and constructive nature of theology.

Pastoral counsellors may hesitate to use this comparative approach because of its postmodern orientation. Postmodern approaches to religious knowledge seem at first to open a deep fissure between first order religious expressions that imply universal faith claims (like confessions of faith, liturgies, prayers, and hymns) and second order languages that provide critical perspectives on religious sources of authority (like theological, historical, and biblical critical perspectives) used within their community of learning at graduate school. When pastoral counsellors experience the liberating possibilities of postmodern approaches to religious knowledge[25], then it can seem as though the same fissure separates them from communities of faith that most often use pre-critical first order religious language. This fissure or gap can be bridged, however, when they practice spiritual care using a relational ethic. Students can learn how to establish relationships in which they step into the

22. It is important to note that "social constructionism is not a singular and unified theory. Rather, it is better seen as an unfolding dialogue among participants who vary considerably in their logics, values, and visions. While there is substantial sharing, there is no single slate of assumptions to which all would adhere. Indeed, to establish a final truth, a foundational logic, a code of values, or a slate of practices would be antithetical to the very unfolding of meaning championed by the movement" (K.J. GERGEN, *Therapeutic Realities: Collaboration, Oppression and Relational Flow*, Chagin Falls, OH, Taos Institute Publications, 2006, p. 17).

23. *Ibid.*, p. 183.

24. GRAHAM, *Transforming Practice* (n. 18).

25. What Sheila McNamee says about psychology applies even more to religious people and communities. See S. MCNAMEE, *Comment on the Incredible Possibilities of Being*, in *Journal of Constructivist Psychology* 18 (2005) 345-348, p. 346: "Yet, in traditional psychology, the focus is, indeed, on the past and its relationship to the present and, by association, its implications for the future. With such an emphasis on the past, there is little room for *imagining* the future in a constructive, proactive manner. The potential to sediment the past, to reify the story, and thereby make it static and immutable is tremendous". Note also these comments by GERGEN, *Therapeutic Realities* (n. 22), p. 20: "Thus, social constructionism first serves an enormous liberating function. It removes the rhetorical power of anyone or any group claiming truth, wisdom, or ethics of universal scope - necessary for all".

pre-critical religious language used within the community of faith, appreciating the psychological, spiritual, and communal need to act as if this shared language points to transhistorical and universal religious truths.

It can be reassuring for pastoral counsellors to realize that in most contexts, people continually shift back and forth among what could be called premodern, modern, and postmodern approaches to knowledge; for example, from precritical or premodern approaches to religious knowledge to modern approaches to scientific knowledge. Using the metaphor of trifocal lenses, I suggest that pastoral counsellors use the lens of premodern approaches to religious knowledge to assess whether people are yearning for an immediate sense of God's presence or a sense of holiness in a pre-critical way similar to how God was experienced in the premodern traditions of Christianity. Pastoral counsellors can help members of Muslim, Jewish, or Christian faith traditions use a modern lens when they are ready to turn to the Koran, the Hebrew Bible or New Testament for help in meaning making; they can be encouraged to think critically about how this source of authority can help them make sense of their lives. Modern psychological approaches to understanding how people use religion to cope with stress can also be helpful in assessing when someone's religious world-making is correlated with stress-related spiritual and psychological growth or struggles[26].

In the long term process of helping people make sense of what is happening to them, pastoral counsellors can assess when people are ready to use a postmodern lens to appreciate the contextual and provisional nature of knowledge, including knowledge of God and that which is experienced as holy. This postmodern lens brings into view the importance of intrinsically meaningful religious and spiritual experiences that emerge from the particular cultural, communal, and family narratives of people[27].

In my use of the terms premodern, modern, and postmodern lenses, I am referring more to styles of religious knowledge and not to historical periods, similar to how Lyotard uses the terms realism, modernism, and postmodernism, all of which coexist and are available in contemporary cultures[28]. Radical shifts in religious world-making occur at historical

26. K. PARGAMENT, *The Psychology of Religion and Coping: Theory, Research, Practice*, New York, NY, Guilford, 1997; ID., *Spiritually Integrated Psychotherapy: Understanding and Addressing the Sacred*, New York, NY, Guilford, 2007.

27. C. DOEHRING, *The Practice of Pastoral Care: A Postmodern Approach*, Louisville, KY, Westminster John Knox Press, 2006.

28. Realism is part of conventional world-making utilizing "a point of view that would give [the world] a recognizable meaning" in order to "decode images and sequences

moments when realism collapses. Vial draws an analogy "between the destruction of the Temple in ancient Israel, which was the locus of the divine and the place of communication and interaction with the divine, and the role the Bible played for Protestants (sola scriptura!) ... The destruction of the Temple (which required a complete re-thinking of divine presence and communication that became rabbinic Judaism) is similar to the way many Protestants experienced the Enlightenment – the rise of science and especially of historical criticism [that] took away the one secure place of revelation and communication [the Bible], and occasioned in the 19th century a massive theological re-thinking of divine presence and human/divine communication"[29]. As religious cultures assimilate symbols that are initially presented in a postmodern style as unpresentable, and as they find ways to analyze and systemically explore these symbols often in ways that imply a sense of progress (using modern approaches to knowledge), the symbols eventually become realistic – equated with what is holy. Some theologians argue that such symbols are idolatrous; it is only when they are broken through some challenge that reveals their otherness, that the now-broken symbols regain the capacity to represent that which is unpresentable[30].

II. Using our Theological Education to Develop Critical Self-Awareness about our Religious World-Making

In order to utilize an intercultural approach to understand the differences between our religious meaning-making and the meaning-making of others, pastoral counsellors need to have a critical awareness of who they are, spiritually and theologically. They need to have resources, relationships, and communities of discourse and accountability that help them critically reflect upon the habitual qualities of their religious world-making which will be unwittingly used as a lens to interpret the religious world-

rapidly ... protect[ing] consciousness from doubt" (J. Lyotard, *An Answer to the Question: What is the Postmodern?*, in Id., *The Postmodern Explained*, trans. D. Barry – B. Maher – J. Pefanis – V. Spate – M. Thomas, Minneapolis, MN, University of Minnesota Press, 1992, pp. 5-6). Modernism and postmodernism "present the existence of something unpresentable. Showing that there is something we can conceive of that we can neither see nor show" (*ibid.*, p. 11). In modernism the unpresentable is "invoked only by absent content, while the form, thanks to its recognizable consistency, continues to offer the reader material for consolation or pleasure" while postmodernism "invokes the unpresentable in presentation itself" (*ibid.*, pp. 14, 15).

29. T. Vial, Personal Communication.

30. R. Neville, *The Truth of Broken Symbols*, Albany, NY, Suny, 1996.

making of those seeking care. A religious and theological education and academic community provides them initially with relational ways of identifying and reflecting upon the spiritual and religious beliefs and practices embedded in their religious world-making since childhood, and the layers of meanings and practices that have accrued over a lifetime. Reflecting critically on the relational matrices that shape their religious world-making can help them identify how they may be using embedded theologies that potentially marginalize or dehumanize others or even themselves.

Their theological education and community of scholars and practitioners thus equip pastoral counsellors to pay attention to what is going on in their religious world-making by monitoring and evaluating theologically whether the religious symbols and practices that are activated under stress are truly life-giving for them in their current context. In order to provide spiritual care that does not violate the other, they have to develop this relational and communal capacity to understand and monitor what is going on in their religious world-making. Without such communal critical reflection, pastoral counsellors risk functioning in theologically naïve ways. Such naïveté is common now among health practitioners without any formal or informal theological education who practice at the intersection of health and spirituality, and who unwittingly impose their religious or spiritual world-making on others because they are not using second order language or participating in a community of theological accountability[31].

The diagram below (p. 169) visually depicts the relational process of religious world-making, along with the matrices that help a pastoral counsellor like myself be critically aware of what is going on in my religious world-making. The box in the center represents my ongoing process of making meaning and putting into practice religious values and beliefs. I have identified four primary relational matrices engaged in this process of religious world-making that arises out of ongoing "conversations" within these four matrices. The upper quadrants represent the relational matrices I have internalized from my formative years. The "conversations" I have, for example, within my family of origin are largely internal and unconscious[32]. These conversations often put into practice an embedded

31. C. DOEHRING, *Theological Accountability: The Hallmark of Pastoral Counseling*, in *Sacred Spaces* 1 (2009), http://www.aapc.org/sacredspaces/185 (accessed June 3, 2009).

32. Gergen describes the influence of such formative relationships as "traces of myriad relationships, past and present, existing or imagined. These traces essentially equip us with multiple and often conflicting potentials for action" (K.J. GERGEN, *Relational Being: Beyond Self and Community*, New York, NY, Oxford University Press, 2002, p. 397).

theology[33] expressed in first-order religious language statements about religious beliefs[34].

The upper right hand quadrant represents relationships formed when I first critically engaged my childhood religion and soon began theological studies in 1975. These relationships gave me initial ways to deliberate over this embedded theology through the second order religious languages of biblical critical and theological studies.

The lower quadrants represent ongoing matrices active in my life now. Participating in my community of faith (lower left hand quadrant) provides a context for me to engage in religious world-making where I can experience a "second naïveté"[35] such that, for moments during communal worship, it is as if my religious world-making is wholly true for me. I can express my religious beliefs and experiences in first order language, realizing that such beliefs are true for me in the moment. The lower right hand corner represents my ongoing communities of theological accountability, which include the ongoing reading and scholarly work I do in

33. Embedded religion is a term used to describe the implicit beliefs, values, and practices we live out in our everyday lives (H. STONE – J. DUKE, *How To Think Theologically*, Minneapolis, MN, Augsburg Fortress Press, 2006, 2nd ed.). They are so woven into our habitual ways of viewing the world and understanding peoples' lives that they are not even aware of them.The process of examining embedded beliefs engages people in the work of deliberative religion. They begin to examine critically which of their beliefs and practices are meaningful to them as adults.

34. Jennings uses the terms first, second, and third order religious language to make distinctions among expressions of religious faith, critical reflections on religious faith, and reflections on methodology (for example, methods of relating different disciplinary perspectives to each other and to the practice of care). See: T.W. JENNINGS, Jr., *Pastoral Theological Methodology*, in R.J. HUNTER (ed.), *Dictionary of Pastoral Care and Counseling*, Nashville, TN, Abingdon, 1990, 862-864. Gergen makes a similar distinction between first-order morality ("the potential for all relations to generate moral goods ... generating first order commitment to the good") and second-order morality ("a non-foundational ethic for sustaining the very possibility of co-creating the good") (GERGEN, *Relational Being* [n. 32], p. 354) (cf. also the Epilogue 'Relational Ethics and Missing Voices' in this volume).

35. Ricoeur distinguishes primitive naïveté from second naïveté: "If we can no longer live the great symbols of the sacred in accordance with the original belief in them, we can, we modern men [and women], aim at a second naïveté in and through criticism. In short, it is by *reinterpreting* that we can *hear* again..." (P. RICOEUR, *The Symbolism of Evil*, trans. E. Buchanan, New York, NY, Harper & Row, 1967 [Original French edition 1960], p. 351). "I believe that [the holy] can still speak to me – no longer, of course, under the precritical form of immediate belief, but as the second immediacy aimed at by hermeneutics. This second naïveté aims to be the post critical equivalent of the precritical hierophany" (*ibid*., p. 352). Ricoeur's notion of a second naïveté has been taken up by Biblical critical scholars, even after Ricoeur himself abandoned this idea. See P. VANDERMEERSCH, *The Failure of Second Naïveté: Some Landmarks in the History of French Psychology*, in J.A. BELZEN (ed.), *Aspects in Contexts: Studies in the History of Psychology of Religion*, Amsterdam, Rodopi, 2000, 235-280. Zygmunt Bauman highlights how "postmodernity can be seen as restoring to the world what modernity, presumptuously, had taken away from it; as a *re-enchantment* of the world that modernity tried hard to *disenchant*" (Z. BAUMAN, *Intimations of Postmodernity*, London, Routledge, 1992, p. x).

religious and theological studies. These relationships help me continually assess whether the religious and theological meanings constructed in my religious world-making and lived out in my practices are part of life-giving, life-limiting, or violent relational webs.

Over the years I have tried to identify the ways in which the values, beliefs, and practices through which I connect with a sense of holiness are shaped by these relational matrices. For example, the "default" way I often use to make sense of personal suffering is a moralistic theology in which I am identified as a sinner, often in shameful ways. Within this moralistic theology I can only reconnect with a sense of holiness through some sort of private repentance that involves being a "good girl". In other words, when "something bad" happens to me, I automatically converse with my childhood ways of making sense of the world and connecting with a sense of holiness, using a pre-critical embedded religion that makes me feel "bad". If I am paying attention, I can draw upon other relational matrices to process this feeling, name the embedded theology that is operant and critically engage it. In this way I can be part of an ongoing relational process that disentangles me from life-limiting or even violent relational webs in which I can become caught or catch others; instead, I can engage in life-giving relational webs that reveal otherness.

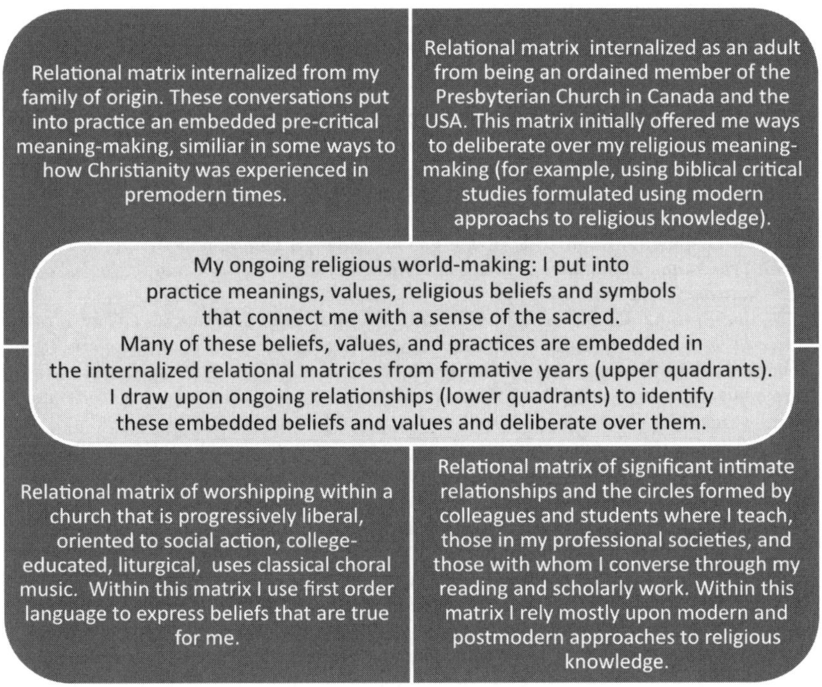

III. Dwelling with the Other

Using a phenomenological comparative approach, pastoral counsellors will more likely experience the otherness of the religious world-making of those seeking care. Their self-awareness about the relational matrices in which their own religious world-making is embedded will help pastoral counsellors identify their usual horizons of meaning. These approaches to the care-seeker's and their own religious world-making will help them transcend habitual ways of thinking about their own and the care-seeker's religious-world-making, so that these are not imposed on the pastoral care encounter in life-limiting or violent ways. Using these approaches and practices, pastoral counsellors are more likely to become immersed in the moment of immediacy[36] that occurs "before the presence of reflective and categorical 'thought'[37]. As Diedrich, Burggraeve, and Gastmans so eloquently note,

> It is in this moment that the other is, or can be, before me in and of herself. Levinas describes this moment as coming into contact with the *face of the other* ... The face is a living, naked presence ... This immediate moment of coming into contact with the face is a moment of transcendence, a kind of deliverance, if you will, from the ordinary structures of being[38].

In other words, pastoral counsellors will use these forms of reflective and categorical thought – a phenomenological comparative approach and theological self awareness – in order to transcend the categories of thought that usually inhibit their experience of the care-seeker's otherness[39]. By not imposing their own religious-world-making on others and

36. Levinas uses the term 'proximity' to describe such immediacy. See E. Levinas, *Otherwise than Being* (n. 3), p. 81.

37. W. Diedrich – R. Burggraeve – C. Gastmans, *A Dialogue between the Thought of Joan Tronto and Emmanuel Levinas*, in *Ethical Perspectives: Journal of the European Ethics Network* 13 (2006) 33-61, p. 42.

38. *Ibid.*, pp. 42-43. See also D. Boileau, *Preface*, in R. Burggraeve, *The Wisdom of Love in the Service of Love: Emmanuel Levinas on Justice, Peace, and Human Rights*, Milwaukee, WI, Marquette University Press, 2002, p. 18 "The face of the other is the discrete but imperative word that affects me and appeals to me neither to use force nor to misuse, violate, totalize, hate or destroy the other: 'Thou shalt not kill'".

39. Nicholas J. Fox makes a distinction between 'care as discipline' (for example, the contract of care that puts into practice professional codes of conduct) and the 'gift of care' "mediated by love, generosity, trust and delight" (N.J. Fox, *Beyond Health, Postmodernism and Embodiment*, London, Free Association Press, 1999, p. 78). Greenwood illustrates this distinction in analyzing an incident between a nurse practitioner and person diagnosed with dementia that he describes using Levinas's notion of the non-intentional where the otherness of the person is experienced (D. Greenwood, *Relational Care: Learning to Look beyond Intentionality to the 'Non-Intentional' in a Caring Relationship*, in *Nursing Philosophy* 8 [2007] 223-232).

by recognizing the otherness of the religious world-making of those seeking care, pastoral counsellors open themselves up to the alterity of the care-seeker's religious world-making.

This opening up of oneself to the other arises from a radical recognition that this obligation to and responsibility for the other comes first[40]. This is a relational way of understanding the very nature of what it means to be human, and the ways in which to be human is to be in these kinds of caring relationships: "To say 'the self is for-the-other' does not mean that first there is a self and then this self becomes 'for-the-other,' but rather that insofar as the self is for-the-other it is itself. Its original way of being is moral"[41]. In a more practical sense, opening one's self up to the other in pastoral counselling means being fully present in the moment and letting go of the usual tools and techniques of pastoral counselling:

> Dwelling-with is a standing open to the being of the other person as radical otherness. Rather than pursuing a particular mode of therapy with a particular client-type in order to realize a particular outcome (utopia), one stands open to genuine otherness – a world of mystery which cannot be adequately appropriated by preconceived categories or totalizing systems ... We offer ourselves up as a 'being-for' in ethical response to the call of the other whom we find here before us: the stranger, the widow, and the orphan[42].

This unconditional ethical responsibility is called goodness by Levinas; it is "neither naive or trivial, but rather the difficult struggle, never with obvious victory, to overcome racism and anti-Semitism, the most extreme forms of moral evil"[43]. For pastoral counsellors, the moment when they surrender to their ethical responsibility for the other has theological meanings:

> The other stands in a position over me because the other is that person who pulls me out of myself, which effects transcendence. The other stands above me as the only one who offers an alternative to dwelling within the labyrinthine circuits of my own interiority[44].

40. For a clarifying discussion of how the asymmetrical relationship of the ethical relationship between the care-seeker and the pastoral counsellor is balanced with the pastoral counsellor's responsibility for what Levinas calls third parties and oneself, see DIEDRICH – BURGGRAEVE – GASTMANS, *A Dialogue between the Thought of Joan Tronto and Emmanuel Levinas* (n. 37), pp. 45-50.

41. COHEN, *Maternal Psyche* (n. 5), p. 42.

42. E. GANTT, *Utopia, Psychotherapy, and the Place of Suffering*, in GANTT – WILLIAMS (eds.), *Psychology for the Other* (n. 5), p. 81.

43. BOILEAU, *Preface* (n. 38), p. 18.

44. DIEDRICH – BURGGRAEVE – GASTMANS, *A Dialogue between the Thought of Joan Tronto and Emmanuel Levinas* (n. 37), p. 50.

Such transcendence allows pastoral counsellors to experience both the radical otherness of the one seeking care and the radical Otherness of whatever they name as transcendent: God or infinity or holiness. This transcendence and experience of alterity creates a relational space in which contextual provisional meanings and ways of experiencing holiness can be co-created, as I represented in the following diagram. I have depicted the way the religious world-making processes of pastoral counsellor and care-seeker interact. I have described this interaction using an action-reflection-action method of theological reflection[45] (p. 73), paraphrasing the way pastoral theologian Loren Townsend describes this method[46].

In what follows, I will develop a brief case study that illustrates this intercultural approach to pastoral care, using the 2003 Québécois film, *Les Invasions Barbares*, directed and written by Denys Arcand[47].

IV. An Illustration

Les Invasions Barbares can be used to provide a lively case study of how a Roman Catholic chaplain in a Montréal hospital, Sister Constance Lazare, offers pastoral care to Rémy, a terminally ill man in his fifties. In addition, a relationship that Rémy has with a young woman named

45. Elaine Graham was one of the first pastoral theologians to describe pastoral practice as an encounter with alterity: "Through pastoral encounter with others, participants will experience the paradox of familiarity and otherness which situates them within, and draws them beyond, the present and immediate. Can we regard authentic pastoral practice, therefore, as that which draws us into encounter with the 'other', towards a deeper understanding of our own identity-in-relation? The process of going beyond the situated and concrete in the encounter with the other may also serve as a metaphor for the human experience of the transcendent. It speaks of an encounter with transcendence and authentic faith occurring at the very point of loss of certainty and self-possession: divine activity and presence encountered in the mystery of alterity" (Graham, *Transforming Practice* [n. 18], pp. 206-207).

46. Loren Townsend describes this method of theological reflection as hermeneutical circulation: L. Townsend, *Introduction to Pastoral Counseling*, Nashville, TN, Abingdon Press, 2009, p. 140.

47. The film takes its title from a scene that replays news footage of the planes crashing into the twin towers on September 11, followed by footage from a commentary by Québec historian Alain Lussier who says that the terrorists "struck at the heart of the Empire. In previous conflicts – Korea, Vietnam, the Gulf War – the Empire managed to keep the barbarians outside its gates, its borders. In that sense people may look back at 9/11, and I stress may, as the beginning of the great barbarian invasion". In the film, Remy also alludes to his cancer and approaching death as a kind of barbarian invasion. In his final moment of life as he drifts into a heroin-induced coma clutching his son's hands, he murmurs "The barbarians are coming".

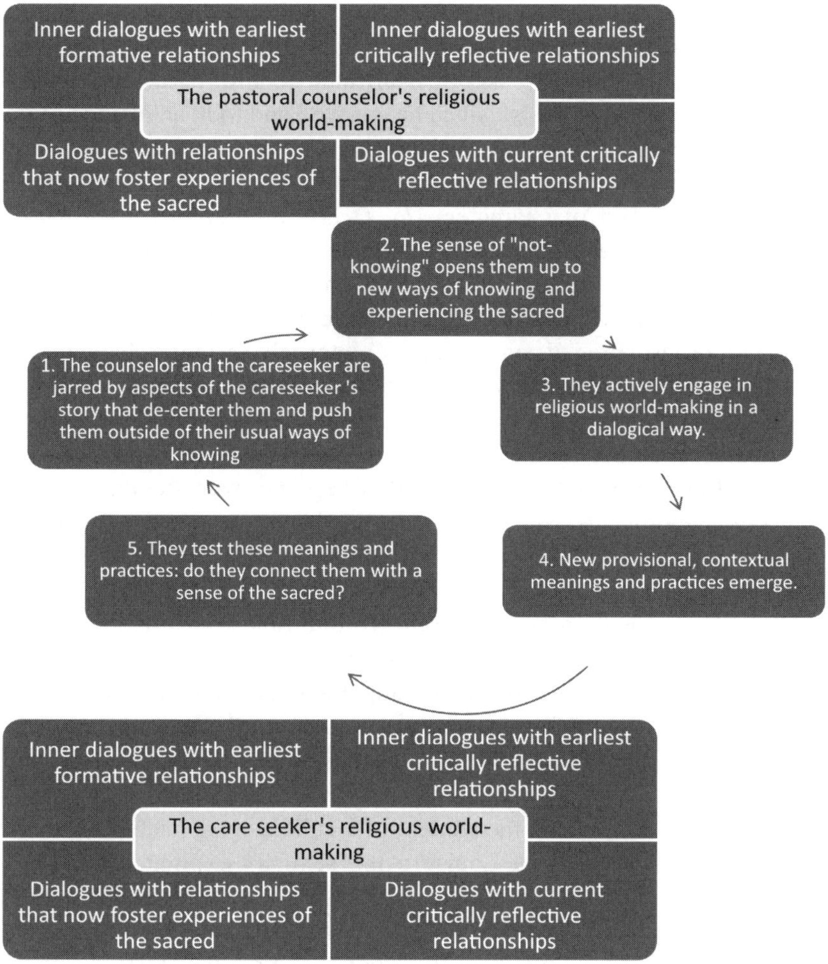

Nathalie offers a form of what we could call existential care. These care-giving relationships provide relational opportunities for Rémy to engage in existential world-making that help him approach death.

Rémy was educated by the Jesuits in a pre-Vatican II era in Québec and then entered young adulthood during Québec's quiet revolution in the mid 1960s. This was a time when many young intellectuals, drawing upon the rigors of their Jesuit education, were catapulted from the kind of premodern religiosity that typified the Duplessis-era[48] in Québec into

48. Maurice Duplessis was Québec's premier from 1936 to 1939 and 1944 to 1959, a period of Québec's history now known as *La Grande Noirçeur* ("The Great Darkness"), in part because of the Duplessis Orphans (*les Orphelins de Duplessis*) – several thousand

the beginnings of postmodern intellectualism. Rémy has been a history professor, and he and many of his circle of friends and colleagues have adopted a philosophically skeptical attitude to life[49]. Rémy describes himself as a sensual socialist, since he enjoyed and took advantage of the sexual revolution of the 1960s and 1970s by having sexual relationships with colleagues and students. As Arcand portrayed in the (1986) movie with this same cast of characters (*Le Déclin de l'Empire Américain*), Rémy enjoyed wine, women, and intellectual banter to excess.

The pastoral care conversations with Constance depicted in the movie illustrate the complex relationship they develop, which includes challenging, humorous, enraged, sorrowful, and intensely caring exchanges. The first two conversations the viewer sees have jarring qualities. The first occurs when the chaplain arrives bearing the sacrament of communion. She addresses Rémy by the wrong name and before she can offer communion, Rémy remonstrates, saying that he is not who she thinks he is. Constance apologizes. She complains that her computer list of Roman Catholic patients is often wrong and then she introduces herself to Rémy as Constance Lazare. He introduces the woman at his bedside as Louise, his wife. Constance offers a consoling word to Louise, saying that it must be hard having her husband in the hospital. Louise is quick to correct Constance's image of her as the distraught and devoted wife, saying that she threw Rémy out fifteen years ago. In the next breathe she says she really doesn't care whether he is in the hospital or having sex with one of his co-ed students. Rémy retorts that his current sexual partner isn't one of his students; she is the student of a colleague. A heated argument erupts between them, with Louise using sexually explicit language to describe Rémy's sexual misconduct with his students. The chaplain looks surprised and quickly bids farewell, saying, "I best continue my rounds! Have a good day!" Rémy cheerily responds, "You, too, Sister".

In this first encounter, Rémy and Louise vigorously jar various images the chaplain has of them. Rémy is not a terminally ill Catholic patient requesting the sacrament. Louise's suffering as Rémy's wife at this moment has less to do with his cancer and more to do with his sexual

orphaned children (often of unwed mothers) who were falsely certified as mentally ill by the provincial government in order to receive federal funds. Many of them were raised in psychiatric institutions.

49. In one humorous scene, Rémy and his friends take turns chanting a list of ideologies they have fervently adopted: "We've been everything ... At first we were existentialists. We read Sartre and Camus. Then [reading] Fanon, we became anticolonialists. We read Marcuse and became Marxists. Marxists-Leninists. Trotskyites. Maoists. After Solzhenitsyn we changed. We were structuralists, situationists, feminists, deconstructionists. Is there an "ism" we haven't worshipped"?

promiscuity with his students and colleagues. It is if they are saying, "Welcome to our worlds and the ways in which we are living with terminal cancer". It would be easy for this chaplain to conclude that this kind of welcome is a way for Rémy and Louise to close the door to further conversations.

As viewers we don't know what happens between this first conversation and the next one we see. We can only conclude that the chaplain has had enough conversations that she is now the one who challenges Rémy. In her opening salvo she declares that he is lucky to have such a caring son and that not many sons remain at their parents' bedsides. She asks Rémy about how he cared for his father when he was hospitalized at the end of his life. Did he visit? Rémy shrugs and protests that his father lived in Chicoutimi and he was in Montréal, about eighty miles away. The chaplain is quick to "remind" Rémy pointedly that his son has come from London, England to care for him. With a steely look she asks whether coming from London and coming from Chicoutimi are the same thing, and whether he is becoming confused. Rémy looks chagrined. In this conversation it is the chaplain who jars Rémy's existential world in order to see if Rémy can break out of his negative stereotypes of his son as an Americanized capitalist and see him in a new light.

These two conversations suggest that Rémy and the chaplain are honest with each other by disclosing what is going on in their religious or existential world-making. In Rémy's existential world-making, he is living out a legacy of sexualizing relationships with students and experiencing the impact of this behavior on his wife and son. His ideologies, which lead him to dismiss his son as a capitalist, are blinding him to the quality of his son's caring. The disclosure of this kind of meaning-making going on in Rémy's world is jarring for the chaplain. She hangs in there with him, jarring him with her religious world-making, and the sense she makes of complex father-son relationships.

The third conversation we see occurs after Rémy has found out that his cancer is inoperable. His son wants to bring Rémy to a hospital in Baltimore where Rémy can receive the best possible care. Rémy refuses to go, shouting ideologies about socialized medicine and castigating his son's kind of caring. Later that night, Rémy is awake, looking frightened and alone. The next day, when Constance visits, Rémy does not talk about his own suffering, fear, and approaching death. Instead, he delivers a lecture about evil. We pick up the conversation in the middle. Constance responds to something he has said about suffering, saying, "You say that because times [right now] are so terrible". Using his walker to hold himself upright as he moves jerkily from window to bed, Rémy declares,

> Not especially terrible. Not at all. Contrary to belief, the twentieth century wasn't that bloody. It's agreed that wars caused 100 million deaths. Add 10 million for the Russian Gulags. How many were killed in the Chinese camps? We'll never know, but say twenty million. So [that's a total of] 130 or 135 million dead. Not all that impressive.
> In the sixteenth century, the Spanish and Portuguese managed without gas chambers or bombs to slaughter 150 million Indians in Latin America. With axes! That's a lot of work, Sister. Even if they had Church support, it was an achievement. So much so that the Dutch, English, French and later Americans followed their lead and butchered another 50 million. [That's] 200 million dead in all! The greatest massacre took place right here. And [there is] not the tiniest Holocaust Museum. The history of Mankind is a history of horrors!

By the end of this speech Rémy is stiff with rage and in the ensuing silence Sister Constance looks deeply troubled.

In this conversation, Rémy has invited Constance into his existential world-making as he draws upon relational matrices in his adult life as a historian in order to express his rage at suffering – not his own but the suffering of the colonized. Her presence as a member of a religious order connects Rémy with the childhood relational matrices formed in his Roman Catholic family and education. At this moment, his existential world-making is fueled by anger and vocalized as a kind of protest theodicy that questions suffering, puts God and the church on trial, and refuses to accept answers. His lament has a liturgical quality, if the rhetoric of the passionate college lecturer can be described as liturgy and Constance can be described as his congregation. She not only bears witness to his rage at the Church; her sadness and distress attest to the ways she, on behalf of the Church and God, accepts the horrors he describes as real. Her sorrow seems to encompass all of those who suffer, including Rémy.

The fourth conversation we view takes place several days later. Rémy's son has bribed the hospital administrator and union members to redecorate a vacant room and make it into a private suite where Rémy can receive hospice care. He has also contacted Rémy's old friends and invited them to visit. In this scene, Sister Constance visits Rémy's suite for the first time and is astonished at the luxurious setting. She jokingly asks whether Rémy is "pals with the Premier [of the province of Québec] or a hockey star?" Rémy's wife says that his son is the one who takes care of him. The chaplain replies, "Yes, I know. And Dumbo won't even thank him". Rémy quickly defends himself, saying, "My son is an ambitious puritanical capitalist. Whereas I was always a sensual socialist". At this point two women enter; they are Rémy's former lovers who were faculty colleagues with him. One of them delightedly exclaims, "Sensual isn't half of it, Sister! Lewd! Bestial! Debauched! Lascivious! Perverse!" After an exchange of kisses, Rémy grinningly declares, "You see, Sister? [I am surrounded by] my exquisite daughter-in-law, my heroic wife and two most charming mistresses. I can die in peace". Rémy places his hands together as if in prayer, looks heavenward and smiles beatifically. Sister Constance pronounces her verdict: "You'll burn in the flames of hell". Rémy's rejoinder is swift: "And I won't be alone. [My wife and daughter-in-law] are safe. But given the depravity of these two [mistresses], they'll roast alongside me. Whereas you'll play the harp on a cloud for eternity, seated between John Paul the second and Mother Theresa...". His wife rolls her eyes and says, "Excuse me, Sister, his malady has affected his brain". Rémy and his two former mistresses chant together a phrase from catechism they learned as children: "For the misfortunes of Poland are proof of God's existence".

In this exchange we see a humorous playing out of Rémy's existential world-making, in which Constance again is aligned with the church and with those who are "good": his wife and daughter-in-law. Rémy jokingly acknowledges his sexual transgressions, and he and his friends easily call to mind the first order language of childhood Catholic catechism. Rémy's humor and wit, which play a large part in his friendships, are much in evidence here, attesting to the ways that the chaplain is now included in the circle of family and friends. Beneath the humor are feelings and questions about death, judgment, and the afterlife. The parody of childhood beliefs, spontaneously sung in unison, reveals the ways in which they are, in face of Rémy's death, re-experiencing embedded childhood beliefs. Their jokes likely trigger some jarring questions for each of them – "What do I believe now?" "How in the world will I make sense of this death?" – especially when Rémy's sudden gasping contortions in response to stabbing pain disrupt the banter. The questions hang in the air as the existential and religious world-making continues. Rémy may be increasingly experiencing the limitations of seeking closeness through humor, intellect, and the sexualizing of relationships.

The second to last conversation we see between Rémy and Constance begins mid-stream, with Rémy sitting upright in bed, shouting, "[Pope] Pius the twelfth [was] sitting on his throne in his gilded Vatican, while Primo Levi was taken to Auschwitz. That's not sad! It's despicable! Hideous!" He slumps back, exhausted. The chaplain, looking tearful and distressed, says in a low voice, "If what you say is true and history is a series of abominable crimes then someone has to exist who can forgive us. That's my belief". Through clenched teeth, Rémy mutters, "I envy you". Once again, Rémy, outraged at his approaching death, finds expression in his protest theodicy. Constance tearfully acknowledges guilt, aligning herself with sinners, and sharing a response from her religious world-making. They are each engaged in a kind of searching for ways of understanding and giving voice to Rémy's rage, pain, fear and sorrow. The meanings they co-construct, to do with atrocities and forgiveness, are provisional and very much in process.

The last conversation that we see takes place as Rémy is being wheeled out of the hospital room on a stretcher. His son is there, packing up Rémy's belongings. Rémy is going with his entourage of family and friends to a house on Lake Memphremagog in the Eastern Townships of Québec, for his final days. This setting is highly significant in the film because it is here that Rémy re-experiences a sense of holiness through the beauty of these natural surroundings. His apprehension of this beauty allows him to be more fully present in the here and now as he approaches death. Constance comes into the room to say goodbye. Grasping his hand, she leans down and gently says, "Adieu!" After gazing steadily at him, she whispers, "Embrace the mystery. Embrace the mystery and you'll be saved". They gaze at each other with great affection. Rémy kisses her hand and then is wheeled away. She turns to Rémy's son, puts her hand on his shoulder and looks at him intently, before saying, "Say you love him. Tell him. And touch him! Touch him"!

The scene discloses the tenderness and intimacy Rémy and Constance experience. Her calm sense of serenity as she says good bye communicates a sense of peaceful acceptance of Rémy's approaching death. This time, she is the one who discloses her religious world-making while Rémy simply listens. Her hope that Rémy will embrace the mystery seems like an alternative theodicy centered on the mystery of God, suffering, and death. We could interpret Sister Constance's counsel to embrace mystery as offering Rémy a way of subsuming his intellectual skepticism within a *via negativa* or negative theology that acknowledges the finitude of all of our human intellectual constructions. Her reference to being saved is jarring to viewers sensitized to comparative religious approaches that impose meanings: is this reference to being saved an imposition of her Christian world-making on Rémy? He doesn't respond as if this is the case. He seems to accept the truth of this for her; perhaps he honors her searching and her provisional meanings in exchange for the times in which she has done this for him.

The pastoral care encounters between Constance and Rémy allow him to dialogue with the church and the God of his childhood Catholicism. These encounters can be juxtaposed with the kind of existential care encounters Rémy has with a young woman named Nathalie. The daughter of one of Rémy's former lovers, she is a heroin addict whom Rémy's son pays to provide his father with heroin, which is 800% more effective than morphine for dealing with pain. The first time they meet, Rémy asks Nathalie whether he remembers that he was "close" to her mother. Nathalie quickly identifies him as one of her mother's married lovers who never stayed until morning. Probably for the first time, Rémy sees what it must have been like for her as a child, saying, "From a child's perspective it must seem sordid. We called it sexual liberation". Prior to this conversation with Nathalie, Rémy might describe the ways he sexualized his relationships with women as a way of breaking free from his Roman Catholic upbringing. At an intellectual level, in humorous reminiscences with his friends, he appreciates the irony of how his Catholic teachings on the sinfulness of sexual desires actually fuelled his fantasies. Before this encounter with Nathalie, he is not able to acknowledge how his sexual liaisons threatened the relational fabric of his life. He has been unaware of how his lifestyle of embracing the "goodness" of the sexual revolution may have wounded his children and the children of his lovers.

When they meet to get high, Rémy talks about his approaching death more candidly than with anyone else. In one such conversation, Nathalie remarks that she will likely die of a heroin overdose. Rémy objects, saying she is young; there is still time to get help. He says he no longer has this kind of time, and he reminisces about how much he has loved life: "Wine, books, music. Women, above all, women. Their smell, their mouths, the feel of their skin". When Nathalie quizzes him on whether he still is able to enjoy all of these pleasures, and he admits he no longer can, she stuns him with her conclusion, "It's not the present you cling to; it's your past life. That life is already dead". Nathalie matter-of-factly recognizes that the passions which used to dominate Rémy's life and connect him with others, however superficially, have already been expended. She challenges him to live fully in the present moment; if Rémy can do this, he may find new ways to engage life, even as he approaches death.

In this exchange we see two people facing a harsh existential reckoning. The time has come for them to let go of the life-limiting ways in which they have grasped life. For Rémy, he has grasped life through his sexual and sensual desires. For Nathalie, she has grasped life by trying to re-experience the self-transcendence she experienced in her first drug-induced high, which she describes as riding the dragon. They both stand on the brink of death: will they choose life?

Rémy learns that he must face the existential questions that have tormented him without using the distractions of women, wine, food, and intellectual compatriots. Can he experience a communion or relational connection that goes beyond the kinds of sexual and intellectual intimacy of his past? Without these distractions and stripped of his self-identity as a sexual, sensual, witty, pugnacious rebel, he is forced to judge the worth of his life. In several conversations with his son and Nathalie, he agonizingly takes stock of his life using standards from his academic identity, and laments that he has no living legacy – no aspect of himself, like books or students, that will survive him. In the brutal honesty of the relational space he and Nathalie have created, Rémy is highly agitated, searching for the purpose of his life and the meaning of his death. He finally acknowledges that he faces death, as he began, like a baby.

His conversations with Constance and Nathalie are both critical to Rémy's existential world-making as he faces death. The chaplain's presence prompts him to re-experience formative relationships in childhood and his embedded Catholicism, and he rages using critical conversations from young adulthood and years as a professor of history. With Nathalie, he reckons with the life-limiting and destructive consequences of sexualized relationships with colleagues and students. With her he searches for a sense of transcendence, a way to be fully present as he faces death, without being able to sexualize, intellectualize, or distract himself with the pleasures of good food and wine. While his searching and questioning do not bring answers, they do bring Rémy to a resting place, where he can face death peacefully.

A significant feature of the pastoral and existential encounters with Constance and Nathalie is that he does not sexualize these relationships when he experiences moments of alterity (as he likely has in the past). Nathalie and Sister Constance remain in their roles as guardians of alterity. Sister Constance engages him with the Otherness he likely experienced at moments through his childhood religion, an otherness which became transposed onto the iconic images of women for whom he felt passionate sexual desire. Nathalie engages him in complex paradoxical ways by first releasing him from pain and introducing him to the physical transcendence of being high on heroin, and then through a brutal reckoning that helps him see beyond his usual horizons of what his life means. In his final moment of life, he tells Nathalie that she is his guardian angel. It is Nathalie, the most vulnerable person in Rémy's circle of family and friends, the one who is closest to death herself, who helps Rémy die. Instead of giving herself the overdose, she gives it to Rémy. She becomes his guardian angel as he crosses from life to death. He becomes her guardian angel as she crosses the line from dangerous overdoes to the relative safety of a methadone program and as she moves into his former home during her recovery.

This case study highlights how pastoral counselling is often one melodic thread in a polyphonic movement where jarring moments in various melodic threads amplify discordant harmonies that can finally break open horizons of meaning and reveal news ways for care-seekers to reconnect with a sense of holiness[50].

> Our being spreads out far beyond us and mingles with the beings of others. We live in other people's thoughts, in their plans, in their dreams. This is as if there were God. We have an infinite responsibility[51].

Iliff School of Theology
Joint PhD Program, Denver University
Office: Iliff Hall 302C
2201 S. University Blvd.
Denver, CO 80210-4798
USA
cdoehring@iliff.edu

Carrie DOEHRING

50. Cf. F. POIRIÉ, *Emmanuel Levinas: Qui êtes-vous?*, Lyon, La Manufacture, 1987, p. 93. See also J. ROBBINS (ed.), *Is It Righteous to Be? Interviews with Emmanuel Levinas*, Stanford, CA, Stanford University Press, 2001, p. 47: "...The true, unquestionable value, and the one that it is not ridiculous to conceive of, is the value of holiness ... It is in the certainty that the other must be given first place in all respects; from the "after you" before the open door to the disposition – hardly possible but holiness demands it – to die for the other".

51. In a novel by Iris Murdoch, a man is contemplating suicide, saying that he doesn't believe in God. His friend tells him that his life doesn't belong to him, describing a relational web of being and an "as if" God. His friend shares this postmodern image of God that emerges from her religious world-making and offers it to him (I. MURDOCH, *Nuns and Soldiers*, London, Penguin, 1980, p. 454).

CARE FOR RECOGNITION IN PASTORAL COUNSELLING

The interdisciplinary book project *After You*, explored in an Expert Seminar held in Leuven, aims at deepening the ethics of encounter by applying the motto 'After You' to the field of pastoral counselling. That title has a number of connotations suggesting different meanings for the expression as it is used in daily life and in professional and academic contexts. What they have in common is that established hierarchies are challenged by the words: 'After You'.

From a gender perspective these words refer to gestures of courtesy, such as men letting women enter a room before them. On those occasions, the social order in which women represent the second sex is overruled and women are first. A Christian scheme of values provides a second meaning, one in which the supreme value of self-sacrificial self-denial is asserted. Here, it is not the naturally dominant *ego* which should prevail, but the other who should come first, since others are of greater importance than the self. Thus, the primacy of the *ego* is put aside by the Christian idea of 'After You'.

A third interpretation, which the organizers of the Leuven symposium had in mind – as they explained in the introductory papers – refers to the professional context in which pastoral workers carry out counselling. Here, 'After You' refers to a certain type of dialogical communication, when pastors do not take the lead in a dominant fashion, but give priority to their client's goals, expectations and outlook on life. This view, eloquently explained in the *oeuvre* of Roger Burggraeve[1], partly derives from the ethical view of the French philosopher Emmanuel Levinas, who radically de-centered the moral subject. Since Immanuel Kant, the moral subject had been regarded as the bearer of moral codes and virtues and

1. Cf. among others *Violence and the Vulnerable Face of the Other: The Vision of Emmanuel Levinas on Moral Evil and Our Responsibility*, in *Journal of Social Philosophy* 30 (1999) 29-45; *The Wisdom of Love in the Service of Love: Emmanuel Levinas on Justice, Peace, and Human Rights*, Milwaukee, WI, Marquette University Press, 2002, 2007 (3[d] ed.); *"No One Can Save Oneself without Others" : An Ethic of Liberation in the Footsteps of Emmanuel Levinas*, in R. BURGGRAEVE (ed.), *The Awakening to the Other: A Provocative Dialogue with Emmanuel Levinas*, Leuven – Paris – Dudley, MA, Peeters, 2008, 13-65; *Affected by the Face of the Other: The Levinasian Movement from the Exteriority to the Interiority of the Infinite*, in I. KAJON – E. BACCARINI – F. BREZZI – J. HANSEL (eds.), *Emmanuel Levinas: Prophetic Inspiration and Philosophy*, Firenze, La Giuntina, 2008, 273-307.

as the one obeying ethical laws of a natural or divine origin. Levinas, on the contrary, stressed the importance of the other (written by Levinas with a capital: 'Other', because of her/his radical otherness), whose face embodied the ultimate ethical command of 'Thou shall not kill'. For Levinas, the main moral imperatives are 'empty', since they consist of *receiving* the commands of the face of other. Thus, the basic ethical attitude is that of receptivity, susceptibility and obedience to the commands that the other gives, or rather personifies, since it is his or her vulnerable face that dictates commands, without speaking a word.

When applied to the field of pastoral counselling, these Levinasian insights have profound consequences, which can be summarized in the dictum 'After You'. When the pastoral counsellor is de-centered, the client occupies the central place. As a result, pastoral counselling is carried out in a listening and dialogical mode. Thus, the traditional pastoral hierarchy collapses. In that hierarchy, the pastoral worker or chaplain is the one who knows best, since he gives moral and spiritual lessons, instructions and guidance in prayer and meditation, and summons the faithful to live according to the laws of God and the Church.

Now, if pastoral workers and chaplains are to counsell in such a Levinasian way, they need a new professional approach. At the symposium in Leuven, the participants tried to reflect on the consequences arising from the dictum 'After You'. It can be asked, however, whether such an innovation is profound enough. When the clients come first and the pastoral counsellors follow, the dichotomy, and with it the accompanying dynamics, still remains intact. It would be an even greater challenge to develop an ethics of encounter and a corresponding ideal of pastoral counselling, which moves beyond the binary dichotomy of two opposite poles, as expressed in 'After You'. It is at this point that the idea of recognition comes in, as it might offer an alternative outlook on what pastoral counselling *is*, and *for whom* it can have results. Let us start here with a provisional definition of recognition to mean 'existing in the eyes of others, while being in the position to notice and value others'.

This essay suggests that the integration of the concept of recognition in the context of pastoral counselling could offer a perspective that goes beyond the dichotomy just mentioned: the dynamics of recognition does not rely on fixed points of supremacy or control, but is a constant re-shuffling of interdependent positions between self and others. A starting point is the German philosopher Axel Honneth and his view on the dynamics of recognition. Since his concept is only partly relevant to pastoral care and counselling, some critics are introduced who complete the concept of recognition so that it becomes more applicable to the pastoral setting. Consequently, the influential forces in the current health care, welfare and pastoral context are pointed out. It is this context that limits the potential that professionals have to get involved in the dynamics of recognition.

The idea which is central to this essay has three facets. The first is that all humans are in need of recognition by others and each human being is able to give recognition to others, even when they are weak and in need. The second facet is that human interaction in the professional domain can also be a locus of social life in which the dynamics of recognition occur. The third facet is the re-interpretation of *the interaction that occurs in pastoral counselling through the lens of recognition*. If re-interpreted in this way, pastoral counselling would gain new significance.

I. The Concept of Recognition according to Axel Honneth

The German philosopher Axel Honneth, who belongs to the so-called Critical School (*Kritische Schule*), integrates the concept of recognition into an encompassing social theory. On this topic his three main works in English translation are *The Struggle for Recognition*, *Reification* and *Disrespect*[2]. Drawing on Georg Wilhelm Friedrich Hegel's early work, and on historians and social psychologists such as George Herbert Mead, Honneth sketches an account of inter-subjective conditions for achieving personal integrity. From the work of these thinkers he concludes that all humans are eager to receive recognition: a precious good that they cannot obtain or buy, but have to receive from other people.

In the English translation, Honneth's first book on recognition is entitled *The Struggle for Recognition: The Moral Grammar of Social Conflicts*[3]. Both the title and subtitle reveal that antagonism and rivalry are central in his intellectual framework, not cooperation and harmony. Honneth sketches an ongoing historical sequence of disrespect, demand for recognition and social change, which he perceives as the developmental logic of collective movements[4].

Honneth puts forward that humans can only build up self-esteem and can only sense that they matter, when others let them know that they are

2. A. Honneth, *The Struggle for Recognition: The Moral Grammar of Social Conflicts*, Cambridge, Polity Press, 1995; Id., *Re-ification: A New Look at an Old Idea*, Oxford, Oxford University Press, 2008; Id., *Disrespect: The Normative Foundation of Critical Theory*, Cambridge, Polity Press, 2007.

3. Id., *The Struggle for Recognition* (n. 2).

4. *Ibid.*, p. 139.

noticed and valued, and when they grant them equal rights. Therefore, one of the most insulting things a person can experience is to be treated as if they are simply *not* there. When people are not recognized, on a social, psychological and ethical level they are structurally excluded, and as a result *their feelings are hurt*, Honneth explains[5]. Consequently, hurt feelings are a main indicator of a shortage of recognition.

Honneth does not pay attention to pastoral interactions or other kinds of relationships between professionals in the health care or welfare sector. He is mainly concerned with socio-political conflicts that have arisen from misrecognition and the struggle that has been fought to correct that situation. He believes that misrecognized groups of people (i.e. colonized people, ethnic groups, women) need a vocabulary that allows them to articulate their personal disappointments and share them with members of their group. Thus, they find a basis for joint social action to claim their rights, and sometimes, as a result of such a social struggle, their rights are recognized and they feel socially included.

Honneth criticizes and complements mainstream social and political philosophy, influenced as it is by Macchiavelli and Hobbes. His outlook is an extension of the prevailing model that explains social change only in terms of the pursuit of (material) interests of atomistic individuals[6]. He rejects that view as being too individualistic and too much based on interest since it assumes that the main factor in social life is the satisfaction of material interests of atomistic individuals.

Honneth offers an explanation of social struggle that is not fought by atomistic individuals and that is not solely about the distribution of resources: he believes that social life is not driven by material interests only, but also by something that is universal and essentially human, namely the quest for *self-realization*. His use of the term is very specific and differs from representatives of humanistic psychologists such as Abraham H. Maslow in *Motivation and Personality*, who defined self-realization as living up to the full potential of one's possibilities[7]. In Honneth's vocabulary, self-realization refers to a complex social process in which is established what it means to exist in the eyes of others and thus become one-self. To Honneth, self-realization means being noticed as 'being there', as someone who matters to others and therefore also to oneself, and who is entitled to equal rights. The value of self-realization,

5. *Ibid.*, pp. 163, 165, 168.
6. *Ibid.*, p. 165.
7. A.H. MASLOW, *Motivation and Personality*, New York, NY, Harper and Row, 1954 (1st ed.), 1970.

so Honneth thinks, is deeply implanted in human nature, and needs to be facilitated socially, politically and economically in order to take shape.

Consequently, social conflicts are not just about the distribution of goods. The 'thing' that social groups have conflicts about, Honneth insists, is recognition. That was, and is, the case in particular for groups that do not take part in the societal domain on an equal basis, such as black people and ethnic minorities in their anti-colonial struggle, and women who fought and continue to fight for civil rights. Social conflicts arise when particular claims to identity and equal rights are denied: under these circumstances these groups are misrecognized. Honneth's aim is not to stimulate the identity politics of various marginal social groups, but to arrive at an integrated community in which all persons participate under conditions of equality of rights and esteem.

There are two evident points in which Honneth's critique on prevailing social theories is relevant to an ethics of encounter in the pastoral setting. His criticism of atomistic individualism can easily be linked to the nature of pastoral counselling, which is an intrinsically inter-subjective event. Besides, the denial that humans are mainly driven by material goods fits with the assumption underlying pastoral care. Pastoral counsellors and chaplains assume that humans are spiritual beings, who long for more than just the pursuit of their material interests. They see it as their task to support the people in their care, especially wounded and vulnerable people, to reach those immaterial goals. When drawing on Honneth's theory, one of these goals can be identified as recognition. In order to elaborate *on the link between recognition and pastoral counselling*, we will have a closer look at Honneth's ideas on the issue.

II. Three Forms of Recognition: Love, Respect and Solidarity

Honneth distinguishes three modes in which recognition is given and received, namely love, respect and solidarity; these modes are paralleled by basic forms of misrecognition[8]. Taken together they represent the basis for a formal conception of ethical life. The first mode of recognition that Honneth mentions is located in the private domain. *Love* is the fundament for the dynamics of recognition, especially the love between a

8. The sketch of Honneth's ideas is based upon the Dutch book Annelies van Heijst published on recognition: *Iemand zien staan: Zorgethiek over erkenning*, Kampen, Klement, 2008, especially Chapter 3, pp. 29-41.

little child and his primary care-giver. Without having been loved as a little child, a person will never be able to receive and to give recognition. A child that is loved will build up a sense of basic trust in itself and the surrounding world. According to Honneth, love is the act of acknowledging the wants and emotional dependencies of a concrete other, and responding to that in an affirmative way. This kind of loving care usually takes place in the relationships between parents and children, and later on in life between friends. The safety of motherly love and affectionate ties with the mother enable the child to live without fear. Only when it has experienced security early in life, will the child dare to express its needs without fear of being left on its own or being rejected by others. While describing love as merely a feeling, Honneth disregards the fact that 'mothering' is also a practice in which the work of loving care has to be done[9]. Love is more than cherishing warm feelings, it is also about doing things which cost effort and energy, time and money.

Honneth argues that love is always directed to a concrete other with whom one is connected through ties of affection, and therefore located in the private sphere. To Honneth, love cannot be stretched out to an undifferentiated mass of people outside the private domain – as, for instance, the Christian conception of neighborly love suggests. Pastoral counsellors, who want to apply Honneth's thinking to their work, should be aware of the limited scope of Honneth's conception of love and also of his main interest in struggle, which will be disputed in the next section.

Honneth's second mode of recognition is *respect*, which he locates in the socio-political realm, outside the private domain. Respect is not a feeling, but a form of principled social equality that all fellow men should grant each other and that every member of a repressed social subgroup is entitled to claim. In the history of mankind, all kind of social groups have struggled to gain respect. In each case their group struggle ended when equal rights were granted. Honneth believes that respect is not linked to any special qualities or characteristics of a given individual. Respect concerns every human being *as a (potential) bearer of equal rights*, which they are entitled to have. Every human deserves this respect from others; they should then respect others as well and grant them their equal rights.

Honneth's second type of recognition is not personal but formal and encompasses many people: all those who are morally accountable and

9. A. HONNETH, *Love and Morality: On the Moral Content of Emotional Ties*, in ID., *Disrespect* (n. 2), 163-179, p. 179.

have the capacity to judge and to act reasonably. He does not seem to notice that his definition (which is in line with Kant's moral subject) excludes categories of people who lack these moral and mental capacities. Does that mean that they are not entitled to receive respect, or that they are not the ones who are able to give respect to their fellow men? It is a question that arises, but that Honneth does not discuss. For professional care-givers and pastoral counsellors, however, it is most certainly an important topic, since they frequently deal with people whose physical and mental capacities are diminished.

Honneth's third form of recognition is also located in the public domain. He calls it solidarity (in German: *Solidarität*), a word that is not very adequate and for which he offers scant explanation. Honneth discusses solidarity only in the domain of paid labour, where colleagues who appreciate each other's work stand side-by-side with each other. A translator of Honneth into English, the philosopher Joel Anderson, has suggested that the third mode of recognition should better be named *social appreciation*, since it has to do with the special merits and efforts of individuals, appreciating them for who they are and what they do[10]. Solidarity or social appreciation is therefore a personal kind of recognition, which takes place in the public domain. The effect of this form of recognition is a sense of self-appreciation. Individuals who receive it will build up a stronger sense of self-esteem and feel valued.

In addition, Honneth identifies three forms of misrecognition expressed in German as *Missachtung*. The antithesis to love is violation of the body. (This is a rather inadequate definition of what happens to people who lack recognition or who are abused and maltreated, as pastoral counsellors may know). The misrecognition of respect is the denial of equal rights. When equality is denied, it leads to social existence on the margins of society. One is denied the facilities that other social groups have. The misrecognition of solidarity/social appreciation is denigration – occurring when someone's individual qualities remain unnoticed, when someone is not valued or when explicit deprecation is communicated. Theologians might remark here that the Christian tradition of self-humiliation has prompted a climate of structural misrecognition. In the Christian milieu, it used to be viewed as a danger to the virtue of humility when one's talents or assets were praised. Thus, a false sense of modesty and a lack of self-appreciation were actually encouraged.

10. J. ANDERSON, *Translator's Introduction*, in HONNETH, *The Struggle for Recognition* (n. 2), p. XV.

III. Honneth's Blind Spot: Professional Loving Care in the Public Domain

Critics of Honneth put forward a variety of arguments. Most relevant for pastoral counselling is the criticism mentioned above, pertaining to Honneth's overlooking weak and vulnerable people who have diminished moral and mental capacities, since these people are a substantial part of the clientele of pastoral counsellors. Other weighty objections to Honneth's theory are his fixation on controversy and the corresponding neglect of harmony, in addition to the sharp boundary he draws between the private and the public realm, since he situates love only in the private domain.

Critic Peter Osborne has argued that Honneth offers a selective reading of Hegel by concentrating only on conflict and ignoring harmony (which together form the movement of thesis, anti-thesis and synthesis in Hegel's work): '(...) it is the conflicted character of recognition in Hegel that Honneth picks up on, rather than the movement towards reconciliation, the justification of which was the motor of Hegel's development'[11]. Michael O. Hardimon asks whether all instances of development and progress are to be explained by reference to the struggle for recognition, as Honneth claimed[12]. Or is that applicable only to some forms of development, or perhaps to many of them?

In an earlier criticism of Honneth, Annelies van Heijst remarked that his pre-occupation with disharmony has prevented him from seeing that the dynamics of recognition is impelled not only by conflicts, but also by generous gifts of love that humans offer to one another, inside and outside the private realm. Honneth does mention parental love as crucial for the dynamics of recognition and has shown that motherly love in many regards takes on the character of a gift. Yet, he fails to grasp the importance of these insights and does not integrate loving generosity in that part of his theory of recognition that deals with public life.

Honneth's amputated conception of love is historically based. The conviction that love is a mere feeling (instead of an action which is practised), and the idea that love does not belong in the public realm and cannot include strangers, arose in the second half of the twentieth century. During that time, the Christian tradition of charity as one of the

11. P. Osborne, *A Paradigm too Far? Review of Axel Honneth's 'Struggle for Recognition'*, in *Radical Philosophy* 80 (1996), November-December, 34-37, p. 35.

12. M.O. Hardimon, *Book review: 'The Struggle for Recognition'*, in *The Journal of Philosophy* 94 (1997 46-54, p. 53.

founding pillars of public life broke down. Instead of being dependent on the benevolence of the wealthy, poor people gained social rights that were enshrined in law. Neighborly love, which for long had been the practice of delivering assistance through institutionalized action, no longer had a role in structuring the social order[13]. Honneth's theory reflects the prevailing late modern view that the correct way to structure today's society was according to the principle of *ex justitia* (justice-driven), instead of *ex caritate* (charity-driven)[14]. He stipulates that love is only possible in the private domain and that the law is the key mediating sphere that holds together the network of inter-subjective conditions for personal integrity (love) and the community-generating values of respect and solidarity/social appreciation.

It will be argued next, that Honneth's basic idea, broadened and enriched by the criticism mentioned above, can be transferred to the professional health care and welfare sector. It is there that professionals give recognition to and receive recogintion from their clients, and a substantial part of pastoral care and counselling occurs.

IV. Professional Interaction as a Locus of Social Life

Social theories such as Honneth's use to hinge around the realms of labor, politics and institutions. From that perspective, the health care and welfare sector (in which a great deal of pastoral counselling takes place these days) is observed as nothing more than the domain of paid labor, in which professionals are the relevant subjects since they work there, and it is labor that matters socio-politically. Another way of perceiving this domain, however, is to view it as a locus of social life, in which relevant social interactions happen between professionals and their clients.

The dynamics of recognition is deeply human and always present in one way or another. Why shouldn't the interactions between the professionals who give nursing care, medical care and pastoral care on the one hand, and the clients or patients who receive the care on the other, count as an integral part of the ongoing societal dynamics of recognition? When doing so, it becomes clear that the struggle for recognition, as well as the gift of recognition, is also going on in nursing homes and hospitals,

13. A. van Heijst, *Models of Charitable Care: Catholic Nuns and Children in Their Care in Amsterdam, 1852-2002*, Leiden – Boston, MA, Brill, 2008.

14. A.G.M. van Melsen, *Evolutie van de caritas: Rede uitgesproken bij de viering van het 50-jarig bestaan van het Sint Laurensziekenhuis te Breda*, Breda, Sint Laurens Ziekenhuis, 1963.

mental wards and prisons, in congregations and in the pastoral face-to-face contact of pastoral workers and chaplains and their clients.

Failures or successes on the level of recognition might have a greater influence on the interaction in pastoral care and counselling than has been observed so far. There is recognition 'going on' not only whenever clients feel they are not being taken seriously and whenever professionals feel denounced, but also when a client experiences that the pastoral counsellor is truly attentive, or when a pastoral worker feels valued because of how she does her work. In other words, the locus of pastoral counselling is at the same time the scene of recognition processes. Sometimes recognition is given generously, at other times it is obtained as a result of demands.

In order to avoid an overly romantic image of recognition processes, we should pay attention to the societal conditions that currently shape health care and welfare professionalism in general, and also affect pastoral counselling and care. Today's reform of health care institutions has strengthened the totalitarian character of modern health care, welfare and pastoral professionalism and has led to the market economy having a strong grip on all types of professional care.

Two early critics of this *totalitarian* character of care professionalism in the modern era are the French philosopher Michel Foucault and the Canadian sociologist Erving Goffman[15]. They have analyzed the architecture of the mental wards and hospitals that developed from the seventeenth century onwards, and the way in which these institutes were run. All aspects of the residents' behavior as well as their thoughts and inner feelings were increasingly watched and controlled. Foucault and Goffman concluded that bodies of professional knowledge function as instruments and techniques of discipline. Foucault's analysis of pastoral care is particularly relevant to pastoral counsellors and chaplains. He argued that the pastoral and moral categories applied by the pastors to the people in their care were internalized, leading to a form of self-control[16]. In his view, self-discipline is the most subtle and stringent form of social control.

Recently, health care and welfare professionalism have developed in new directions, a result of the grip of the *market economy*. A growing number of pastoral care-givers and counsellors have to live and function within that reality. In order to make care giving effective and efficient,

15. E. GOFFMAN, *Asylums: Essyas on the Social Situation of Mental Patients and Other Inmates*, New York, NY, Doubleday, 1961.

16. M. FOUCAULT, *Madness and Civilization: A History of Insanity in the Age of Reason*, London, Pantheon Books, 1967; ID., *Discipline and Punish: The Birth of the Prison*, New York, NY, Random House, 1975.

the care process has been organized to maximize the results. Professionals deal in an increasingly rationalized and instrumental way with the deficiencies of body, mind and soul of their clients, residents or patients. The time and space that they have for adding a personal touch to their work has been annihilated. It scarcely matters who they are, as long as they carry out the functions for which they were trained and skilled. It is the professional's task to conquer and defeat illness, anger, hurt, grief and pain and to postpone death - to the greatest extent possible. Consequently, professionals who work in large institutes are reduced to being executors of 'functions'; they are replaceable by others and serve as a means to an end, as the French philosopher François Dubet remarked[17].

Today's hyper-specialization in health care professions, together with marketplace driven interests, has turned health care interventions into a product to buy and sell. The de-personalization of professionals is accompanied by an estrangement of the clients. It would be imprecise to argue that the clients are objectified, since each mission statement advertises its patient-centeredness. What is objectified, however, are the clients' defects and deficiencies, which are diagnosed and singled out as 'objects' for treatment and cure. Because of that approach, clients may *feel* reduced and objectified, since it is just their defective part that is noticed, while the rest of them doesn't seem to matter.

Professionals are obliged to carry out the work of mending and repair as effectively and efficiently as possible, in order to reduce costs. The clients or patients are defined by the deficiencies that they display in order to be cured, mended or restored. The expert professional has the responsibility of solving the problems of the non-expert client. Although it is not the professionals' intention, this approach leads to a social split between the professionals who are in control on the one hand (seemingly invulnerable and unharmed themselves) and the 'caste' of clients and patients on the other hand. The latter certainly is the case for care-needing people who are chronically or terminally ill, or are in the last stage of their life.

Practices of help and healing have lost their awe and wonder. The awareness that humans share a common ground of fragility and transience has evaporated. That awareness was rooted in the Christian tradition of charity, the Enlightenment and in the French Revolution with its idea of the brotherhood of man. Until the twentieth century, most interactions of help and support (as well as the professional help for which patients paid) were considered a manifestation of neighborly love, not merely an

17. F. DUBET, *Le déclin de l'institution*, Paris, Seuil, 2002.

economic transaction. At that time, it was not only pastoral workers who acted from such ideological motivation, but also physicians, nurses, schoolteachers and social workers. In the late modern context, however, the common bonds of fragility, which urged humans to help each other, seem to have become rather irrelevant.

Care giving is reduced to an act of applying the appropriate methods, techniques, medication and other means. What rules nowadays, is a stripped-down pragmatism. The main dimensions that remain and are seen as relevant are technocratic (is everything arranged well?) and economic (what is the balance between profit and loss?). As a result, chaplains and pastoral counsellors face new challenges and difficulties, as Larry VandeCreek remarked: "If chaplaincy does not produce a product, how can this ministry be described to skeptical administrators?"[18].

An early corrective response to the objectifying and tunneled approach in health care and well fare professionalism arose in the 1960s. A plea for a *holistic* approach to clients was voiced; since a human being is a rich entity, all the facets of clients should be acknowledged – their minds, bodies and souls. In the current, ever-more-specializing professional environment, the holistic approach no longer solves the problem. Keeping an eye open for the dimension of recognition might make a difference in this respect. In order to point out its meaning, we should look into approaches which have come up in pastoral care and counselling in the past decades and the discourse which is used to describe their goals and methods.

V. Effective and Efficient Pastoral Therapy, Aiming at Cure of the Soul

The history of the practice of pastoral care and counselling has been described in terms of 'the *cure* of souls', a discourse that is highly therapeutic[19]. A similar jargon has been used by William Clebsch and Charles Jaekle in *Pastoral Care in Historical Perspective*, who also defined pastoral care as the curing of souls[20]. Charles F. Kemp even

18. L. VandeCreek, *If Chaplaincy Understands Health Care Reform, Will It Hurt the Profession Less?*, in *Journal of Pastoral Care and Counselling* 56 (2002) 351-361, p. 360.

19. J.T. McNeill, *A History of the Cure of Souls*, New York, NY, Harper and Brothers, 1951, p. 4.

20. C.F. Kemp, *Physicians of the Soul: A History of Pastoral Counselling*, Englewood Cliffs, NJ, Prentice-Hall, 1964.

expanded the medical impact when he compared pastoral counsellors to medical doctors in *Physicians of the Soul: A History of Pastoral Counseling*[21]. The therapeutic goal mentioned here is not of a bodily but of a psychotherapeutic nature. E. Brooks Holifield, in *A History of Pastoral Care in America: from Salvation to Self-Realization*, distinguished between pastoral care (aimed at sustaining a congregation of believers) and pastoral counselling (a face-to-face relationship between a pastor and a person in need)[22]. The title of Alisson Stoke's book even referred to evident psychoanalytical influences; it was called *Ministry after Freud*[23].

Today the profession of pastoral workers is undergoing a profound change (at least in the Dutch context, from which this essay is written). In former days, pastoral counsellors and chaplains were primarily holders of religious office carrying out an ecclesiastical task. In a changing and multiform world, in which the individualization of religions is increasing, the spiritual care-giver turns into an existential counsellor, who offers support to his clients, patients or residents, irrespective of their religion or outlook on life. Additionally, various groups of pastoral workers – especially those who work in the healthcare ministry, have to deal with the ideology and terminology of the market place which is adopted institutionally. The impact of these changes is the commercialization of pastoral care and counselling, which has to be as effective and efficient as possible[24].

It is in this changing context that the evidence-based model of diagnosis-and-intervention has become dominant. Recently, books and articles have appeared which state that pastoral counselling is a specific kind of therapy, to be carried out in an evidence-based way, and embedded in the matrix of diagnosis-and-intervention[25]. Douglas Anderson typified pastoral counselling as 'a restorative response': an echoing process which takes place at the human level, although the restorative Grace of God is present between therapist and client "opening the ears

21. Id., *Physicians of the Soul: A History of Pastoral Counseling*, New York, NY, The Macmillan Co, 1947.

22. E. Brooks Holifield, *A History of Pastoral Care in America: From Salvation to Self-Realization*, Nashville, TN, Abingdon Press, 1983.

23. A. Stoke, *Ministry after Freud*, New York, NY, Pilgrim Press, 1985.

24. T.D. Rosell, *Pastoral Products or Pastoral Care? How Marketplace Language Affects Ministry in Veterans Hospitals*, in *The Journal of Pastoral Care and Counseling* 60 (2006) 363-367.

25. J.J. Gleason, *Evidence-Based Standards of Care in Pastoral Practice*, in *The Journal of Pastoral Care and Counseling* 60 (2006) 195-199.

and eyes of both of them"[26]. These words reveal that the author models his thoughts on the discourse of 'diagnosis and treatment'. Anderson equates listening with 'diagnosing', and his assumption is that the pastor has to identify what is problematic, sick, or otherwise wrong, and that his aim is to restore or mend the 'soul'. The means that are used for that end lie in the personality of the pastoral counsellor: he or she responds with the totality of his or her life experience, which shines through in his or her presence. Such sharing of one's own life-experiences could be helpful and result in the self-acceptance and self-love of the client.

Another example is an influential (Dutch) book of Johan Bouwer on pastoral diagnosis[27]. In addition, there are articles published calling for pastors to be accountable for their work and for its effectiveness to be statistically measured, for example, "a preliminary proposal for a scale to measure the effectiveness of pastoral care with family members of hospitalized patients"[28]. The general tendency in this type of literature is that pastoral workers and chaplains are encouraged to give a precise account of the results of their works. Consequently, they will begin to view their clients as bearers of physical, mental, social or spiritual deficiencies which should be offered restorative and mending interventions, to be measured in terms of effectiveness and efficiency. Some pastoral counsellors and chaplains support that tendency, others oppose it[29].

Nonetheless, the current crisis in the sector of health care and welfare and pastoral care is more than a problem of logistics, managerial options or a shortage of money. At stake is the moral underpinning of the social interaction in which a particular social group (called 'professionals') helps out its fellow men (called 'clients' and 'patients'). This type of professionalism, which is based upon competent and skilled capacities, should rediscover that it is rooted in a general sense of sharing fragile and transient human life. All creatures are part of the relational network

26. D.A. ANDERSON, *Pastoral Counseling as an Echoing Process: A Transformative Therapy Hour*, in *Journal of Pastoral Care and Counseling* 56 (2002) 3-9, p. 3.

27. J. BOUWER, *Pastorale diagnostiek: Modellen en mogelijkheden*, Zoetermeer, Boekencentrum, 1998.

28. K.J. FLANELLY – K. GALEK – H.P. TANNENBAUM – G.F. HANDZO, *A Preliminary Proposal for a Scale to Measure the Effectiveness of Pastoral Care with Family Members of Hospitalized Patients*, in *Journal of Pastoral Care & Counseling* 61 (2007) 19-29.

29. For a discussion on the issue of the 'Diagnostic Schema for Religious/Spiritual Concerns' see the Supplement 2005 of the *Journal of Pastoral Care & Counseling*, Vol. 59, No. 5, 425-454, in which Wesley L. Brun proposes a pastoral elaboration of the Fourth Edition of the *Diagnostic and Statistical Manual of Mental Disorders* (Washington 1994), and is responded by Donald D. Denton, George Fichett, Bruce M. Hartung, and H. Newton Malony.

without which they would never have been born and would not be able to survive and exist as true human beings. Professionalism is just one of the range of social manifestations in which that human vulnerability and dependency is handled. Most certainly *pastoral* professionalism should be more than a set of skills and techniques which experts know how to apply in order to treat the defective parts of other people. One might expect that pastoral counsellors and their clients would not forget the dependent condition of human life, since Judaism, Christianity and Islam all assert that human life depends on JHWH, God or Allah, and that all humans are children of God.

VI. How Recognition Could Modify the Ethics of Pastoral Encounter

It was argued, to complete Honneth's theory, that recognition is not just a struggle but has also the character of a generous gift. The latter is something that Honneth, like most male social theorists, did not acknowledge, since it is divergence that arouses their intellectual curiosity, not harmony. The interaction between professionals and clients was re-claimed as a substantial part of social life in which the dynamics of recognition are operative. Therefore, recognition is relevant to pastoral counselling as it works in two ways. The first way is the recognition offered by the pastoral counsellor to the client.

Several facets of recognition in pastoral counselling can be distinguished here. The starting point is the professional availability of the pastoral counsellor: they are there for every client that may need them, that is to say, for those who are in the institutional setting and entitled to their help. The offer does not exclude certain clients, but is open to everyone. This has to do with recognition in the form of respect, as Honneth explained it, but for Christian pastors there is more to it. Their professional welcoming attitude which excludes nobody, is inspired by the ideal of neighborly love, which believers show for their fellow men, especially for those who are in need and in despair. Another form of recognition is offered when the pastoral worker and the client get involved in the process of counselling. Then, the hope and grief of the client are also recognized; to his or her personal features and life story the pastoral counsellor responds.

A pastoral counsellor welcoming a client who was a stranger until that moment, recognizes the other as someone who matters. The care-seeker is not left alone, his suffering is accepted, he is not rejected as unworthy of help. Here we have a basic form of recognition that the professional gives to the client. It is not social struggle that prompts this acceptance; it is, rather, a kind of gift, even though the client has to pay for the work what the pastoral counsellor will do with and for him.

On the part of the clients there is a basic form of recognition as well. It lies in their entrusting themselves to the care of the pastor, thus affirming the professional and personal identity of the pastor. Without clients, patients, residents or believers, a pastoral worker wouldn't be much of a pastor; they would not be able to do their work. Here, too, recognition has the character of a gift: clients, by entrusting themselves to the care of the pastor, hope the pastor will prove trustworthy.

On top of this basic dynamics of recognition, which ground the pastoral interaction, a more personal communication develops, which is also two-way. Most of the time, pastors who are in the process of counselling clients begin to appreciate certain aspects of the latter's personality and life-stories. Reciprocally, clients develop their own thoughts and judgment on their pastoral care-giver. To most pastors it matters a great deal how their clients feel about them. It is here that the social ranking of the mastering professional versus the mastered clients is effaced. Clients are the ones to form an opinion on the pastors, even when they are traumatized, in great pain or in misery, or are socially marginalized. Most pastors are susceptible to the judgments of their clients; they are touched by how their clients feel about them, and their self-esteem is linked to how the clients experience and value them. This sensibility is not an unwanted weakness, but a sign of the underlying common humanity that grounds the pastoral interaction[30].

That common humanity is the need for recognition, as it is operative in social life in general as well as in the subject-subject relation between pastors and clients. Therefore, when the dynamics of recognition is taken seriously and acknowledged, the binary opposition between professional and client, self and other, is not simply reversed. It is rather transcended or transgressed. Here we get a glimpse of the profound ethical significance of recognition, which goes beyond the dictum 'After You'. Within the dynamics of recognition, the most powerful party – the professional pastor – is reminded of his humbleness, since it is not he himself who is able to assert his professional identity; it is the client who does so, or who doesn't. The more vulnerable party – the client – is put in the position of offering something to the care-giver, or of refusing it. Thus, the binary dichotomy of 'After You', is destabilized and transgressed: it is

30. A. VAN HEIJST, *Professional Loving Care: An Ethical View of the Healthcare Sector*, Leuven, Peeters, 2011.

because givers are turned into receivers, and receivers are turned into givers, that the concept of recognition, when introduced in pastoral counselling, grounds the ethics of encounter.

Tilburg School of Humanities
Tilburg University
Room D 248 PO Box 90153
NL-5000 LE Tilburg
Netherlands
j.e.j.m.vheyst@uvt.nl

Annelies VAN HEIJST

ASYMMETRY AND POWER IN PASTORAL COUNSELLING

THE NEED FOR ETHICAL ATTITUDES

In their moral intuition, pastors could dislike asymmetry in the pastoral relationship and reject the idea that they have power over their conversation partners. Influenced by a Christian concept of brotherhood and sisterhood, pastors might think they should be friends with their conversation partners. This intuitive idea can be dangerous if pastors would tend to deny the asymmetry and the power in their own pastoral counselling. It is better to be fully aware of it.

The aim of this article is to make a critical ethical reflection on asymmetry and power in pastoral counselling. The research question is how pastors can deal in an ethical and responsible way with the asymmetric relationship and the power imbalance in pastoral counselling? Our reflection is based on a study of literature and on our experience in ethical advising and pastoral supervision. First, we describe the asymmetric positions and the subsequent imbalance of power in the pastoral relationship. Then we present one possible response to this challenge, namely the development of a coherent pattern of ethical attitudes for the pastor. We believe that the pastor's ethical attitudes are a good way to prevent the abuse of power and to enhance empowerment in pastoral counselling.

I. ASYMMETRY AND POWER IN PASTORAL COUNSELLING

1. *Pastoral Counselling*

Before we address the challenge of asymmetry and power in pastoral counselling, we should clarify the underlying concept of pastoral counselling. There are many possible concepts of pastoral counselling[1]. The

1. In our concept of pastoral counselling we combine ideas of several authoritative definitions: G. HEITINK, *Practical Theology: History, Theory, Action Domains. Manual for Practical Theology*, Grand Rapids, MI – Cambridge, Eerdmans, 1999, pp. 6-9; G. LYNCH, *The Relationship between Pastoral Counseling and Pastoral Theology*, in J. WOODWARD – S. PATTISON (eds), *The Blackwell Reader in Pastoral and Practical Theology*, Oxford, Blackwell, 2000, 223-232; ID., *A Critique of Pastoral Care*, London, SCM, 2000 (3rd ed.), pp. 5-18; J. PATTON, *Pastoral Counseling*, in R.J. HUNTER (ed.), *Dictionary of Pastoral Care and Counseling*, Nashville, TN, Abingdon Press, 1990, 849-854.

point of departure of our view is the human person's quest for meaning in life and/or the search for faith. We consider human persons as existential beings, challenged by the questions of meaning of their existence and by the answers given by philosophical or religious traditions. This presumes an existential view on the human person: the parameters of existence are time and space[2].

The time line is the historical progress, which human persons make between the moment of their birth and the moment of their death. This is their life history. People try to interpret the fragments of their life history in a manner that blends into a meaningful whole. As part of this process, they pose existential questions about their origin and their destination. Who am I and where do I come from? Where am I going and what is my future? People can find intuitive answers in everyday life and reflective answers in philosophical or religious frames of reference. The particular tradition of Christian faith proclaims, in general terms, that the origin of human beings is their creation by God and that the destination is their return to God. Can this faith inspire people in their search for meaning in their life history?

The space line is the relational tension human beings experience between their individuality and their relatedness with others. This is their life world. Most people want to be independent and to make own choices. At the same time, they are related with others in a network of relationships within the context of a social environment. Again, people can ask questions about their individuality and their relatedness. How can I develop myself and live with others in a community? Where are the boundaries of my freedom and responsibilities? Once more, people can find answers in everyday life and in philosophical or religious frameworks. Christian faith, generally considered, proclaims that through creation human beings are fundamentally relational, free and at the same time responsible. Can this faith help people in the search for meaning of their living together with others?

Human persons are living at the intersection of time and space, at the cross roads of their life history and their life world, searching for meaning and faith in their life. This existential view on the human person is the foundation of our concept of pastoral counselling. Hence, we define pastoral counselling as an empowering companionship between a pastor

2. A. LIÉGEOIS, *Values in Dialogue: Ethics in Care*, in progress. This view is also inspired by E. VAN DEURZEN, *Everyday Mysteries: Existential Dimensions of Psychotherapy*, London, Routledge, 1998, pp. 93-128; T. VAN KNIPPENBERG, *Towards Religious Identity: An Exercise in Spiritual Guidance*, Assen, Van Gorcum, 2002, pp. 95-116.

and a conversation partner, whereby the pastor, inspired by the Christian tradition, community and spirituality, supports the conversation partner in his or her own quest for meaning and/or faith in life[3].

This concept of pastoral counselling is fundamentally relational because the relationship or the companionship between the pastor and the conversation partner stands central. The pastor is a companion, a friendly and professional person, who shares the conversation partner's quest for meaning and/or faith. But it is a qualified relationship, namely an empowering companionship. The aim of pastoral counselling is that the pastor, through this relationship, empowers the conversation partner. We understand empowerment in an ethical way as giving another person more power so that he or she is better able to assume responsibility in his or her life. So the pastor empowers the conversation partner by supporting him or her in the own quest for meaning and/or faith in life.

This latter distinction between meaning and life is also important. Pastoral counselling is not always directly related to faith. Pastors often give support to 'non-believers', to people who are simply wrestling with the meaning of their own existence. Therefore, the support can be a process of clarifying and/or of deepening. Clarification means that the pastor supports the conversation partner in the search for meaning or faith, whereas deepening means that the pastor supports the conversation partner to understand or experience this faith and/or meaning more intensely once it has been found. The aim of pastoral counselling is open and inclusive. It comprises all persons, regardless of their religious faith or convictions.

Consequently, the nature of pastoral counselling is not to be found in the faith or convictions of the conversation partner. The identity of pastoral counselling is created by the pastor her- or himself: it is the unshakable association of the pastor with the above mentioned Christian tradition, Christian community and Christian spirituality which determines the specific form which the pastor gives to his or her companionship with the other person. The counselling is a real pastoral counselling because the pastor is inspired by the Christian tradition, representing a Christian community and moved by Christian spirituality.

2. *Asymmetry and Power in the Relationship*

Pastoral counselling is grounded in a relationship between a pastor and a conversation partner. One of the most important characteristics of this

3. A. Liégeois, *Pastoral Counselling in Care Services: Between Confidential Space and Integrated Care*, in *Counselling and Spirituality* 25 (2006) 127-140, p. 129.

relationship is its asymmetry and power imbalance[4]. The relationship may well be a mutual one, in the sense that both partners are involved with each other and communicate with each other. Moreover, both partners can be considered as 'equal', in the sense that they both enjoy the same dignity as human persons. However, they are unequal in terms of their relative position within the pastoral relationship: the one is the pastor and the other is the conversation partner. Asymmetry is the quality of the relationship that both partners have an unequal position in that relationship.

To begin with, the pastor holds an official position, a ministry in the Christian community[5]. This gives the pastor the authority to act and speak on behalf of the community. In some cases this authority may originate from an even more exalted source, since the conversation partner may regard the pastor as being the direct representative of God himself, which can lead to ascribe all kinds of 'superhuman' qualities to the pastor. Moreover, the pastor not only holds a ministerial position, but also has a professional status. The pastor is a theological expert as well as a professional counsellor in matters of meaning and faith. This implies a lot of knowledge and skill in these matters.

The conversation partner who seeks pastoral counselling is placing great reliance on the position, the expertise and professionalism of the pastor. At the same time, the conversation partner is in a vulnerable and dependent position[6]. The conversation partner is vulnerable because he or she has a question, a need or a problem that is difficult to solve on his or her own. Therefore, the conversation partner would like to share it with a pastor in order to get some support. This makes the conversation partner dependent on a pastor who is available for such support. Moreover, the conversation partner is vulnerable because he or she should reveal a personal matter and describe at least a part of the context of his or her life history and life world.

4. See C. DOEHRING, *Taking Care: Monitoring Power Dynamics and Relational Boundaries in Pastoral Care and Counseling*, Nashville, TN, Abingdon Press, 1995, pp. 74-103; R. GULA, *Ethics in Pastoral Ministry*, New York – Mahwah, NJ, Paulist Press, 1996, pp. 65-90; K. LEBACQZ, *Professional Ethics: Power and Paradox*, Nashville, TN, Abingdon Press, 1985, pp. 109-123; ID. – J. DISKRILL, *Ethics and Spiritual Care: A Guide for Pastors, Chaplains, and Spiritual Caregivers*, Nashville, TN, Abingdon Press, 2000, pp. 72-77; C. NEUGER, *Power and Difference in Pastoral Theology*, in N.J. RAMSAY (ed.), *Pastoral Care and Counseling: Redefining the Paradigms*, Nashville, TN, Abingdon Press, 2004, 65-85; T. TRULL – J. CARTER, *Ministerial Ethics: Moral Formation for Church Leaders*, Grand Rapids, MI, Baker Academic, 2004, pp. 90-97.

5. HEITINK, *Practical Theology* (n. 1), pp. 310-324.

6. A. VAN HEIJST, *Professional Loving Care and the Bearable Heaviness of Being*, in H. LINDEMANN – M. VERKERK – M. URBAN WALKER (eds.), *Naturalized Bioethics?*, Cambridge, Cambridge University Press, 2009, 199-217.

This unequal position creates an inequality or imbalance in the relationship. This imbalance is inevitably a power imbalance. Power means the ability to influence or control other persons. Obviously, the pastor has more power. But in particular situations the conversation partner can also exercise limited power on the pastor and the pastor can feel very powerless and helpless. Despite this possibility, the power imbalance is mostly in favour of the pastor because of the structure of their relationship.

Indeed, the unequal position and the power imbalance are structural facts. They are inescapable facts in the pastoral relationship as well as in any other caring and helping relationship. Unequal position and power imbalance belong to the inherent structure of any professional relationship. They anticipate the manner in which pastor and conversation partner relate to each other. They are structural facts and not immediately an ethical matter.

3. *An Ethical Reflection*

In a critical ethical reflection, it is helpful to make a distinction between the 'premoral' dimension on the one hand and the 'moral' dimension on the other hand[7]. We consider the unequal position and the power imbalance as premoral evil. They are evaluated as 'evil' because on a philosophical and anthropological level all human beings are considered as fundamentally equal[8]. Unequal position and power imbalance are qualified as 'premoral' because they are inevitable facts in the human actions. These facts are not immoral or unethical, but premoral of preethical. They become moral or ethical through human actions.

The reason is that the morality or the ethical character of human actions depends on three 'sources of morality': the intention of the person who acts, the object associated with that act and the circumstances surrounding the act[9]. These three elements determine the moral

7. R. GULA, *Reason Informed by Faith: Foundations of Catholic Morality*, New York – Mahwah, NJ, Paulist Press, 1989, pp. 269-270; L. JANSSENS, *Ontic Evil and Moral Evil*, in *Louvain Studies* 4 (1972-73) 115-156, pp. 133-156; ID., *Ontic Good and Evil: Premoral Values and Disvalues*, in *Louvain Studies* 12 (1987) 62-82, pp. 70-82. In the tradition of moral theology, the distinction between premoral and moral is based on and develops the distinction between *malum physicum* (physical evil) and *malum morale* (moral evil).

8. ID., *Artificial Insemination: Ethical Considerations*, in *Louvain Studies* 8 (1980) 3-29, pp. 12-13. Janssens elaborates a personalist view on the human being, in which fundamental equality is an important dimension.

9. GULA, *Reason Informed by Faith* (n. 7), pp. 265-267; JANSSENS, *Ontic Evil and Moral Evil* (n. 7), pp. 116-132. In the moral theological tradition, the three sources of morality are the *finis operantis* (intention), the *finis operis* (object), and the *circumstantiae* (circumstances).

or ethical character of human actions. The morality of human actions depends on how these actions are intended by human persons in particular circumstances. Consequently, the ethical or moral character of the imbalance of power depends on the way the persons concerned deal with this unequal power in a particular situation. If they use the imbalance of power in pastoral counselling for their own benefit or to the disadvantage of the other, then the human actions are unethical and the asymmetric relationship becomes unethical. The ethical character hinges on the way people deal in a free and responsible way with the power imbalance.

When we return to our concept of pastoral counselling, it becomes clear that the concept was fundamentally relational and based on a relational ethics. We described pastoral counselling as an empowering companionship or relationship. The pastor does not engage in this relationship for his or her own benefit, but for the benefit of the conversation partner. The pastor's aim is to empower the conversation partner, to make him or her more powerful. So the conversation partner is better able to assume his or her own responsibilities. At the same time, the pastor can redress the imbalance of power within the pastoral relationship. In short, the qualification of empowering companionship expresses the true goal of pastoral counselling: the empowerment of the conversation partner in his or her own quest for meaning and/or faith in life.

An important consequence of these ethical reflections on power is that the person who has the greatest power in the relationship also bears the greatest responsibility towards that relationship. Because of the fact of the unequal position, the pastor has the greatest power and the greatest responsibility. This imposes a twofold responsibility on the pastor: the responsibility not to abuse the power or harm the conversation partner, and the responsibility to empower the conversation partner in his or her quest for meaning and/or faith in life.

II. The Need for Ethical Attitudes

1. *The Use of Moral Rules and Guidelines*

Now the challenge is how we can improve the responsibility of the pastor towards the conversation partner, so that there is no abuse of the power but on the contrary empowerment of the other. A quite evident approach is that of moral norms and rules. They are practical guidelines for the human actions and make clear what is good or evil. These rules and guidelines are expressed in professional codes of ethics. But mostly, these professional codes are very short in warning for exploiting the power imbalance and involving into dual relationships[10]. In our opinion, the most interesting and significant rules are formulated in the *Code of Professional Ministerial Responsibility,* proposed by Gula. We quote his rules concerning the use of power:

1. "We do not minimize or ignore the unique power that we have over those seeking pastoral service, but we strive to use our power in ways that respect the dignity of persons by empowering them to come into their own freedom and so to participate more fully in the mission of the church.
2. We should be sufficiently self-disciplined so as to maintain clear boundaries in our pastoral relationships and restrain from exploiting the trust and the dependency of those who seek our service by not using them to satisfy our needs for attention, acceptance, and pleasure.
3. We strive to avoid, to the extent possible, those dual relationships (e.g. with our employees, students, friends, business relationships) which could impair our professional judgement, create conflicts of interest, or lead to exploiting the relationship for our own gain. When dual relationships are inevitable, we must lessen their potential for conflicts or interest and exploitation by monitoring our role and boundaries and by being clear about whose needs are being met[11].

These moral rules and guidelines are interesting, but in our opinion, they are not sufficient to influence profoundly the practice of pastoral counselling. They concern what pastors should do and mostly all pastors know that they should not exploit the power imbalance and should better not involve in dual relationships. Nevertheless, it seems so difficult to respect these rules and guidelines. Therefore, we develop another approach, inspired by ethical attitudes.

10. These guidelines are generally accepted in the ethical codes of all professional groups. For specific codes of ethics for pastors we refer to: AMERICAN ASSOCIATION OF CHRISTIAN COUNSELORS, *Code of Ethics*, 2004, art. 1.102; 1.130, www.aacc.net; AMERICAN ASSOCIATION OF PASTORAL COUNSELORS, *Code of Ethics*, 2010, art. III.E; III.H, www.aapc.org; CANADIAN ASSOCIATION FOR PASTORAL PRACTICE AND EDUCATION, *Code of Ethics for Chaplains, Pastoral Counselors, Pastors, Pastoral Educators and Students*, 2009, art. 1.4; 1.6, www.cappe.org; NETHERLANDS ASSOCIATION OF SPIRITUAL COUNSELLORS IN CARE INSTITUTIONS, *Professional Standard Spiritual Counsellors*, 2005, art. 8; 18, www.vgvz.nl.

11. GULA, *Ethics in Pastoral Ministry* (n. 7), p. 148.

2. *The Importance of Ethical Attitudes*

Ethics is often associated with the external dimension of human actions guided by rules. But to focus on actions is not sufficient for ethical reflection. As we have seen, there are several 'sources of morality': not only the actions, but also the intention in particular circumstances[12]. Actions are the expression of what human persons intend. Ethics is equally concerned with the internal dimension, namely who human beings are. This internal dimension is closely related to virtues or attitudes. In the ethical tradition, a virtue or an attitude is a fixed habit or a personal quality which focuses our actions on what is good[13]. Because of the moralistic connotations of the word virtue, we prefer to speak of attitudes.

It seems very important to make a shift from an ethics of doing, based on rules, to an ethics of being, inspired by attitudes. These attitudes express who we are, and they underline and determine what we do. They are the driving force of our actions. From a psychological point of view, these attitudes are a resource of motivation for our actions. But from a theological point of view, they are a source of inspiration too. Spirituality endows pastors with an inner conviction and an inner strength which make them able to really perform their pastoral counselling. For this reason, ethical attitudes are the motivational and the spiritual foundation of ethics in pastoral counselling. Moreover, they are not only qualities of the person, but also abilities. The attitudes provide the pastors also with knowledge and skill to act in an ethical way.

Human actions can be seen as the concrete, outward expression of our ethical attitudes: they are the fruit of the tree. In this respect, the attitude is more fundamental than the action. Nevertheless, it can sometimes be difficult to identify and articulate these attitudes, and often we learn most about them by analysing and interpreting the ensuing actions: by their fruits you shall know them. Consequently, there is an interaction between attitudes and actions, but it is always the attitudes which provide the basic inspiration and motivation for our deeds. In this sense, ethics flow automatically from the good attitudes which inspire and motivate our actions. If our attitudes are not good, our actions will lose their ethical quality or character. This explains the great importance of sound ethical attitudes.

12. See note 9. In the tradition of moral theology, a distinction has been made between the *actus interior* (inner act) and the *actus exterior* (exterior act).

13. J. KEENAN, *Virtue Ethics*, in B. HOOSE (ed.), *Christian Ethics: An Introduction*, London – New York, Continuum, 84-94; S. PINCKAERS, *Plaidoyer pour la vertu*, Paris, Parole et Silence, 2007.

It is possible to identify a number of attitudes which can be said to be fundamental for pastors[14]. But we need to be careful. By describing these attitudes we may create the impression that pastors need to be almost perfect people. This, of course, is not the case. Ethical attitudes are virtues or characteristics of the person: they describe who we should strive to become, not necessarily who we 'must' be. From an ethical perspective, it is important that pastors should seek to embody these fundamental attitudes, but in the full realization that it will seldom, if ever, be possible to succeed in this quest. In this respect, it is worth noting that mildness is one of these ethical attitudes, and it is an attitude that we should be prepared to apply to ourselves.

These ethical attitudes can be related to some recent theories concerning virtues and attitudes, namely the theories of love, presence, compassion and mercy[15]. These theories present one fundamental virtue or attitude, but by a closer look it is a synthesis of a range of attitudes. We prefer to introduce a pattern of interrelated attitudes and to describe these attitudes individually, in terms of their own dynamic. We elaborated a pattern of nine attitudes for pastoral counselling, inspired by literature and our experience in ethical advising and pastoral supervision. In these nine attitudes, we can discern three sets of three attitudes. The first three attitudes concern a receiving movement, the next three a responding and the last three a guiding movement towards the conversation partner.

Finally, we should remark that these attitudes are not specific for dealing with asymmetry and power, but they are general attitudes for good pastoral counselling. Good pastoral counselling is inspired by these ethical attitudes and is at the same time the best way to prevent abuse of power and to empower the conversation partner.

3. *Openness, Attentiveness and Mildness*

The first three attitudes form a receiving movement. It is clear that pastors first have to be open and to receive other persons before they can respond to and guide them. The main receiving attitude is attentiveness

14. See A. Liégeois, *Values in Dialogue, Ethics in Care*, in progress.

15. See A. van Heijst, *Professional Loving Care: An Ethical View of the Health Care Sector*, Leuven, Peeters, 2011; A. Baart – F. Vosman, *Relationship Based Care and Recognition.* Part One: *Sketching Good Care from the Theory of Presence and Five Entries*, in C. Leget – C. Gastmans – M. Verkerk (eds.), *Care, Compassion and Recognition: An Ethical Discussion*, Leuven, Peeters, 2011, 183-200; M. Nussbaum, *Upheavals of Thought: The Intelligence of Emotions*, Cambridge, Cambridge University Press, 2001.

to others. This attentiveness can be qualified with mildness. It is a mild attentiveness to the conversation partners. The assumption of such a mild attentiveness is a basic openness towards others.

The most fundamental of the receiving attitudes is openness[16]. It is a precondition for all the other attitudes. Openness is the quality and ability to open oneself for other persons, to be available to and touchable by the others. Synonyms for openness could be approachability, accessibility, availability, receptivity or touchability. Openness enables pastors to encounter their conversation partners and to be touched by them. This entails that the pastors try to push their own concerns and preoccupations to one side, or at least to put them on 'hold'. In this sense, the pastors need to create an inner and free space, a space in their own minds. In this inner and free space, they can welcome and receive their conversation partners. There, they can be touched and affected by the others personality and life story. Openness therefore implies a willingness to listen and to enter into dialogue.

Openness is a necessary prerequisite for attentiveness[17]. It is the quality and ability of paying attention to other persons, to listen carefully and with interest. Synonyms for this attitude are understanding, empathy, sympathy or compassion. Attentiveness means that pastors are involved with and really interested in their conversation partners. They listen with attention and concentration to the other persons' story. They try to be understanding and sensitive to the experiences, feelings and thoughts, motives and needs of their conversation partners. This entails that pastors move from their own position or perspective to the position of the other persons and try to understand them from their own perspective. In this respect, attention is a broader concept than empathy. This last concept is a specific term in the field of counselling and psychotherapy. It focuses on feelings and less or not on thoughts, and it is associated with special skills and techniques to get inside the minds of other people. Compassion and sympathy are ethical terms, but according to their etymological meaning, they emphasise too much the suffering in life and do not include enough the joy of life.

Mildness can be seen as an important qualification of attentiveness[18]. It is the quality and the ability to accept other persons in benevolent way,

16. See N. PEMBROKE, *The Art of Listening: Dialogue, Shame and Pastoral Care*, Grand Rapids, MI, Eerdmans, 2002.

17. See E. HOUSSET, *L'intelligence de la pitié: Phénoménologie de la communauté*, Paris, Cerf, 2003.

18. See L. BASSET, *Moi, je ne juge personne: L'Évangile au-delà de la morale*, Genève, Labor et Fides, 1998.

without blaming or condemning. Other words are acceptance, kindness, gentleness, benevolence or generosity. Mildness implies that the pastors do accept their conversation partners as they are. Pastors are kind and gentle towards others. They receive their conversation partners with a positive and benevolent regard. They endeavour to perceive the positive elements in the others' person and life, and not to fix their attention to the more negative aspects. They do not blame or condemn their conversation partners for particular feelings, thoughts or actions. Pastors accept their conversation partners as human persons in a generous way. This does not mean that pastors approve and agree with all their convictions and behaviour. However, pastors are prepared to continually give their conversation partners new chances, so that there is always hope for future improvement.

4. *Recognition, Responsibilization and Truthfulness*

After receiving the conversation partners with an open and mild attentiveness, we move on to responding them. Here two attitudes are on the foreground, namely recognition and responsibilization. These attitudes are interrelated and should be in a good balance. A precondition for expressing these attitudes is truthfulness.

The first responding attitude is recognition of other persons[19]. Giving recognition is the quality and ability to respect, appreciate and confirm other persons as valued human beings. Other words are respect, esteem, appreciation, approval and confirmation. Recognition is a more active concept than respect and mildness. Respect can be interpreted as the passive acceptance and tolerance of others. Mildness is a receiving attitude of benevolent acceptance of the others as they are. Recognition on the contrary, is a responding attitude that not only accepts the other persons as they are, but also appreciates them for the valuable human beings they are. Recognizing pastors express this appreciation. They approve and confirm the others persons as valuable human beings. Recognition is a prerequisite for the creation of a pastoral relationship, since it underlines the essential value of the other person, irrespective of their abilities and limitations, their life and behaviour.

Giving recognition could be understood as accepting and confirming persons in the situation they live. It might even be interpreted as paternalism, as protecting persons in their current life situation without challenging

19. See A. HONNETH, *Kampf um Anerkennung: Zur moralischen Grammatik sozialer Konflikt*, Frankfurt am Main, Suhrkamp, 1992.

them to change this situation. Therefore, it is important to counterbalance recognition by responsibilization[20]. The attitude of responsibilization is the quality and ability to give other persons freedom of choice and to enhance their responsibility. Synonyms could be emancipation, assertion, encouragement or empowerment. Indeed, responsibilization expresses the empowering character of pastoral counselling. Pastors have the task to strengthen their conversation partners. They support and encourage their conversation partners, so that they can find the strength and courage to take their own responsibility. The pastors try to foster as much self-responsibility to the conversation partner as possible, thereby further developing the conversation partner's own sense of personal responsibility. The pastors only take responsibility themselves if it is absolutely necessary.

Truthfulness is a prerequisite for recognition and responsibilization[21]. A good balance between recognizing and responsibilizing other persons is only reasonable if these persons experience the pastor as being truthful. Truthfulness is the quality and ability to act in correspondence with truth, so that there is a correlation between intentions and actions. Synonyms for truthfulness are genuineness, honesty, sincerity and veracity. Truthfulness entails that there is a correlation between the opinions and the behaviour of the pastors, between what they think and feel on the one hand and what they say and do on the other hand. So the conversation partners are able to see pastors as persons who are trustworthy and reliable. Truthfulness also implies that pastors do not place their faith in false or so-called 'absolute' truths. They seek to discover the truth through dialogue, in which they examine the different perspectives of all those involved, thereby broadening their own perspective.

5. *Wisdom, Self-Reflection and Integrity*

Receiving the conservation partners and responding to them, belongs to the core of pastoral counselling. Sometimes pastors can also guide their conservation partners in making choices. Two attitudes are essential for this guiding movement, namely wisdom en self-reflection. The precondition to realise these attitudes is integrity.

20. See A. LIÉGEOIS, *The Perspective of Mental Disability Care on Asymmetry in the Care-Relationship: Towards Empowering Compassion*, in LEGET – GASTMANS – VERKERK (eds.), *Care, Compassion and Recognition* (n. 15), 117-130.

21. See J. BUSH, *Gentle Shepherding: Pastoral Ethics and Leadership*, St. Louis, MO, Chalice Press, 2004, pp. 70-105.

The first guiding attitude is wisdom[22]. It is the quality and ability to make sensible decisions and to give good advices based on reason and experience. Other words are advisability, prudence, conscientiousness and good judgement. It is a practical wisdom which pastors need in order to transform in a well-considered manner theoretical knowledge into sensible practice for their conversation partners. Wisdom requires a fine balance between intelligence and emotion, and a strong feeling for the human aspects of the situation. Wisdom in this sense relates to the classical virtue of prudence. This is the character of being reasonable and careful when assessing situations or taking important decisions. This wisdom is inspired through a person's own conscience. This is the sense of what is good and evil and the endeavour to do good and avoid evil.

Wisdom goes hand in hand with self-reflection. This attitude is the quality and ability to critically examine and assess one's own choices and actions. Other possible words are self-criticism and self-questioning. Pastors can ask critical questions to themselves. What are we choosing and why are we choosing it? What are we doing and why are we doing it? These questions help to prevent pastors from becoming bogged down in routine. Self-reflection challenges in a constructive manner the pastors' attitudes, knowledge and skills. It encourages comparison of their own practices with the good practices of other pastors. It stimulates the search for new scientific insights which can improve the own insights. Self-reflection ensures that pastors measure their own perspective against the perspectives of their conversation partners and of significant others.

A prerequisite for guiding other persons and realising the attitudes of wisdom and self-reflection is integrity[23]. This is the quality and ability to act in correspondence with ethics. Other words for integrity are reliability, righteousness, rectitude and incorruptibility. Integrity is related to the attitude of truthfulness, but is nevertheless different. It entails that there is unity, consistency or correlation of the pastors' choices, actions and behaviour on the one hand and their beliefs, values and norms on the other hand. Integrity therefore implies that there is no discrepancy between what pastors postulate in ethical terms and what they actually do. If pastors possess integrity, they will be regarded as being reliable and trustworthy. Pastors lose their integrity if they cease to be faithful to

22. See T. BEAUCHAMP – J. CHILDRESS, *Principles of Biomedical Ethics*, Oxford – New York, Oxford University Press, 2001, pp. 32-39; R. GULA, *Conscience*, in B. HOOSE (ed.), *Christian Ethics: An Introduction*, London – New York, Continuum, 110-122.

23. See B. MUSSCHENGA, *Integrity – Personal, Moral and Professional*, in ID. – W. VAN HAAFTEN – B. SPIECKER – M. SLORS (eds.), *Personal and Moral Identity*, Dordrecht, Kluwer, 2002, 169-201.

their own values and norms, or if they compromise their own sense of impartiality and/or incorruptibility.

6. *A Prerequisite: Emotional Integrity*

Ethical integrity presupposes that pastors have already attained a high level of emotional integrity. This means that pastors experience harmony and well-being in their emotional life. Two means are required to reach this emotional integrity, namely self-knowledge and self-care.

Self-knowledge is necessary for pastors in order to be aware of their own desires and needs, and the role which these can play in the processes of transference and countertransference[24]. By transference, the conversation partners project in an unconscious way onto their pastors a number of unfulfilled wishes or unresolved problems stemming from relationships with other important people in their life. On the contrary, by the process of countertransference, pastors can also project unconsciously a number of their own unfulfilled wishes and unresolved problems back onto the conversation partners. As a result, the pastors can sometimes use or abuse the conversation partners to satisfy their own desires and find solutions to their own problems. If they are conscious of their use or abuse, their acts are even more disgusting. The use of power for the pastors' own benefit distorts pastoral counselling which has as its purpose the empowerment of the conversation partners. Therefore, pastors should learn during their education and training how to deal with their own desires and problems in the pastoral relationship.

This brings us to the question of the pastor's self-care. One of the pastors' tasks is to ensure their own emotional well-being and integrity. Being comfortable and content with their own private and professional life is an important precondition for keeping unfulfilled feelings and needs detached from their pastoral relationships. If the pastors are not able to do this, they may need external guidance and help. Pastors can seek this support in an informal way from a colleague or a friend. They can also use formal procedures as supervision or intervision to approve their emotional functioning in pastoral counselling. In severe cases, they can undergo psychotherapy. The advice of an outsider might help the

24. B.M. HARTUNG, *Transference*, in HUNTER (ed.), *Dictionary of Pastoral Care and Counseling* (n. 1), 1285-1286; L. ROBINSON, *The Abuse of Power: A View of Sexual Misconduct in a Systemic Approach of Pastoral Care*, in *Pastoral Psychology* 52 (2004) 395-404, pp. 400-404.

pastors to clarify their own desires and needs, allowing them to function more effectively in both their personal and a professional life.

III. Conclusion

We addressed the research question how pastors can deal in a responsible way with the asymmetry and power in pastoral counselling. We defined pastoral counselling as an empowering relationship. In fact, the relationship is asymmetric. The pastor and the conversation partner have an unequal position and this creates an imbalance of power. However, this power imbalance is structural and premoral and becomes moral depending on the way the pastor and conversation partner deal with it. Because the pastor has the greatest power, he or she bears the greatest responsibility, namely not to abuse the power but to empower the conversation partner. For that reason, pastoral counselling is qualified as an empowering relationship.

Rules are not sufficient to influence profoundly the praxis of pastoral counselling. Because attitudes are the driving force of actions, we developed a pattern of nine interrelated ethical attitudes consisting of three groups of three receiving, responding and guiding attitudes. But are these attitudes sufficient to incite pastors not to abuse power and to empower their conversation partner? Certainly, the theoretical knowledge of these attitudes is mostly not sufficient. Pastors need more practical support to realise these attitudes in their praxis. First, a prerequisite is the necessary psychosocial support to attain emotional integrity. Secondly, they need practical training and supervision to develop these attitudes. Finally, they need a personal spirituality that nourishes them with an inner conviction and an inner strength to adopt these attitudes. It would be interesting to continue research in these fields.

Research Unit Pastoral Theology
Faculty of Theology and Religious Studies
KU Leuven – Catholic University of Leuven
Sint-Michielsstraat 4 box 3101
B-3000 Leuven
Belgium
axel.liegeois@theo.kuleuven.be

Axel Liégeois

DOING JUSTICE IN PRIMARY RELATIONSHIPS

INTERSUBJECTIVITY, SOCIAL IDENTITY AND POWER IN PASTORAL COUNSELLING, IN DIALOGUE WITH THE THOUGHT OF IVAN BOSZORMENYI-NAGY

Most often, it is the relation with a counsellor that is the most helpful for a counsellee. Therefore, it is important to search for what could be called a 'just counselling relationship' or a just relationship of pastoral care. In this contribution I focus on how the contextual thought of Ivan Boszormenyi-Nagy (1920-2007)[1] can contribute to this subject and how it is related to other theories about pastoral counselling, such as the work of Pamela Cooper-White and reflections on 'power'.

I. CONTEXTUAL PASTORAL WORK

Since 1986 many pastoral ministers in the Netherlands have been trained in what we call 'contextual pastoral work'[2]. Here, the term 'contextual' refers to the 'contextual thinking' of the Hungarian-American psychiatrist Ivan Boszormenyi-Nagy. In the eighties and the nineties of the last century, his work became very popular in the Netherlands. It was well received by psychotherapists, educationalists, social workers and by pastoral ministers. In Belgium, the ideas of Ivan Boszormenyi-Nagy also had an influence in these areas. The Dutch social worker Ammy Van Heusden (1920-1986), who translated Nagy's work into Dutch, introduced Nagy in the Netherlands. Together with Else-Marie Van den Eerenbeemt she wrote 'Balans in beweging' (*Balance in motion*), an introduction to contextual therapy[3]. Nagy also visited the Netherlands and Belgium several times for masterclasses and workshops. The Dutch-Belgian organisation *Leren over Leven*

1. I. BOSZORMENYI-NAGY, *Foundations of Contextual Therapy: Collected Papers of Ivan Boszormenyi-Nagi*, New York, NY, Brunner – Mazel, 1987; ID. – J. GRUNEBAUM – D. ULRICH, *Contextual Therapy*, in A. GUMAN – D. KNISKERN (eds.), *Handbook of Family Therapy* (vol. 2), New York, NY, Brunner – Mazel, 1991, 200-238.

2. H. MEULINK-KORF – A. VAN RHIJN, *De onvermoede derde: Inleiding in het contextueel pastoraat*, Zoetermeer, Meinema, 2002, p. 12.

3. A. VAN HEUSDEN – E.-M. VAN DEN EERENBEEMT, *Balance in Motion: Ivan Boszormenyi-Nagy and His Vision of Inidvidual and Family Therapy*, New York, NY, Brunner – Mazel, 1987.

vzw is one of the main promoters of Nagy's ideas – but courses in 'contextual thinking' are offered by various therapeutical institutes, mostly framed within broader training in systemic or family therapy. Nagy's theory, however, offers an approach that balances between family therapy and individual therapy. Simultaneously with its reception in the social sciences, Nagy's theory influenced theories on pastoral ministry. Hanneke Meulink-Korf and Aat van Rhijn introduced a two-year formation course of contextual pastoral care organised by the University of Amsterdam in Doorn, the Netherlands. Nowadays, the training is given by Henk Vrielink and Nel van Doorn. Since 2010 a similar type of training has been conducted in Romania.

In this contribution I will present some elements of contextual pastoral care and the contextual theory of Nagy in general, in order to investigate the meaning of 'justice' in a pastoral relationship and in primary relationships such as the family.

The lens through which I look is the 'relational paradigm' as presented by the American theologian Pamela Cooper-White[4]. I will analyse to what degree the approach of contextual pastoral care, following Nagy, and Cooper-White's approach are similar and complementary. Cooper-White presents a 'relational paradigm' for pastoral care and counselling, which takes a middle way between objectivism and constructivism and which recognises the subjectivity of both the care-giver and the care receiver. I will use the terms 'counselling', 'counsellor' and 'counsellee' throughout this contribution. These terms can refer to a therapist (in Nagy's own thought, as Nagy does not speak about pastoral care himself), to a pastoral counsellor or a pastor offering pastoral care in various settings.

II. Basic Principles of Contextual Thinking

When reflecting on the contextual (or 'intergenerational') thinking of Nagy, it is important to distinguish the two relationships in which 'dialogue' takes place and about which Nagy has written. Dialogue refers both to the relationship between the counsellor and counsellee and to the relationships between family members. The insights about dialogue between family members are important in so far as they make clear how counsellors should best deal with counsellees and how the dialogue between counsellor and counsellee may be qualified. In this contribution,

4. P. Cooper-White, *Shared Wisdom: Use of the Self in Pastoral Care and Counselling*, Minneapolis, MN, Fortress Press, 2004.

I will analyze aspects of relations in families and in counselling processes, showing how the two are interwoven.

1. *Loyalty*

In 'contextual work' it is important that the counsellor takes into account the dynamics in each family, even when he or she only works with one individual. Nagy considers loyalty between family members very important. Loyalty does not refer to feelings, a 'sense of loyalty' or to a form of obedience to someone in a hierarchical position. It is "a preferential commitment to a relationship, based on indebtedness born of earned merit"[5]. A child is always loyal to his or her birthmother and birthfather, because they have given life to the child. Even if they could not care for the child and have given the child up for adoption, there is often a strong loyalty from the child – as we can see in the common 'root-seeking' of adopted children. When a father or mother cares for their children, they gain their children's loyalty. The title of Nagy's first book, *Invisible loyalties*[6], explains how the dynamics of loyalty are often hidden, but nevertheless important. A boy who is not allowed to see his father, who has divorced his mother, may act in a destructive way, such as using an excessive amount of drugs and alcohol as a hidden way to react against the situation, Nagy says. Couples usually do not appreciate their partners' criticism of parents-in-law, even if they agree with the criticism. Here, loyalty also plays a role.

2. *Respecting Loyalty and Each Person's Position in Counselling*

For a counsellor, it is very important to take into account the counsellee's loyalty mainly towards parents, but also to other family members. A contextual counsellor will ask questions that aim to (re)connect family members. The counsellor asks questions that help the clients to think about their relationships, especially from the point of view of the other ('how do you think your mother would feel if she knew what you did?') or from the perspective of the client's own positive contribution to the other ('How do you think you can help your father, now that he is old and ill?'). This leads to Nagy's main insight for counselling, which is the

5. I. Boszormenyi-Nagy – B.R. Krasner, *Between Give and Take: A Clinical Guide to Contextual Therapy*, New York, NY, Brunner-Mazel, 1986, p. 15.
6. I. Boszormenyi-Nagy – G.M. Spark, *Invisible Loyalties: Reciprocity in Intergenerational Family Therapy*, Levittown, PA, Brunner-Mazel, 1973.

attitude of multidirected partiality. This means that the counsellor takes the position of everyone involved in the (family) system (present or not) – not at the same time, because a bird's eye view is impossible, but one after another. The counsellor has an eye for each person's (constructive) entitlement, but also tries to give a voice to the injustices that have occurred in the system. The counsellor does not consider anyone a monster, even if family members blame each other. This openness for each one's positive possibilities is based on a positive anthropology. One of the central ideas in Nagy's thought is the concept 'destructive entitlement' that functions as a way to understand why some people act in a destructive way. If people suffer from injustice, Nagy says they are 'destructively entitled': they may expect something back from others or from life, because of their own suffering. 'Destructive entitlement' (among other things) occurs when parents fail to recognise the giving that comes from the child, as when the child "receives mistrust, deceit and mystification in return for his trust and devotion", or when "the child is eventually blamed for adult, relational failures"[7]. When this kind of exploitation occurs, a "child is justified in seeing the adult world as his debtor"[8]. Unfortunately, it often happens that people 'use' this destructive entitlement and 'take' from others, often third parties such as their own partner or children, what they did not get during their own childhood. Nagy does not legitimise this, but the concept 'destructive entitlement' can help people to see that others do not act negatively because they are 'monsters', but are often influenced by their experiences, such as being badly treated themselves. Nagy considers it important to recognise people's destructive entitlement. In situations where it is very difficult to credit someone for his or her actual merits, one can refer to destructive entitlement in order to see that the person is not totally bad. A contextual counsellor will ask each person to try to find merits in the other, and to name them.

Crediting is not something for the counsellor alone, it is most of all something the family members have to do themselves. Here we arrive at another important element in contextual work. The main aim is to empower individuals in their relationships, and thus also to empower families. The means through which this goal should be reached are, according to Nagy, the actions of family members among themselves and only secondarily through counselling. It is not the relationship between

7. BOSZORMENYI-NAGY – KRASNER, *Between Give and Take* (n. 5), p. 415.
8. *Ibid.*

counsellor and counsellee that is central in contextual work, but the relation between family members.

One of Nagy's co-authors, Barbara Krasner, has published much about 'direct address': the relevance of speaking directly to family members, and not only speaking about them in counselling[9]. Direct address refers to the basic idea that it is not the counsellor who has the main role in counselling, but the family members themselves, who are admonished to speak directly towards each other and to share each others' 'truth'. Krasner and Joyce call 'direct address' the "cornerstone of dialogical possibilities"[10]. It can stimulate real dialogue between family members. Direct address can take many forms, "a word, a tear, a touch, a look, a gift, a tone, a question posed"[11]. If direct address does not succeed – which is very possible, as it is a demanding process – something may be lost. Krasner and Joyce describe this as "the truth of each person's side"[12]. Between parents and children it may be sometimes difficult to come to 'direct address', as many children have perceived the message 'not to disturb the parents', 'not to talk to the parents in an explicit way', and may have internalised these messages, even when they are adults themselves[13]. Loyalty may then become 'binding' – which may lead to a loss of freedom and real dialogue. However, when family members are able to speak in a direct way to each other, this may stimulate the 'ethical imagination' they need so as to be able to take the position of the other and to credit the other for his or her entitlement.

III. Objectivity and (Inter)Subjectivity in Contextual Therapy

1. *Justice in Relationships – the Concept of the Justice of the Human Order*

The aim of these 'techniques' or 'methods' – direct address and multi-directed partiality – is to favour the autonomy and the trust of clients, so that counselling becomes superfluous[14]. Nagy recognises the value of the role of the counsellor (his or her "capacity to empathize with each family member's justifications and to credit their relational merit is likely to

9. B.R. Krasner – A.J. Joyce, *Truth, Trust and Relationships: Healing Interventions in Contextual Therapy*, New York, NY, Brunner-Mazel, 1995.

10. *Ibid.*, p. xxi.

11. *Ibid.*, p. xxiii.

12. *Ibid.*, p. xxii.

13. *Ibid.*

14. Boszormenyi-Nagy – Krasner, *Between Give and Take* (n. 5), p. 113.

have a catalytic effect"[15]), but at the same time he argues that "[f]amily members have to find their own ways toward earning constructive entitlement. (...) The therapeutic task is to guide family members towards self-rewarding avenues of autonomy and trustbuilding. It is this self-reinforcing process rather than therapeutic acknowledgement *per se* that ultimately functions as a healing source"[16].

Nagy wants to stimulate justice in relationships. Justice does not refer to a fixed constellation of values and norms, or specific family orderings, but to what he calls 'the justice of the human order'[17]. This concept is derived from Buber's 'human order of being'. The 'justice of the human order' can be considered as a combination of Buber's concepts of the 'order of the human world' and the 'justice of the order of being'[18].

Nagy's conceptual framework is based on the assumption that human relationships are intrinsically ethical. Relationships are not mere transactions, they have a deeper meaning that refers to this 'justice of the human order'. This does not have to do with actual values and norms[19]. Nagy is afraid of been seen as moralistic. He has a rather narrow idea about what he calls "the common usage of the term 'ethics'"[20]. He associates this with "an individual's selfless, even self-sacrificing, consideration of persons or principles"[21]. Nagy's own conception of relational ethics deals with "the equitable distribution of the benefits and burdens of all partners in a given situation"[22].

The concept of the justice of the human order is similar to a constructivist view of values and norms as it leaves a lot of space for interpretation, but it also refers to a reality that is more than a mere construction. I consider 'constructivist' here in a similar way as does Pamela Cooper-White[23]. She distinguishes between the extremes of constructivist and positivistic approaches. Whereas the positivist position believes in the possibility of knowing 'reality out there' and is based on the 'correspondence theory' of truth, the constructivist position does not acknowledge that there is a

15. *Ibid.*

16. *Ibid.*, pp. 113-114.

17. I. BOSZORMENYI-NAGY, *Foundations of Contextual Therapy: Collected Papers of Ivan Boszormenyi-Nagy*, New York, NY, Brunner-Mazel, 1987, p. 308.

18. M. BUBER, *Guilt and Guilt Feelings*, in ID., *The Knowledge of Man: Selected Essays*, ed. and trans. M. FRIEDMAN – R.G. SMITH, New York, NY, Harper & Row, 1965, 121-148, pp. 127, 146.

19. BOSZORMENYI-NAGY, *Foundations of Contextual Therapy* (n. 17), p. 275.

20. ID. – KRASNER, *Between Give and Take* (n. 5), p. 173.

21. *Ibid.*

22. *Ibid.*

23. COOPER-WHITE, *Shared Wisdom* (n. 4), p. 45.

reality out there. For constructivists there are only 'truths' that are "multiple, fluid, local, particular, changing, and cocreated"[24]. Most contemporary thinkers about (pastoral) care and counselling (including Nagy) can be situated in the middle position that is given the umbrella name 'postpositivism' by Coooper-White. This middle position – where 'social constructionism' also has a place[25] – is characterised by the belief that reality exists 'out there' but that one cannot know it directly. Truth is always influenced by contextual factors.

Contextual thinking is very much centred on what happens between people, on the relationship. The 'ethical' is not dependent on cultural values, but more on what is considered as 'just' in the interaction between people. On the other hand, Nagy thinks there is something 'out there' that is more than only a subjective interpretation of what happens. This point of reference that goes beyond subjective interpretation, however, cannot be considered at all similar to a positivistic approach. Nagy's approach is in line with Cooper-White's 'relational and intersubjective paradigm' (based on a postpositivistic epistemology).

Nagy speaks about an ethical dimension in addition to the dimensions of facts, psychology, and interaction. This fourth, ethical dimension that centres around 'justice of the human order' is a way of considering elements of the other three dimensions. A divorce (in the dimension of facts) of the parents can be seen, for example, within the fourth relational ethical dimension as a form of 'destructive entitlement' a child receives.

2. *Transference and Countertransference*

From the approach developed by Cooper-White, Nagy's insights about interpretation and co-constructing reality in relation to the meaning of the 'justice of the human order' seem very much related with what Cooper-White calls the 'relational paradigm', focusing on intersubjectivity in pastoral care and counselling. When Nagy speaks about transference and countertransference, however, he is more hesitant than Cooper-White. Nagy's interpretation of transference and countertransference is narrower than the one of Cooper-White[26]. Nagy clearly wants to prevent possible negative consequences of transference and countertransference, mainly

24. *Ibid.*

25. Cooper-White refers to the work of Kenneth J. GERGEN, *The Social Constructionist Movement in Modern Psychology*, in *American Psychologist* 40 (1985) 266-275. See COOPER-WHITE, *Shared Wisdom* (n. 4), p. 44.

26. For an overview of the history of the concepts of 'transference' and 'countertransference', see COOPER-WHITE, *Shared Wisdom* (n. 4), pp. 26-34.

on the basis of his concern to deal with difficulties and positive elements within the actual family relations (cf. 'direct address'). His focus on the existential loyalty of each child towards his or her parents and the loyalty within family relations in general makes him aware of the danger that a therapist becomes a 'better parent' for the client. He acknowledges that transference may be important in therapy ("Freud's description of transference and its therapeutic use obviously has much merit"[27]), but he also cautions against this process ("emotional entanglement is also the substrate of a client's real dependence on a therapist"[28]). Nagy writes about the "disloyalty connotations of therapeutic alliances and of transference"[29]. The therapist may use the emotional openness of a client in a manipulative way. He calls emotion a "two-edged sword"[30].

Nagy considers 'countertransference' in a rather negative way, and clearly describes his method and attitude of multidirected partiality as a way to 'protect' the therapist "from becoming unilaterally attached to one person via countertransference"[31]. He recognises the feelings a counsellor may have, but these "emotions are best channeled into a mode of altering, inclusive partiality that can provide guidelines for how family members might credit each other"[32].

Nagy's warning about the dangers of transference and countertransference seems an expression of striving for more objectivity, as described by Pamela Cooper-White. It also seems contrary to Cooper-White's positive re-appreciation of transference and countertransference. Cooper-White argues that countertransference should not necessarily be seen as something negative, as it has traditionally been conceived. The counsellor's own subjectivity plays an important role in counselling. The counsellee brings his/her own subjectivity as well, such that we can speak of a form of mutuality. This does not mean that the relationship is totally symmetrical. Cooper-White warns strongly against a "blurry form of mutuality in which roles and boundaries are merged"[33].

Nevertheless, although Nagy reacts against countertransference, two arguments can be given to show that Nagy's view is not totally in opposition to Cooper-White's relational paradigm. Nagy's idea of counselling is first of all not a strong defence of neutrality and secondly, like

27. BOSZORMENYI-NAGY – KRASNER, *Between Give and Take* (n. 5), p. 398.
28. *Ibid.*
29. *Ibid.*, p. 25.
30. *Ibid.*, p. 399.
31. *Ibid.*, p. 52.
32. *Ibid.*, p. 310.
33. COOPER-WHITE, *Shared Wisdom* (n. 4), p. 179.

Cooper-White, he develops a model that integrates both asymmetry and mutuality.

First, Nagy's approach does not favour objectivity, as his focus on multidirected partiality shows that the counsellor is not just neutral. There is no bird's eye view where one can survey all different positions. Multidirected partiality means being 'partial' – but without taking into account only one perspective. The balance of give and take refers to what people themselves experience as just in relation to the concrete situation, not only in relation to cultural or objective norms. The idea of the 'justice of the human order' brings in an element of objectivity, but this remains so vague that it can only be seen as a formal category.

Second, Nagy combines asymmetry with a form of mutuality, but he focuses mainly on parent-child relations to clarify this position. The relationship between parents and children can, however, be compared with the relationship between a counsellor and counsellee – which does not mean at all that patriarchal structures in both areas should be copied. The acknowledgement of the asymmetric relationships in parent-child relations and in counselling relations may however lead to interesting insights. Nagy's ideas about the asymmetrical relations between parents and children can help us to see that mutuality does not stand in opposition to the recognition of asymmetry and that the recognition of asymmetry is essential in order to respect the dignity of people and to avoid power abuse.

Nagy's main idea of a 'fair balance of give and take' gives the impression of a strong focus on mutuality[34]. The existential loyalty of children goes together with a responsibility of the parents, simply through the fact of giving birth to those children. Thus, the relationship between parents and children is always asymmetrical. It is very important to recognise that children can give to their parents. They can, however, never give back everything they have received from their parents. Nevertheless, it is important to speak about justice in the parent-child relationship. Nagy speaks about 'due care', the 'balance of give and take' and the 'intrinsic

34. A. DILLEN, *Infinite Responsibility and 'Good Enough Parenting': The Challenge of Levinas's Thought for Family Ethics*, in R. BURGGRAEVE (ed.), *The Awakening to the Other: A Provocative Dialogue with Emmanuel Levinas*, Leuven, Peeters, 2008, 89-112. The differences and analogies between the ideas of Nagy and Levinas are elaborated systematically in H. MEULINK-KORF – A. VAN RHIJN, *De Context en de Ander: Nagy herlezen in het spoor van Levinas met het oog op het pastoraat*, Zoetermeer, Meinema, 1997, 1998 (2d ed.). See the Summary: "The Context and the Other: Re-reading Nagy following in the track of Levinas, with a view to pastoral care and pastoral theology" (pp. 484-488).

tribunal'[35]. When someone cares for someone else, he or she 'gives' to the other. All giving leads to 'constructive entitlement', which is a term for a kind of merit that motivates people to go on giving in a constructive way. At the same time, people also have a right to receive from others. Nagy even speaks about the duty to receive, because it is important that others' giving is recognised and accepted. Sometimes people give too much to others or are unable to give to others, due to particular relational factors. Then one can see that the balance of give and take is disturbed. This can go in both directions, parents can give too much or too little to children and vice versa.

The ideas of Nagy about parent-child relations, asymmetry, give and take and justice, may enrich our reflection about pastoral relations. In pastoral relationships, the position of the pastor brings an essential asymmetry. Nevertheless, it is important to find out if the pastor is open to receiving from the other and crediting him or her for the giving, if the pastor is not giving in an inadequate way, not really taking into account the needs of the counsellee, for instance. The pastor's own family relations may have an influence. For instance someone may have been obliged to give during his or her own life to an ill mother (a form of 'parentification': the child had to take up the role of the parent[36]), and will continue this 'caring attitude' in pastoral relationships, causing problems concerning adequate receiving or for delineating boundaries. Pastors can be assisted in looking at the relationships in their own families[37] in order to reflect on what is 'fair' in their pastoral relationships. Within the literature on contextual pastoral care, we find reflections on the 'parentified pastor'. Some pastors are really searching for valuation through caring. They absolutely want to help people and feel good that they are relevant to others.

3. *Feelings*

Although Cooper-White and Nagy are similar in their relational thinking and their focus on asymmetry that goes together with a form of mutuality, there are differences as well. Nagy's focus on 'relational ethics'

35. BOSZORMENYI-NAGY – KRASNER, *Between Give and Take* (n. 5).

36. Parentification is not always destructive. It is very important that the giving of the 'child' is recognised by the 'parent'. When enough recognition is given, parentification does not have to be problematic.

37. See e.g. also R.W. RICHARDSON, *Becoming a Healthier Pastor: Family Systems Theory and the Pastor's Own Family* (Creative Pastoral Care and Counselling), Minneapolis, MN, Fortress Press, 2005.

sounds much more 'rational', whereas Cooper-White more explicitly integrates emotions and feelings in her view on counselling. Nagy's multidirected partiality exists in crediting everyone who is affected by the counselling for his or her constructive or destructive entitlement. Constructive entitlement is clearly distinguished from 'feeling entitled'. It refers to the 'relational ethics' within a relationship, and especially to the entitlement one earns when caring for someone else. Destructive entitlement refers to the relational ethical balance of being "justified in seeing the world as his debtor"[38]. Nagy explicitly states that this crediting is different than sympathy and empathy. It is not just valuing someone, giving compliments or positive labelling. Crediting someone is not just expressing that one values what the other does, maybe because it benefits someone, but it also makes clear that one sees that the action is an investment by the other. On the other hand, whereas empathy is more focused on recognising the feelings of the other, Nagy's 'crediting' is mostly focused on what he calls the relational-ethical dimension. Empathy can, however, be part of crediting. Crediting by the therapist is, however, only a secondary means in contextual work. The focus lies on stimulating people to credit each other for their entitlement[39].

Cooper-White calls for a "recuperation" of the "diagnostic usefulness" of empathy[40]. She also warns, however, against equating empathy with care or warmth[41]. Empathy is "careful perspective taking"[42]. It is "not mere sympathy or concern"[43]. It "requires an effort to stand in the other person's shoes"[44]. Cooper-White warns counsellors about their sometimes invasive desire for caring. She claims that it is very important to refrain from a "rush to momentary gratification". Empathy requires considering all consequences of the feelings that come up when "taking the perspective of the other". It is merely a way of considering things rather than a way of acting. Nagy's critique of the concept of empathy is more or less the same as Cooper-White's critique, although Nagy prefers to speak about crediting and Cooper-White chooses to clarify the meaning of 'empathy'. We learn from Nagy that 'taking the perspective of the other' is not enough. It is also important to take the perspective of different others, not only the client, but also his or her mother, father,

38. BOSZORMENYI-NAGY – KRASNER, *Between Give and Take* (n. 5), p. 415.
39. *Ibid.*, p. 413.
40. *Ibid.*, p. 174.
41. *Ibid.*, pp. 178-179.
42. *Ibid.*, p. 178.
43. *Ibid.*, p. 179.
44. *Ibid.*

brother, sister, child, and so on (multidirected partiality). Nagy criticises a relational anthropology that does not take into account a 'third'; one that is mainly dyadic. His concept of loyalty implies that people are not just connected with other people, but that there is always a "priority of 'bonding'", in Nagy's terms: "the preferring one, the preferred one and the one who is not preferred"[45].

Cooper-White focuses more on the complexity of the subject him or herself. A person is not just a monolithic identity. Nagy takes up this idea, borrowed from object-relational therapy, but broadens it to real people 'out there'. A person is not only related to others within his or her mind, but is so most of all in concrete reality. Cooper-White's relational theology, based on a Trinitarian approach, could be further developed when she takes the idea of multidirected partiality into account.

IV. Power and Contextual Pastoral Care

So far, I have discussed contextual work in light of the relational framework of Cooper-White. The concept of multidirected partiality is a main element in contextual pastoral care that maintains the possibility of a balance between 'neutrality' and strong emotional involvement and helps to direct the client towards his or her own context. Thus far, contextual pastoral care seems to present a nuanced and balanced model for the relationship between the counsellor and the counsellee. Nevertheless, contextual pastoral care and the concepts around 'relational ethics' within this model have been critiqued as well. One of the critiques comes from a feminist point of view and concerns 'power dynamics' within relationships.

Nagy considers 'power' as an aspect of the third dimension, the dimension of interactions. This dimension is important in the life of humans, but the fourth dimension of relational ethics is more fundamental. Power struggles can be considered in the light of give and take, loyalty and entitlement. In one of the basic books of contextual pastoral care[46], one reads how contextual work does not start with the diagnosis of power balances or what goes wrong in families, but with the positive elements of enjoying life. 'Power' is considered in a rather negative way, here, linked with manipulation and 'power-over'.

Feminist theologians critique Nagy's neglect of power aspects in the broader social context and the factual hidden forms of power within

45. *Ibid.*, p. 418.
46. Meulink-Korf – van Rhijn, *De onvermoede derde* (n. 2), p. 176.

family relations and the consequence that contextual therapy may work in favour of the most powerful. Nagy claims that his concepts are universally applicable whereas those who criticise his work make clear that a 'universal theory' about relationships is impossible. Both claims should be honoured. Nagy's general framework might be universal in the sense that, although it originated in a Western context in relation to traditional nuclear families, this does not say anything about the validity of his concepts elsewhere. Although a theory is generated within a particular context, it might apply to different contexts. This is, in general, the case with Nagy's concepts about loyalty, give and take, and so one. Nevertheless, what loyalty means, how it is expressed and to whom people are loyal may differ within various contexts. For instance, in some cultures the eldest brother may take the position of the father in western cultures. Expressions of loyalty may be very different. The idea of loyalty within family relations and loyalty conflicts in general are relevant for most cultures. Feminists are right, however, that the ideas of Nagy are not sufficient for a 'just way of doing pastoral care'.

It is important to take into account the context in the broadest meaning possible, as people are not only influenced by family relations. Various elements of people's social identity need to be considered such as gender, ethnicity, age, class, culture of sexuality, and religiosity. The last aspect, religiosity, is an aspect that tends to be part of pastoral counselling, but the other aspects of people's social identity are not always seen. Further, it is not only important to know what it means to speak as a woman to a male pastor, for instance, or to speak as a white counsellee to a black counsellor. The various aspects of social identity come together in one person, as is made clear by intersectionalist thought[47]. A counsellee may be a homosexual women from upper-middle class, a Christian and about 30 years old. All these elements interact with each other, as well as her position in the family and the balance of give and take in her familial context. If contextual counselling wants to be really 'contextual', it has to integrate serious reflection on intersectionalism and power. The various interacting aspects of social identity are linked to various levels of power. In a particular culture, being homosexual may give someone more limited access to ways of expressing his or her voice. Being a man or coming from a middle or upper class may bestow privileges and power. These elements are often hidden, since many counsellors and scholars themselves come from privileged positions, blinding them to the disadvantages

47. A. Brah – A. Phoenix, *Ain't I a Woman? Revisiting Intersectionality*, in *Journal of International Women's Studies* 5 (2004), no. 3, 75-86.

of others. Various pastoral theologians, however, especially from a feminist and womanist perspective, have made clear that counsellors need to be aware of their own social identity and that of their counsellees.

This is important for various reasons. First of all, counselling is not just an interrelational talk that occurs within a vacuum. Counselling is part of society and is not only influenced by it, but may also influence society in general. Surely, when we speak about pastoral counselling within a broader church community, we can say that this church community has a prophetic task as well, the task not only to comfort people, but also to urge critique towards unjust aspects of society. Pastoral counsellors should be open to the story of the counsellee, but this does not mean that they cannot have any critical voice when it comes to gender-inspired balances of power, for instance. Through the method and attitude of multidirected partiality, the contextual pastor has a good instrument for raising awareness of other perspectives. Nagy himself wants contextual work to prevent the 'revolving slate' passed on from generation to generation. He wants to stop injustices against the next generation. This general aim makes clear that therapy and pastoral care, inspired by the contextual paradigm, should not be limited to the actual client, but have consequences that reach much further. Contextual work itself is strongly focused on the consequences of what happens in families. Its relational ethics (fourth dimension) gives a strong frame for analysing what happens between family members and other important people. But it could be complemented by an analysis of power dynamics in society more broadly and the mutual influences of family dynamics and social aspects.

A second reason why the awareness of elements of (social) power is important within pastoral care and counselling is to provide adequate support for the people who are directly influenced by the pastoral care or counselling. Taking into account power differences between family members, influenced by elements of their social identity such as age, gender, education or social class, can give deeper insight into the aspects that allow people to bring new dynamics to the balance of give and take. This expresses how both approaches, the one based on a 'power analysis' and on the recognition of 'privileges', and the other based on relational ethics, need each other to be operational.

Taking into account the perspective of 'power' means asking 'in whose interest' a position is defended. This is true for the counsellor who might question family members or an individual to see how the most disadvantaged can be given more justice. In this way, multidirected partiality is a tool for researching power (im)balances. Nevertheless, one could critically ask whether this principle might not also causing a certain blindness, especially for ideologies that favour the most powerful. Imagine a woman who ran away from her husband, but returns under the (hidden) pressure from her husband, or a young girl who does not want to speak about the incestuous acts of her stepfather. These are examples of situations where there is loyalty, and where a counsellor who supports this loyalty all too easily may stimulate the most powerful, while neglecting the needs of the woman or girl. This situation may be true if a contextual counsellor does not take into account power differences and ways in which people are socialised. Women or children who have always been told to obey will easily be obedient even in situations where their own wellbeing is threatened. Counsellors should be aware of cultural and ideological positions that legitimise the power of some persons over others, as is the case, for instance, with specific religious beliefs about sacrificial love, images of the perfect woman or ideas about the 'normalcy' of corporal discipline for children.

In defense of contextual therapy one could, however, say that the risk of overlooking the most vulnerable within the therapeutic process is taken into account by Nagy's focus on the relevance of timing in the method of multidirected particality. He writes: "As a general rule, a priority of consideration is most effectively assigned to the most decisively wounded person. It makes little sense to expect someone who is bitterly hurt to offer generous concern to a partner who has been unfair"[48]. In order to be able to recognise patterns that may hurt someone or the vulnerability of someone for being hurt, it is important to recognise how social aspects of one's identity and related power balances interact with patterns in the family.

A third reason why it is important to recognise power differences in the context of pastoral care is related to the relation between the counsellor and counsellee. The recognition of differences in social identity between the counsellor and the counsellee are very important, in order to be aware of hidden hypotheses that are at play when the counsellor asks questions, for instance about socio-economic situations, age or gender.

V. Conclusion

In order to come to a form of pastoral counselling that does justice to everyone involved in the counselling process it is important to strive for 'connection', but to notice at the same time one's own subjectivity. The

48. Boszormenyi-Nagy – Krasner, *Between Give and Take* (n. 5), p. 303.

basic idea about the aim of human development in contextual thinking can be described as searching for just relationships while standing on one's own ground. Multidirected partiality is one of the attitudes that can help a counsellor to reach this goal within the counselling process itself and to stimulate it in the life of all those involved or afflicted by the counselling. This attitude is based upon the idea that every human person is valuable, has his or her merits and should be credited for his or her entitlement. Nobody is a monster – we learn this both from Nagy and from Christian theology. People may commit cruel deeds, but it is important to search for the person and his or her story that lies behind the deeds. Whereas in Nagy's theory the focus lies on the family context, it is – in light of a broader approach of justice in counselling – also important to take into account the broader social context and power balances that are mirrored within counselling and family processes. Power differences within families and between social groups in society may make it difficult to directly speak with others. Nevertheless, 'direct address' is, as mentioned before, the 'cornerstone' of real dialogue and worth striving for in order to come to justice in relationships.

Research Unit Pastoral Theology
Faculty of Theology and Religious Studies
KU Leuven – Catholic University of Leuven
Sint-Michielsstraat 4/3101
B-3000 Leuven
Belgium
annemie.dillen@theo.kuleuven.be

Annemie DILLEN

FROM 'GOOD MORNING' TO THE RESPONSIBILITY FOR THE RESPONSIBILITY OF THE OTHER

A LEVINASIAN PERSPECTIVE ON PASTORAL CONVERSATION AS ETHICAL EVENT

In this essay we would like to shed light on pastoral conversation as an ethical event from the perspective of Emmanuel Levinas (1905-1995)[1]

1. For the references to the works of Levinas, the following abbreviations will be used throughout the essay: **AS**: *Autrement que savoir* (Interventions in the discussions and *Débat général*), Paris, Osiris, 1988; **AT**: *Alterity and Transcendence*, New York, NY, Columbia University Press, 1999; **BV**: *Beyond the Verse: Talmudic Readings and Lectures*, Bloomington, IN – Indianapolis, IN, Indiana University Press, 1994; **CPP**: A. LINGIS (ed.), *Collected Philosophical Papers*, Dordrecht – Boston, MA – Lancaster, Martinus Nijhoff Publishers, 1987; **DF**: *Difficult Freedom: Essays on Judaism*, Baltimore, MD, The Johns Hopkins University Press, 1990; **EE**: *Existence and Existents*, The Hague, Martinus Nijhoff, 1978; **EI**: *Ethics and Infinity: Conversations with Philippe Nemo*, Pittsburgh, PA, Duquesne University Press, 1985; **EN**: *Entre Nous: Thinking-of-the-Other*, London – New York, NY, Continuum, 2006; **ET**: *The Ego and the Totality*, in **CPP** 25-45; **FC**: *Freedom and Command*, in **CPP** 15-23; **GCM**: *Of God Who Comes to Mind*, Stanford, CA, Stanford University Press, 1998; **GDT**: *God, Death, and Time*, Stanford, CA, Stanford University Press, 2000; **HO**: *Humanism of the Other*, Urbana, IL – Chicago, IL, University of Illinois Press, 2003; **IFP**: *Interview with François Poirié*, in **IRB** 23-83; **IRB**: J. ROBBINS (ed.), *Is It Righteous to Be? Interviews with Emmanuel Levinas*, Stanford, CA, Stanford University Press, 2001; **NT**: *New Talmudic Readings*, Pittsburgh, PA, Duquesne University Press, 1999; **NTR**: *Nine Talmudic Readings*, Bloomington, IN – Indianapolis, IN, Indiana University Press, 1994; **OB**: *Otherwise than Being or Beyond Essence*, The Hague – Boston, MA – London, Martinus Nijhoff Publishers, 1981; **OS**: *Outside the Subject*, London, The Athlone Press, 1993; **PIF**: *Philosophy and the Idea of Infinity*, in **CPP** 47-59; **PM**: *The Paradox of Morality* (interview with T. Wright, P. Hugues, A. Analy), in R. BERNASCONI – D. WOOD (eds.), *The Provocation of Levinas: Rethinking the Other*, London, Routledge, 1988, 168-180; **PN**: *Proper Names*, Stanford, CA, Stanford University Press, 1996; **PPS**: *Pour une philosophie de la sainteté*, in M. DE SAINT-CHERON, *Entretiens avec Emmanuel Levinas 1992-1994*, Paris, Livre de Poche, 2006, 21-52; **RTJD**: *La révélation dans la tradition juive* (suivi de 'Discussion d'ensemble'), in D. COPPIETERS DE GIBSON (ed.), *La révélation*, Bruxelles, Facultés Universitaires Saint-Louis, 1977, 55-57; 207-236 ('Discussion d'ensemble'); **SM**: *Sociality and Money*, in R. BURGGRAEVE, *Proximity with the Other: A Multidimensional Ethic of Responsibility in Levinas*, Bangalore (India), Dharmaram Publications, 2009, 115-123; **TH**: *Transcendence and Height*, in A.T. PEPERZAK – S. CRITCHLEY – R. BERNASCONI (eds.), *Emmanuel Levinas: Basic Philosophical Writings*, Bloomington, IN – Indianapolis, IN, Indiana University Press, 1996, 11-31; **TI**: *Totality and Infinity: An Essay on Exteriority*, The Hague – Boston, MA – London, Martinus Nijhoff Publishers, 1979; **TN**: *In the Time of the Nations*, Bloomington, IN – Indianapolis, IN, Indiana University Press, 1994; **VVP**: *Visage et violence première: Entretien avec Emmanuel Levinas sur phénoménologie et éthique* (H.-J. Lenger), in D. COHEN–LEVINAS (ed.), *Levinas et l'expérience de la captivité*, Paris, Lethielleux – Collège des Bernardins, 2011, 135-149.

on the face and on responsibility[2]. Since he did not see it as his task to develop a concrete, applied ethics but rather to expose the fundamental dynamics and the 'meaning' of the ethical event itself as 'inter-personal' (EI 90), we may not expect any tips, methodologies or strategies for concrete practice from our Levinasian interpretation but rather a view on the foundational aspects of pastoral conversation as an ethical event. This does not mean, however, that – in a second instance – no concrete aspects or applications can be derived from it, as will be made apparent in various places in this essay. Inspired by Levinas, the following foundational aspects of pastoral conversation are discussed: the otherness and the mastership of the client; the ethical dynamics of the pastoral face-to-face, beginning with the vulnerability of the other and the temptation to violence in the pastor; and followed by the delineating and positive dimensions of responsibility for the client. Special attention will finally be given to the description of pastoral responsibility as responsibility for the responsibility of the client.

I. In Line with Dialogical Thought

Before we map out the view of Levinas on conversation, and its implications for pastoral conversation, we would first like to reflect on the position taken by Levinas on the I-other-relationship. He situates himself entirely in line with dialogical thought as developed in Germany by Buber and Rosenzweig and in France by Gabriel Marcel. Particular to dialogical thought is that it fundamentally deviates from the Western, and especially modern, philosophical tradition that puts "the unity of the I, and self-sufficiency, and immanence" on centre stage (GCM 137). In contrast to enlightened thought that links meaning, sense and truth to the consciousness and the thought of the 'I', an entirely new source of meaning was discovered especially by Martin Buber and Gabriel Marcel in the encounter (TI 40)[3]. In contrast to consciousness that enters into

2. See also: M. Riemslagh, *The Face-to-Face as Asymmetrical and Reciprocal Revelation: Founding the Ethics of the Process of Pastoral Counselling in the Footsteps of Emmanuel Levinas*, in R. Burggraeve (ed.), *The Awakening to the Other: A Provocative Dialogue with Emmanuel Levinas*, Leuven, Peeters, 2008, 191-214; I. Neumann, *"Bitte nach Ihnen" : Der Vorrang des Anderen in der Ethik von Emmanuel Levinas als Herausforderung für Seelsorge und Beratung*, Düsseldorf, Impressum No. 5 (Schriftenreihe der Gesellschaft für Interkulturelle Seelsorge und Beratung), 2000, 22 p.

3. Indeed, their dialogical philosophy did not just fall from the sky. They themselves mention some elements of its prehistory. Martin Buber (1878-1965) thus declares how he found concrete indications in a few fragments of letters from Friedrich Heinrich Jacobi (1743-1819), a German philosopher of feeling and writer of epistolary novels, like 'Eduard

Allwills Papiere' (1775-1776) and especially 'Woldemar' (1779). The foremost source of Buber's dialogical philosophy, however, was Ludwig Feuerbach (1804-1872) who in his resistance against the monologues of idealism posed the "Notwendigkeit des Du für das Ich" and even went so far as to label the 'I' and 'thou' as 'God'. In his work 'Das Problem des Menschen' Buber refers to a passage from the second part of Feuerbach's "Grundsätze der Philosophie der Zukunft": "Der einzelne Mensch für sich hat das Wesen des Menschen nicht in sich, weder in sich als moralischen, noch in sich als denkenden Wesen. Das Wesen der Menschen ist nur in die Gemeinschaft, in der Einheit des Menschen mit Menschen enthalten – eine Einheit, die sich aber nur auf die Realität des Unterschieds von Ich und Du stützt". After Feuerbach, Buber also cites Kierkegaard as a source of his I-thou-philosophy precisely because on a religious level he described the relationship of humans to God as an I-Thou-relationship. What is remarkable is that after Feuerbach and Kierkegaard, nothing more happened for 70 years. The dialogical theme would have resounded but nothing further was developed. It was only around the year 1920 when the Jewish thinkers Hermann Cohen and especially Franz Rosenzweig, with his 'Stern der Erlösung' (1921), again noticed the theme and began to use it. In the period before and during Buber's 'Ich und Du' (1923), *the* manifesto of dialogical thought, the theme of inter-human encounter also came to the fore in the works of Ferdinand Ebner, Hans and Rudolf Ehrenberg, Eberhard Griesbach, and last but not least Eugen Rosenstock-Huessy (1888-1973). The latter interpreted the meaning of speech in his own very unique manner as 'man's matrix' that precedes thinking and contains it and therefore orients human and religious (Christian) life as conversation of partners who speak and listen to each other, as his motto likewise expresses: 'Respondeo etsi mutabor' – 'I answer even though I have to be changed', which implies that the meaning of the dialogue does not lie in the past but in the future (cf. some of his works: *Speech and Reality*, 1969; *The Origin of Speech*, 1981; *I am an Impure Thinker*, 1970). It cannot be denied that the appearance of Buber's work 'Ich und Du' was a revolutionary event that would influence Western thought once and for all. This first work, which strongly deviates with its almost aphoristic and at times poetic tone from the explicative systematicity and logical clarity common to academic writing, was expounded in a more university style in later works, which in turn were compiled in "Das Dialogische Leben" wherein "Zweisprache" (1930) and "Das Probleem des Menschen" (1943), among others, were included. Especially the latter, which contained the written report of the lectures that Buber gave in Jerusalem in 1938 under the title "Baajat ha-adam", is the most systematic elaboration of his 'I-Thou-thought'. In this work he takes up once again his view in a direct and radically critical confrontation with Heidegger's view on the 'Mitsein' and the 'Fürsorge' in "Sein und Zeit" (1927). Parallel with, but independent of, Buber (and other German authors), Gabriel Marcel (1889-1973) developed in France the concepts 'intersubjectivity', 'coexistence' and 'encounter'. In the foreword to the English edition (1956) of his study on the metaphysics of Josiah Royce, he thus declares how these helped him discover the 'thou' (*tu*) as a necessary correlative of the 'I' (*je*). Marcel first offered the theme of intersubjectivity as *'condition humaine'* in his "Journal métaphysique" (1927) and then continued to develop it further in, among others, "Position et approches concrètes du mystère ontologique" (1933), "Homo Viator" (1945), "Le mystère de l'être I & II" (1951), "La dignité humaine" (1964), and in numerous stage plays. Levinas met Marcel regularly, in the course of several years, during the famous Saturday evening gatherings in the 1930s at Marcel's home, where the philosophical avant-garde could elucidate and test his ideas without constraint and unsystematically. Marcel put emphasis on the *'co-présence'*, coevality, the mutual presence to each other of the 'I' and 'Thou'. What is essential for him is that this co-presence is mediated by the 'body', not the 'body-object' (*corps objet*) but the 'body-subject' (*corps sujet*): the I's being-toward-itself is immediately a *being exposed to others*. Our incarnation makes possible that we are connected to each other and are able to participate in each others' being and living, which for Marcel is the foundation of all encounter with the other, human and God: "participation founding all relation" (OS 27).

dialogue with itself in and through thinking, in the inter-human relationship as language and dialogue an irreducible and even superior form of spirituality opens up: "beyond the sufficiency of the being-for-itself another possibility of excellence is shown in the human dimension that is not measured by the perfection of the consciousness-of-self. In effect, early in his work, Gabriel Marcel denounced in his *Journal Métaphysique* what he called 'the eminent value of *autarchy*', or the sufficiency unto oneself, in order to affirm that 'only a relation of being to a being can be called spiritual'" (GCM 143).

Buber distinguishes between two movements that make being-human possible: away from and back to the 'world' (an encompassing term for surrounding reality): 'Urdistanzierung' and 'In-Beziehungtreten'. The first constitutive condition for being-human is that the human person is able to distance oneself from one's surroundings and that thereby a 'reality' comes to be as 'across'. Buber calls this the *fundamental anthropological fact*. In the world there is a being that is not so much a being amongst other beings but an utterly unique being that knows the world as world and that knows itself as the one who has knowledge of this knowing and thereby takes distance from the world (PN 24). There is, however, also a second movement back to the world, the 'In-Beziehungtreten': to enter into relationship with the other than oneself. With this second movement begins concrete being-human, history. The entering into relationship realises the concrete becoming human. Stronger still, being-human is essentially entering-into-relationship. The human is no beingness or substance in and of itself, an 'Ich-an-sich' that only afterwards enters into relationship with being, nature, history, people, God. From the very outset, the human is constituted as 'relation', 'relationship' (*Beziehung*). The movement itself of relating-oneself is, in other words, the 'soul' (essence) and 'ensoulment' (dynamics) of the self.

In the world there are also two fundamental ways of being-in-relationship, namely the 'I-It' and the 'I-Thou' (TI 68), likewise characterised by Buber as two 'primary words'[4]. When the human enters into relationship with the things that are arranged, the objects that are used, the tools

4. M. BUBER, *Ich und Du*, in ID., *Werke. I. Band – Schriften zur Philosophie*, Heidelberg, Schneider, 1962, p. 79: "Die Haltung des Menschen ist zwiefältig nach der Zwiefalt der Grundworte, die er sprechen kann. Die Grundworte sind nicht Einzelworte, sondern Wortpaare. Das eine Grundwort ist das Wortpaar Ich-Du. Das andere Grundwort ist das Grundwort Ich-Es. (...) Somit ist auch das Ich des Menschen zwiefältig. Denn das Ich des Grundworts Ich-Du ist ein anderes als das Grundworts Ich-Es". In his first major work *Totalité et Infini* (1961) Levinas distinguishes, in line with Buber's bifurcation between 'I-It' and 'I-Thou', between the economic, totalising relationship of the 'I' with the world and the social relationship of the 'I' with the other.

that are utilised, and thereby necessarily activates one's observation and imagination, the human enters into relationship with the other as 'Es' (It). The I-It-relationship (PN 21) expresses "the knowledge of an I investing an 'object' in its neutrality submissive to the act of knowledge that assimilates it". The 'I-It' designates "the *subject* of idealist philosophy in relation with the world, referring to things and to humans treated as things". Even the human can belong to the world of the 'It', namely insofar as one belongs to the world of 'givenness' and is therefore spoken of in the third person ('he', 'she', 'they'), with its unavoidable functional and utilitarian relationships, without there being any mention of a true presence before the other as a thou: "The *I* experiences these entities, exploring no more than their surfaces, not becoming engaged with them with his or her whole being, and not truly coming out of his or her self". Radically distinct and equally original as the I-It, there is the primary word 'I-Thou', which is for Buber "the Relation *par excellence*" (PN 22). When the *I* affirms itself fully, it is inconceivable without the *Thou*. The *I* finds itself in connection with the *Thou*. And this relationship is so original that it is also primary: "the primacy of the *I-Thou* over the *I-It*" (PN 22). Consequently the *I-Thou*, understood as dialogical relationship, precedes factual or practical dialogue (OS 26). It is no coincidence that Levinas links this 'dialogue [as condition] before all dialogue [as practice]' with the idea of universal human brotherhood: "prior fraternity of humanity" (OS 16). And entirely in line with this he considers the 'face-to-face' or the 'I-other-relationship' as the foundational condition of our being-human, which precedes all practice of this inter-human connectedness. Especially in his second major work *Otherwise than Being* (1974) he affirms and explores this 'human condition' of fraternity and solidarity, preceding all consciousness, all knowledge, choice and practice: "The neighbour concerns me before all assumption, all commitment consented to or refused. I am bound to him, him who is, however, the first one on the scene, not signalled, unparalleled; I am bound to him before any liaison contracted. He orders me before being recognised. Here there is a relation of kinship outside of all biology [...]. The neighbour is a brother. A fraternity that cannot be abrogated, an unimpeachable assignation, proximity [...]" (OB 87).

For Buber the I-Thou-relationship is "the principle and the basis of all dialogue", in the sense that it is "the dialogue that brings one into dialogue" (OS 16). His philosophy of dialogue teaches that to invoke or to summon the other man as a *you* (*tu*), and to speak to him, constitutes the basis and the meaning of dialogue, without a form of knowledge or communication of ideas having to precede it. The fact that people speak to each other (speaking 'about' each other belongs to the order of the 'I-It') is an utterly original event, in a phenomenological sense a miracle: "Ich werde am Du; Ich werdend spreche Ich Du"[5]. When the addressed 'Thou' directs itself in turn to the addressing 'I' as to a 'Thou', the typical human dialogue arises. Only in this reciprocity of the dialogue, whereby the one human does not treat the other as a thing but addresses and treats the other as a 'Thou', does the human come to fullness[6]. The other speaks to me and I respond: not the indicative but the vocative rules the speaking here. I do not only think that the other is, I address him. I no longer ask questions about the other, I question him. In this speaking to each other – through which an 'I' and a 'Thou', stronger still an 'I-Thou-relationship', precisely is – the greeting, and thus also the acknowledgement, precedes all knowledge. Buber exactly calls this the 'dialogical principle', in the sense that the I-Thou-relationship is constitutive for our being-human and is not something that may or may not come round as a coincidental, non-necessary possibility.

Levinas agrees entirely with Buber's radical thesis concerning the priority and originality of the I-Thou-relationship as source of orientation and meaning. Perhaps with a bit too much modesty, Levinas goes so far as to say that he, in comparison with Buber and Marcel, does not even have much that is new or original to offer. Below, it will become clear how in his own unique manner he analyses the *face-to-face* phenomenologically as an original dialogical event and qualifies it as "a dialogue of transcendence" (GCM 147), namely as the dialogue of the 'I' with the 'other', who is wholly other. This dialogue of transcendence contrasts radically with "the dialogue of immanence" (GCM 139), namely "the dialogue of the soul with itself", just as Plato has seen and explored. Levinas sees his own contribution especially on the level of ethics (TH 20), in the sense that for him the encounter and conversation between the 'I' and the other has from the very beginning an ethical structure which can only fulfil itself as the responsibility of the one for the other. From this ensues directly that ethics is the soul of conversation: "The

5. BUBER, *Ich und Du* (n. 4), p. 85.

6. Levinas expresses this in his own terminology as follows: "Language in its expressive function is addressed to, and invokes the other. It does non consist in invoking him as something represented and thought, but this is just why the distance between the same and the other, in which language occurs, is not reducible to a relation between concepts that limit one another, but describes transcendence, where the *other* does not weigh on the same, but only places it under an obligation, makes it responsible, that is, makes it speak. The relationship set up in language is not reducible to that which links thought with an object given to thought. Language cannot take in the other; we are now making use of the concept of the other, but the other is not invoked as a concept, but as a person. In speech we are not only thinking of the interlocutor, but speaking to him" (ET 41).

Relationship where the I encounters the You is the original place and circumstance of the ethical coming about [avènement]" (GCM 147). This does not mean that Buber pays no attention to the ethical dimension of the dialogue, meaning to say to authenticity and inauthenticity. It means rather that Levinas puts the ethical dimension at the centre, or rather the essential ethical modality of the I-Thou-relationship, and moreover radicalises it, namely by emphasising the asymmetry between the 'I' and the other. In order to understand what he means by this, we must return to Buber. He strongly affirms the immediacy of the presence of the partners of the relationship, the 'I' and the Thou, to each other. Both direct themselves directly and without mediating intermediary terms to each other. The most essential characteristic of this direct presence is reciprocity. In contrast to the I-Thou-relationship, whereby the object for the subject is not what the subject is for the object, the I-Thou-encounter appears as a reversible reciprocity. The 'I' is for the Thou what the Thou is for the 'I': the 'I' says 'Thou' to a Thou insofar as this Thou is an 'I' that can respond 'Thou'. Both have the same status, in the sense that the two are both the interpellators as well as the interpellated. Here, Levinas makes the critical comment that this reciprocity cannot disregard the asymmetry between both partners. Both are not 'I's that stand before or are connected with each other. That is an abstract and 'transcendent' perspective that looks at the I-Thou from the outside and thus neglects the concrete reality of an 'I' that stands before an irreducible other. In concrete experience – from the inside – there is always an 'I' – a 'myself' – that stands before an other: 'I' and the other relate to each other in an essential difference to each other. Furthermore, Levinas is apprehensive of an important misunderstanding with regard to reciprocity, a misunderstanding that according to him is active especially on the ethical level. Saying-Thou to me by the other can in no way be seen as a condition for my saying-Thou to the other. My ethical commitment to the other would then be dependent on the ethical commitment of the other, which would then get us bogged down in a utilitarianism, albeit a noble utilitarianism. My ethical relationship to the other, as responsibility for the other, is unconditional in the sense that my commitment is not determined by the commitment of the other as precondition, which would simply be a selfish 'do-ut-des'. In such a conditional symmetry I would only be ethical if I know or am assured that the other will also be ethical towards me. Indeed the unconditionality also applies equally to the other, who like me is responsible for me as an other. His ethical commitment is unconditional and thus not dependent on my 'good-will'. This does not mean that the other would not be addressable regarding his ethical attitude towards me, but I cannot demand this ethics from the other. That is the essence of the ethical asymmetry, namely that I am fully obliged to be responsible for the other, notwithstanding whether the other takes up his own responsibility (OB 84). It is precisely this ethics of the unconditional responsibility of the one for the other that introduces inter-personal relationships as an 'I-other-encounter'. It is apparent from all this how it is Levinas's main intention to "bring out the ethical meaning [of the inter-human *I-Thou*] without questioning the reciprocity on which Buber always insists" (PN 32).

II. Foundation of Pastoral Conversation: The Other Who Speaks to Me

After situating Levinas's mode of approach to dialogical thought, especially that of Buber, we now turn our thoughts to pastoral conversation as an ethical process. The starting point for that can be found in Levinas's view on the asymmetrical relationship between the 'I' and the 'other' as dialogue and ethics. He always reflected on the relationship to the other from the perspective of the self, which is brought into contact with the other through the epiphany of the face. Applied to pastoral conversation, this means that the pastor stands in the position of the 'I' and the client in that of the 'other'. Hence in the remainder of our essay, the terms 'I', 'self', 'myself' represent the pastor while 'other' then refers to the client. In its turn, the pastoral conversation will appear as a unique and eminent clarification of Levinas's view on the ethical dynamism of the inter-personal relationship. Indeed the pastor is not only obliged to relate ethically to the client as a fellow human being; he is even more obliged to do so as a professional (care-giver) and as one who is sent (in God's Name)[7].

The starting point for every pastoral conversation is a simple act, or rather a 'radical fact' or an 'absolute or pure experience', that at the same time is also an 'heteronomous experience coming from elsewhere' (TI 67) – "a traumatism of astonishment" (TI 73) –, namely the fact that the pastor is confronted with the client as 'other'. Put in a Levinasian manner: in the direct encounter with the client, the pastor is faced with the 'epiphany of the other'. In the encounter, which forms the basis for pastoral

7. My thanks go to Marina Riemslagh for her suggestions in amending and concretising the text of this entire essay, in the light of her pastoral expertise and academic research contribution to the doctoral project: "After You: The Ethics of the Pastoral Counselling Process".

conversation, the other reveals itself not only as separate but also as distinct from the pastor. That is precisely what Levinas calls the radical alterity of the other. In his first major work *Totality and Infinity* (1961) he speaks of the 'exteriority' of the other, by which he does not mean a spatial distance that can be bridged or not, but rather a qualitative difference of irreducibility: "the alterity of the other person is the only model of exteriority, where space does not come in between" (RTJD 225).

In the concept of 'alterity' lies both a negative and a positive dimension. The negative dimension means a denial of the knowability of the other. The alterity of the other lies precisely in the fact that the other constantly transcends our observation and our knowledge. What is constitutive of alterity is that the other never coincides with the image and the presentation that we make of him. As an other, the client always eludes, up to infinity, the image formed by the pastor. The distance of this surplus remains fixed, notwithstanding all attempts at bridging the gap. The other presents himself to me as a 'withdrawing' movement, or rather as a 'withdrawal in the withdrawal', a withdrawal that never weakens. The client is always infinitely more than the images, presentations and interpretations that the pastor can design of the other. Even though the other has his physiognomy and personality, and thus his recognisable calculability, his epiphany still consists in shattering his own image and appearance time and again. The other escapes essentially from every typology, characterology and classification, in short from all (professional) attempts by the pastor to understand and fathom the client. In this sense the face of the other is essentially, and not provisionally, a movement of retreat (*anachoresis*). It is a veritable paradox: the other appears by means of disappearing, stronger still by means of withdrawing himself from his appearance as an inaccessible secret or mystery. The other is a presence that immediately renounces itself: an apostate or 'heretic' to itself. The client is literally 'extra-ordinary' and 'e-norm-ous', beyond all order and norm, the purest 'anachronism', an essential conundrum: the unsurpassed enigma that brings the pastor to confusion. The epiphany of the other confronts me with the other as a stranger, or better as 'the stranger' par excellence. The epiphany of the client makes any kind of curiosity ridiculous (OB 90-91).

This rather negative description of the alterity of the other, parallel to negative theology that attempts to approach God by describing what the Other is not, has a clearly positive meaning, however. The basis for the unknowability and irreducibility of the other to his image and appearance is indeed his "manifestation kath'auto" (TI 65), and that is precisely what Levinas labels as the face. The face is at the same time a form and a shattering of this form. It is 'expression', or stronger still 'self-expression': "it is a presence before me of a self-identical being" (FC 41). The other manifests himself out of himself, and not on the basis of his (psychological, relational, economic, social, cultural) context: "The sensible presence of this chaste bit of skin with brow, nose, eyes, and mouth is not a sign making it possible to ascend toward the signified, nor is it a mask which dissimulates the signified. Here the sensible presence desensibilises to let the one who only refers to himself, the identical, break through directly" (FC 41-42).

According to Levinas, the expression of the face occurs in an eminent manner in the look. The possible nakedness of the other can be covered or disguised by using cosmetics or makeup. However, there is one zone of the face that cannot be made-up or embellished, namely the eyes (even when the area around the eye – the eyelid and the eyebrow – can be made-up): "The eyes break through the mask – the language of the eyes, impossible to dissemble. The eye does not shine; it speaks" (TI 66)[8]. The concrete shape of this direct presence is the look: "This way for a being to break through its form, which is its apparition, is, concretely, its look, its aim. There is not first a breakthrough, and then a look; to break through one's form is precisely to look; the eyes are absolutely naked" (FC 20). They are the most unprotected part of the face. Thus the look is the most direct and personal presence of someone else who looks at me. Hence for a pastoral conversation it is of utmost importance that the client gets the chance to look at the pastor, which implies that the pastor will also look at the client: to divert one's eyes would then mean a refusal of contact and encounter. When both look at each other, they encounter each other directly. The look of the client is the other itself, that gazes at the pastor in absolute directness and frankness, and thereby speaks to me. In other words, both do not originally stand beside each other (*Miteinander*), as Heidegger posits, but facing each other: 'eye to eye'. And it is precisely this directness of facing each other that makes possible both the sincerity of the encounter as well as the invitation to it[9].

8. Could this be the reason why the eyes of a dead person are closed? The eyes of a dead person no longer can see; they no longer shine with a lively gaze. Dead eyes that remain open can be disturbing precisely because eyes that are open mean that someone should be looking at us, but that is no longer the case because the other is dead ... and that is unbearable: "Someone who dies: a face that becomes a mask. The expression disappears" (GDT 12).

9. With this, not everything has indeed been said about the look and looking at each other. This is only possible when it is placed in an ethical perspective. Sartre has pointed out that the look can be objectifying and thus deadly. It is only when conversation partners look at each other in ethical benevolence, namely in the acknowledgement and confirmation

The expression of the look refers, as was already made apparent inadvertently in the description above, to language or rather to conversation. "The epiphany of a face is wholly language" (PIF 55). This language, however, should not primarily be understood as an objective linguistic system but rather as the fact that the other speaks to me and vice-versa. This is not about a discourse but an 'invocation' and 'response' between two people who direct themselves to each other and speak to each other. "The claim to reach the other is realised in the relationship with the other that is cast in the relation of language, where the essential is the interpellation, the vocative. The other is maintained and confirmed in his heterogeneity as soon as one calls upon him, be it only to say to him that he cannot speak to him, to classify him as sick, to announce to him his death sentence; at the same time as grasped, wounded, outraged, he is 'respected'. The invoked is not what I comprehend: *he is not under a category*. He is the one to whom I speak" (TI 69). By means of the fact that either the pastor or the client addresses the other, the pastor and the client are detached from themselves and appealed for a response. The word of the one elicits the counter-word of the other. And the fact of this conversation that precedes every content is the first and most fundamental 'miracle' of the encounter between two people, between client and pastor (ET 28).

This reciprocity of speaking to each other, however, is neither neutral nor formal, but a qualified reciprocity in the sense that the conversation is marked by the primacy of the other. The other comes before me: his speaking is the basis for the pastoral conversation. With this we reach the most fundamental and general significance of the expression: "after You". Both the fact that the other speaks to the pastor and what the other consequently says establish the pastoral dialogue itself. The other is my master: by means of speaking to me the other does not only express himself but he also 'teaches' me. Even though it is possible that by means of his address the pastor elicits the word of the other, still the word of the client comes first. By means of speaking, the other indeed determines and orientates the conversation. In this regard, the speaking of the other can in no way whatsoever be reduced to one or the other form of Socratic maieutics (TI 171). The word and the first content of this word, namely the alterity of the other, comes to me from elsewhere and contributes

of the other, that the look becomes human (cf. infra). This means that the look, the looking of the other, can be perverted ethically. According to Buber as well, lying with the eyes is a strong form of inauthenticity: pretending as if one is favourably disposed by projecting an insincere kindness via the eyes!

more to me than what I find and contain in myself (TI 51). The word of the client does not arouse any idea that was already slumbering in the pastor; it teaches the pastor something completely new: "the absolutely new is the other" (TI 219). If the other were not to speak to me I would neither experience nor know the other in his alterity. In that sense is the other my teacher, who educates me masterfully about himself, without my having possessed this education already in the depths of myself – as a source of affinity and recognisability – or my being able to let it simmer up from within me (TI 69). Hence Levinas states, making use of religious language, that the other who speaks to me 'reveals' himself and thus is a radical, heteronomous – not religious but experiential – form of 'revelation'. Hence the first teaching of the other is the fact of his insurmountable alterity: "the first teaching of the teacher is his very presence as teacher" (TI 100). The pastor cannot foresee or predict the word of his or her client entirely. He or she is not the designer who takes initiative; on the contrary, the pastor is the one who receives, listens, obeys – literally the one who gives ear (TI 69). This means that listening is the first way of answering, of being literally 'repons-ible'[10]. It also implies that the spoken word takes priority over the written word: "Oral discourse is the plenitude of discourse" (TI 96). The one who speaks assists himself in order to illuminate his word (TI 98) and to correct or even to contradict the interpretations of his word (by the pastor) (TI 91). This possibility of 'contra-dicting' – speaking again, or literally anew – is essential for pastoral conversation as conversation.

The pastor is no longer the 'lord and master' of the conversation. Ideally speaking, pastors learned from their professional formation and position to discern and to adjust their position as a superior. To be pastor requires a constant conversion in the literal sense of the word, namely a reversal of the order: by means of his epiphany and speaking, the client becomes the master and teacher to whom the pastor must listen humbly. It is not I, the pastor, who stands at the centre of attention but the other, the client. The other appears as the superior who exercises authority[11] over me: "To approach the other in conversation ... is to *receive* from the other beyond the capacity of the I" (TI 51). Perhaps the pastor indeed has something to offer, but first the client must acquire the space to express himself and to speak. Every pastoral relationship must thus begin

10. The contribution of Lisbeth Lipari therefore focuses on 'listening' as the occurrence, and performance of the ethical relation [red.].

11. Authority should not be confused with power, although the temptation to do so lurks round the corner (cf. *infra*).

– and begin time and time again – with a form of humility and modesty. The client must 'teach' the pastor about that which concerns him the most. This is a wholly different learning than Greek learning, based on 'know thyself' (*gnothi seauton*). In the relationship to the client, the pastor learns not by descending into himself and drawing out from one's deepest interiority the wisdom about all things, but by stepping out of oneself and standing open attentively for the other who reveals himself by speaking to the pastor. The relationship to the client as other is pre-eminently not an autonomous but a heteronomous event, that is based on the pastor's awareness of one's not-knowing. In this regard, the alterity of the client as the starting point for the learning of the pastor is not only external but also prior and superior. As radical other, the client brings the pastor round to lay down all pretence and to approach the client with diffidence and respect[12], so that the other can reveal his alterity in all freedom, at the authority of his alterity itself.

III. Ethical Dynamics of the Pastoral Face-to-Face as Crisis

With this, however, we have already arrived inadvertently at the ethical discourse. It is thus high time that we now direct our attention explicitly to the ethical dynamics of pastoral conversation as an I-other-relationship (or even better as an other-I-relationship).

Before we enter into the positive dynamics of respect, acknowledgement and responsibility in their different forms, we must first reflect on the negative ethical dynamics, namely the lower limit, that Levinas summarises on the basis of the first prohibition of the second table of the ten commandments: 'You shall not kill'. Here he would like to state that a qualitatively ethical relationship between people – just as a qualitatively ethical pastoral conversation – is impossible without examining the real possibility of an unethical relationship.

1. *The Vulnerability of the Client*

Concretely speaking, we follow Levinas in his analysis of the ethical vulnerability of the other, whereby we focus on the vulnerability of the

12. This reminds us of the biblical 'fear of the Lord', that is not based on a flinching fear of the omnipotence of the Infinite One but rather ensues from the mature respect for the wholly Other-yet-narrowly-Near who summons 'the fear for (and for the sake of) the other'. See BV 95-97.

client at the same time. Above, we spoke of mastership and thus about the authority and the strength of the other as 'master and teacher'. But the strength of the face is also characterised by weakness, a very specific ethical vulnerability. Stronger still, the mastership of the face is based, upon closer inspection, on that vulnerability. The 'hard and unrelenting' alterity of the face consists in that the other is irreducible and unassailable in his being-other. But actually that is already an ethical statement, since the face can in fact be assailed, meaning to say it can be stripped of its alterity and thus be violated. The paradox is that the face appears in its epiphany as invulnerable, while at the same time it can be negated and humiliated in its alterity. Hence, according to Levinas the face also reveals itself as a "strangeness-destitution" (*étrangeté-misère*) (TI 75). In the nakedness of its face the other appears as the biblical 'stranger, widow and orphan' (TI 251) or as the 'proletarian' who is homeless and has no stone upon which to lay his head (GCM 9). Since the other comes 'from elsewhere', he falls outside the horizon of the familiar world of the 'I'. The other is literally a 'foreigner': utterly dependent on himself and abandoned to his fate, completely defenceless, in need of help and without refuge, "not autochthonous, uprooted, without a country, not an inhabitant" (OB 91). The nakedness of his face runs through up to the nakedness of his body, which suffers cold and is subject to disease and ailments. And he is embarrassed by his nakedness, which also drives him to camouflage his nakedness by means of all sorts of 'false pretences'. In short, through the face – and his entire body is face – the other is exposed to all kinds of weather, to disease or old age and decline, and thus to loneliness, suffering and death: "Existence *kath'auto* is, in the world, a destitution" (TI 75).

2. *The Temptation to Murder*

By means of his essential and factual poverty the face of the other elicits in the 'I' the 'temptation to murder' (EI 86). Although with this bold statement Levinas goes directly against the positive self-image that we cherish narcissistically, an honest appraisal of reality – especially the reality of ourselves – still requires that we acknowledge our potential violence towards the other. It is only by means of this humility and wisdom that we shall be able to prevent and heal our violence (TI 237).

The question now is, what allows for the fact that the 'I', in this case the pastor, can be tempted to violence. For the answer to this question we must turn to the way in which Levinas describes the dynamics of existence of the 'I' (and thus of the pastor as an 'ordinary' person – a person like other persons). Well then, just like all other earthly beings the 'I' – as a being – is marked by the attempt-to-be. With a term from Spinoza, Levinas speaks of the *conatus essendi* (OB 4-5): "the natural tension of being on itself that I have alluded to as egoism. Egoism is not an ugly vice of the subject's, but is ontology, as we find in the sixth proposition of Part III of Spinoza's *Ethics*: 'Every being makes every effort insofar as it is in it to preserve in its being'; and in Heidegger's expression about existence existing in such a way that its Being has the very Being as an issue" (PN 70-71). The existence of the 'I', and thus of the pastor, is no blank page, no trouble-free existence, but a threatened, fearful and worried existence that displays the inclination – especially when threatened – to fold back into itself whereby it precisely becomes a subjective existence, an I-existence: 'as-far-as-I-am-concerned' (*quant-à-moi*). The attempt-at-being is from the very beginning an 'effort-at-being', literally an effort in order to be, a 'struggle for life' to use an expression of Darwin (AS 80-83). In this struggle to exist the 'I' does not remain turning within itself and affirming itself (I am I), but steps outward in order to transform the other, namely the world, into its means, its house and environment (TI 116). Even knowledge is introduced in this project of self-unfolding that ensues from the finitude of the 'I', in the sense that the 'I' literally gets a grasp onto the world by means of developing and applying its knowledge as 'understanding'. It is knowledge, therefore, in the service of the economic transformation of nature into a life world for humans as egos. In this manner, the 'I' realises itself as an *animal rationale*: the animality of the struggle for life is raised to the human level of rationality, but this rational humanity remains at the service of animality (PM 169-172).

This dynamism of the attempt-at-being, however, does not only relate to the 'other' in nature but also to other people in the world. In his egocentric interest the 'I' is inclined to introduce even other people into his project of self-unfolding – or, if necessary, if they form too great a threat, to eliminate them. This leads us seamlessly to the 'temptation to murder', which Levinas repeatedly refers to when he explores the relationship between the 'I' and the other. The ethical benevolence toward the other is not self-explanatory; it is no spontaneous natural given for it must elevate itself time and again above the egocentric selfishness of the 'I' that as a 'for itself', in its fear for limitation, suffering and death, fights with suppressed energy and with all its means for its own existence.

3. *The Many Faces of Violence*

The 'temptation to murder', according to Levinas, is based on the self-interestedness of the 'I', which strives 'to reduce the other to itself'.

This reduction is the core of all violence, whatever the form may be in which it incarnates itself: visible and direct or indirect, hidden and subtle; bodily or psychologically and socially; mild or extreme; individual or collective; profane or spiritual and religious. The concrete forms wherein Levinas discovers this violence are especially the following: the use and abuse of the other, tyranny and enslavement, racism and anti-Semitism, hate and murder. This enumeration can give the impression that only specific or gradual differences between these forms of violence exist. Notwithstanding the relatedness, namely that it always concerns a reduction of the other to the same, Levinas also sees a radical difference, whether or not that reduction ends up in denial and destruction. That is why for him, murder is a 'unique passion' (TI 232) precisely because it strives to assail and destroy the other in its existence: "total negation" (TI 198), "unlimited negation" (TI 225). Killing is radical: one does not dominate (appropriate, use and consume) but annihilate the other. Murder, then, renounces absolutely all 'com-prehension' of the other, for one no longer wishes to include the other in the 'same' – that is, in one's own project of existing – but, on the contrary, to exclude him, because he is 'too much' in the way of my struggle for life. Murder manifests itself as the effort and realization of an inexorable struggle for omnipotence: the I plays not 'all *or* nothing' but 'all *and* nothing.' It promotes itself to 'all' so that the other must be reduced to 'nothing' or 'no one,' which is also to say to 'is-no-longer,' in not only the factual but also, and above all, the active sense of 'is' no-longer (TI 198). In other forms of violence we distinguish an ambiguity, which is no longer to be found in the passion of murder. It is namely the ambiguity to deny the other in one way or the other or to rid it of its alterity, without likewise destroying the other. In the manner in which we approach the other and reduce it to ourselves, we want at the same time not to rob the other entirely of its alterity, because in one way or the other we need the acknowledgement by the other of our own power over the other. That is precisely the paradox that Levinas discovers strongly in hate (TI 239). Through his hate one wants at the same time both to radically negate the other and also not to do so entirely. From its offensive height, hate wishes to humiliate and crush the other, but without destroying him completely. On one hand, hate aims at making the other suffer, such that he would then be reduced to pure passivity. But on the other hand, hate wishes that the other in this passivity will remain at his most active, so that he can bear witness to this hate. Only the suffering of the other reveals the destructive, reductive power of the I at work in hate. Whoever hates wants to be the cause of a suffering of which the hated person is the living proof. This is what makes hate so absurd and sordid.

Hate wants the death of the other, yet without killing him; it holds the other, still living, at the verge of destruction, so that through the terrible pain of rejection and denial the other testifies to the triumph of hate. A similar ambiguity also applies to the use of the other and to tyranny (see further): they cannot use or overpower the other if that other does not remain existing as other. If the other no longer is, there can be no mention of use or domination. On the other hand, it cannot be denied that in the non-lethal forms of violence lies a tendency that leads to the destruction of the other or to murder. This tendency manifests itself in racism and anti-Semitism. As forms of hate, they endeavour to deny and exclude the other as a 'stranger' in such a way that that other still can bear witness to his exclusion and thus to the power of the racist and Jew-hater. Ultimately, they strive for extermination and genocide, just as the *Endlösung* or the so-called 'final solution' of the Jewish problem and other mass exterminations in history demonstrate.

In the framework of our Levinasian interpretation of the pastoral conversation, we reflect on a few 'milder', non-lethal forms of violence. Although they seem a far cry from murder and destruction, this does not mean that they would be 'not serious', meaning to say they would not imply any real violation of the other. Precisely in order to promote the ethical quality of pastoral conversation, they must be taken very seriously. Because they are not so serious as murder and killing, one could be tempted not to make much of a fuss about them and perhaps even in certain circumstances consider them acceptable, although they can cause much damage to the other – the client.

4. *The Temptation to Diagnostic Violence*

Firstly, with Levinas we can point to 'diagnostic reduction', meaning to say to the inclination of the 'I' (pastor) to reduce the other (client) to his appearance (cf. supra). Thanks to my spontaneous or methodical and professionally developed observation – 'vision' in the literal sense of the word – I endeavour to focus on or get an image of the other, and to know and to understand him (VVP 141-142). By means of his face, which expresses itself physically in and through its plastic form, we get a view of the other thanks to his appearance, meaning to say thanks to his physiognomy, glance, facial expression – and, in extension, thanks to his psychological and social body, namely thanks to his character, relational network, social and cultural milieu. On the basis of our attempt-at-being and its egocentric interestedness we are inclined to approach the other in his observable and objectifiable appearance. Thus the other becomes accessible and understandable to us. Thus I come to know how to deal with the other and how to exercise power over him, so that he 'contributes' to my own happiness and self-unfolding. If the pastor can make clear to his client how well he understands him or her, he can then obfuscate how much his pastoral action stands in service of the reinforcement of his own positive self-image as a person and as a professional. In the words of Levinas himself: "You turn yourself toward the other as toward an object when you see a nose, eyes, a forehead, a chin, and you can describe them. [...] When one observes the colour of the eyes one is not in ethical relationship with the other. The relation with the face can surely be dominated by perception, but what is specifically the face is what cannot be reduced to that" (EI 85-86). It is of vital importance for every pastor to realise how in the endeavour to gain good knowledge of the other, on the basis of one's own perception, one can inadvertently end up in the risk of diagnostic reduction, and thus in the risk of a real, although not always acknowledged form, of violence. In this regard, coming to awareness that one is liable to be tempted to diagnostic reduction is already an ethical awareness, namely that such a reduction is not allowed, in other words that one should not 'kill' (which will be discussed further).

5. *The Temptation of Rhetoric*

Another temptation is that of rhetoric, "the art that is supposed to enable us to master language" (OS 135), and this art can corrupt conversation in its true nature of 'face-to-face'. Here Levinas follows in particular the view of Plato, who among others in the Phaedrus (273d) states[13] that in our conversations we often rely on rhetoric in order to approach the other as "an object or an infant, or a man of the multitude" (TI 70). For that, rhetoric makes use of figures of language itself, so that the saying can appear in beauty – as a form of 'appearance': eloquence (OS 139). This applies not only to our pedagogical and psychological or other conversations offering assistance, but also and especially to our conversations that are involved with meaning and the creation of meaning, namely with pastoral conversations that make room for "the existential concern, the world-view and religious experience of the

13. Levinas also refers to the Phaedrus 261d-e and the Gorgias 463d and 465c: on the basis of rhetoric, this semblance abides not only in philosophy and morals but also in jurisprudence and especially in politics. Politics then becomes an ideological linguistic art form that attempts to convince the citizens that politicians are 'the saviours of the poor' (sic!) (GCM 7-8).

conversation partner" (Riemslagh)[14]. Precisely because the pastoral conversation lends itself in terms of content to the path of sense questions, feelings and experiences, it becomes necessary to make much use of metaphors – and thus of rhetoric – in order to convey the trans-empirical field of meaning. Or as Levinas himself puts it succinctly: "the famous – and easily rhetorical – quest for the 'meaning of life'" (GCM 174; EN 111). The risk of this metaphorical rhetoric is that one tries to convince the interlocutor by means of flattering and charming him: rhetoric, thus, as a form of linguistic magic (GD5 168-169). And as in all rhetoric, one ends up in the temptation to approach the other with a ruse – but that ruse is at the same time embellished in beautiful and elevated language (*'belletterie'*) (DF 277), whereby it is not always simple to unmask it as a form of abuse of power, or even of terror. Rhetoric can degenerate into a form of violence, in the sense that it attempts to penetrate into reason via wordplays rich in imagery and hyperbolic figures of speech conveyed with the necessary pathos (OB 19), so that the conversation partner begins to think and act differently, no longer in conformity with reason but according to the power of the speaker – and this, according to Plato, turns the speaker into a 'despot'. In rhetoric – the violent and less violent but subtle forms – language is transformed into a form of art, namely the art to 'persuade' the other by means of presenting the content of the argument as beauty with the intention – or the consequence – that it is clad with the semblance of truth. Rhetoric would never be able to seduce so many people if in its reasons and reasoning no hint of plausibility were present. The deception of rhetoric consists precisely in that one attempts to get the other to one's side by arousing trust, namely the trustworthiness of the partial truth, so that the other is then prepared to take along the beautifully embellished lie in the guise of truth (NTR 64). Making use of diplomacy, flattery, subtlety, demagogy and propaganda, rhetoric endeavours to win the other over and corrupt him, meaning to say to seduce the other to become docile and agree with what is presented. Levinas can then also state that rhetoric does not approach the other 'face-to-face' but rather indirectly and obliquely. This does not mean that rhetoric reduces the other to an object. Rhetoric remains a conversation where despite – or by means of

14. Levinas is very much aware of the fact "that in our time the effects of eloquence are everywhere, dominating our entire lives. There is no need to go through the whole sociology of our industrialised society here. The media of information in all forms – written, spoken, visual – invade the home, keep people listening to an endless discourse, submit them to the seduction of a rhetoric that is only possible if it is eloquent and persuasive in portraying ideas and things too beautiful to be true" (OS 139).

– the ruse and tricks of all kinds of figures of speech, one still remains addressing the other. But precisely by addressing the other as other, rhetoric competes for his 'yes' which constitutes exactly rhetoric's ambiguity: a face-to-face wherein violence is done to the other at the same time. Rhetoric is therefore a specific form of violence and injustice, in the sense that one acknowledges the other by means of speaking to him, but at the same time one tries to seduce the other to give himself over to the speaker. Rhetoric is thus not about a form of violence whereby one launches frontally onto the other as an object or inert reality. The eloquent 'I', in this case the pastor, launches onto the other, in this case the client, as a free being. Via the use of evocative, metaphorical language and reasoning as such, one attempts to penetrate the freedom of the other so that the other will agree freely with what is presented so beautifully and meaningfully in elevated and spiritual language. At any rate, rhetoric will go at lengths to give the impression of free consent to the other. Against this background it is understandable that Levinas argues for the use of simple and direct everyday language (OS 138), even though he is aware that that language cannot do without rhetoric[15], just indeed as no conversation is possible without rhetoric (TI 70). And if we were to keep silent in order to avoid rhetoric, that silence also becomes a form of rhetoric (BV 28). In extension to this, we thus argue for the use of sufficiently sober and brief, 'naked' everyday

15. Levinas points out how we are confronted today with an invasion of a remarkable form of rhetoric in everyday language in the form of a pronounced 'anti-rhetoric' (OS 139-140). In our society we notice how a "struggle against eloquence" dominates, clad in a particular linguistic style. We find eloquent discourse suspicious and hence we take recourse in everyday parlance, precisely "to bring down and profane the heights of eloquence and the verbal sacredness it engenders". Stronger still, "everyday speech is found to be not everyday enough, not straight enough. The decency of words, the noble cadence of oratorical speech, the respectability of books and libraries must be debunked. Bring in the filthy words, interjections, graffiti – make the walls of the city cry out". Ordinary, everyday language is still too decent and clean, and that is why one takes recourse to "a language purposely crude that hopes to achieve straightforwardness in a certain vulgarity". To regain one's lost sincerity, ordinary language is not enough, and has to be enhanced by words and phrases more negative and more destructive than negations. "Hence the development of the whole frightening and nihilistic arsenal of scatology: shouts, curses, obscene poems". But this simply is a new rhetoric: "language directed against eloquence in turn becomes eloquence". The rhetoric degradation of everyday parlance into brutal, impolite and uncivil speech can go so far that, just like classic rhetoric, it becomes too horrible to reflect reality. Stronger still, such an anti-rhetorical language then even becomes more deceitful than ordinary rhetoric, precisely because it is clad in the guise of what is absolutely not beautiful and attractive. Then indeed there is no more 'semblance', as in traditional rhetoric, that can make us distrustful. It all sounds so direct and upright that we no longer realise that it is simply a rhetorical and thus embellished directness and uprightness.

language in pastoral conversation, certainly when it is about spiritual matters related to meaning. In that way, the misleading ideological use of all too grandiloquent religious metaphors can be avoided[16]. And, by means of the use of simple, everyday language, the encounter itself between me and the other, between pastor and client, can especially remain primary – without being flooded by all sorts of eloquent forms and manners of speaking. One is then no longer concerned about the art of speaking but about the encounter with the other himself, whereby the presence and the word of the other take first place: "In everyday language we approach the other instead of forgetting him in the 'enthusiasm' of eloquence" (OS 142).

6. *Temptation to Domination and Tyranny*

Another milder form of inter-human violence, which can also creep into the pastoral relationship, can be called instrumental functionalisation. Concretely, this happens whenever I try to make the other person subordinate to me as 'food', or to press him into one or another form of service, hence to 'consume' the other, to instrumentalise him and to use him for my – even spiritual – purposes. For this, I can of course apply all the riches and power which I have assembled for myself in my struggle for existence. I can use all possible means – or better, *mis*use them – in order to draw the other to myself as a 'function' or a 'means' of my own self-development.

What is remarkable is how the functional approach to the other is often coupled with forms of the exercise of power and domination, which in turn come forth out of self-protection and fear for the power of the other who can equally be a selfish 'I'. In the pastoral relationship, the exercise, or better the abuse of power by the pastor remains a permanent temptation especially when one feels threatened. Moreover, the

16. With Levinas, we refer here to the Rabbinic texts that, as expressions of Jewish wisdom, concentrate on preserving the style of their master Moses "who was slow of speech and slow of tongue" (NTR 181). This should not be considered as a personal shortcoming but as an objective manner of thinking and speaking that is not capable of the art of rhetoric, or rather that does not want to avail itself of the ruses of rhetoric. The Rabbinic discourse remains below par when compared to rhetoric: intentionally below par. It wants to avoid losing contact with complex and contradictory realities by means of its embellished performance. That is why it distrusts a rhetoric 'without stuttering and without stammering' and remains stubbornly faithful to its chief prophet Moses who stuttered and was an awkward, entirely uninspiring speaker (BV 136). In short, inspired by Moses, the Rabbinic masters gave preference to "a sermon in valley, in the valley of tears. A sermon without eloquence" (NTR 181).

possible misuse of power goes hand in hand with the power position of the pastor as a professional. This is no such temptation that a pastor can put behind himself or herself once and for all by means of a one-time decision at a certain moment. It can crop up time and again, since the pastor is not immune and perfect but rather a fragile being that can be pushed into the defensive on account of the context and the circumstances. Hence, vigilance and conversion remain necessary in order to accord the client with the deserved priority: 'after You'.

With Levinas we must also be aware that the striving for domination, which is intertwined with the instrumental functionalisation of the other, can be tempted towards the 'terror of tyranny'. Following Plato, Levinas labels tyranny as a despotic and unlimited expression of the effort of existing (FC 15-17). Tyranny consists in an 'I' trying to subjugate others – but without killing them – in such a way that in one way or the other they give up their freedom to him, in exchange for the satisfaction of their needs (TI 229). This tyrannical penetration into, and seizure of freedom makes of its victims not only 'slaves,' but in its extreme form also 'enslaved spirits.' One no longer has an individual will; one loses his or her freedom to think and act. In its consistent form, this means that even the 'capacity' to obey an order – which implies freedom – is eradicated. An enslaved spirit acts out of 'blind' obedience. Here, 'blind' means literally that the 'servile soul' not only loses the experience of his or her autonomy but also of his or her obedience. There is no longer any 'conscious' obedience, but only an inner, irresistible 'inclination' and 'drive' to accommodate oneself to the powerful (TI 237). The inclination to submit becomes second nature, whereby the tyranny exercised no longer appears as terror (DF 149).

For an ethically authentic pastoral conversation it is therefore extremely important that the pastor is aware of his or her possible striving for domination, and of the possible inclination towards the subjugation and subordination of the client. In his existential situation of need, the other can feel so weak and impotent that he would be prepared to become attached to the pastor who is assisting him. And the pastor can be tempted, in one way or the other, to bind and subjugate the client to himself or herself, that is to say to intimidate and manipulate the client so that the client surrenders himself emotionally and spiritually to the pastor. Even though it appears at first sight rather far fetched and exaggerated, tyranny is in no way whatsoever impossible in a pastoral relationship, precisely because the terror exercised can hide behind the pretence of the docile obligingness and unconditional trust of the client.

7. *The Ethical Shock Experience 'Thou Shall not Kill'*

The description of all these facets of the 'temptation to violence' was no neutral description, in the sense that they already proceeded inadvertently from an important ethical presupposition, namely the 'prohibition against violence', which has been interpreted time and again by Levinas in the unrelenting prohibition: 'Thou shall not kill' (EN 30). With this prohibition begins all responsibility and care for the other, and thus also of pastoral conversation as a specific form of pastoral care. This does disturb our romantic and naïve image of pastoral conversation, as if it would be based spontaneously, constantly and entirely on goodness, care and benevolence. Our analysis, in line with Levinas, of a few modalities of violence has demonstrated unambiguously how even pastoral conversation can be subjected to violence and inauthenticity. A pastoral conversation is not automatically non-violent because it is pastoral. Just like every human conversation it is potentially violent. Pastors who are not aware of this run a great risk – greater than the risk of those who are indeed aware – of ending up in one or the other shrouded or direct form of violence. That is why an ethically qualitative pastoral conversation begins with the awareness that violence is possible and prohibited.

We would now like to elucidate further what this prohibition signifies, paying special attention to its implications on pastoral conversation. At the moment that I, on the basis of my attempt-at-being, am tempted by the naked and vulnerable face to reduce the other to myself, meaning to say to its appearance or into a means of my self-unfolding, I realise that that which is possible is actually not allowed. This is precisely the core of the fundamental ethical experience that is aroused within me as pastor by the face of the client. I feel shocked in my self-complacency, which via knowledge and capability wants to move forward. In the face I discover myself as potentially violent vis-à-vis the other. The face appears as opposition and resistance: it poses itself before me as a radical 'halt' or 'no', as an absolute resistance against all my capacities (PIF 55). This is not about a physical but rather an ethical resistance: a resistance of that which actually has no resistance. The banal factuality of violence "reveals the quasi-null resistance of the obstacle" (TI 198). Even though the face is not capable of resisting the factual violence, it still stubbornly remains speaking – without words or in an almost inaudible whisper – the defenceless word: 'Thou shall not kill' (OS 94).

Something very paradoxical is apparent here, namely that pastoral conversation – as an incarnation of inter-human ethics – begins as a shock experience, i.e. as the possibility *and* the prohibition to cause damage to the client, the other, by means of inflicting violence on him in one way or the other. The pastoral encounter begins not with a commandment that prescribes what we must do, but with a prohibition that indicates what is certainly not allowed. In the conversation that the pastor initiates with the client, he or she is not primarily faced with the task 'to do' something, but rather with the warning 'not to do' something. An ethically qualitative conversation begins not as straightforwardness and generosity, but as reservation and caution. The fundamental ethical feeling that is aroused by the prohibition against violence is a remarkable form of fear and 'shuddering' (OB 84, 87, 192, 195), now no longer the fear and concern for oneself (the dynamics of the *conatus essendi*) but the fear of wanting to kill the other. In this regard, Levinas likewise speaks of a scruple. Literally, the Latin *scrupulus* means a stone in the shoe whereby one cannot remain standing but is irked to start moving. Scruple is thus an unrest that has a bothersome effect, which is also characterised by Levinas as discomfort and shame: I am anxious that I might in one way or the other grasp and do violence, neglect, violate or damage, use and abuse, reduce to his image or diagnosis, manipulate rhetorically, maltreat, dominate or subjugate deny, in short 'kill' and inflict injustice to the other in his irreducible and wholly being-other, whereby he is given over to me (GCM 169). We can also label this first ethical movement toward the vulnerable other as "the apparently negative movement of restraint" (NT 126). Confronted with the principal affectability and factual vulnerability of the client, the pastor is demanded to restrain and to withdraw himself or herself. An ethically qualitative conversation begins as the paradox of the shrinking or 'self-contraction' of the pastor. It is not with impetuous haste that enthusiastically drives forward and thus threatening to crush the client, but with trembling and inhibition that the pastor approaches his or her conversation partner. Or to put it differently still, the ethical relationship of the pastor to the client begins as hesitation, embarrassment about oneself, a movement of self-questioning: 'Oh my, what am I doing…? Am I perhaps too obtrusive, too rough, too self-assured and unconcerned? Or am I too concerned with myself and my own image?' The appearance of the other traumatises me so that I begin to feel uncomfortable (OB 51). "[The face of the other] calls into question the naïve right of my powers, my glorious spontaneity as a living being. Morality begins when freedom, instead of being justified by itself [being sure of itself in its naïve spontaneity], feels itself to be arbitrary and violent" (TI 84). Conscience begins as a bad conscience, namely as "the consciousness of my own injustice – the shame that freedom feels for itself" (TI 86).

All this implies that an ethically qualitative pastoral conversation cannot tolerate any form of violence by the pastor towards the client. This demand for non-violence is the primary ethical task of the pastor, whatever the context of the pastoral conversation may be. It is such a fundamental ethical task that it precedes all other ethical modes of approach to the client. Its fundamental character is at the same time wholly paradoxical since by not killing or by not using any (direct or indirect) form of violence, one has in fact not yet done anything. If one refrains from violence, everything else still remains to be done, whereas through obedience to the prohibition the conditions for a salutary pastoral conversation have been created.

By means of the prohibition 'Thou shall not kill' and the ethical scruple or reservation that has been aroused within me, the radical asymmetry between me and the other – between the pastor and the client – still becomes more visible than was already demonstrated above. The ethical prohibition instigates the "curvature of the intersubjective space" (TI 291). By means of the prohibition, the 'I', the pastor, and the other, the client, are distinguished from each other in a radical way, not only phenomenologically but also ethically, precisely because they are placed before each other in non-in-difference. This difference does not depend on their respective, distinct qualities nor on their coincidentally unequal psychological dispositions and moods during the pastoral encounter (TI 215). It lies in the 'I-other-conjunction' itself: by means of its demanding – forbidding – character, the face of the other – the client – stands as an authority above me, that out of its ethical 'highness' comes towards me with an appeal. With Levinas we can also call this the 'sacred' and 'divine' character of the face of the client (PIF 56). As such, the client as other is not my equal, but my superior: not only my master who teaches me and reveals something radically new, as we saw above, but also my 'lord' who as a 'You' commands me unconditionally from his eminent height: "The interlocutor is not a Thou, he is a You [*pas un Toi, il est un Vous*]; he reveals himself in his lordship" (TI 101). That is precisely the paradox of the epiphany of the face of the client: as the factually lesser and 'needy' one, the client as the irreducible other that speaks to me and appeals to me ethically is my superior, by whom the pastor must let himself or herself be orientated. This refers at the same time to the loftiness and majesty of God, the wholly Other. Thus, the mastership of the other, the client, sketched above, is reinforced or rather ethically qualified. Thus the 'after You' – the primacy of the other – likewise acquires its full ethical weight. The other comes first, not because he is better or occupies a more interesting social position, but rather because in and through his face as ethical appeal he exercises authority over me, to be sure a disarmed authority because by means of its prohibition the face cannot force me but only appeal to me.

IV. Ethical Dynamics of the Pastoral Face-to-Face as Responsibility

It is only by means of obedience to the prohibition against violence that space is created in pastoral conversation for the positive interpretation of the ethical relationship toward the client, the other.

1. *Creative Responsibility for the Vulnerable Client*

Levinas characterises the positive ethical relationship toward the other with the synthetic term responsibility. It is a responsibility that allows a client to raise her or his voice: the voice of the irreducible, lofty other, the true master and teacher for every pastor. This responsibility is more than not killing or not using violence. It is also the attitude of acknowledgement and respect for the being-other of the client. Concretely, the pastor acknowledges the client by believing in that other. This means no subjugation of the other but a turning towards the client that confirms its alterity. By means of acknowledging the client, the pastor respects and confirms its face as an expression of its unique being-other: "to show respect is to bow down before a being that commands me". Hence, Levinas can state that "speech is a relationship between freedoms which neither limit nor negate, but affirm, one another". By speaking to each other they bind themselves to each other, but at the same time they are not swallowed up in this conversation: they remain transcendent with regard to each other. The reciprocity of this respect is no formal relationship of someone who speaks to someone else. On the contrary, it is about an ethically qualified reciprocity in the sense that the client, who is confirmed in its unique being-other and mastership by the pastor, responds to this acknowledgement with its word and story and thus also gives acknowledgement to the pastor (which does not mean that this returning acknowledgement becomes the condition for the acknowledgement by the pastor) (ET 43).

An essential and at the same time concrete form of acknowledgement in pastoral conversation consists in paying the necessary and deserved attention: "the eminently sovereign attention in me is what *essentially* responds to an appeal. The exteriority of its point of departure is essential to it: it is the very tension of the I" (TI 99). This attention to the other, however, should not be misunderstood, namely as an observation. If from within ourselves we depart towards the other, as we stated above, then on the basis of our scrutiny we will try to get to know the other by means of observing, in order thus to be able to describe its characteristics, by which we can also understand and handle the other. In order to avoid the violence that is entrenched in that observation, we must, according to Levinas, give preference to listening to the other. Its starting point no longer lies with me and my sensory perception but in my being open to the word of the other. An ethically qualitative pastoral conversation is primarily based not on what we see of the other but on what the other says to us – which appeals to us to listen attentively and with an open mind. Or to put it paradoxically: "The best way of encountering the other is not even to notice the colour of his eyes" (EI 85). A pastoral conversation is an ethical event precisely because before everything else the client is given and granted the word. This is made possible by the attentive and sympathetic listening by the pastor to the client. For that, a certain reserve from the side of the pastor is necessary, in the sense that he or she guards oneself from speaking all too much and thus determine, or even through the overflow of eloquent words 'terrorise', the other. The ethical asceticism of listening more than speaking also implies the 'silence' of the pastor, to be sure on condition that it is not an indifferent, all too politely distant, rhetorical, or even an icy and aggressive silence, but rather a silence that contributes to the creation of a 'terror-free zone' (Riemslagh) wherein the client is given the chance to be present and to speak as other. Listening implies being able to keep silent, but the silence must also be a sincere listening, otherwise the moments of silence, whether long or short, become unbearable. And it is also this ethical approach, which gives preference to and creates space for the word of the client, that orientates and inspires the looking at the other into an affirming, acknowledging and mild look.

From this brief analysis of the acknowledgement, and the listening that is intimately connected to it, it is apparent how the ethical relationship, from which pastoral conversation derives its quality, requires a fundamental option and attitude of benevolence, namely desiring the good for the other, promoting the well-being of the client. This general ethical orientation contains the entire array of dimensions and aspects, where Levinas bridges the two extremes in one sentence: "One must yield to the other the first place in everything, from the *after You* before an open door right up to the disposition – hardly possible, but holiness demands it – to die for the other. In this attitude of holiness, there is a reversal of the normal order of things, the natural order of things, the persistence in being of the ontology of things and of the living" (IFP 47).

The foundational benevolence for the other, the client, is attained not only and even often not in the first place through all sorts of great and heroic deeds of care and responsibility for the other. It is realised both in daily life as well as in the concrete course of the pastoral encounter usually on the basis of small deeds – or words, which are actually also deeds that bring about something. Thus for Levinas, the expression 'after You' not only indicates the principal and radical primacy of the other (cf. supra), but it also refers to the usually anecdotic, hardly spectacular, everyday gesture of letting someone pass first when both happen to be at an entrance at the same moment. That is a form of politeness, which is more than etiquette, precisely because it is ethically laden. Hence, Levinas speaks of an 'ethical courtesy': "To respect the other, to take the other into account, to let him pass before oneself. And courtesy! Yes, that is very good, to let the other pass before I do; this little effort of courtesy is also an access to the face. Why should you pass before me? That is very difficult, because you, too, encounter my face. But courtesy or ethics consists in not thinking that reciprocity" (IFP 49)[17].

As an extension of this small ethical politeness Levinas also pays attention to the small word of greeting at an encounter: "the first miracle is the fact that I say *bonjour*!" (IFP 59)[18]. "Is not the first word *bonjour*? As simple as *bonjour*" (IFP 47). We give preference to 'good morning' rather than the common English translation 'hello' because in the latter

17. With the last sentence of the quote, Levinas refers to a problem that is coupled with the application of the fundamental principle 'after You'. If both the one as well as the other says, and keeps on saying, 'after You', then they block each other and see to it that in the end no one takes precedence, or no one enters the door first. Hence Levinas maintains 'after You' as a fundamental principle but at the same time links its application in practice to the entrance of the 'third party' and the necessity of justice, which organises all things in fairness and proportion, and thus makes arrangements to bring back to balance the asymmetry and thus the original imbalance of the I-other-relationship. Cf. OB 157-160. We ourselves suggest still another possibility, which lies in line with goodness. Even though I in principle am faced with the ethical calling to let the other go first, I can – as an expression and act of goodness – forgo my ethical privilege of letting the other go first. By giving in to the insistence of the other who wants me to go first, I give the other the chance to realise his ethical task, namely to let me pass first, and as such act in an ethically good manner. By means of my generosity, which does not put first adamantly my own ethical goodness but on the contrary withdraws from it modestly, I give the other the chance to be generous toward me. By acknowledging this generosity via a simple 'thank you' and 'you're welcome', an *'entre-nous'* is created, a benevolent space for listening and speaking, hesitant or outspoken, questioning or affirming, calling forth – literally 'pro-vocative'.

18. Cf. also VVP 140: "On dit: 'Bonjour!' avant de parler avec quelqu'un. Ce souhait ouvre et rend possible tout ce qui va suivre".

the finesse of both wish and blessing are lost. For indeed, to address someone with 'good morning' is to pronounce a wish, stronger still to pronounce a blessing over the other: "When I say to you, *bonjour*, I have blessed you before knowing you; I am concerned with your days, I enter into your life beyond the order of simple knowledge" (IFP 49). 'Good morning' is thus no neutral communication that the weather is beautiful today, but a way of wishing the best for the other, a wish of peace: "I wish you peace, I wish you a good day, expression of the one who worries for the other. It underlies all the rest of communication, underlies all discourse" (IFP 47). In the pastoral encounter as well, a salutation by name and a 'good morning' sets the conversation on the ethical tracks of benevolence: "*Bonjour* as benediction and my being available for the other" (IFP 47). Not only does the pastor wish the client all things good, his or her greeting also expresses how reality is orientated by the good: "The greetings addressed to the other is an invocation. I therefore insist on the primacy of the well-intentioned relation toward the other. Even when there may be ill will on the other's part, the attention, the receiving of the other, like his recognition, mark the priority of good in relation to evil" (AT 98).

The responsibility of the one (the pastor) for the other (the client) realises itself not only in sympathetic words but also requires concrete and tangible deeds of goodness. Responsibility is not sentimentalism or naïve romanticism in being moved by the vulnerability of the other. Its affectivity must become efficaciousness, its turning toward the other into 'works' of care for the other (HO 25-29). Without such incarnation, responsibility for the other remains empty and inauthentic. Or to put it with a biblical image: it is not enough to love the other with all our heart, all our reason and all our will, we must also 'roll up our sleeves' and 'get our hands dirty' (SM 121-122). In short, our word of proximity to the other must – via our body – become flesh, and that in earthly, appropriate forms (AS 81). Even in pastoral conversation, we can be appealed to turn our words into deeds and to make sure that not only the spiritual but also the material needs of the client are being met, even if perhaps we will have to refer to other agencies and assistance to do so.

Responsibility for the other does not stop with 'giving', as we just described. Responsibility 'infinitises' itself into a goodness full of longing. By means of its appeal, the face arouses in me not only the sobering up and the shame of my attempt-at-being, that goes forth unabashed without looking left or right. The face also awakens in me the desire to dedicate myself unselfishly to the well-being of the other (HO 29-30): "The infinity of responsibility denotes not its actual immensity, but a responsibility increasing in the measure that it is assumed; duties become greater in the measure that they are accomplished" (TI 244). And this dedication develops – or rather is called forth to develop – into the 'radical generosity' of the one, the pastor, who assists the other, the client, in his suffering and dying. At this, Levinas puts the classic approach to death on its head. In a modern or enlightened mind, strongly influenced today by Heidegger, 'one's own death', our very own dying and mortality, take centre stage. Perhaps that is ultimately our great concern, unless we flee to the everyday insouciance of the 'babble' and the 'man' (*das Man*) of the 'market place'. The great task is to take seriously one's own 'being unto death' and thus come to authenticity – to be sure, a heroic task. According to Levinas, however, the human being comes to true humanity when one changes perspective and in the first place becomes concerned with the death of the other: "when its fear of death is inverted into fear of committing murder" (TI 244). This 'fear for the mortal and dying other' lies at the foundation of our responsibility for the other (PPS 37). I am so moved by the death of the other that I hold myself responsible for the ultimate violence that the other suffers because of his mortality. The extreme vulnerability of the other's mortality appeals and provokes me to enter "into the concern-for-the-death-of-the-other" (GCM 164). Concretely, I am called not to let the other stand alone when he looks death in the eye, even though I have no power at all against this unrelenting enemy and I can only respond with the 'here I am' of the lingering and caring proximity that eases his dying and makes it bearable (EN 79-81). In short, in the appearance of the death of the other, the duty to offer hospitality to the other and to meet the other with giving and serving hands (AS 76) becomes the duty to truthful goodness and pure love of neighbour 'without covetousness and selfishness'. This is a non-indifference *par excellence*, that in no way whatsoever seeks for a reward in return; it is a non-mutual goodness that in the face of the relentlessness of death even bears to be in vain and to no avail (EI 118-119).

With this, we touch at the same time an essential dimension, or rather the very core, of all pastoral dealings with people. The epiphany of the face consists precisely in the appeal not to abandon the other, the client, who ends up in one or the other existential 'need', to its fate. This appeal towards non-indifference and towards responsible proximity shows itself most clearly when the client is beset with irreversible suffering whereby its death is announced or becomes imminent. The pastor experiences a radical appeal to unconditional, non-reciprocal goodness, namely not to leave the other alone in its suffering and dying, even though the client can no longer give something in return – and when the pastor himself or herself can no longer do anything effective anymore. Then the gesture of holding the hand of the sick or the dying replaces the word, or rather the gesture of the touch itself becomes the word: a wordless word of tangible proximity that does not abandon. The Jewish tradition calls this 'true mercy', the only mercy that one can still demonstrate to someone who is delivered up to the unrelenting enemy, death: a lingering, gratuitous, non-reciprocal goodness (GCM 186). With Levinas we can also call this true consolation, which stands in stark contrast with the promise of compensation: 'Don't worry, it will all get better tomorrow'. Authentic comfort does not flee from the present, from the actual suffering of the other, in order to hold up one or the other (illusory) vision of recovery. Consolation comes to stand in the present of the experience of suffering of the other, to touch the other here and now and be near, without empty promises (not even of the life after death as compensation for this vale of tears): "The caress of the consoler which softly comes in our pain does not promise the end of suffering, does not announce any compensation, and in its very contact, is not concerned with what is to come *afterwards* [...]; it concerns the very instant of physical pain, which is then no longer condemned to itself, is transposed 'elsewhere' by the movement of the caress [...]. [True salvation] must concern the very instant of pain, and not only compensate for it" (EE 91).

2. *Responsibility for the Responsibility of the Client*

And still with all this, not everything has been said about the responsibility of the one, the pastor, for the other, the client. In his second major work, *Otherwise than Being* (1974), Levinas radicalises the idea of responsibility by describing it as "responsibility for the responsibility of the other" (OB 117). We can distinguish two aspects therein, on the one hand, the care for the responsibility of the other for itself, and on the other hand, the care for the responsibility of the other for others.

The first aspect dovetails with the incarnational dimension of responsibility, as we have already sketched above. Our responsibility for the other indeed shows a remarkable paradox. Thanks to its heteronomous and altro-centric origin and orientation, it implies a transcendence of the attempt at being of the 'I', the pastor. But this transcendence directs itself at the same time to the attempt-at-being of the other, the client. The responsibility of the other only becomes real when it directs itself not only to the person of the other but also to his or her well-being. It is not only the acknowledgement of the other that is important, but also the care for the ups and downs of the other in its very concrete being. And these ups and downs of the other do not only concern its bodily and material needs, but also the unfolding of its 'attempt-at-being' into an independent and free existence. In the pastoral encounter, attention for the other must be such that the other is not reduced to an 'object' of responsibility, but rather be promoted to a 'subject' of responsibility. In that sense the claim of the client does not stand at odds with the radical heteronomous responsibility of the pastor, but the one has need of the other. The responsibility of the pastor sees to it that the 'mastership' of the client, the other *par excellence*, which was made explicit above, takes on its true ethical form. By means of his or her responsibility for the client as 'other before me', the pastor makes the ethical mastership of the other effectively possible. The responsibility for the client implies indeed the essential care for his or her being independent and becoming mature, otherwise there is no encounter or conversation possible. The I-other-relationship is indeed, according to Levinas, only possible when the partners of the encounter are radically separate from each other and are not swallowed up in the relationship (and the conversation), but remain separate: "Simultaneously, in dialogue is hollowed out an absolute distance between the I and the You, absolutely separated by the inexpressible secret of their intimacy, each being unique in its kind as *I* and as *You*, each one absolutely other in relation to the other. [...] On the other hand, it is also there that unfolds [...] the extraordinary and immediate relation of dia-logue, which transcends this distance without surpassing it or recuperating it" (GCM 144). Or formulated still more pithily: "The same and the other at the same time maintain themselves in relationship and *absolve* themselves from this relationship, remain absolutely separated" (TI 102). What is remarkable here is that the relationship and separation do not stand side by side, but are mutually dependent on each other. The irreducibility between the partners of the dialogue is the condition for a non-fusional, non-violent encounter. And it is in and through the encounter that they receive their separateness as well. Thus the alterity of the client becomes, thanks to pastoral conversation and thanks to the responsibility of the pastor, confirmed and promoted. With Levinas we can call this the true miracle of pastoral conversation, and of all authentic conversations. We would also like to call it the emancipatory dimension of the heteronomous responsibility 'by and for the other', whereby the evil – the real risk of paternalism and moralism – in pastoral conversation can be prevented. Or rather, this needs to be avoided at all costs in order to guarantee the ethical quality of pastoral conversation. The awareness that one can be inclined, precisely from one's 'power position' as pastor, to emphasise only the 'neediness' of the client and as such make the other dependent or keep the other imprisoned in (the yearning for) dependence, forms an essential part of an ethically qualified pastoral responsibility. The pastor who takes on correctly his or her responsibility for the client throughout the course of the conversation creates space and possibilities for the affirmation and development of the independence and responsibility of the client for itself. This of course is not the same as denying unrealistically the dependencies and alienations that afflict the client, since this is probably the reason why the client has approached the pastor. It rather means that one does not identify the client with these dependencies and alienations, so that precisely in and through the encounter and the conversation, space is created in order to tap the potentialities of growth of the client. That is also why it is an essential condition for an ethically qualitative conversation that the pastor does not approach the client as an 'interesting object' that merely contributes to his or her own self-development in a professional pastoral performance. Responsibility for the client rather means that one stimulates the other to express itself and make itself present in its unique being-other, so that the conversation can unfold into a true partnership – without thereby destroying the ethical asymmetry: an asymmetric reciprocity. This emancipatory approach to the client as subject of its own being and speaking likewise implies that the pastor appreciates not merely by acknowledging and by 'resonating' or 'mirroring' the contribution of the other, but that he or she also dares to react with questions and reflections that contribute to the client's being able to express itself more and better. Only thus can the banal and pitying sentimentalism of a merely 'accommodating' conversation be avoided. A real and robust, at the same time circumspect and respectful, conversation is based on the face-to-face of two unique persons that approach each other with an open view and that confirm each other in their unique alterity in and through this directness.

We need now to go a step further, perhaps a step further than Levinas himself takes in his philosophical view on responsibility, even though he remains our inspiration for this new step. Namely we would like to broaden the asymmetrical responsibility of the pastor for the client and also regard it from the perspective of the responsibility of the client for others. We call it a chiastic responsibility, in the sense that it concerns two forms of responsibility that intersect each other. The responsibility of pastors for their clients is only integral if it grows forth into a responsibility for the responsibility of those clients not only for themselves (cf. supra) but also and in particular for others. Levinas affirms explicitly that an ethically excellent existence consists in this: "to elevate the *care-for-self* of living beings to the *care-for-other* in man" (TN 1). In other words, if we only apply the idea of responsibility for the other to the pastors, our analysis falls short and gives rise to a one-sidedness with dangerous consequences. It is indeed not impossible that the engagement of pastors for their clients ends up in an egocentric and utilitarian result in the clients. The caring responsibility for the other, the client, can be very altro-centric and unselfish, but this can unintentionally entail as well that one leads the client – the goal of our responsibility – to a conventionally smug, self-sufficient life wherein what is only or mainly important is the care for oneself. To put this pastorally, the altruism of the one can lead directly to a promotion of the egotism of the other. Not only the 'I' but also the other, the client as 'alter ego', can be selfish, indifferent, rude, dominant, manipulative, exploitative, violent, tyrannical, racist, immoral in one way or another … Precisely for that reason, the emancipatory promotion of the other to free self-determination and creative self-expression, as sketched above, should never have the final word. Pastoral conversation must go farther. Not only must it be the expression of self-transcendence in the pastor, but also in the client. Through the epiphany of the other, who come in their vulnerable existence, pastors are made responsible for the responsibility of the other, not only for itself but also for others. In other words, the pastor is faced with the challenge to take up his or her responsibility for clients in such a way that they are helped and stimulated to acknowledge and take up in turn their heteronomous responsibility for others. If this does not happen, the pastoral guidance ends up contradicting itself, destroying even its own dynamism and meaning: in an extreme ethical attention for the client as radical other, that other is then only led to pose itself centrally at the cost of others.

Concretely speaking, this implies for pastoral conversation that, if necessary, one also confronts the client with the boundary rule mentioned above of 'Thou shall not kill' as an expression of the prohibition against violence, abuse, consumption, humiliation, indifference, exclusion, denial … In the non-violent space of pastoral conversation, everything can be said by the client, but this does not mean that everything is allowed. If in the pastoral conversation the pastor adopts only a 'compliant' and 'understanding' attitude and does not remain critically alert to the non-allowable boundary transgressions by the other, he or she then corrupts one's calling to responsibility. The client as well is responsible for 'his' or 'her' others, both those who are near in one's relational and social network as well as those who are far with whom one is only linked indirectly via the mediation of organisations, structures, and institutions. Hence, in his or her responsibility for the client the pastor must not be led to the temptation by the uniqueness of the other to close up oneself in an exclusive in-crowd of the 'I-you' with the client. He or she must be alert time and again for the others with whom the client is also connected, beginning with the 'hidden' others of the client's family, social and cultural milieu. If one neglects the real responsibilities and connections of the client with those absent third parties, then one inadvertently encourages the egocentric utilitarianism which we have argued against above. An ethically qualitative pastoral conversation should never enclose itself in the cosy in-crowd of only a mutual 'I-you'. The pastor is tasked not only 'to hear' the voice of the vulnerable client but also 'to awaken' the other to a manifold responsibility, not only for oneself but also for others, not only for those who are near but also for the absent others with whom one is invisibly but no less really connected[19].

V. Conclusion in a Religious Perspective

Even though it is not the theme of this essay, and thus cannot be developed but only briefly referred to in it, we still do not want to conclude this essay without referring to the religious possibility and dynamism of pastoral conversation as the ethical event of the I-other-relationship. In line with Buber, and with the entire dialogical thought, for Levinas it is not so much the nature of 'being' but rather the inter-human encounter that is *'le lieu divin'*, namely *the* context par excellence where God comes to mind in an authentic manner: "wenn Gott fällt uns ein" – "descent of God" (IRB 282). As a way of entering ethically in relationship with the other, pastoral conversation puts us on the trail of the wholly Other, the Infinite One, who at the same time narrowly comes near to us by entrusting us to one another. At the end of his fundamental study on 'the dialogue' (1980) Levinas expresses the religious perspective of conversation as follows: "The I as the I is the servant of the You in Dialogue. An inequality that may appear arbitrary; unless it be – in the word addressed to the other man, in the ethics of the welcome – the first religious service, the first prayer, the first liturgy, the religion out of which God could first have come to mind and the word 'God' have made its entry into language and into good philosophy. It is not, of course, that

19. In their retrospective essay "Relational Ethics and Missing Voices" at the end of this book Kenneth J. Gergen and Mary M. Gergen reflect further on the implications of the client's eventual immorality or unethical behavior for the counselling, i.c. pastoral relationship [red.].

the other man must be taken for God or that God, the Eternal Thou, be found simply in some excession of the You. What counts here is that, from out of the relation to the other, from the depths of the Dialogue, this immensurable word signifies for thought, and not the reverse" (GCM 151). It is thanks to the ethical relationship to the other, as it is incarnated – or rather must and may be incarnated – among others in pastoral conversation, that the human person is put on the path towards God: "For-the-other-man and thereby unto God" (GCM XV).

Department of Theological Ethics
Faculty of Theology and Religious Studies
KU Leuven – Catholic University of Leuven
St.-Michielsstraat 4/3101
B-3000 Leuven
Belgium
roger.burggraeve@theo.kuleuven.be

Roger BURGGRAEVE

EPILOGUE

RELATIONAL ETHICS AND MISSING VOICES

From an historical perspective, the preceding chapters suggest that we are entering a new space of ethical concern. In many respects this is also a dangerous space, as it subtly undermines the traditional view of the individual as an autonomous, moral decision maker – one who can, and should, act in terms of his or her own moral criteria. In these pages we begin to approach a more dialogical view of ethics in care-giving relationships. Care-givers[1] are invited to embrace the needs, wants, and beliefs of their clients *in their own terms*. No longer does the care-giver enter the relationship as "the knower" of the good life, and how to intervene in the client's life so as to institute such a state. Rather, these chapters celebrate acts of "responsive listening", and empathic understanding of the client's life world. This position is particularly well developed in the chapters by Burggraeve (Chpt. 12), Lipari (Chpt. 2), McNamee (Chpt. 1), Riemslagh (Chpt. 7), Rober (Chpt. 4), van Heijst (Chpt. 9), and Doehring (Chpt. 8). On this account, to serve others is not to lead them in directions already embraced – independent of the other's existence – but is indeed to follow "after you". These discussions provide enormously valuable resources in thinking through the implications of care-giving, whether it be in (pastoral) counselling, therapy, social work, or in policy making relevant to those in need. These are also contributions to globe-spanning dialogues on the relation between the *haves* and the *have nots* throughout the world. They speak cogently to contemporary circumstances, in which differing cultures are increasingly thrown together, and in which competing value claims – always volatile – now threaten global relations. It is indeed time to listen, to comprehend, and to appreciate. We are speaking, then, about an ethical stance toward relationships in a world of difference.

I. In Search for a Fully Relational Ethic

In this final chapter we wish to expand on this emerging vision of a relational ethic. Responding in our relations to the 'face of the other', as

1. 'Care-givers' in this essay can be understood in an inclusive way, namely as therapists, social workers and pastoral counsellors.

Levinas[2] described it, is surely an essential step in the right direction. However, as we see it, this is but a beginning in coming to understand and practice a fully relational ethic. We must press further. The challenge to expand our deliberations begins when we ask about the missing voices in the dialogue between care-giver and client. Thus far we have placed refreshing emphasis on the voice of those in need. But consider: it is one thing to listen and embrace, but what does this say about the voice that the care-giver brings to the relationship? Chapters by Bergum (Chpt. 5) and Bertau (Chpt. 3) both carry this concern. As care-givers we often confront those whose forms of life are not congenial with what we bring to the relationship as personal values. It is one thing to listen to and accept the "no" of the client, as in Rober's perceptive discussion (Chpt. 4). But what if we find the values and life patterns of the client distasteful, unethical or evil[3]? Should we bend an empathic ear, for example, to a tyrannical and abusive father, a sexist employer, a pedophile, a racist commentator, or a bully – those who engage in behavior that may be perfectly acceptable to themselves, but not to others? What if our clients support terrorism, man-boy relations, or neo-Nazism? Should we as care-givers remain silent, curious, accepting, and hoping only to make a contribution to the client's good in his or her own terms? If the relationship is truly a dialogue, then why should we as care-givers not expect the client to grant to us the right to voice; why should our "face" be obliterated in the inter-change?

There is more: The relationship between care-giver and client may be very important to the client's ultimate well-being. However, this is a highly circumscribed relationship, focused as it is on the dyad. Depending on the outcome of the dyadic process, many others may be affected – for good or ill. To what extent, for example, will the client's gain represent a loss for others? Such losses may be experienced not only among family members and friends of the client, but also within the client's community, workplace, or place of worship. Similarly, the care-giver does not remain unaffected by the therapeutic exchange, and the results may have reverberating effects on the network of those to whom he or she is responsible. And where shall we draw the line in terms of ethical concerns? Is it only the social world immediately shared by care-giver and client to which we should attend? In transforming relationships

2. E. LEVINAS, *Totality and Infinity: An Essay on Exteriority*, trans. A. Lingis, The Hague – Boston, MA – London, Nijhoff, 1979, pp. 197-201.

3. See also the last part of Burggraeve's contribution and his idea on being responsible for the other's responsibility, to be understood as the confrontation of the other with the prohibition against being violent.

we are transforming cultures, and in turn, their relationship to other cultures. Such questions are all the more challenging, as not all parties will agree on the value of *any* therapeutic outcomes. The wife of a client may be very pleased at the results of her husband's treatment, while his children may be dismayed. A client's self-esteem may be bolstered, but family members may encounter hurtful neglect. A bigot is helped, while the victims are hurt, and so on. Where are the voices of the extended network of those who may have a stake in the (pastoral) counselling relationship?

Clearly, these are not easy questions. There have never been universally commanding criteria for the virtuous life. However, continuing dialogue is essential. What we propose in the following pages is to extend the discussion initiated in these chapters by first considering more carefully the relational process and its implications for conceptions of self and other. In this discussion we will raise challenges to the conception of independent selves and autonomous moral actions. Then, with a more fully relational conception of self in place, we will examine the origins of human value – moral and otherwise. At this point we can consider the potentials of a fully relational ethical stance and its implications for care-giving practices.

II. The Relational Genesis of Meaning

At the outset, let us ask what it is to offer help or support to anyone? More specifically, can those in care-giving roles themselves determine that their actions indeed offer help or support? Can a care-giver listen sensitively to the other, without the other's affirmation that they have done so? And if the voice of the other is to count in determining the meaning of the care-giver's actions, then a dramatic re-visioning of both the individual and ethical action is invited. Consider: a client speaks at length of her feelings of loneliness, isolation, and insignificance. The therapist listens intently, opening himself to feeling the significance of these utterances. Slowly he responds, "What you are saying really moves me, and I can feel you are valiantly wrestling with intense depression". The client then replies, "That's all very well and good, but I don't need your sympathy. I need a prescription for anti-depressants". Or, consider a second client, who might reply, "I just have to tell you how relieved and grateful I am. I feel you truly appreciate the depth of my depression. And this means maybe I can also trust you to help me find a way out … a way to quietly leave this life". In effect, we find the meaning of the therapist's [or the pastoral counsellor's] actions are not contained within his utterances themselves. Their meaning is born in the client's response.

Yet, we should not thus conclude that it is the client who creates the meaning of the therapist's response. For the client's response is not itself meaning/full alone. Should the therapist pay no attention to it, and proceed with a line of questioning, the client would fail in giving meaning to the therapist's comment. Should the therapist begin to speak of the harmful side-effects of anti-depressants or the harmful social consequences of suicide, he would be disqualifying the utterance of the client. Should he offer a prescription for drugs – to aid in depression or suicide – he would affirm the client's utterances. Yet, neither the actions of the client nor the therapist depend on the interchange in itself. Both are participants in conversational traditions, and their ability to generate intelligibility depends on their compliance with the relevant rituals of conversation that precede them. Or, more generally, we not only require each other to 'make meaning', but we also depend on a preceding tradition of social coordination.

From this account we may conclude that we are not the origins of the meaning of our actions, but meaning takes shape within a continuous process of coordinated action – one that both precedes and follows the actions themselves. Nor should we confine the process of generating meaning to linguistic collaboration alone. Coordination will often include bodily movements, such as posture, gaze, or gesture, which can often be more significant than verbal content. Further, the process of coordination may also include surrounding objects, along with particular contexts of space and time. In the same way that coordination in the use of words brings them into meaning, so are the various objects with which we surround ourselves brought into significance. This 'cup' becomes a vessel for drinking tea; this 'clock' a device for counting time together. To paraphrase Wittgenstein, meaning issues from the forms of life in which we are collectively engaged. Within this process all that we take to be real, rational and good is brought into being. All that we take to be significant in life, to be sacred, objectively true, or worthy of commitment is born in relationship[4].

Such a view also raises fundamental questions regarding the traditional conception of the autonomous individual and of moral action. If all meaning is born within coordinated actions, then the very concepts of 'the individual', 'individual minds', and 'moral thought' are problematized.

4. K.J. GERGEN, *Relational Being, beyond Self and Community*, New York, NY, Oxford University Press, 2009.

All are byproducts of relational traditions. Likewise, moral action is never accomplished alone. Actions become moral or immoral within relational traditions, and the meaning of any action is open to continuous reinterpretation, as traditions and relationships are transformed over time. Let us turn, then, to traditions of moral action, and the challenges they pose in the care-giving relationship.

III. Orders of Moral Action

If it is neither individual action, nor social inter-action from which human intelligibility emerges, but a process of coordinated action, what are the implications in the context of multiple and conflicting visions of the good? Let us approach this problem by inquiring first into the origins of good and evil in a relational key.

1. *First Order Morality: The Dangers of Dissonance*

We commonly suppose the world suffers because there are people who possess a flawed sense of conscience, who pursue their goals without regard for the consequences to others, or who lack character or intelligence. From a relational standpoint, however, we may entertain the opposite hypothesis: There is no absence of good in the world; rather, in important respects we suffer from its plenitude. How is this so? If we trace all that we hold meaningful in life to relationships, then we must also view relationships as the source of our presumptions of good and evil. At a basic level, we may say that virtually all relationships will generate at least rudimentary understandings of good vs. bad. They are essential to sustaining patterns of coordination. Deviations from accepted patterns may constitute a threat. When we have developed harmonious ways of relating – of speaking and acting – we place a value on 'this way of life'. That which encroaches upon, undermines, or destroys this form of life becomes defined as 'not good', or evil.

Let us view this movement from rudimentary coordination to value formation in terms of *first order morality*. To function within any viable relationship requires embracing the values inherent in its patterns, whether we articulate our values or not. When preparing dinner with one's spouse, for example, we recognize that first order morality is at work. We establish and perpetuate what becomes the 'good for us'. There are no articulated rules in this case, no moral injunctions, no 'bill of rights' for husbands and wives. The rules are all implicit, but they touch on virtually everything we do, from the tone and pitch of our voices, to our bodily movements around the kitchen, to how the food is cooked, and to when and if we give tidbits to the dog. One false move in our dinner dance, and each of us can become 'morally superior' to the other.

It follows that, if fully immersed within a particular relationship, one cannot step outside the existing patterns of coordination to do otherwise. To do so would be unintelligible. To return to the kitchen, neither of us would throw food at the other, spit on each other, or smack the other with a pan. We do not engage in these activities primarily because they are unintelligible to us; they would never occur as options for ethical deliberation. We continue to carry on normal domestic life because it is our way of life. In effect, morality of the first order is essentially being sensible within a particular way of life. In the same vein, most people do not deliberate about murdering their best friend, not because of some principle to which they were exposed in their early years, and not because it is illegal. It is virtually unthinkable. We live our lives largely within the comfortable houses of first order morality.

To what, then, do we attribute the source of immoral action? We must again look to first order morality. Wherever people come into coordination first order morality is in the making. As we strive to find mutually satisfactory ways of going on together, we begin to establish a local good, 'the way we do it'. As a result there are myriad traditions of the good, and everywhere people congregate successfully they will set in motion new possibilities. This condition is not only descriptive of countless localized traditions of family, friendship, and community, it also applies to the major religions of the world, as well as governments, the sciences, education, art, and so on. In this sense, the sciences and the arts are similar to religion. All sustain visions of the good, some sacred and others secular, some articulated and others implicit.

It is in the multiplication of the good that the stage is set for social conflict. In a pluralist world of goods, any action will be judged according to a multiplicity of alternative traditions. All ways of life can be alien or odious to those who do not participate. And if these ways of life seem to impede or threaten one's own traditions, the response is resistance. It may be minimal, as in disregard, avoidance, and hateful gossip, or moderate, as in ostracizing the other, divorce, or disinheritance. In the case of more threatening actions, the impulse is toward elimination. This is typically accomplished through various forms of defense (surveillance, policing) curtailment (imprisonment, torture), or more radically, through extermination (death penalty, invasion, bombs). In all these ways a hardened shell comes to separate the good shared within, from the evil without. Those within can derive value and nurturance from punishing and destroying those without. At the same time, those outside may be moved to resistant action. Their own traditions are now under threat. At this point we enter a familiar pattern of sustained attack and counter-attack, all in the name of the good. Once this dance of death is underway, it is not the other who comprises the major enemy, but the tradition of choreography.

Of course, the traditional care-giving relationship never reaches such deadly proportions. However, most of those in the care-giving professions will recognize the often subtle voices of antipathy they carry for many of those they treat. They encounter ways of life in which failure, weakness, wastefulness, laziness, insensitivity, oppression, cruelty, prejudice, and irresponsibility prevail. As a consequence, they avoid them, dismiss them, and try to explain them away. There is the voice of the other, calling for attention, but there is also the moral counter-voice of one's own traditions. The challenge, then, is between conflicting forms of life, each valued by their constituents.

2. *Second Order Morality: Coordinating Coordination*

In applying the account of relational process to the question of moral pluralism, we find that the very production of the good also establishes the conditions for the less than good, or evil. In effect, so long as differing groups of people coordinate their actions to generate harmony and fulfillment, there will be confrontations between good and evil. Given the rapid development and proliferation of communication technologies – email, cell phones, twitter, internet social networks, and the like – we might anticipate that such differences will only increase. With each communicative connection, new formations of valuing (and devaluing) may be thrust into orbit. Agonistic tension is virtually inevitable. The challenge is not that of creating a conflict free existence, but of locating ways of approaching conflict that do not bend toward mutual extermination. Given the circumstances of human coordination, how do we go on?

Here let us return again to the sketch of relational process, in this case to introduce the potential of a second order morality. As outlined above, first order morality may be essential to a satisfying life; it is a source of harmony, trust and direction. At the same time, because of its enormous potentials for variation and multiplicity, we also confront the continuous production of evil. We are moved to control, punish, incarcerate, and ultimately to eliminate that which we have been instrumental in creating.

Conflict is endemic. At the same time, it is important to note that first order morality rests on a logic of distinct units. In western culture the unit is the individual; it is from the individual's capacity for reason and sense of conscience that moral action springs (or not). It is the individual who is typically held responsible for untoward actions, whether in the petty exchanges of everyday life or in courts of law. Much the same logic is employed in holding larger units morally responsible. Variously condemned are political parties, businesses, unions, lobbyists, religions, terrorist groups, armies, and nations. Its representatives may be punished, tortured or destroyed out of simple membership in the unit.

From a relational standpoint a major outcome of first order morality is often the severing of communicative connection. And this in effect, the process of coordination from which reality, rationality and a sense of the good derives can often be destroyed. The potentials for the continuous generation of first order morality are thus terminated. As the eliminative impulse is set in motion, and we move toward mutual annihilation, we slouch toward the end of meaning. To eliminate all those whose values are not identical to one's own, would leave but a single voice – one's own. It is precisely here that we require the presence of *second order morality*, that is, a process that can restore the possibility of first order morality. It is to realize from one's past immersion in first order morality, that without each other there are no values, nothing worth living for. When first order moralities conflict, we slouch toward the end of moral meaning altogether. We must protect and restore the process of collective valuing together. In effect, to engage in second order morality is to sustain the possibility of morality of any kind.

Second order morality rests not on a logic of discriminate units, but of a relational process of co-action. There are no acts of evil committed by a single individual on this account because the meaning of all action is derived from relationship. Holding individuals responsible for untoward actions is not only misguided, but results in alienation and retaliation. In the case of second order morality, individual responsibility is replaced by *relational responsibility*, that is a responsibility derived from relational participation. It is only together that we can bridge the gap of alienation and mutual destruction. When the wheels of individual responsibility are set in motion, relationships typically go off track. Blame is followed by excuses and counter blame. In relational responsibility we step outside this tradition, and recognizing the value of relationship becomes primary. In relational responsibility we avoid the narcissism implicit in ethical calls for 'care of the self', and as well, the negation of traditions resulting from the imperative to 'care for the other'.

IV. Toward Second Order Moral Practices

What then of an orienting ethic for the care-taking relationship? For the care-giver, simply listening to and appreciating the life-world of the client is insufficient; nor is it satisfactory to use the care-giving relationship to vindicate and extend the reach of one's own tradition. In both cases one sustains the divisive conditions of first order morality. The challenge, then, is to develop dialogic forms that move toward second order morality, that is, ways of going on that place primary value on the generative process of relating itself. This is focally a challenge for the participants in the care-giving relationship. "How can we, with our differences, build in directions that we both can value"? However, the responsibility for relationship then expands. "How does our relationship here draw in those not present, but who are near and dear"? And subsequently, "How are we here being responsive to the broader community in which we reside; are there ways we can be sensitive to the global community, so that our relationship contributes to mutually viable forms of life"?

These are not easy challenges, and their very novelty in the care-giving world makes it difficult to draw extensively from our existing traditions. However, to stimulate dialogue on these matters, let us touch briefly on a range of micro-practices that we find rich in potential in care-giving relationships:

– *Sharing stories*: Drawing from the ground-breaking work of the Public Conversations project (www.publicconversations.org), it becomes clear that a major means of gaining an appreciation for another's otherwise alien form of life is to listen to his or her stories. "Here is why I have come to do these things, to believe these things, etcetera". Of course, this is perhaps the primary way in which care-givers come to empathize with their clients. They listen to stories, and in doing so, come to appreciate the life-world of the other. However, in the service of second order morality, the same practice is available to the care-giver. They too may share stories of their lives that would give insight into alternative values. One may learn a great deal from a client who tells a story about why parents should not 'spare the rod and spoil the child'; however, the client may also learn much from a therapist or counsellor who tells a story about parenting that does not require physical punishment.

– *Opening the vocabulary of selves*: We all harbor a multitude of values, many of them conflicting. For every action in which we engage, we can locate reasons for our not acting in this way. For everything we do, we also find value in not doing it. Exploring these often suppressed values can be an effective way of crossing boundaries of meaning, and bringing the many traditions of which one is part into active play. If a client is an irresponsible drinker or gambler, for example, he or she harbors many reasons for not being so. Bringing the traditions represented by these values into salience may bring the client into a more promising relationship with others. At the same time, care-givers may also draw on their multiplicitous histories, raising questions about the particular values they are espousing at any given time. By broadening the field of voices, one avoids antagonisms between opposites.

– *Letter writing*: Among others, Peggy Penn[5] has made effective use of letter writing as a means of re-establishing clients' relationships with those from whom they are alienated. For example, a daughter who has cut herself away from an abusive father may be encouraged to write to him, not necessarily with the intent of sending the letter, but of experiencing what it would be like to bare her feelings to him. Then, she may later be asked to take the father's part in answering such a letter. By role-playing through this exchange, a significant thawing in relationships may take place.

– *Establishing others' presence*: In the same way we carry multiple values, we also carry with us the voices of those about us. In important respects they supply our vocabularies of being. The therapist Karl Tomm makes active use of these vocabularies, by asking clients to give voice to others who are not present[6]. For example, if a client is highly critical of a spouse, an employer, or neighbor, the therapist may ask the client to take the part of the devalued other. What would he or she say, what story would he or she tell? Some therapists approach a similar goal by setting a chair in the room to represent the absent other. The absent person is now made salient in the ensuing dialogue.

– *Appreciative questioning*: Joan Chadbourne and Tony Silbert[7] have developed ways for care-givers to co-create intimate dialogues that strengthen emotional ties, build relationships, help overcome conflicts, and bring peace and comfort to dying people and their families. Through appreciative questioning, especially, people gain the trust and confidence to share stories of the past with others; care-givers learn to listening deeply and quietly to their patients, and also learn to accept others

5. P. Penn, *Joined Imaginations*, Chagrin Falls, OH, Taos Institute Publications, 2009.

6. K. Tomm – M. Hoyt – S. Madigan, *Honoring Our Internalized Others and the Ethics of Caring: A Conversation with Karl Tomm*, in M. Hoyt (ed.), *The Handbook of Constructive Therapies*, San Francisco, CA, Jossey-Bass, 1998, 198-218.

7. J. Chadbourne – T. Silbert, *Healing Conversations Now: Enhancing Relations with Elders and Dying Loved Ones*, Chagrin Falls, OH, Taos Institute Publications, 2011.

listening to them. Often the energy and love that is created in these conversations creates new relational possibilities for those involved, whether it is a dyad or a larger family group[8].

– *Reflection on repercussions*: Drawing from developments in philosophical counselling, perhaps the most apparent means of addressing the broader network of relationships is through direct dialogue. "What are the repercussions of what you are doing for your family, community, or the world at large?" Such a discussion could well bring into play issues of value, the meaning of one's life, and the responsibility to relationship.

These few practices are but illustrations of the possibilities for moving from a first to a second-order ethics in the care-giving relationship. They open a space for realizing multiple visions of the good, and the significance of the relational process from which they arise[9]. They bring disparate voices into play, creating ways of living in which they may be integrated. Given the birth of individual being within relational process, they can nurture a process that is life-giving for us all.

331 Rogers Lane
Wallingford PA 19086
U.S.A.
info@taosinstitute.net

Kenneth J. GERGEN
Mary M. GERGEN

8. Also see www.healingconversationsnow.com.
9. Cf. R. RORTY, *Philosophy and Social Hope*, London, Penguin, 1999, p. 79: "Moral development in the individual, and moral progress in the human species as a whole, is a matter of re-making human selves so as to enlarge the variety of the relationships which constitute those selves".

LIST OF CONTRIBUTORS

Vangie BERGUM, PhD Education University of Alberta (1986), is professor emerita at the John Dossetor Health Ethics Centre & Faculty of Nursing, University of Alberta, Edmonton, Alberta, Canada. She is the author of *Relational Ethics for Health Care*, in J. STORCH – P. RODNEY – R. STARZOMSKI (eds.), *Toward a Moral Horizon: Nursing Ethics for Leadership and Practice*, Toronto, Pearson Prentice Hall, 2012; co-author of V. BERGUM – J. DOSSETOR, *Relational Ethics: The Full Meaning of Respect*, Hagerstown, MD, University Publishing Group, 2005.

Marie-Cécile BERTAU, Dr. Philosophy University of Munich (1996), is cultural-historical psycholinguist and staff member at the Institute of Phonetics and Speech Processing, University of Munich, Germany. She is the author of *Developmental Origins of the Dialogical Self: Early Childhood Years*, in H.J.M. HERMANS – T. GIESER (eds.), *Handbook of Dialogical Self Theory*, Cambridge, Cambridge University Press, 2012, 64-81; co-author of M.-C. BERTAU – M. GONÇALVES – P. RAGGATT (eds.), *Dialogic Formations: Investigations into the Origins and Development of the Dialogical Self*, Charlotte, NJ, Information Age, 2012.

Roger BURGGRAEVE, Dr. Theology KU Leuven (1980), is emeritus professor of Theological Ethics and Levinas Scholar at the Faculty of Theology and Religious Studies, Catholic University of Leuven (KU Leuven), Belgium. He is visiting professor at the International Institute 'Lumen Vitae' (Bruxelles) and Dharmaram College, Bangalore (India). He is the author of *Proximity with the Other: A Multidimensional Ethic of Responsibility in Levinas*, Bangalore (India), Dharmaram Publications, 2009; *Passion for Mercy and Justice: Biblical and Ethical Perspectives on Prophetic Pastoral Care and Counseling*, in A. DILLEN – A. VANDENHOECK (eds.), *Prophetic Witness in World Christianities: Rethinking Pastoral Care and Counseling*, Münster, LIT-Verlag, 2011, 61-90.

Jozef CORVELEYN, PhD Psychology KU Leuven (1983), is professor in clinical psychology and psychology of religion at the Faculty of Psychology and Educational Sciences and at the Faculty of Theology and Religious Studies, KU Leuven (University of Leuven) and part-time professor of psychology of religion at the Free University of Amsterdam (VU Amsterdam). He is the co-author of C. THORNE – J. CORVELEYN – C. PEZO DEL

PINO – T VELAZQUEZ – R. VALDEZ, *Buenas practicas en la prevención y atención de la violencia social: Sistematización de la labor realizada por instituciones y organizaciones peruanas*, Lima, Fondo Editorial Pontificia Universidad Católica del Perú, 2011; E.N. JOSEPH – P. LUYTEN – J. CORVELEYN – H. DE WITTE, *The Relationship between Personality, Burnout, and Engagement among the Indian Clergy*, in *The International Journal for the Psychology of Religion* 21 (2011), no. 4, 276-288.

Annemie DILLEN, Dr. Theology KU Leuven (2005), is associate professor of Pastoral Theology and head of the Academic Centre for Practical Theology at the Faculty of Theology and Religious Studies, Catholic University of Leuven, Belgium. She is the co-editor of A. DILLEN – D. POLLEFEYT (eds.), *Children's Voices: Children's Perspectives in Ethics, Theology and Religious Education*, Leuven, Peeters, 2010; A. DILLEN – A. VANDENHOECK (eds.), *Prophetic Witness in World Christianities: Rethinking Pastoral Care and Counseling*, Münster, LIT-Verlag, 2011.

Carrie DOEHRING, PhD Pastoral Psychology Boston University (1992), is associate professor of Pastoral Care and Counselling, Joint PhD Program, Iliff School of Theology, Denver University, Colorado USA. She is the author of *The Practice of Pastoral Care: A Postmodern Approach*, Louisville, KY, Westminster John Knox Press, 2006; *An Applied Integrative Approach to Exploring How Religion and Spirituality Contribute to or Counteract Prejudice and Discrimination*, in K.I. PARGAMENT – A. MAHONEY – E. SHAFRANSKE (eds.) *APA Handbooks in Psychology: APA Handbook of Psychology, Religion, and Spirituality*. Vol. 2, Washington, DC, American Psychological Association (in preparation).

Kenneth J. GERGEN, PhD Psychology Duke University (1963), is a founding member and President of the Taos Institute and a Senior Research Professor of Psychology at Swarthmore College. Swarthmore, Pennsylvania USA. He is the author of *Realities and Relationships: Soundings in Social Construction*, Cambridge, MA, Harvard University Press, 1994; *Relational Being: Beyond Self and Community*, Oxford, Oxford University Press, 2009.

Mary M. GERGEN, PhD Psychology Temple University (1980), is a founder, board member and treasurer/secretary of the Taos Institute, Chagrin Falls, Ohio USA, and Professor Emerita of psychology and Women's Studies, Pennsylvania State University, Brandywine USA. She is the author of *Feminist Reconstructions in Psychology: Narrative, Gender and Performance*, Thousand Oaks, CA, Sage, 2001; co-author of M.M. GERGEN – K.J. GERGEN, *Playing with Purpose:*

Adventures in Performative Social Science, Walnut Creek, CA, Left Coast Press, 2012.

Axel LIÉGEOIS, Dr. Theology KU Leuven (1988), is professor of Pastoral and Practical Theology at the Faculty of Theology and Religious Studies, Catholic University of Leuven, Belgium. He is also ethical advisor, Brothers of Charity Gent, Belgium. He is the author of *Pastoral Counselling in Care Services: Between Confidential Space and Integrated Care*, in *Counselling and Spirituality* 25 (2006) 127-140; *Values in Dialogue. Ethics in Care* (in progress).

Lisbeth LIPARI, PhD in Communication with a minor in Liguistics Stanford University (1996), is associate professor at the Department of Communication, Denison University, Granville, OH, USA. She is the author of *Listening, Thinking, Being: Toward an Ethical Ontology of Listening*, in *Communication Theory* 20 (2010), no. 3, 348-362; *Listening Others*, in A. CARLYLE – C. LANE (eds), *On Listening*, London, CRiSAP (Center for Research into Sound Arts Practice), 2012 (in press).

Sheila MCNAMEE, PhD Communication University of Massachussets/ Amherst (1983), is professor of Communication at the University of New Hampshire, Durham, New Hampshire USA, and Vice President, Founder, and Board Member of the Taos Institute. She is the co-author of S. MCNAMEE – K.J. GERGEN, *Relational Responsibility: Resources for Sustainable Dialogue*, Thousand Oaks, CA, Sage, 1999; S. MCNAMEE – D.M. HOSKING, *Research and Social Change: A Relational Constructionist Apporach*, New York, NY – Oxford, Routledge, 2012.

Darcia NARVAEZ, PhD Educational Psychology University of Minnesota (1993), is professor of psychology at the University of Notre Dame, Indiana USA. She is editor of the *Journal of Moral Education*. She is the co-editor of D. NARVAEZ – D.K. LAPSLEY, *Personality, Identity, and Character: Explorations in Moral Psychology*, Cambridge, Cambridge University Press, 2009; author of *The Neurobiology and Development of Human Morality*, New York, NY, W.W. Norton & Company, 2013.

Marina RIEMSLAGH, PhD Practical Theology KU Leuven (2011), is CPE Supervisor, PMA Coach and PSYCH-K Facilitator, Trainer in Pastoral Care and Counselling, Bornem, Belgium. She is the author of *Cronicle about the Expert Seminar 'After You': The Ethics of the Pastoral Counselling Process*, in *Ephemerides Theologicae Lovanienses* 86 (2010), no. 1, 531-534; M. RIEMSLAGH – F. CUVELIER – J. CORVELEYN – A. LIÉGEOIS – R. BURGGRAEVE, *The 'METHODIC' Exploration of Ethics and Pastoral Dimension in Interaction: The Cycle of Encounter*, in *Journal of Pastoral Care & Counseling* 66 (2012), no. 3, 1-11.

Peter ROBER, Dr. Psychology UGent (2006), is professor at the Interfaculty Institute for Family and Sexuality Studies, Faculty of Medicine KU Leuven. He is clinical psychologist, family therapist and family therapy trainer. He is the author of *The Therapist's Experiencing in Family Therapy Practice*, in *Journal of Family Therapy* 33 (2011) 233-255; co-author of P. ROBER – M. SELTZER, *Avoiding Colonizing Positions in the Therapy Room*, in *Family Process* 49 (2010) 123-137.

Annelies VAN HEIJST, Dr. Theology Katholieke Universiteit (Radboud University) Nijmegen (1992), is professor of Care Culture and Charity at the School of Humanities, Tilburg University, Netherlands. She is the author of *Models of Charitable Care: Catholic Nuns and Children in Their Care in Amsterdam, 1852-2002*, Leiden – Boston, MA, Brill, 2008; *Professional Loving Care: An Ethical View of the Healthcare Sector*, Leuven, Peeters, 2011.

INDEX OF NAMES

INDEX OF SUBJECTS

BIBLIOTHECA EPHEMERIDUM THEOLOGICARUM LOVANIENSIUM

SERIES III

131. C.M. TUCKETT (ed.), *The Scriptures in the Gospels*, 1997. XXIV-721 p. 60 €
132. J. VAN RUITEN & M. VERVENNE (eds.), *Studies in the Book of Isaiah. Festschrift Willem A.M. Beuken*, 1997. XX-540 p. 75 €
133. M. VERVENNE & J. LUST (eds.), *Deuteronomy and Deuteronomic Literature. Festschrift C.H.W. Brekelmans*, 1997. XI-637 p. 75 €
134. G. VAN BELLE (ed.), *Index Generalis ETL / BETL 1982-1997*, 1999. IX-337 p. 40 €
135. G. DE SCHRIJVER, *Liberation Theologies on Shifting Grounds. A Clash of Socio-Economic and Cultural Paradigms*, 1998. XI-453 p. 53 €
136. A. SCHOORS (ed.), *Qohelet in the Context of Wisdom*, 1998. XI-528 p. 60 €
137. W.A. BIENERT & U.KÜHNEWEG (eds.), *Origeniana Septima. Origenes in den Ausein andersetzungen des 4. Jahrhunderts*, 1999. XXV-848 p. 95 €
138. É. GAZIAUX, *L'autonomie en morale: au croisement de la philosophie et de la théologie*, 1998. XVI-760 p. 75 €
139. J. GROOTAERS, *Actes et acteurs à Vatican II*, 1998. XXIV-602 p. 75 €
140. F. NEIRYNCK, J. VERHEYDEN & R. CORSTJENS, *The Gospel of Matthew and the Sayings Source Q: A Cumulative Bibliography 1950-1995*, 1998. 2 vols., VII-1000-420* p. 95 €
141. E. BRITO, *Heidegger et l'hymne du sacré*, 1999. XV-800 p. 90 €
142. J. VERHEYDEN (ed.), *The Unity of Luke-Acts*, 1999. XXV-828 p. 60 €
143. N. CALDUCH-BENAGES & J. VERMEYLEN (eds.), *Treasures of Wisdom. Studies in Ben Sira and the Book of Wisdom. Festschrift M. Gilbert*, 1999. XXVII-463 p. 75 €
144. J.-M. AUWERS & A. WÉNIN (eds.), *Lectures et relectures de la Bible. Festschrift P.-M. Bogaert*, 1999. XLII-482 p. 75 €
145. C. BEGG, *Josephus' Story of the Later Monarchy (*AJ *9,1–10,185)*, 2000. X-650 p. 75 €
146. J.M. ASGEIRSSON, K. DE TROYER & M.W. MEYER (eds.), *From Quest to Q. Festschrift James M. Robinson*, 2000. XLIV-346 p. 60 €
147. T. RÖMER (ed.), *The Future of the Deuteronomistic History*, 2000. XII-265 p. 75 €
148. F.D. VANSINA, *Paul Ricœur: Bibliographie primaire et secondaire - Primary and Secondary Bibliography 1935-2000*, 2000. XXVI-544 p. 75 €
149. G.J. BROOKE & J.D. KAESTLI (eds.), *Narrativity in Biblical and Related Texts*, 2000. XXI-307 p. 75 €
150. F. NEIRYNCK, *Evangelica III: 1992-2000. Collected Essays*, 2001. XVII-666 p. 60 €

151. B. DOYLE, *The Apocalypse of Isaiah Metaphorically Speaking.A Study of the Use, Function and Significance of Metaphors in Isaiah 24-27*, 2000. XII-453 p. 75 €
152. T.MERRIGAN & J.HAERS (eds.), *The Myriad Christ.Plurality and the Quest for Unity inContemporary Christology*, 2000.XIV-593 p. 75 €
153. M.SIMON, *Le catéchisme de Jean-Paul II.Genèse et évaluation de son commentaire du Symbole des apôtres*, 2000. XVI-688 p. 75 €
154. J. VERMEYLEN, *La loi du plus fort. Histoire de la rédaction des récits davidiques de 1 Samuel 8 à 1 Rois 2*, 2000. XIII-746 p. 80 €
155. A. WÉNIN (ed.), *Studies in the Book of Genesis. Literature, Redaction and History*, 2001. XXX-643 p. 60 €
156. F. LEDEGANG, *Mysterium Ecclesiae. Images of the Church and its Members in Origen*, 2001. XVII-848 p. 84 €
157. J.S. BOSWELL, F.P. MCHUGH & J. VERSTRAETEN (eds.), *Catholic Social Thought: Twilight of Renaissance*, 2000. XXII-307 p. 60 €
158. A. LINDEMANN (ed.), *The Sayings Source Q and the Historical Jesus*, 2001. XXII-776 p. 60 €
159. C. HEMPEL, A. LANGE & H. LICHTENBERGER (eds.), *The Wisdom Texts from Qumran and the Development of Sapiential Thought*, 2002. XII-502 p. 80 €
160. L. BOEVE & L. LEIJSSEN (eds.), *Sacramental Presence in a Postmodern Context*, 2001. XVI-382 p. 60 €
161. A. DENAUX (ed.), *New Testament Textual Criticism and Exegesis. Festschrift J. Delobel*, 2002. XVIII-391 p. 60 €
162. U. BUSSE, *Das Johannesevangelium. Bildlichkeit, Diskurs und Ritual. Mit einer Bibliographie über den Zeitraum 1986-1998*, 2002. XIII-572 p. 70 €
163. J.-M. AUWERS & H.J. DE JONGE (eds.), *The Biblical Canons*, 2003. LXXXVIII-718 p. 60 €
164. L. PERRONE (ed.), *Origeniana Octava. Origen and the Alexandrian Tradition*, 2003. XXV-X-1406 p. 180 €
165. R. BIERINGER, V. KOPERSKI & B. LATAIRE (eds.), *Resurrection in the New Testament. Festschrift J. Lambrecht*, 2002. XXXI-551 p. 70 €
166. M. LAMBERIGTS & L. KENIS (eds.), *Vatican II and Its Legacy*, 2002. XII-512 p. 65 €
167. P. DIEUDONNÉ, *La Paix clémentine. Défaite et victoire du premier jansénisme français sous le pontificat de Clément IX (1667-1669)*, 2003. XXXIX-302 p. 70 €
168. F. GARCÍA MARTÍNEZ, *Wisdom and Apocalypticism in the Dead Sea Scrolls and in the Biblical Tradition*, 2003. XXXIV-491 p. 60 €
169. D. OGLIARI, *Gratia et Certamen: The Relationship between Grace and Free Will in the Discussion of Augustine with the So-Called Semipelagians*, 2003. LVII-468 p. 75 €
170. G. COOMAN, M. VAN STIPHOUT & B. WAUTERS (eds.), *Zeger-Bernard Van Espen at the Crossroads of Canon Law, History, Theology and Church-State Relations*,2003. XX-530 p. 80 €
171. B. BOURGINE, *L'herméneutique théologique de Karl Barth.Exégèse et dogmatique dans le quatrième volume de la Kirchliche Dogmatik*, 2003. XXII-548 p. 75 €
172. J. HAERS & P. DE MEY (eds.), *Theology and Conversation: Towards a Relational Theology*, 2003. XIII-923 p. 90 €

173. M.J.J. MENKEN, *Matthew's Bible: The Old Testament Text of the Evangelist*, 2004. XII-336 p. 60 €
174. J.-P. DELVILLE, *L'Europe de l'exégèse au XVIe siècle. Interprétations de la parabole des ouvriers à la vigne (Matthieu 20,1-16)*, 2004. XLII-775 p. 70 €
175. E. BRITO, *J.G. Fichte et la transformation du christianisme*, 2004. XVI-808 p. 90 €
176. J. SCHLOSSER (ed.), *The Catholic Epistles and the Tradition*, 2004. XXIV-569 p. 60 €
177. R. FAESEN (ed.), *Albert Deblaere, S.J. (1916-1994): Essays on Mystical Literature – Essais sur la littérature mystique – Saggi sulla letteratura mistica*, 2004. XX-473 p. 70 €
178. J. LUST, *Messianism and the Septuagint: Collected Essays*. Edited by K. HAUSPIE, 2004. XIV-247 p. 60 €
179. H. GIESEN, *Jesu Heilsbotschaft und die Kirche. Studien zur Eschatologie und Ekklesiologie bei den Synoptikern und im ersten Petrusbrief*, 2004. XX-578 p. 70 €
180. H. LOMBAERTS & D. POLLEFEYT (eds.), *Hermeneutics and Religious Education*, 2004. XIII-427 p. 70 €
181. D. DONNELLY, A. DENAUX & J. FAMERÉE (eds.), *The Holy Spirit, the Church, and Christian Unity. Proceedings of the Consultation Held at the Monastery of Bose, Italy (14-20 October 2002)*, 2005. XII-417 p. 70 €
182. R. BIERINGER, G. VAN BELLE & J. VERHEYDEN (eds.), *Luke and His Readers. Festschrift A. Denaux*, 2005. XXVIII-470 p. 65 €
183. D.F. PILARIO, *Back to the Rough Grounds of Praxis: Exploring Theological Method with Pierre Bourdieu*, 2005. XXXII-584 p. 80 €
184. G. VAN BELLE, J.G. VAN DER WATT & P. MARITZ (eds.), *Theology and Christology in the Fourth Gospel: Essays by the Members of the SNTS Johannine Writings Seminar*, 2005. XII-561 p. 70 €
185. D. LUCIANI, *Sainteté et pardon*. Vol. 1: *Structure littéraire du Lévitique*. Vol. 2: *Guide technique*, 2005. XIV-VII-656 p. 120 €
186. R.A. DERRENBACKER, JR., *Ancient Compositional Practices and the Synoptic Problem*, 2005.XXVIII-290 p. 80 €
187. P. VAN HECKE (ed.), *Metaphor in the Hebrew Bible*, 2005. X-308 p. 65 €
188. L. BOEVE, Y. DEMAESENEER & S. VAN DEN BOSSCHE (eds.), *Religious Experience and Contemporary Theological Epistemology*, 2005. X-335 p. 50 €
189. J.M. ROBINSON, *The Sayings Gospel Q. Collected Essays*, 2005. XVIII-888 p. 90 €
190. C.W. STRÜDER, *Paulus und die Gesinnung Christi. Identität und Entscheidungsfindung aus der Mitte von 1Kor 1-4*, 2005. LII-522 p. 80 €
191. C. FOCANT & A. WÉNIN (eds.), *Analyse narrative et Bible. Deuxième colloque international du RRENAB, Louvain-la-Neuve, avril 2004*, 2005. XVI-593 p. 75 €
192. F. GARCÍA MARTÍNEZ & M. VERVENNE (eds.), in collaboration with B. DOYLE, *Interpreting Translation: Studies on the LXX and Ezekiel in Honour of Johan Lust*, 2005. XVI-464 p. 70 €
193. F. MIES, *L'espérance de Job*, 2006. XXIV-653 p. 87 €
194. C. FOCANT, *Marc, un évangile étonnant*, 2006. XV-402 p. 60 €
195. M.A. KNIBB (ed.), *The Septuagint and Messianism*, 2006. XXXI-560 p. 60 €

196. M. SIMON, *La célébration du mystère chrétien dans le catéchisme de Jean-Paul II*, 2006. XIV-638 p. 85 €
197. A.Y. THOMASSET, *L'ecclésiologie de J.H. Newman Anglican*, 2006. XXX-748 p. 80 €
198. M. LAMBERIGTS – A.A. DEN HOLLANDER (eds.), *Lay Bibles in Europe 1450-1800*, 2006. XI-360 p. 79 €
199. J.Z. SKIRA – M.S. ATTRIDGE, *In God's Hands. Essays on the Church and Ecumenism in Honour of Michael A. Fahey S.J.*, 2006. XXX-314 p. 90 €
200. G. VAN BELLE (ed.), *The Death of Jesus in the Fourth Gospel*, 2007. XXXI-1003 p. 70 €
201. D. POLLEFEYT (ed.), *Interreligious Learning*, 2007. XXV-340 p. 80 €
202. M. LAMBERIGTS – L. BOEVE – T. MERRIGAN, in collaboration with D. CLAES (eds.), *Theology and the Quest for Truth: Historical- and Systematic-Theological Studies*, 2007. X-305 p. 55 €
203. T. RÖMER – K. SCHMID (eds.), *Les dernières rédactions du Pentateuque, de l'Hexateuque et de l'Ennéateuque*, 2007. X-276 p. 65 €
204. J.-M. VAN CANGH, *Les sources judaïques du Nouveau Testament*, 2008. XIV-718 p. 84 €
205. B. DEHANDSCHUTTER, *Polycarpiana: Studies on Martyrdom and Persecution in Early Christianity. Collected Essays.* Edited by J. LEEMANS, 2007. XVI-286 p. 74 €
206. É. GAZIAUX, *Philosophie et Théologie. Festschrift Emilio Brito*, 2007. LVIII-588 p. 84 €
207. G.J. BROOKE – T. RÖMER (eds.), *Ancient and Modern Scriptural Historiography. L'historiographie biblique, ancienne et moderne*, 2007. XXXVIII-372 p. 75 €
208. J. VERSTRAETEN, *Scrutinizing the Signs of the Times in the Light of the Gospel*, 2007. X-334 p. 74 €
209. H. GEYBELS, *Cognitio Dei experimentalis. A Theological Genealogy of Christian Religious Experience*, 2007. LII-457 p. 80 €
210. A.A. DEN HOLLANDER, *Virtuelle Vergangenheit: Die Textrekonstruktion einer verlorenen mittelniederländischen Evangelienharmonie. Die Handschrift Utrecht Universitätsbibliothek 1009*, 2007. XII-168 p. 58 €
211. R. GRYSON, *Scientiam Salutis: Quarante années de recherches sur l'Antiquité Chrétienne. Recueil d'essais*, 2008. XLVI-879 p. 88 €
212. T. VAN DEN DRIESSCHE, *L'altérité, fondement de la personne humaine dans l'œuvre d'Edith Stein*, 2008. XXII-626 p. 85 €
213. H. AUSLOOS – J. COOK – F. GARCÍA MARTÍNEZ – B. LEMMELIJN – M. VERVENNE (eds.), *Translating a Translation: The LXX and its Modern Translations in the Context of Early Judaism*, 2008. X-317 p. 80 €
214. A.C. OSUJI, *Where is the Truth? Narrative Exegesis and the Question of True and False Prophecy in Jer 26–29 (MT)*, 2010. XX-465 p. 76 €
215. T. RÖMER, *The Books of Leviticus and Numbers*, 2008. XXVII-742 p. 85 €
216. D. DONNELLY – J. FAMERÉE – M. LAMBERIGTS – K. SCHELKENS (eds.), *The Belgian Contribution to the Second Vatican Council: International Research Conference at Mechelen, Leuven and Louvain-la-Neuve (September 12-16, 2005)*, 2008. XII-716 p. 85 €
217. J. DE TAVERNIER – J.A. SELLING – J. VERSTRAETEN – P. SCHOTSMANS (eds.), *Responsibility, God and Society. Theological Ethics in Dialogue. Festschrift Roger Burggraeve*, 2008. XLVI-413 p. 75 €

218. G. VAN BELLE – J.G. VAN DER WATT – J. VERHEYDEN (eds.), *Miracles and Imagery in Luke and John. Festschrift Ulrich Busse*, 2008. XVIII-287 p. 78 €
219. L. BOEVE – M. LAMBERIGTS – M.WISSE (eds.), *Augustine and Postmodern Thought: A New Alliance against Modernity?*, 2009. XVIII-277 p. 80 €
220. T. VICTORIA, *Un livre de feu dans un siècle de fer: Les lectures de l'Apocalypse dans la littérature française de la Renaissance*, 2009. XXX-609 p. 85 €
221. A.A. DEN HOLLANDER – W. FRANÇOIS (eds.), *Infant Milk or Hardy Nourishment? The Bible for Lay People and Theologians in the Early Modern Period*, 2009. XVIII-488 p. 80 €
222. F.D. VANSINA, *Paul Ricœur. Bibliographie primaire et secondaire. Primary and Secundary Bibliography 1935-2008*, Compiled and updated in collaboration with P. VANDECASTEELE, 2008. XXX-621 p. 80 €
223. G. VAN BELLE – M. LABAHN – P. MARITZ (eds.), *Repetitions and Variations in the Fourth Gospel: Style, Text, Interpretation*, 2009. XII-712 p. 85 €
224. H. AUSLOOS – B. LEMMELIJN – M. VERVENNE (eds.), *Florilegium Lovaniense: Studies in Septuagint and Textual Criticism in Honour of Florentino García Martínez*, 2008. XVI-564 p. 80 €
225. E. BRITO, *Philosophie moderne et christianisme*, 2010. 2 vols., VIII-1514 p. 130 €
226. U. SCHNELLE (ed.), *The Letter to the Romans*, 2009. XVIII-894 p. 85 €
227. M. LAMBERIGTS – L. BOEVE – T. MERRIGAN in collaboration with D. CLAES – M. WISSE (eds.), *Orthodoxy, Process and Product*, 2009. X-416 p. 74 €
228. G. HEIDL – R. SOMOS (eds.), *Origeniana nona: Origen and the Religious Practice of His Time*, 2009. XIV-752 p. 95 €
229. D. MARGUERAT (ed.), *Reception of Paulinism in Acts – Réception du paulinisme dans les Actes des Apôtres*, 2009. VIII-340 p. 74 €
230. A. DILLEN – D. POLLEFEYT (eds.), *Children's Voices: Children's Perspectives in Ethics, Theology and Religious Education*, 2010. X-450 p. 72 €
231. P. VAN HECKE – A. LABAHN (eds.), *Metaphors in the Psalms*, 2010. XXXIV-363 p. 76 €
232. G. AULD – E. EYNIKEL (eds.), *For and Against David: Story and History in the Books of Samuel*, 2010. X-397 p. 76 €
233. C. VIALLE, *Une analyse comparée d'Esther TM et LXX: Regard sur deux récits d'une même histoire*, 2010. LVIII-406 p. 76 €
234. T. MERRIGAN – F. GLORIEUX (eds.), *"Godhead Here in Hiding": Incarnation and the History of Human Suffering*, 2012. X-327 p. 76 €
235. M. SIMON, *La vie dans le Christ dans le catéchisme de Jean-Paul II*, 2010. XX-651 p. 84 €
236. G. DE SCHRIJVER, *The Political Ethics of Jean-François Lyotard and Jacques Derrida*, 2010. XXX-422 p. 80 €
237. A. PASQUIER – D. MARGUERAT – A. WÉNIN (eds), *L'intrigue dans le récit biblique. Quatrième colloque international du RRENAB, Université Laval, Québec, 29 mai – 1er juin 2008*, 2010. XXX-479 p. 68 €
238. E. ZENGER (ed.), *The Composition of the Book of Psalms*, 2010. XII-826 p. 90 €
239. P. FOSTER – A. GREGORY – J.S. KLOPPENBORG – J. VERHEYDEN (eds.), *New Studies in the Synoptic Problem: Oxford Conference, April 2008*, 2011. XXIV-828 p. 85 €

240. J. VERHEYDEN – T.L. HETTEMA – P. VANDECASTEELE (eds.), *Paul Ricœur: Poetics and Religion*, 2011. XX-534 p. 79 €
241. J. LEEMANS (ed.), *Martyrdom and Persecution in Late Ancient Christianity. Festschrift Boudewijn Dehandschutter*, 2010. XXXIV-430 p. 78 €
242. C. CLIVAZ – J. ZUMSTEIN (eds.), *Reading New Testament Papyri in Context – Lire les papyrus du Nouveau Testament dans leur contexte*, 2011. XIV-446 p. 80 €
243. D. SENIOR (ed.), *The Gospel of Matthew at the Crossroads of Early Christianity*, 2011. XXVIII-781 p. 88 €
244. H. PIETRAS – S. KACZMAREK (eds.), *Origeniana Decima: Origen as Writer*, 2011. XVIII-1039 p. 105 €
245. M. SIMON, *La prière chrétienne dans le catéchisme de Jean-Paul II*, 2011. XVI-290 p. 70 €
246. H. AUSLOOS – B. LEMMELIJN – J. TREBOLLE-BARRERA (eds.), *After Qumran: Old and Modern Editions of the Biblical Texts – The Historical Books*, 2012. XIV-319 p. 84 €
247. G. VAN OYEN – A. WÉNIN (eds.), *La surprise dans la Bible. Festschrift Camille Focant*, 2012. XLII-474 p. 80 €
248. C. CLIVAZ – C. COMBET-GALLAND – J.-D. MACCHI – C. NIHAN (eds.), *Écritures et réécritures: La reprise interprétative des traditions fondatrices par la littérature biblique et extra-biblique. Cinquième colloque international du RRENAB, Universités de Genève et Lausanne, 10-12 juin 2010*, 2012. XXIV-648 p. 90 €
249. G. VAN OYEN – T. SHEPHERD (eds.), *Resurrection of the Dead: Biblical Traditions in Dialogue*, 2012. XVI-632 p. 85 €
250. E. NOORT (ed.), *The Book of Joshua*, 2012. XIV-698 p. 90 €
251. R. FAESEN – L. KENIS (eds.), *The Jesuits of the Low Countries: Identity and Impact (1540-1773). Proceedings of the International Congress at the Faculty of Theology, KU Leuven (3-5 December 2009)*, 2012. X-295 p. 65 €
252. A. DAMM, *Ancient Rhetoric and the Synoptic Problem: Clarifying Markan Priority*, 2013. Forthcoming
253. A. DENAUX – P. DE MEY (eds.), *The Ecumenical Legacy of Johannes Cardinal Willebrands (1909-2006)*, 2012. XIV-376 p. 79 €
254. T. KNIEPS-PORT LE ROI – G. MANNION – P. DE MEY (eds.), *The Household of God and Local Households: Revisiting the Domestic Church*, 2013. Forthcoming
255. L. KENIS – E. VAN DER WALL (eds.), *Religious Modernism of the Low Countries*, 2013. Forthcoming
256. P. IDE, *Une Théo-logique du Don: Le Don dans la* Trilogie *de Hans Urs von Balthasar*, 2013. Forthcoming
257. A.A. DEN HOLLANDER – W. FRANCOIS (eds.), *"Wading Lambs and Swimming Elephants": The Bible for the Laity and Theologians in Late Medieval and Early Modern Era*, 2012. XVI-406 p. 84 €

PRINTED ON PERMANENT PAPER • IMPRIME SUR PAPIER PERMANENT • GEDRUKT OP DUURZAAM PAPIER - ISO 9706

N.V. PEETERS S.A., WAROTSTRAAT 50, B-3020 HERENT